Happier Days:

Paramount Television's
Classic Sitcoms 1974–1984

MARLEY BRANT

BILLBOARD BOOKS
An imprint of Watson-Guptill Publications

Executive Editor: Bob Nirkind
Project Editor: Patricia Fogarty
Production Manager: Katherine Happ
Cover Design: John Clifford/Thinkstudio
Interior Design: Sivan Earnest

First published in 2006 by Billboard Books,
An imprint of Watson-Guptill Publications,
A division of VNU Business Media, Inc.,
770 Broadway, New York, NY 10003
www.watsonguptill.com

Library of Congress Cataloging-in-Publication Data
The CIP data for this title is on file with the Library of Congress
Library of Congress Control Number: 2006923285

ISBN-13: 978-0-8230-8933-8
ISBN-10: 0-8230-8933-9

Every effort has been made to obtain permission for the material in this book. The
author, editors, and publisher sincerely apologize for any inadvertent errors or omissions
and will be happy to correct them in future editions.

Printed in the United States

First printing, 2006

2 3 4 5 6 7 8 9 / 14 13 12 11 10 09 08 07 06

ACKNOWLEDGMENTS

Richard J. "Dick" Winters was a terrific guy. Not only was he an excellent publicist, but he possessed a remarkable heart. Most everyone who knew Dick liked him, and I was one of those who not only called him boss but also considered him my friend. I worked as Dick's assistant in our two-person Paramount Television Publicity office in the late seventies through the early eighties. Dick allowed me opportunities that surely enriched my professional and personal life, and without him this book would not have been possible. At least not by this author.

I thank the actors, producers, writers, directors, casting directors, crew members, and assistants who shared their thoughts over the years regarding the Paramount Television sitcoms that have come to define the remarkable television comedy that was produced throughout the time span 1974–1984. I was privy to many of the incidents and events contained in this recounting, but others who were there experienced so much more. Many people were so kind to share their familiarity and knowledge with me, and I treasure and appreciate their memories. Some folks spoke off the record back when all this was happening, and it's not possible for me to thank them here by name. Others who helped with or supported the book or who were simply a delight to re-connect with have my heartfelt thanks, especially Jim Burrows, Randy Carver, Pam Dawber, Corey Feldman, Michael Gross, Clint Howard, Donna Pescow, Suzi Quatro, Rose Marie, Misty Rowe, Howard Storm, and Henry Winkler. Thanks to Ron Howard, Henry Winkler, Ronny Hallin, Garry Marshall, Lowell Ganz, Jerry Paris, Bobby Hoffman, Robin Williams, Pam Dawber, Donna Pescow, Bob Hays, Robin Chambers, Jim Burrows, Danny DeVito, Marilu Henner, Chris Lloyd, and Tony Danza for being so nice to me back in the day and making my job so much easier and so much fun.

Thanks, as always, to Bob Nirkind, Executive Editor of Billboard Books, for consistently finding a way to make things work. Thanks to editor Patricia Fogarty, who I'm sure is hoping that her next author knows the proper use of a comma. I'd also like to thank Henry Winkler and Jim Burrows for their continued inspiration through quality work and personal integrity.

I thank God for the wonderful opportunity I had at Paramount and for everything else with which He has blessed me. Jesus always holds my hand through life's adventures. My family has to be the best in the history of mankind. I love them incredibly and thank them for their unwavering love and support. Thank you, Dave, for your daily inspiration and encouragement; Kathie, for your tenacious phone abilities and unfaltering, enduring friendship; Willie, for your legwork (now finish *your* book—I can't wait for it to be published); Cha, for your constant companionship; and Tim (my Rambling Wreck, of whom I'm extremely proud and love watching develop into a wonderful writer and thinker of great creative thoughts). It sometimes gets lonely being a writer, and it means the world to me to have supportive friends and family who tug my sleeve to occasionally leave "The Hermitage" to experience *real* life and engage in activities that create new adventures and memories. They'll never know how much I appreciate their support of my career, so thanks especially to John, Jennifer, Will, Carol, Jeannieweenie (an inspiration to us all), The Big A, Francieface (my hero), Jo, Ubie, Aunt J, Janel, John, Linda, Steve J., Cheryl, Sam, Donna, Dusty, Ansley, Buddy, "The Guys": Dave, Mike, Ron, Buzz, and Kevin, Rosie, Patti, Cheri, Jim, Caren, Steve and Cheryl A., Bonnie, Phil, Auntie Vera, Marie, Betty, Abby, Dorothy, Harriett, Gary and Nancy G., Jake, Kelly, Judy, Shelley, Jamie, Susie, Ralph, George M., Nancy P., Wig, Greg, Debbie, Steven, Shelley, and Monika (I miss you, friend). And to Mom (for your repeated encouragement to "hang in there") and Dad (for making me prove to you I had something unique to offer). I miss you both tremendously.

CONTENTS

For my family: I love you guys immeasurably. You are my world.

Dedicated to Richard J. Winters with my respect and appreciation.

In memory of Jerry Paris, Pat Morita, Wendie Jo Sperber, Phil Foster, Debralee Scott, Elizabeth Kerr, Andy Kaufman, and Gary Nardino.

INTRODUCTION

Nineteen seventy-four was quite a year for the United States. The war in Vietnam was nearing an end, Patty Hearst was kidnapped by the SLA, Richard Nixon resigned from the presidency, and the previous year's oil embargo by OPEC ended. Contributions in entertainment were significant: Hank Aaron hit his 715th home run, Stephen King published his first novel, *Carrie*, moviegoers flocked to see *The Godfather: Part II*, which would win the Academy Award for Best Picture, and the first issue of *People* magazine hit the stands. As society forged ahead into a year of unpredictability and change, a group of creative television forces cast a glance back to the relative calm and safety of the fifties. *Happy Days*, a half-hour show based in that era and sweeter than apple pie, took the country by storm and provided America with an extended family every bit as lovable and involving as those of Lucy and Desi, Samantha and Darrin, Laura and Rob, Pa Cartwright and his boys, and Andy and Opie. *Happy Days'* Cunningham family, in fact, even *had* Opie. Well, it had Ron Howard, the actor who portrayed Opie on the popular *Andy Griffith Show*. *Happy Days* provided its audience with a comfortable, familiar locality on Tuesday nights. Who said you can't go home again?

During the years 1974–1984, the movie lot at Paramount in Hollywood was the place to be. Paramount Pictures was producing films such as *Chinatown, Day of the Locust, The Godfather: Part II, Saturday Night Fever*, and *Raiders of the Lost Ark*. The television area of the lot was active with the dramatic shows *Star Trek, Petrocelli, Paper Moon*, and *Little House on the Prairie*, as well as an abundance of made-for-television movies and mini-series, such as *Shogun*. Then there were the sitcoms: *Happy Days, Laverne & Shirley, Mork & Mindy, Taxi, Angie, Bosom Buddies, Family Ties, Cheers*, and a dozen or so shorter-lived series. Creative talent was drawn to Paramount like chocoholics to a brownie.

In the ten years that *Happy Days* would reign as one of the leading shows in television, Paramount Television produced a solid package of comedy series written by some of the best and brightest the industry would ever know: Lowell Ganz, Bob Brunner, Ed. Weinberger, Les and Glen Charles, Gary David Goldberg, Michael Leeson, Dale McRaven, Stan Daniels, Brian Levant, Earl Pomerantz, David Angell, and hundreds more who would keep America connected and laughing out loud. The producers who were selected to serve as the foundations of the shows were extremely adept at employing top-notch directors and writers and at casting little-known actors with a flair for capturing an audience and creating characters with whom America would love to spend time. These were men and women who understood television and knew comedic appeal: Garry Marshall, Tom Miller, Eddie Milkis, Bob Boyett, Gary David Goldberg, David Davis, Mark Rothman, Bruce Johnson, Leonora Thuna, and a dozen other resourceful wunderkinds. The directors came from such television classics as *The Dick Van Dyke Show*, *The Mary Tyler Moore Show*, *Rhoda*, and *The Odd Couple*, and included the incredible talents of Jerry Paris, Jim Burrows, Howard Storm, Joel Zwick, Jeff Chambers, and Garry Marshall.

And the actors. The actors came from film, television, stage, comedy clubs, and out of the blue: Ron Howard, Henry Winkler, Robin Williams, Penny Marshall, Danny DeVito, Andy Kaufman, Pam Dawber, Tom Hanks, Ted Danson, Donna Pescow, Kelsey Grammer, Michael J. Fox, Michael Gross, and on and on—actors who may have been known only slightly, if at all, when they were cast but whose opportunities through their association with Paramount Television productions would create a place for them to detonate their talent and become household names.

Some of the actors involved in the Paramount sitcoms, like Robin Williams and Tom Hanks, would go on to become superstars, appearing in television only as guest stars as their film careers skyrocketed. Others, like Tony Danza, Kelsey Grammer, Ted Danson, Scott Baio, and Kirstie Alley, would remain in television as the singular stars of their own series. Corey Feldman, Henry Winkler, Michael McKean, Christopher Lloyd, and Michael J. Fox would all experience success in both film and television. Ron Howard, James Brooks, Penny Marshall, and Danny DeVito became renowned film directors. Jim Burrows, a regular on the Paramount lot, would become the television director with the track record for the most pilots that developed into series. The talent of the Paramount sitcom players knew no bounds. Most would remember fondly that their association with a Paramount Television series was a magical, once-in-a-lifetime experience.

The Paramount sitcoms were filmed before studio audiences, allowing the fans of the shows to come on the lot and share the fun. It wasn't unusual for visitors to the set of *Mork & Mindy* to see Robin Williams delight and astonish with his improvisation and employment of a variety of personalities and countless voices. *Taxi*'s Andy Kaufman was another loose cannon. "Try to ignore him," Jim Burrows once said to me, "even though you can't." Henry Winkler, who through his character, Fonzie, became one of television's biggest stars, always took time to meet his fans and sign autographs after a taping. Tom Hanks and Peter Scolari would often visit other of the Paramount television stages, dressed as women for their roles in *Bosom Buddies*. The interaction between the dozens of actors and other creative talent on the lot was remarkable.

But not everything at Paramount Television was entertaining. The fights between Penny Marshall and Cindy Williams on the *Laverne & Shirley* set were common knowledge on the lot. Scott Baio, a teen idol through his *Happy Days* character, Chachi Arcola, received a death threat. Shelley Long had a serious problem with the character Dr. Frasier Crane. David Lander faced a battle with multiple sclerosis. The bridges that Andy Kaufman burned along the path of his rise to stardom were innumerable as he pulled out all the stops to make himself as obnoxious—and noticed—as possible. Drugs happened, and Robin Williams was at the head of the line. Egos flared, sometimes out of control, as many actors were exposed for the first time to the naturally competitive environment of the television business. The networks that aired the shows created tension and heartbreak as they shifted their programming schedules and caused more than one of the hit series to finally collapse under the weight of their constant tinkering. As the popularity of the Paramount sitcoms and the stars they created rose, so did the unpredictability and problems.

The legendary guest stars also became part of the story. Cameos, bit parts, and memorable appearances were written for the likes of Tom Selleck, Martin Mull, Carol Kane, Pat O'Brien, Danny Thomas, Crispin Glover, Amy Irving, David Letterman, Tate Donovan, Hank Azaria, Andy Griffith, Johnny Carson, and even Danny DeVito's mother, Julia. Robin Williams was fascinated by Jonathan Winters, who joined the cast of *Mork & Mindy*, playing the couple's son, Mearth. I once heard Robin comment that Winters was "so talented, it's fucking scary." In light of Winters's previous bouts with mental illness, perhaps it was, but Winters together with Williams was pure magic. Raquel Welch appeared as a delicious alien guest star on that show but didn't check her diva behavior at the Paramount gate. During the course of her guest-starring stint she suggested outlandish changes to the script and once, realizing that I was a studio publicist, threw me out of her trailer. Carol Kane's appearance as Latka Gravas's girlfriend, Simka, on *Taxi* brought an excited merriment to the set through her unique comedic ability and the hilarious language she and Kaufman created. The friends of the stars, some of them legendary entertainers themselves, would periodically drop in to watch the tapings. With such a wide and diverse group of extremely talented actors, *anything* could happen on the Paramount lot. It was, simply put, an exciting time.

The sitcoms produced at Paramount Television during the golden years 1974–1984 were a springboard for sophisticated comedy and successful entertainment careers. It was a unique environment that culminated in programming that set the standard by which sitcoms would be judged for years to come. I was blessed to be a small part of the excitement in my role as assistant to Paramount Television's Vice President of Publicity, Dick Winters. I savor my days and nights on the various sets and my interactions with the amazingly creative people who brought these series into our homes. From 1974 through 1984 the comedy productions of Paramount Television truly were lightning in a bottle.

—Marley Brant, 2006

Chapter 1

BEFORE A LIVE AUDIENCE

The live audience tapings at Paramount Television were an institution. The fans who wanted to watch the shows be taped would wait out on the street until the doors opened late in the afternoon. They entered the huge sound stages with enthusiasm. The public was ready to be entertained. Those present watched their favorite television stars at work, while the shows' producers secured their positive reactions and taped their "live" laugh track. Many times the actors stayed after the taping to sign autographs and chat with members of the audience. The tapings were a magical time for those who were allowed in to share the magic but were fairly routine for the casts involved. Yet what happened behind the scenes on those sets from week to week was anything *but* routine.

The Paramount Television audiences instinctively knew that if they attended a *Happy Days* taping they were in for laughs and good-natured family entertainment. Teasing among the cast members and the occasional prank or two were standard fare. In character as Fonzie, Henry Winkler, in his appearance and the lines he delivered, would evoke both cheers of appreciation and enthusiastic laughter. Winkler was a master of expression. His double takes, sidelong glances, and raised eyebrows often had fellow actor Ron Howard on the floor. Winkler rarely, if ever, broke character once he donned his signature leather jacket. He would strut around the set, and a mere glance from "The Fonz" would send some of the female on-lookers into an audible swoon. Ron Howard had great curiosity about the mechanics of filmmaking, and his interest would take him in and out of the character Richie Cunningham throughout the taping. When called on to act, Howard acted. When he wasn't on-screen, Howard was busy watching the director and cameramen, trying to pick up bits of information that would benefit him in his future behind-the-camera career. His serious approach to production aside, Ron Howard always appreciated a blooper or on-set joke. One of Henry Winkler's favorite surprises was to place unscripted characters behind the fictional Cunningham family's front door. On one occasion when Richie opened the door expecting to greet his friends Ralph and Potsie, a half-dressed stripper stood before him. The studio audience (on most nights about 300 people) roared as Howard turned crimson and blew his lines.

Garry Marshall would famously say, "Some people teach with their shows. I do recess." Even so, the *Happy Days* viewership consisted of children, teenagers, and adults, and the program's producers and writers were comfortable using their storylines as vehicles for educating their audience. Marshall was proud to recount that one of *Happy Days*' most well-received episodes was the show in which Fonzie gets his library card; it was given credit for boosting U.S. library card applications by 500 percent. The ABC-TV television special "Henry Winkler Meets William Shakespeare" combined the popular character Fonzie with Winkler's desire to make a contribution to the lives of his young fans.

Happy Days, full of mischief, practical jokes, and lessons in responsible behavior, was a fun set. The show remained relatively scandal-free until long after production ceased. In the nineties, Erin Moran, the young actress who played cute little Joanie Marie Cunningham during all those successful years of the show, reportedly accused her fellow cast members of unprofessional behavior toward her during the time she was involved with *Happy Days*. That wasn't the way the cast and crew remembered it. Aside from that isolated incident, those involved with *Happy Days* remained loyal friends long after the cameras stopped rolling. Moran would be welcomed back into the family for televised reunion specials, with little or no comment on any of her assertions.

The set of *Laverne & Shirley* was quite different from *Happy Days* and often *not* a fun set. Tensions ran high on that show, which filmed on Stage 20 next door to *Happy Days*. Audiences who lined up outside the studio anticipating an enjoyable evening watching *Laverne &*

Shirley were sometimes diverted to the filming of another show. Despite the producers' efforts to lighten the sometimes dismal mood that pervaded the set, Penny Marshall and Cindy Williams often just didn't like each other come time to tape the show. The competition between the two actresses was intense, and the show's other actors, and the crew, were sometimes drawn into the fray. Marshall and Williams were frequently not speaking, which sometimes made the set of *Laverne & Shirley* a difficult place to be. On several occasions the women almost came to blows. These fights often ended with each actress stomping off to her dressing room; doors would slam, production would temporarily shut down, and precious time would be lost. Although that was usually during rehearsal, it was imperative that the cast and crew work together to plan the moves that would make the taping of the show go off with as few hitches as possible. It was anybody's guess what would happen the night of the taping. The producers could count on one thing: it was rare that the taping was completed before every member of the cast and crew was exhausted and irritated. Working on the set of *Laverne & Shirley* meant that cast and crew members occasionally had to take sides. Sometimes least among Penny Marshall and Cindy Williams's fans was Penny's father, *Laverne & Shirley*'s executive producer Tony Marshall. The elder Marshall was once heard screaming at the two women, "Would you two act like professionals?"

It may have been the scene of a tempestuous coupling, but *Laverne & Shirley* most often offered its audience the very finest in entertainment. The two young women in the lead roles were extremely talented, especially in the art of physical comedy. This aspect of Williams and Marshall's talent was emphasized almost as much as the dialogue they so cleverly delivered. Garry Marshall would later say that whether they were learning to fly an airplane beside an unconscious pilot or dressed as Christmas elves in a toy store, Laverne and Shirley were reinventing physical comedy. Marshall and Williams, regardless of their squabbles, were having the time of their lives interacting with some extremely talented co-stars, including veteran actors Phil Foster and Betty Garrett and hilariously funny up-and-comers Michael McKean and David L. Lander. *Laverne & Shirley*, while not always a *fun* set, was certainly an interesting adventure for all involved.

Tapings of the show down the road on Stage 4 were often edgily hilarious. Nobody knew what to expect on the set of *Mork & Mindy* any more than they knew what to expect from the show's star, Robin Williams, who had a background in stand-up comedy, a venue quite different from family television comedy. His comedy was eccentric, often bizarre, as his repertoire of strange voices and even stranger personalities attested. There was some initial concern that Williams wouldn't be able to successfully tackle television comedy, but he certainly wanted to take a crack at the medium. Robin Williams was always up for a challenge.

To the producers' surprise and relief, Williams was able to adjust to the role of television comedian fairly easy. Williams worked hard bringing the character Mork to life, but there was still plenty of time to have fun with his fellow cast members and *Mork & Mindy*'s many guest stars. One of his favorite targets was his co-star, Pam Dawber. Williams would constantly slip off-color remarks and jokes into the dialogue to shock Dawber and throw her off her lines. Dawber was new to the business, yet she was respected as a skillful actor. She confided to the crew that she wanted to *just once* beat Williams at his own game. One night during a lull in the taping, the crew helped Dawber achieve her goal. They gave her the punch line to one of Williams's current gags. When Williams stopped in the middle of a scene and asked Dawber, "What do you get when you cross a donkey and an onion?" she didn't pause before coming back with, "A piece of ass that will make your eyes water!" While Williams was surprised at the comeback, he was amused and not deterred. Dawber learned early in their professional relationship to expect the unexpected from Williams. Another time Mork was to welcome Mindy wearing a dress. Mindy opened the door to greet Mork. She was greeted in turn, as was the studio audience, by the sight of Robin Williams with an uplifted dress revealing that underwear was *not* part of his costume. The cameraman caught the entire incident on tape, but Williams later thought better of it and asked that the taped incident be destroyed lest it fall into the hands of a tabloid.

Sometimes the comedic energy wouldn't be what the producers of the show expected. Jonathan Winters, one of Williams's comedy idols, was asked to guest star in an episode of *Mork & Mindy*. (Winters would later appear in a co-starring role in the series.) Garry Marshall thought that Winters's presence would inspire Williams and encourage additional viewers to tune in to the show. During the warm-up, Winters and Williams had everyone on the floor in hysterics. When the taping began, the risqué material that the two used earlier wasn't acceptable, and they were forced to stick to the scripted lines. Even so, some fascinating interplay ensued between the two brilliant comedians. Winters's appearances with Williams served to reinforce the belief that anything and everything might happen on the *Mork & Mindy* set.

The show that taped on Stage 3 was of a similar complex nature. Where *Mork & Mindy* and *Laverne & Shirley* centered primarily around two main stars, *Happy Days* was more of an ensemble. *Taxi* was another such show, relying on seven-plus players for its character-driven plotlines. It was one of the first of its kind to approach comedy in such a manner, and each character featured a different comedic personality and delivery.

The talent behind *Taxi* was superb. The show was created by James L. Brooks, Stan Daniels, David Davis, and Ed. Weinberger, and was directed by the very talented James Burrows. Brooks, Daniels, Davis, Weinberger, and Burrows were alumni of the enormously successful *Mary Tyler Moore Show* and *Room 222*. After the success of those shows, the talented writers and producers grew tired of formulaic storylines and were anxious to break away from MTM Enterprises to form their own company. (MTM was created by actress Mary Tyler Moore and her husband, Grant Tinker, to develop and distribute television programming.) All five men possessed a bent, off-center humor. They decided to embark on the adventure of creating a television comedy that would reflect their own peculiar jocundity. This atypical brand of humor extended even into the naming of the new production enterprise: the John Charles Walters Company, a name derived from an English pub. There was no John Charles Walters involved with the venture, and the guys had a private chuckle anytime someone feigned familiarity with their non-existent company head.

The actors who were cast in the comedic company that was *Taxi* were eclectic and extremely gifted. The first to be cast was a character actor named Danny DeVito. DeVito is a consummate prankster, and his audition threw the producers off guard. He came in, took a couple of steps, threw the script on the table, and said, "One thing I wanna know before we start is, who wrote this shit?!" There was dead silence, and then the producers laughed uproariously.

The cast of characters *had* to include the standard-issue career cabby, but the writers decided that their character would have a certain strong moral fiber that would make him a pseudo father figure to the other drivers. Actor Judd Hirsch, a veteran Broadway actor who had enjoyed some success as the star of CBS's *Delvecchio*, was cast. Of course, there needed to be an attractive female driver, and the role of Elaine Nardo, a straight-shooting single mother, was created. The producers auditioned almost forty actresses before deciding on Broadway and television actress Marilu Henner. The producers found the perfect actor to fill the role of a wannabe boxer who was supplementing his income driving a cab. Real-life middleweight boxer Tony Danza had previously auditioned for a couple of boxing-related and street-savvy roles. He was screen-tested after he came to the attention of Jim Brooks. Danza's puppy-dog charm appealed to the *Taxi* producers, and Danza was cast for the role of Tony Banta. The character had initially been named Phil Banta. Danza laughingly said he initially thought it was nice that they changed the character's name to Tony in his honor, but later thought maybe it was because they thought he wouldn't answer to Phil.

Jeff Conaway joined the cast fresh from the hit Broadway musical *Grease* to play the role of aspiring actor Bobby Wheeler. Conaway's ability to sketch out the dream-laden and optimistic Wheeler was right on the money. One character took everyone by surprise. Brooks and his partners had not originally planned to include Latka Gravas. The idea of an extremely strange, funny-talking, ostensibly foreign misfit had not crossed their minds when some of the creators of the series went to see performance artist Andy Kaufman at LA's Comedy Store. Little did the producers know that Kaufman's troubled psyche would later bring them untold hours of unimaginable entertainment, concern, and distress. Kaufman would routinely disappear into his numerous personas and become either uncommunicative or obnoxiously verbal. He would stare or glare at various production and studio employees, making the atmosphere of the set unsettled. No one knew when another Andy tirade might be forthcoming.

Later, the character Reverend Jim Ignatowski was created. Stage actor Christopher Lloyd was cast as the unpredictable, excitable, questionably religious mechanic. Lloyd took to the role with a vengeance. "Chris was an actor who stayed in character a lot," laughs Jim Burrows. Academy Award nominee Carol Kane would also join the show to play opposite Andy Kaufman as Latka's equally bizarre girlfriend. Such were the characters of the Sunshine Cab Company.

The chemistry of the *Taxi* actors, executives, and crew was comfortably right, yet the actors' variations in approach to their craft often caused a strange vibration on the set. This was not a set that could be categorized as a family unit like *Happy Days*, an unpredictable pressure cooker like *Laverne & Shirley*, or a hysterical romp such as *Mork & Mindy*. The *Taxi* set was unique. Hirsch was often in a corner studying lines and glowering at Kaufman, a man he didn't seem to like. Conaway might be busy entertaining his legions of female fans, and Henner might be huddled elsewhere with a current boyfriend, John Travolta or Frederic Forrest. DeVito would sometimes encourage Kaufman's weird behavior as he greatly enjoyed watching the others' reactions to Kaufman's strange antics. Lloyd would carefully defuse any volatile situations with comedy, and Danza would attempt to be the peacemaker, striving to keep everything settled so that the work could be done. The *Taxi* set was one to be approached with caution.

Another of Paramount Television's unique shows was *Bosom Buddies*, a takeoff on the film classic *Some Like It Hot*. The premise was that two young male advertising executives lived in an all-female hotel. The characters, who cross-dressed so they would remain unrecognizable as males, and their attraction to and interaction with members of the opposite sex created a multitude of comedic scenarios. Tom Hanks and Peter Scolari, the production's lead actors, were fairly new to the business but very professional in their approach. The same was true of the cast of another show on the lot at that time, *Angie*. Robert Hays and Donna Pescow, fresh off her success in *Saturday Night Fever*, were always easy to work with, as was consummate actress Doris Roberts.

Another series that had potential for Paramount Television was *The Associates*. This show came from the producers of *Taxi* and offered great promise. The cast consisted of several very good actors who would later star in extremely popular television comedies or create hilarious personas: Alley Mills, Joe Regalbuto, and Martin Short. *The Bad News Bears'* cast was mainly children, headed by Corey Feldman and Billy Jacoby.

The cast of *Family Ties* ranged in age and experience, but all the actors brought a reliable professionalism to the set. Michael J. Fox, Meredith Baxter, and Michael Gross could easily swing from comedy to drama. The actors all seemed to like and respect each other, and while they got their work done, they still had time for personal interaction and fun. And then came a little show called *Cheers*, which provided an opportunity for several gifted comedians and writers and would establish television award records during its eleven-year run. That set offered just about everything that could happen during the making of a television show. The actors obviously enjoyed their work and each other. The atmosphere was comfortable and inspiring . . . and many times downright hilarious.

The television lot at Paramount was indeed a happening place during the years 1974–1984. Usually the viewing public was invited in to share the magic during the tapings. Other than the fact that the audience could expect to be entertained, the "before a live audience" tapings were anything but predictable. The different approaches to comedy, the variations in the casts, and the extremely large amount of talent enabled Paramount Television the unique opportunity to have the best of all worlds. During times of frustration and concern for the mental well-being of their comedians, producers, directors, and writers, the Paramount Television brass were comforted by knowing that most of their shows not only were colossal hits with television viewers but also provided a tremendous amount of revenue. If the producers could hold the casts of extraordinary actors together, each show would enjoy a long and fruitful run. Ah yes, but holding them together was often not an easy thing to do.

Chapter 2

THREE CREATIVE FORCES EXPLODE

Garry Marshall is quite a guy. It's not a secret that he has a wonderful sense of humor. He *did* write for such legendary comedians as Lucille Ball, Joey Bishop, Danny Thomas, and a host of others who had tremendously successful television shows in the early 1960s. In addition to Marshall's humor, the man has vision. Garry Marshall has produced more than a thousand television shows, written more than a hundred television scripts, directed eight movies, and written three plays. He has won Emmys, Golden Globes, and Writers Guild Awards. Marshall donated the money that made possible the Northwestern University Marjorie Ward Marshall Dance Center, named for his mother, who died of Alzheimer's in 1983. He also donated the Barbara and Garry Marshall studio wing for film and television production at Northwestern and the Marshall Center for Arts and Athletics at the Harvard-Westlake School in Los Angeles. Garry Marshall is an accomplished man. Actor Tom Bosley says that Marshall is clever and energizing. Ron Howard calls him a natural teacher. Henry Winkler says unabashedly that Marshall is a genius.

How someone obtains the ability to succeed with untried but promising new endeavors is anybody's guess, but the story of Marshall's dynasty at Paramount Television began when Garry Kent Maschiarelli was born on November 13, 1934, in the Bronx. His mother, Marjorie, aspired to be a dancer and taught dance to the children of the neighborhood. Marshall's father, Anthony Wallace (a middle name he made up because it sounded distinguished), known as Tony, was an advertising executive who graduated from New York University. Garry was very close to his family, especially sisters Penny and Ronny.

As a young man, Marshall was often sick in bed with severe allergies and would use his downtime to develop his natural appreciation for a good laugh. He would clip cartoons from newspapers and comic books, and rate them according to his own ha-ha factor. During the long hours of recuperating from an allergic reaction, Marshall learned an important lesson: nothing could replace laughter as a means to get through life's rough patches. After testing his approach to humor through a column he wrote for his De-Witt Clinton High School newspaper and work as a sports stringer for the *New York Journal-American*, Marshall decided to attend Northwestern University to study journalism. He served as night editor and proofreader of the *Daily Northwestern*. After graduating from Northwestern in 1956, Marshall enlisted in the Army. While stationed in Seoul, Korea, Marshall worked for the American Forces Korea Network as a sound editor and writer. He also enjoyed playing basketball and supplying the backbeat as he performed on drums with a band he formed with his fellow soldiers. Though he likely didn't realize it at the time, Marshall's most important free-time activity was successfully telling jokes during Army talent contests. He honed his craft with partner Jim Anglisano and placed third in the All-Army Entertainment Contest, held in Virginia.

Soon after his release from the Army, Garry Marshall decided to try his luck as a joke writer in New York City. He first secured an entry-level job with the *Daily News*. The first professional money Marshall earned was for writing jokes for transsexual celebrity Christine Jorgensen and children's personality Shari Lewis. As aspiring comedy writers, Marshall and his partner, Fred Freeman, soon found a champion in comedian Phil Foster. Foster was impressed with the young men's talent and introduced the joke writers to the very funny Joey Bishop, who appeared regularly on *The Jack Paar Show*. Writing comedy bits for the comedian garnered Marshall and Freeman their first television writing credits. In 1960 Phil Foster hired the pair to write for his NBC radio show *Monitor*. Marshall continued to write jokes for *The Jack Paar Show* and honed his comedic talents to advance his career. From 1962 through 1966, Marshall wrote for *The Joey Bishop Show*, *The Bill Dana Show*, *The Danny Thomas Show*, *The Dick Van Dyke Show*, and *The Lucy Show*. Jerry Belson was Garry's new writing partner, and the two became a sought-after team. The result was in: Garry Marshall was a success as a professional comedy writer.

Happy Days' Ron Howard with legendary producer Garry Marshall. Photo courtesy of Globe Photos, Inc.

Garry and his wife Barbara Marshall's first child, daughter Lori, was born in 1963. The couple has two other children: Kathleen and Scott. The Marshall clan was a close one. Garry and Barbara are married to this day. Marshall, his parents, and his siblings remained close. The family's propensity for being funny was both present and abundant. As devoted to his family as Marshall was, he was also devoted to a career involved with quality television. His writing credits include specials and episodic television, such as *Gomer Pyle*, *I Spy*, and the television movie *Evil Roy Slade*, starring Mickey Rooney.

In 1966 Marshall and Belson sold their first pilot to Warner Bros. and the NBC television network. *Hank*, starring Dick Kallman and Howard St. John, lasted only one season. (Kallman, who went on to play roles in other television shows, such as *Batman* and *Medical Center*, was murdered in 1980 in New York City.) The show may not have been successful, but Marshall and Belson's next series, NBC's 1966 *Hey, Landlord*, received some notice. The series starred television's "Sugarfoot," Will Hutchins, and comedian Sandy Baron. Richard Dreyfuss, Rob Reiner, and Sally Field made appearances on the show. Marshall had the opportunity to work with other up-and-comers: writer James L. Brooks and director Jerry Paris. Paris would later work closely with Marshall on one of Marshall's most successful shows, and Brooks would helm the sitcom

Taxi on the same Paramount lot where Marshall would base his future television productions.

In 1970 Garry Marshall adapted, produced, and served as head writer for his first hit series, *The Odd Couple*. Neil Simon's play was fertile comedy ground for the writers and for stars Tony Randall and Jack Klugman. It was there that writers Lowell Ganz and Mark Rothman would first work with Marshall. Marshall took the opportunity to cast his sister Penny Marshall as Oscar Madison's secretary, Myrna. The show was very well received.

The Odd Couple would run for five seasons, but Marshall didn't let grass grow between his toes. From 1970 to 1974, he would be involved in the creation of three other sitcoms: *Barefoot in the Park*, with Bess Armstrong and Dick Arnold, *Me and the Chimp*, starring Ted Bessell and Tami Cotler, and *The Little People*, with Brian Keith and Shelley Fabares. The quality of the shows that Marshall wrote and created was important to him. He wanted them to counter-balance the negativity of some of the shows already on television, and he wanted to produce shows that he could watch with his children. Life was good for Garry Marshall, but it was about to get better.

Rising on the scene was a young man with ambition and initiative: Michael Eisner. Eager to make his mark, Eisner found the field of entertainment right up his alley. Michael Dammann Eisner was born on March 7, 1942, in Mount Kisco, New York, with the proverbial silver spoon in his mouth. He grew up on Manhattan's Park Avenue with his older sister, Margot, and their parents, Lester and Maggie. Lester was a demanding father who expected much from his son. Eisner's early years were filled with the adventure of riding the subway to various spots in the big city, and playing glockenspiel in the orchestra and quarterback on the football team of the Allen-Stevenson School. Although watching television in the Eisner household was restricted to one hour a day, young Michael loved such sitcoms as *Father Knows Best* and *The Adventures of Ozzie and Harriet*. These feel-good television series would remain in Eisner's memory, tucked away for future recollection and use. It was possibly a love of these traditional family exchanges that inspired Eisner to pursue a career as an all-American doctor, like that of Jim Anderson on *Father Knows Best*. He enrolled as a pre-med student at the small, liberal arts Denison College in Granville, Ohio.

While at Denison, Eisner changed his major to English and discovered that he loved writing plays. He even had a couple produced and presented by the school's drama department. Back home in New York City, Eisner was thrilled when he landed a summer job as an NBC

Television page. Having whetted his appetite for the world of entertainment, Eisner next took a job as a traffic clerk at NBC, where his tasks involved logging commercials. He also signed on to work weekends for WNBC Radio. Eisner wanted more responsibility and moved on to CBS Television when he was offered a more expansive job in the Traffic Department. He soon was transferred to the game show division of the network, where he pitched an idea for a show he called *Bet Your Bottom Dollar* to legendary television executive Fred Silverman. The show didn't get produced, but ideas for television programming continued to run through Eisner's mind.

As Michael Eisner sent out resumes in an attempt to be hired for a more significant position within the television industry, another young talent was on the rise. Barry Diller had graduated from mail clerk at the William Morris Agency to a position in the programming department at ABC Television. It was Diller who first saw Eisner's letter seeking employment at ABC. The two men would fashion interesting paths through the jungle of Hollywood throughout their entertainment careers.

Barry Diller was not one to waste his time on things he found unimportant. He was quite aware of the opportunities open to those in television and film. The son of a real estate developer, Diller was born in San Francisco on February 2, 1942. His family moved to southern California, and he attended Beverly Hills High School. He was a student at UCLA when he decided that college wasn't offering him as much as a career in the entertainment industry might. Diller dropped out of school in 1966 to take a job at the William Morris Agency. The young man was hired after an interview arranged by Danny Thomas, the father of Diller's long-time friend Marlo Thomas. By 1964 Diller had worked his way up to the position of junior agent. His ability to learn quickly, go-getter attitude, and ability to grasp the intricacies of the complex business of entertainment began to come to the attention of various people in the industry. One of those people was ABC-TV executive Leonard Goldberg, who offered Diller a job in New York City as his assistant. It was in this capacity that Diller came across Michael Eisner's resume.

Although the men were complete opposites in personality, it was through his interview with Barry Diller that Michael Eisner was hired at ABC-TV as assistant to Special Programming's Ted Fetter. By 1966 Eisner was promoted to Talent and Specials manager, working for Gary Pudney. Eisner impressed his superiors with his aggressiveness and creativity, and he moved up the network ladder quickly. He soon had the job of Prime-time Development director. Diller, in the meantime, was working with studio executives to acquire the rights to movies for the network and soon was developing Movies of the Week and mini-series.

By 1969 Michael Eisner was heading the Feature Films and Program Development department and reporting to Barry Diller, who was now head of prime-time programming for ABC. For a short time, Diller worked out of Hollywood while Eisner remained in Manhattan. Eisner evidently wasn't delighted to be working for, or even with, Diller. Their approach to business was very different, and the two men were highly competitive. Diller was more a "people" type of guy, and Eisner, while he could get along with people, was more ruthless in his approach. Success was important to both men. During this time Eisner also made some advances in children's programming for the network and was involved in game show development. By 1973 Eisner was working in Hollywood, as Vice President of Prime-time Programming for ABC.

Meanwhile, Barry Diller was setting his sights on a career outside of ABC. When Gulf + Western Chairman Charlie Bluhdorn offered Diller a job working for Paramount Pictures president Frank Yablans, Diller said he wasn't interested. Bluhdorn was so impressed with Diller that he offered him the job of chairman, working *alongside* Yablans. Diller accepted the position, but the relationship didn't work. Yablans left Paramount, and Diller was soon running the studio himself.

Michael Eisner, in his position at ABC, helped introduce some quality mid-season replacements for the network in January 1975. *Baretta* and *Barney Miller* were both unique enough to garner strong viewer attention. Eisner couldn't have been delighted when CBS programming genius Fred Silverman was brought in to work *his* magic at ABC. Eisner needed to come up with something special to show those at ABC that he was a force in television programming himself. A chance conversation with Paramount development head Tom Miller led to something that would become a major factor in Eisner's career development.

Michael Eisner and Tom Miller were delayed at the Newark airport one wintry night while on a business trip and passed the time discussing their favorite television shows. Each of the men liked family-driven television and missed the types of shows that revolved around family values and togetherness. Once back in Hollywood, Eisner remembered the conversation and was soon writing a development concept for a new television series centered on the idea of family interaction. He titled the proposal "New Family in Town." And thought of Garry Marshall.

Chapter 3

LOVE IN THE HAPPY DAYS

The alliance of Michael Eisner, Tom Miller, and Garry Marshall provided a wealth of ideas and creative talent. Marshall has called Michael Eisner one of the best television minds around. When Eisner and Miller discussed classic family television that night at the airport, Eisner cited his favorite television show, *Mama*, a CBS series starring Peggy Wood and Judson Laire that ran from 1949 to 1957. Tom Miller was a bit more contemporary with his favorite, *Father Knows Best*, starring Robert Young and Jane Wyatt. That show was based on the popular radio program of the same name and ran on NBC from 1954 through 1960. Both shows exuded family interaction and featured half-hour morality plays interlaced with light comedy. Both were steeped in the post–World War II wholesomeness of the fifties.

Soon after the airport conversation with Tom Miller, Michael Eisner drafted a four-page outline for a television show he titled "New Family in Town." He thought the premise of the show he had in mind, a family living somewhere in suburbia USA, would be a nice throwback to those family-oriented shows that television viewers seemed to remember so fondly. Eisner felt that Garry Marshall, who had some quality television under his belt and was currently enjoying success with *The Odd Couple*, would be a good match to produce what he and Miller had in mind.

Garry Marshall thought the idea of situations revolving around an average family sounded promising. Marshall and his current writing partner, Jerry Belson, had been producing television under their Wendell Henderson banner. The first thing to be addressed was where to set the show. Marshall wanted to base it in his hometown, the Bronx, but Eisner and ABC thought that locale might be too regional and ethnic. Eisner thought the viewing audience would be more comfortable with a midwestern family. Tom Miller was from Wisconsin, so Eisner suggested to Marshall that that locale might be more appealing. Wisconsin it was. The natural inclination in television development is to set shows in the present, but Garry Marshall thought setting the show in the fifties might be fun. When Tom Miller suggested the era to Eisner, Eisner thought it was a great idea. When Marshall spoke to Belson about the idea, Belson said he didn't much like the fifties experience and didn't think that era would make for interesting television. Marshall decided that it wouldn't hurt to work with Tom Miller to see where the idea might take them. If the show came together, he could produce it under Henderson Productions, while Belson would continue with his other projects using the Wendell name.

Garry Marshall and Tom Miller worked with Miller's colleague Eddie Milkis—young but already accomplished in television—to flesh out the premise. Edward K. Milkis had begun his career as a film editor in the fifties and had done memorable work on television's *Star Trek*, *The Brady Bunch*, and *The Odd Couple*. Garry Marshall wrote a script incorporating the trio's ideas and named the show "Cool." Test audiences didn't seem to like the title, so Tom Miller rechristened it *Happy Days*. Eisner loved it. He couldn't wait for the powers that be at ABC to have a look at the script and give the project the green light.

Michael Eisner thought the purchase of the proposed series by ABC was in the bag. He was in for a surprise. The network didn't want to finance the pilot. They didn't find the fifties interesting. The script was brought to the attention of Paramount Television, and it was suggested that Marshall's treatment be used for an episode of ABC's popular series *Love, American Style*. ABC agreed to $100,000 for an episode, titled "New Family in Town," that would center on a Milwaukee family who was the first on their block to own a television set. Tom Miller was calling it "Love in the Happy Days." The show would air in February 1972. It was Eisner's intent that, after filming was completed on the episode, the executives at ABC would realize that the show would be wonderful as a stand-alone series and not just as an episode of *Love, American Style*. What would happen with the finished product down the line was anybody's guess.

Marshall, Miller, and Milkis joined forces to put the episode together. The *Love, American Style* episode was first cast featuring Ron Howard, Marion Ross, and Dennis Weaver. Weaver dropped out of the episode, and it was recast, retaining Howard and Ross but adding Tom Bosley in place of Weaver. Susan Neher played little Joanie Cunningham, Ric Carrott was cast as Charles Cunningham, and Tanis Montgomery appeared as Richie's girlfriend, Arlene.

Tom Miller thought that Ron Howard, the now-grown moppet from the popular television series *The Andy Griffith Show*, would be perfect in the role of the teenage son. Howard had been adored as Opie Taylor and was known in the industry as a hardworking young actor. Now a teenager, Howard was more interested in attending film school than continuing to act, but he found the script appealing. He thought he might have fun with the role of Richie Cunningham, named after a nice young man who had gone to church with Garry Marshall back in the Bronx. Robbie Benson and Donny Most also read for the role of Richie. Benson didn't really want the role, and Miller, Marshall, and Eisner all knew that with Ron Howard came a degree of professionalism upon which they could rely.

Ron Howard wasn't just any teenage actor. There was a good reason why he was chosen for this Americana-influenced pilot. He was born Ronald William Howard on March 1, 1954, in Duncan, Oklahoma, to actors Rance and Jean Howard. Rance, born in 1928, was a drama major at the University of Oklahoma. The former Jean Speegle was also interested in acting, although she wouldn't make her film debut until 1975 in the made-for-television movie *Huckleberry Finn*. In 1956 Rance landed a role in the western *Frontier Woman*, and the director cast Howard's eighteen-month-old son, Ronny, in the film as well. Ronny's first bonafide role came as the character Billy Rhinelander in the 1959 film *The Journey*, which featured the all-star cast of Yul Brynner, Deborah Kerr, E. G. Marshall, Jason Robards, and Anne Jackson—quite good company in which to start an acting career. Young Ronny was awarded the role after doing a scene from *Mr. Roberts* for the film's director, Anatole Litvak. Ronny had been doing the scene for his family since he was two and a half years old, and it finally paid off. Howard's mother and father weren't the usual stage parents. They told Ronny that if he wanted to do the part, they'd take the money, put it in the bank, and he'd never have to act again if he didn't want to. Rance and Jean debated whether they wanted their son to get started in the family business so young, but since it was a great opportunity for Ronny to travel to Vienna to shoot the movie, they decided why not?

Ronny Howard's first television role was the pilot "Barnaby and Mr. O'Malley" with Bert Lahr, which aired on December 20, 1959. Howard soon began appearing regularly on television's *Playhouse 90* and in 1960 was cast as the precocious Opie Taylor in the series *The Andy Griffith Show*. Ronny Howard was a tremendous success as the only child of a widowed southern sheriff. More than an adorable little face, Howard quickly became a consummate young actor. While he appeared on *The Andy Griffith Show* throughout its eight-year run (1960–1968), Howard attended public school in Burbank, California. He appeared in many movies throughout his childhood, including the hit musical extravaganza *The Music Man*. Howard's mother, Jean, told a reporter that she was giving up acting so that the two men in the family could make their mark in the entertainment world. After *The Andy Griffith Show* went off the air in 1968, Ronny did *The Smith Family* television series with Henry Fonda and Janet Blair.

Howard would later say that during his teenage years he grew tired of being rejected in favor of older actors. When he was fifteen, he decided to take a break from acting to play varsity basketball, but the young man didn't completely abandon his Hollywood roots. He picked up a Super 8 camera and shot little movies starring his family. Howard was deeply intrigued by the film-making process, and upon graduation from high school he entered the University of Southern California's film school. Then came the offer to appear in a little movie newcomer George Lucas was producing and directing titled *American Graffiti*.

George Lucas is originally from the small farming community of Modesto, California. As an up-and-coming screenwriter, he realized that the small-town dynamics of Modesto would be interesting to explore on film. During the time that Lucas was a teenager, Modesto youth could often be found admiring each others' cars, hanging out at the local drive-in restaurant, and engaging in the other forms of teenage adventure enjoyed by the young people of rural America. Writing with Gloria Katz and Willard Huyck, Lucas centered a story on the last night of summer vacation.

George Lucas admired the acting talents of Ronny Howard. The red-haired, all-American-looking actor was perfect for the lead role in *American Graffiti*. Fred Roos, a friend of Garry Marshall's, was casting the film and asked Marshall if Lucas could view the "Love in the Happy Days" episode to see Ron Howard playing a fifties-era charac- ter. Tom Miller says that he showed George Lucas the un-aired pilot of *Happy Days*. When asked later, Lucas wouldn't really deny that the Ron Howard character in that pilot had been an inspiration for the same actor's character in *American Graffiti*. The many components of Lucas's ode to teenage angst made *American Graffiti* a box-office smash.

The *Happy Days* cast gathers for their first group photo, 1974: Top (left to right): Donny Most (Ralph), Anson Williams (Potsie), Gavan O'Herlihy (Chuck). Bottom (left to right): Marion Ross (Marion), Tom Bosley (Howard), Erin Moran (Joanie), Ron Howard (Richie), Henry Winkler (Fonzie). Photo courtesy of Globe Photos, Inc.

All in the family, 1977. Producer Tom Miller (center) relaxes on the *Happy Days* set with (from left to right) Ron Howard, Scott Baio (Chachi), and Henry Winkler. Photo courtesy of Globe Photos, Inc.

Although *American Graffiti* actually took place on a summer evening in 1962, the teenagers featured experienced their adolescence in the fifties. At this same time, a new play also featuring teens, but this time firmly set in the fifties, was opening on Broadway. *Grease* would also be a big hit. The fifties were once again a hot commodity. Was the television industry listening to the buzz? Yes, it was. The powers that be at ABC made an inter-office call to Michael Eisner. "Remember that Garry Marshall pilot . . . ?"

Looking back, there are many similarities between *American Graffiti* and what evolved into the *Happy Days* series. Of course, there is Ron Howard and his character. Another hit film of the time that was influential in the formation of *Happy Days* was the movie *Summer of '42,* starring Jennifer O'Neill and Gary Grimes. Each of these movies captured the essence of their decades, and *Happy Days* could—and would—do the same. The show could be a big hit with television viewers. Also, thought Garry Marshall and Tom Miller, if the show does all right and goes into reruns, it won't look dated.

Michael Eisner was anxious to bring a hit series to the network. The network liked the "New Family in Town" episode, but they didn't think it was quite good enough to sustain a series. They asked that it be remade. There were some concerns that Ron Howard and actor Anson Williams were too old to play teenagers, and they were asked to come in and test. Howard says he was a little offended being asked to test, but he liked Garry Marshall and decided he could do that if that was what ABC was asking. Howard said he'd commit to what was now being called *Happy Days* but only if he could age each year the show was on the air.

On Thanksgiving Day 1973, actors Ron Howard, Marion Ross, Anson Williams, and Tom Bosley were informed that the series was a go. Michael Eisner told Tom Miller that he would like to air the first episode in five weeks. That meant a lot of work, but Marshall wanted to do the show, and he committed. Now to develop a storyline, put together a crew, and flesh out the cast. A *lot* of work. It was a good thing Marshall was a television professional. (Some of the footage from "New Family in Town" would appear as a flashback in a future *Happy Days* episode.)

Garry Marshall had three small children at the time he began to produce *Happy Days* and was very interested in doing a show that would be something they could watch and enjoy. At the time *Happy Days* aired in the 1973–1974 television season, television broadcasts were filled with social conflict and politics. *Happy Days* was perceived as a comedy vehicle that could transport the audience back to a happier time. Marshall decided that physical humor wasn't the approach he wanted for the cast he had assembled, but rather that a short-scene, visual style comedy would be the most successful way for the show to go. It was important to Marshall to fully develop the characters and make them "friends" whom the audience would want to visit each week. Marshall says ultimately a television show wants to develop characters with whom people are comfortable spending time. One of Marshall's television tenets was that when an audience laughs, it means the actor has done something funny. When they cheer, it is because they love the character. To Marshall funny is in equal parts writing and acting. The cast chosen was one that certainly worked well to accomplish those goals.

Influenced by the tough guys in *Grease* and *American Graffiti*, Eisner and Tom Miller decided that *Happy Days* needed a gang. Marshall didn't like that idea. He felt it was too similar to the play and the movie. Eisner thought the show wouldn't work without it, so Marshall compromised and said he would write in one tough guy. Tom Miller said he knew just the guy for the part, a New York actor named Henry Winkler. Miller had evidently heard about Winkler's performance in *The Lords of Flatbush* (although the film would come out three months after *Happy Days* was on the air) and thought he would be great in the part. Winkler says he was nervous about reading for the role. He remembers he made a choice to make the person he was reading with sit down so that he would be the last person standing. He managed to pull it off, but there were concerns. After Winkler left the audition, Marshall said to Miller, "*This* is my Fonzie?" Marshall later said that there were concerns that Winkler was too short to bring authority to the role. Other actors were brought in to audition, including Micky Dolenz and Mike Nesmith. Nobody knocked Garry Marshall out, though. Reluctantly, Marshall finally agreed to cast Henry Winkler. Marshall would come to change his opinion about Winkler being too short to portray Fonzie. When he saw Winkler develop the character, his height didn't matter any more. Garry Marshall thought Henry Winkler "acted like he was ten feet tall." It was a great choice. Winkler would receive more than 50,000 fan letters a week at the height of the series' run.

The character Arthur Herbert Fonzarelli, a name that producer Bob Brunner came up with, was oddly silent in the first episode. His initial hipness was somehow apparent due to the fact that "Fonzie" had a bevy of females around his motorcycle, which was parked at Arnold's Drive-In. (In the premiere episode, Arnold's is named Arthur's.) The image was cemented when Fonzie stepped to the bathroom mirror in Arnold's. It was important to Winkler to not portray Fonzie as the standard-issue tough guy. Fonzie was a member of first the Demons and then the Falcons, but the "gang" members would never appear on the show. Winkler promised himself his character wouldn't chew gum, have cigarettes rolled in his sleeve, or comb his hair on camera, unlike previous film tough guys. While the producers were okay with that likely unverbalized promise, they did ask that Fonzie comb his hair in the mirror in that first episode. Winkler protested but was encouraged to stick to what was in the script. Winkler, in character, approached the mirror but just couldn't comb his hair after raising the comb. Fonzie looked into the mirror, saw that his hair was already perfect, threw out his arms, and walked away. Winkler says the idea just came to him as a way he could be true to himself as an actor and also to what was written in the script. It was in that moment, Winkler says, that Fonzie was really born. Although Fonzie was intended to be a side character, Henry Winkler's portrayal of the cool yet caring motorcycle loner immediately endeared him to viewers. Winkler himself says that The Fonz was everything that Winkler wanted to be—the epitome of cool. Fonzie was enough of an enigma that those who were watching that premier episode of *Happy Days* seemed to want to stick around to see more of the character. (By the way, the only one who was ever allowed to call Fonzie "Arthur" was Mrs. Cunningham.)

Henry Winkler might have been the last person to believe that he would make his initial acting claim through portraying a street tough, even though he says he was born to be an actor. When Winkler, at age eight, saw Jimmy Stewart in the film *Rear Window*, he was spellbound. The actor, though dyslexic, had earned a masters degree at the Yale School of Drama.

Henry Franklin Winkler was born on October 30, 1945, in New York City to Harry and Ilse Winkler. He has an older sister named Beatrice. Before World War II, Winkler's parents had been living a very comfortable life in Germany. Because of the war they left their homeland and started over again in New York City. Harry and Ilse Winkler were well-educated, and Harry became head of a prosperous international lumber company.

As a boy, Henry was a daydreamer. He was raised in a strong Jewish tradition, and many of the kids in school teased him. Winkler's first stage appearance was as a tube of toothpaste in a play at Hilltop nursery school. From that point on, Winkler wanted to be an actor. His father was deadset against it. His mother was sure he would forget about it and move on to other, more worthy things. Winkler was sent to McBurney School for Boys, a college prep school. He says he was surrounded by over-achievers and received the lowest grades in his class. Though Winkler was interested in the school's drama productions, the drama coach, who was also the headmaster, told him that he had no talent and would never be an actor. Winkler questioned if acting was still what he wanted to do and decided it was.

Winkler remained true to his dream and decided to study drama at Emerson College in Boston. His parents said he could participate in drama as long as he studied something else as well. Winkler majored in child psychology. He says that he was obsessed with becoming an actor, as he felt that was the best way for him to most clearly communicate. He appeared in plays while attending Emerson, and his work was very well received. Winkler's mother saw how much his heart was in acting and began to entertain the thought that perhaps Henry could achieve his dream. When it came time to graduate from college, Winkler sought the support of his parents to continue in the acting field. His father told him that if he wanted to become a serious actor he should get a master's degree in theater. Winkler was admitted to the Yale School of Drama as a graduate student and earned his degree there. He was recommended for the Yale Repertory Theater and stayed with that entity for a year and a half.

Winkler was able to pick up several jobs acting in off-Broadway productions and commercials before making his screen debut in 1974's *The Lords of Flatbush*. He replaced Richard Gere in the role of Butchey Weinstein when Gere dropped out of the picture. Winkler heard that an actor was leaving the role and asked his agent to see if he could read for it. After Winkler finished work in the film, his agent felt that Winkler had done about all he could do in New York City and suggested the young man relocate to try his luck in Los Angeles. Winkler wasn't crazy about the idea but agreed to the new experience. Within two weeks, he was hired for a role on *The Mary Tyler Moore Show*. Two bit parts in films and a couple of appearances on *The Mary Tyler Moore Show* and *The Bob Newhart Show* followed *The Lords of Flatbush*, though the film had yet to be released. (When he received good reviews for his work in *The Lords of Flatbush*, Winkler sent a copy of the notices to the McBurney headmaster—evidently he *could* act.)

Winkler was pretty much an unknown in the entertainment business when he was cast as The Fonz. He had been in Los Angeles only a couple of months when he was called to read for the role. Winkler at first had a hard time believing that he could play a chick magnet as he saw himself as "a short Jewish kid with a big nose." He didn't expect to be cast as Arthur Fonzarelli.

In addition to Fonzie being a man of few words in the early episodes of *Happy Days*, the character Arthur Fonzarelli is noticeably different in other ways from the character that would evolve. Even Fonzie's name was to have been something else. The Fonzie character was originally named Arthur Maschiarelli after creator Garry Marshall's real last name. His nickname was to have been "Mash." The character's name was changed in the original script because ABC didn't want people being reminded of CBS's hit show *M*A*S*H*.

It's interesting to look at the first season of *Happy Days* and watch the transformation of Fonzie. Winkler's delivery of his lines early on is a softer, less confrontational approach than the too-cool-for-school, don't-you-dare-doubt-the-word-of-The Fonz attitude that would develop over the run of the series. Henry Winkler said that he originally modeled Fonzie's speech pattern after Sylvester Stallone, with whom he co-starred in *The Lords of Flatbush*. The early Fonzie also smiles more than The Fonz of later shows. Most notable in those first episodes, of course, is the lack of a leather jacket.

While Fonzie and his leather jacket would make television history when the jacket was enshrined in the Smithsonian Institution in 1980, ABC didn't always embrace the concept. Scott Baio, who would later come on the show to play Fonzie's nephew, Chachi, told reporter Dan Snierson that it was taboo to try on the leather jacket. Some things, after all, are sacred. (Interestingly, in the pilot Richie is wearing a leather jacket, though it is black, not brown.) But for those first episodes, Fonzie was wearing . . . a windbreaker. (The leather jacket Winkler wore on *Happy Days* was stolen sometime during the second year of the show. The jacket that was given to the Smithsonian was the jacket worn during the second year through 1979. Henry Winkler is especially proud of the fact that Fonzie's jacket resides in so prestigious a place as the Smithsonian. He parents had experienced great hardship and escaped Nazi Germany, and they were in the audience at the presentation in Washington, D.C. As Winkler himself put it, "What a journey.")

Seasoned veteran Tom Bosley would continue with the role of Howard Cunningham, the average dad who serves as a moral compass for his children but who isn't above demonstrating his quick wit and sometimes acting goofy. Tom Bosley was born in Chicago on October 1, 1927. He attended DePaul University after a wartime stint in the Navy. Bosley worked in Community Theater and off-Broadway before making his mark on the Great White Way in the role of New York Mayor Fiorello LaGuardia in the 1959 musical *Fiorello!* Bosley was so impressive in the role that he won a Tony Award. Other Broadway appearances followed.

Bosley's first big-screen appearance was in 1964's *Love with the Proper Stranger*. Appearances in films such as *The World of Henry Orient* and *Yours, Mine and Ours* followed. Bosley had been appearing in small television roles since 1952, and he landed the series *The Debbie Reynolds Show* in 1968. Roles in *The Sandy Duncan Show* and *Wait 'Til Your Father Gets Home* followed.

Tom Bosley portrayed Howard Cunningham as a dad with whom the viewers could identify: someone whose advice would be valuable but who would often fall into the "my dad is a wiener" category. Howard's comments to his son Richie are based in common sense and serve as the impetus for informative conversations. At the same time, Howard serves as the Grand Poobah of his lodge and wears a silly hat. Bosley made Howard a believable character. Howard Cunningham would be ranked number 9 in *TV Guide*'s 2004 list of the 50 Greatest TV Dads of All Time. The actor said the *Happy Days* cast was so close that it was like having a second family. He said that it was easier to parent the kids on *Happy Days* than his real-life children as he had the scripted words to deal with, whatever problems arose.

The role of Marion Cunningham née Kelp, who would come in at number 2 in the *TV Guide* Greatest TV Moms list, was brought to life by popular screen actress Marion Ross. Ross brought grace and experience to the role. She was born Marian Ross but changed the spelling of her name to Marion at the age of thirteen to fit with her future plans to become an actress; she believed that the change of vowel would have greater marquee appeal. The future *Happy Days* mom hails from Albert Lea, Minnesota. Ross enrolled in San Diego State College after her family moved to California. While a freshman, Ross was named the school's most outstanding actress. She was awarded a contract with Paramount Pictures at the age of twenty-two after a successful run with the La Jolla Summer Stock Theater.

Marion Ross's debut on the silver screen was with Ginger Rogers in *Forever Female*. Roles in such films as *The Glenn Miller Story*, *Sabrina*, and *Operation Petticoat* followed. Ross found success in television, playing the maid in the hit series *Life with Father*, which debuted in 1953. She also appeared on *The Burns and Allen Show* and several other television series. Ross was ideal to play the ditzy yet responsible maternal head of the Cunningham family. Capricious as she could sometimes be, Marion also had great common sense and more than a little intelligence. She had, after all, majored in archaeology in college. Ross fleshed out the role nicely and made Marion a character that didn't easily fade into the background. One of Ross's favorite episodes was the one in which "Mrs. C" dances the tango with Fonzie. Henry Winkler would later say that Marion Ross was one of the great women of the twentieth century. Extremely flexible as an actress, Ross brought a lot of spark to the show. Ross says that playing Marion Cunningham was like playing house. She says that the character Marion Cunningham was basically her own personality: a compulsive, sweet person who likes to please people.

Every successful television teen character has to have a group of "zany" friends, and the friends Marshall and his writers had in mind perfectly complemented Richie Cunningham. First, Richie needed a best friend. Warren "Potsie" Weber, as goofy as he was, served as a loyal sounding board for the sometimes confusing situations in which Richie found himself. Warren had been nicknamed Potsie by his mother because when he was a child he liked to make things out of clay.

Anson Williams, with his limited acting experience, showed the producers that he could bring what was needed to the role of second banana. There was a certain spunk to the young actor. He was born Anson William Heimlick on September 24, 1949, in Los Angeles. His father was an art director who ran an Orange Julius store during Anson's high school years. Williams attended Pierce Junior College, where he discovered drama. He dropped out of school to pursue a career in acting. Community stage appearances in *The Sound of Music* and *The Music Man* followed. Soon the young man was appearing in a McDonald's commercial and on such television shows as *Marcus Welby, M.D.* and *Owen Marshall: Counselor at Law.*

There had to be the stereotypical class clown, that guy who not only finds the humor in the mundane process of growing up but who also can be counted on to have something inane to say. Ralph Malph, as indicated by his perfectly selected name, would provide a lot of the comic relief on *Happy Days*. Actor Don "Donny" Most had just the kind of background that Garry Marshall was looking for to play this character.

Donny Most had already experienced some success as an actor, but it was his swift delivery that caught the attention of the producers. His timing and quick wit were a delight. Donald Most was born in Brooklyn on August 8, 1959, to an accountant father and homemaker mother. Most's favorite movie as a child was *The Al Jolson Story*, which he claims to have seen more than fifty times. Most was performing at various resorts in the Catskill Mountains by the age of fifteen. He began to take acting lessons and appear in commercials while a student at Erasmus High School, where he was also co-captain of his swim team.

After graduation from high school, Most attended Lehigh University in Pennsylvania as an engineering major, although he later switched to business. He ended his college career after his junior year, when he appeared in bit parts on television's popular shows *Emergency!* and *Room*

222. Most auditioned for the role of *Happy Days'* Potsie Weber and was well received by the producers, who enjoyed his humor. The problem was that Most, like Ron Howard, had red hair, and Garry Marshall didn't want to cast another redhead as Richie's best friend. The role of Ralph was originally conceived as a dumb football jock. That character ended up being Richie's brother, Chuck. The character Ralph was turned into the class comedian to fit Don Most's comedic ability. The role was written larger after Most was given the job.

No family in the fifties would be complete without the smart-aleck little sister. Richie needed someone to mentor and also someone who would serve as a pesky nuisance. Erin Moran fit the role nicely. She was a very young actress—only twelve at the time she was hired for *Happy Days*—but she already had experience and was perfect as the wise-ass little sister. Moran, the youngest of six children, was born in Los Angeles on October 18, 1961. She appeared in a commercial for First Federal Bank at the age of five. Moran furthered her career by landing roles in television's *Daktari* and *The Don Rickles Show*. She also appeared in feature films such as *How Sweet It Is* and *Watermelon Man* and on television in such series as *My Three Sons*, *The Courtship of Eddie's Father*, and *Family Affair*. Moran would win hearts as *Happy Days'* hula-hoop-spinning Joanie. Moran was pleased to be associated with a show that had, in her words, "great values and morals."

If the Cunninghams were to reflect the average midwestern family, it was believed they should have those 2.5 children the nation's statisticians were claiming for the era. Marshall decided to add an older brother for Richie. The character Chuck Cunningham was one of the show's few failures. In the beginning, it is established that Chuck is a college student, though where he goes to school and what he is studying aren't ever made clear. Chuck isn't very bright and seems interested only in eating sandwiches and dribbling basketballs. He seems more like a visitor to the Cunningham house than a valued member of the family—and not a very well-liked visitor at that. In those first episodes, the character seems tolerated more than embraced. Chuck's relationship with Howard, for instance, is not only under-developed, but we almost feel sorry for Chuck as he seems to be not a concern of Howard's but rather a disappointment to his father. This aspect of the Chuck dynamic tends to make us uncomfortable with his presence and detracts from both the warmth and the worthiness of the Cunningham family.

When the character Chuck Cunningham was first cast, the role was played by Gavan O'Herlihy, son of Dan O'Herlihy, a noted film and television actor who appeared in dozens of films, including such classics as

Imitation of Life, *The Virgin Queen*, and *Kidnapped*. He was nominated for an Academy Award in the category of Best Actor for 1954's *The Adventures of Robinson Crusoe*. Gavan O'Herlihy was a tennis player who attended Trinity College in Dublin, Ireland. Paul McGuinness, future manager of the band U2, approached the young man about taking a role in one of the college's productions. Although he would become Irish National Tennis Champion, O'Herlihy decided to pursue acting by joining Ireland's leading theater, The Abbey. He worked on stage for two years and decided at the age of twenty to head to Hollywood to see what future he might have in acting. Within five months of O'Herlihy's arrival in California, he had a role on *The Mary Tyler Moore Show*.

It was interesting that an Irishman—although O'Herlihy was actually born in Los Angeles—was asked to play such a critical role in *Happy Days'* all-American family. O'Herlihy wasn't that fond of his role as Chuck. Since the Cunninghams' eldest son was a college student, the young actor realized that the role was going to be little more than a reoccurring bit and likely wouldn't receive a lot of screen time. After only a few episodes, O'Herlihy asked that he be written out of the show. He told Garry Marshall that he was moving to Ireland to focus on poetry, and his request to leave was granted. O'Herlihy must have changed his mind, as he soon was seen in roles on such television shows as *The Six Million Dollar Man* and *Police Woman*.

Randolph Roberts took over the role of Chuck after O'Herlihy left. Roberts was a young actor who had appeared on the series *Gunsmoke* and in the movie *Wicked, Wicked*. Roberts didn't seem to get much out of the role either. The producers and writers didn't really know what to do with Chuck because Fonzie was already serving as an older brother to Richie. (Ron Howard and Henry Winkler themselves were already feeling a brotherly bond. Winkler said he will never again have an acting partner like Howard. They continue to be great friends.)

One of the talented professionals who produced and wrote for the show was Lowell Ganz; he had been a writer on *The Odd Couple* and had a terrific sense of comedic television. Ganz was born August 31, 1948, in New York City and grew up in Queens. He and his writing partner Babaloo Mandel would become important to *Happy Days*. It was Ganz who later said that it became one of the goals of the show to focus on the relationship between Richie and Fonzie. Ganz claims that this relationship was the "romance" every show needs. The producers decided to drop the useless character Chuck, who mysteriously disappeared after the second season, never to return. (Chuck almost seemed to have been a figment of the viewing audiences' imagination. Years later when *Happy Days* was winding down, Howard and Marion talk about raising their "two children," and no mention is made of Chuck. Whenever Garry Marshall was asked what happened to Chuck, he would reply that Chuck was on a twelve-year basketball scholarship at the University of Outer Mongolia. The disappearance of Chuck Cunningham became a pop culture joke. It was referenced some thirty years later when *Entertainment Weekly* compared the "disappearance" of *The O.C.*'s Caitlin character to Chuck's disappearance from *Happy Days*. In the movie *The Cable Guy*, Jim Carrey's character says he is the long-lost Chuck Cunningham.)

Now that the Cunningham family and Richie's close friends were cast, there was a need for supporting characters other than Fonzie and the teenager's buddies. Garry Marshall didn't want the show to get too authoritarian in tone, so bringing in more adults was tricky. There was the opportunity to develop the friends' parents, but that detracted from the parenting done by Howard and Marion. The parents of Potsie and Ralph were introduced later in the series. (Ironically, Ralph's parents are named Minnie and Mickey Malph, which is amusing in light of the development of Michael Eisner's career.) Since the kids perceived their parents as uncool, there needed to be some adults with whom the kids would feel comfortable. Enter Arnold, the first-season owner of the local drive-in restaurant and hang-out.

Although Arnold was seen as humorous but stern by the teenagers, he did provide the opportunity to show the kids how foolish they could be, without having to moralize like their parents. The actor chosen to play Arnold Takahashi needed to be believable in his out-of-context position as the Japanese owner of a gathering spot for suburban Wisconsin youths. To keep the character from being *too* fish-out-of-water it was important that the actor have a comedic spark, and Pat Morita had all that and more. He was born Noriyuki Morita, on June 28, 1932, in Isleton, California. Morita suffered from spinal tuberculosis as a child and said that for nine years he was in a cast from his shoulders to his knees. He was told he would never walk again. He overcame that disability but was then interned in a Japanese-American camp during World War II. Ron Howard would later say that Morita had seen a lot of life and it wasn't pretty, yet he was never angry or resentful. After graduating from Armijo High School in Fairfield, California, Morita worked as a computer programmer and at his parents' restaurant. Looking to make his life more interesting, he entered show business as a stand-up comic known as "the Hip Nip." During one of his nightclub performances, legendary stand-up comedian Redd Foxx made note of Morita and cast him as Ah Chew on his show *Sanford and Son*. Morita made his screen debut in the film *Thoroughly Modern Millie* and was soon appearing on other television series, including *M*A*S*H*. Arnold would be a popular *Happy Days* character, although he didn't appear often. (Only when the writers of the show attempted to have Arnold get married did the laughs for the character fall flat. Morita was nervous during this episode. Ron Howard told him to relax, as this was Morita's show and he had the best supporting cast in the world. It was not the character that didn't work, but rather the desperateness of having a wedding. Morita left the show to pursue other roles; in 1976 he starred in *Mister T and Tina*.)

Several of the names of characters in *Happy Days* were inspired by people and places Garry Marshall had known. Potsie Weber was said to have been a friend of Marshall's wife, Barbara, and the future Chachi Arcola was named after the street on which the Marshalls' first house was located. When the Marshall family car broke down in Atascadero, California, one day, the name stuck in Marshall's mind and later was the influence for the naming of Pinky Tuscadero.

As soon as Michael Eisner received footage of *Happy Days* from Miller and Marshall, he started flooding the network markets with promos for the new show. Eisner loved the characters and even was said to identify with Potsie Weber. Garry Marshall was baffled by Eisner's choice of characters with whom to identify. It seemed out-of-character for the hard-driving television executive.

"Rock Around the Clock," by Bill Haley and the Comets, was used to establish the show's era and served as the theme song, but the original 1955 recording of the hit song was used only for the first episode. Bill Haley and the Comets recorded a new version of their classic for the show that served as *Happy Days*' theme for the remainder of the first season. The "*Happy Days* Theme" that the viewing audience would come to love wasn't introduced until the 1975–1976 season, with a new arrangement in 1983. That theme was written by Pratt and McClain and sung by Ron Hicklin, although in the show's final season the song was sung by Bobby Avron. (When the original "*Happy Days* Theme" was released as a single in 1976, it reached number 5 on the pop charts.) The show featured the popular songs of the fifties decade on the jukebox at Arnold's. Some of the more expensive-to-clear songs were actually sung on tape by Anson Williams, who had a very nice singing voice. After the *Happy Days* writers heard Williams singing backstage, Potsie Weber started to sing on the show. (Of course, Richie Cunningham was always singing his signature song, Fats Domino's "Blueberry Hill." One of the highlights of the show was when Richie, Fonzie, Ralph, and Potsie all sang the song together during one episode. Howard says he is still known to hum the tune to this day.)

Happy Days' group of actors, writers, and producers was solid. Garry Marshall made sure that the set was a comfortable, positive place to work for both the actors and the crew. "Garry Marshall is a force to be reckoned with," says actress Suzi Quatro, who would play Leather Tuscadero. "He had a vision and saw it through. He was always present at rehearsal and final shoots. He was always checking the lines, the laughs, the tears, and the message. What a lovely man."

Another of *Happy Days'* greatest assets was director Jerry Paris, whose first calling wasn't directing but acting. Such a background was helpful when directing a fairly large, ensemble cast. Jerry Paris was a natural communicator. Born in San Francisco on July 25, 1925, William Gerald Paris served in the Navy during World War II and upon discharge entered New York University and then UCLA, from which he graduated. He then studied at the famed Actors Studio in New York City. Paris began his acting career in 1949 on stage, but soon was enjoying roles in such legendary films as *The Wild One*, *The Caine Mutiny*, *Marty*, and *The Naked and the Dead*. In 1959 Paris appeared as a regular on television's *The Untouchables* and was cast in 1961 to play Dick Van Dyke's neighbor and buddy Jerry Helper on *The Dick Van Dyke Show*. "He was a very funny man," recalls actress Rose Marie, one of Paris's co-stars on the show, "with a great sense of humor and a great sense of comedy for television."

While Paris was appearing on *The Dick Van Dyke Show*, producer Carl Reiner saw to it that Paris was allowed to direct some of the shows. Paris had previously directed an episode of *The Joey Bishop Show*. Jerry Paris decided directing was his true calling. In 1968 he directed the film *Viva Max*, with Peter Ustinov and Jonathan Winters. His next directing project was *Star-Spangled Girl*, with Sandy Duncan and Tony Roberts. Paris decided that he liked working in television better than film and directed some episodes of *The Odd Couple*. Jerry Paris and Garry Marshall had met while working on *The Dick Van Dyke Show*. When Garry Marshall was considering who would be a good director for *Happy Days*, Jerry Paris immediately came to mind. (Paris wasn't immediately available. Mel Ferber would direct Episode #1. Ferber was a veteran director from *Mary Tyler Moore*, *The Odd Couple*, and other notable television shows.)

Marshall says Paris brought consistency, warmth, and dedication to the show. Jerry Paris became a beloved director with the cast of *Happy Days*. He would often even appear in scenes. Paris was giving and supportive, but he had come from the theater and the early days of television, where "more" was the standard. "Jerry Paris was the director, and he screamed so much they gave him a megaphone," remembers actress

Misty Rowe. "Then he would scream through the megaphone. I think the great successes of *Happy Days* were one, the casting, and two, the direction. It was just a wonderful, wonderful time." Marion Ross remembers Paris as being "the one who was fun." Paris would film gags for the amusement of the cast, such as when he had Marion Cunningham kiss Fonzie on the mouth. Marshall would later say that Paris became "the heart" of *Happy Days*. Ron Howard remembers Paris talking from the heart to his young cast members when sometimes the going got rough. Howard says that Paris would say that of course doing a television show is hard; if it was easy, everybody would be doing it. Paris would easily defuse situations and encourage and calm the cast. (Jerry Paris remained with the show through the eleven years it was on the air. He also directed the popular *Police Academy* movies. In 1985 Paris developed cancer and suffered from a brain tumor. On March 31, 1986, the sixty-year-old director died in Los Angeles.)

Other people were added to the *Happy Days* team, including Garry Marshall's sister Ronny Hallin, who was brought in as one of the associate producers. Hallin had a degree from Northwestern and joined her brother in Hollywood as a secretary for the Screen Actors Guild. Ronny knew quite a bit about contracts and unions from that experience and thus was a welcome addition to Marshall's production staff. The Marshalls' dad, Tony, was one of the producers of the show. As to the allegations of nepotism that Garry Marshall had to endure, he readily admitted that he worked with his family because they made him comfortable *and* they were talented.

ABC Programming Vice President Fred Pierce guided the show as network liaison during the first year. The network was solidly behind the series. Paramount's Stage 19 was home to *Happy Days*. (The exterior shots of the Cunningham home were of a house located on Cahuenga Boulevard in Hollywood.) The *Happy Days* set was relaxed and positive. Visitors enjoyed the family atmosphere and welcoming air offered by those associated with the show. In spite of the fact that the show would gain popularity with viewers very quickly and the teenagers in the cast were experiencing great fame for the first time, the young people didn't let their almost-instant celebrity go to their heads.

Michael Eisner continued to champion the show and was positive he had a hit on his hands. ABC decided to use *Happy Days* as a mid-season replacement, putting it up against such hit series as NBC's *Adam 12* and CBS's *Maude*. The first episode of *Happy Days* aired on Tuesday, January 15, 1974, at 8:00 P.M. As Don Most later said, *Happy Days* was a seventies look at a fifties family. Those who had experienced the fifties would no doubt enjoy the show, plus they could use it to introduce the decade to their children. Ron Howard says that the show was timeless.

The first episode of *Happy Days* has "worldly" Potsie Weber arranging a date for the innocent Richie and an alleged "fast girl." Fonzie is surrounded by his usual group of starry-eyed girls, but other than demonstrating that he is cool, he has little to do and nothing to say. Ralph Malph is introduced as a loudmouth braggart. The Cunningham family is a bit edgier in that first episode than they would later be portrayed. Little sister Joanie remains a smart aleck, and Chuck makes his perfunctory appearance. Howard Cunningham seems a bit jaded by fatherhood, and Marion appears a little intimidated by her husband. (These characterizations would change in future episodes.) Richie is the young man Opie Taylor might have become. He has integrity, yet the inexperience of a teenage boy. We can see that he is someone worth knowing, and right from the start Richie is projected as a role model for the young people in the viewing audience.

The character Richie Cunningham was brought to life very successfully by Ron Howard. While Howard has said that he is more sophisticated and smarter than Richie, he has also said Richie stood up to people more easily than Ron himself could. Basically, Ron Howard and Richie Cunningham are of the same mind-set. Richie was "Mr. Nice" and so was Ron. The similarity and classification of the character Richie was actually addressed in a future episode, with Richie saying he is tired of being considered "Mr. Nice." Richie says that he would probably be voted the nicest kid in the class. "Pat Boone, Kate Smith, Captain Kangaroo, and me." Ron Howard would develop the same reputation, sometimes to his chagrin. (Richie's niceness was acknowledged on the television show *NewsRadio* when a character was said to be so normal he made Richie Cunningham look like a crack-smoking porno freak.)

Some people in Hollywood had initially thought that Howard taking on the role of Richie was a bad career move. They thought that after his success in *American Graffiti* Howard should concentrate on film roles. Howard himself has said he was pleased to have the opportunity to work on *Happy Days* as his time on the show gave him the chance to learn the art and craft of television production so that he might further his knowledge and someday work as a director. Taking on the role of Richie also made the actor eligible for a draft deferment since the livelihoods of so many people depended on the show's success. Howard would later say that he didn't want to go to Canada and didn't want to fight in Vietnam, so being deferred for the work in *Happy Days* was the nudge he needed to accept the role. In the long run, the deferment didn't really matter much; the draft ended shortly after *Happy Days* went into production.

According to Penny Marshall, Ron Howard was a bit nervous about doing situation comedy. She says that on the first day of shooting Howard pulled Garry Marshall aside and expressed concern about "being funny." Making people laugh wasn't something the young actor was used to doing. Yet Howard was surrounded by some outstanding talent, and he would quickly learn comedic timing and delivery. Richie Cunningham would be a success.

Henry Winkler's Fonzie became such a draw for *Happy Days* that Winkler's billing was quickly moved from fifth to third, then second to Ron Howard's. Fonzie's trademark "aaayyyy" and "whooooa" (which Henry Winkler says simply came from horseback riding) became national buzz words. And *everyone* was using the thumbs-up gesture. All the little nuances that Winkler brought to his character paid off. Fonzie was a hit. "I remember going on the set and meeting the three guys and The Fonz," says Misty Rowe, who played Wendy the Carhop. "I had such a crush on him. I think he thought I didn't like him or something because he tried to talk to me and I was like duh . . . But I was so young and so naïve, and I just had such a crush on Henry Winkler I couldn't speak. All the makeup and hair people would say, 'Stay away from Henry. Everybody's after Henry.'"

When the attention started to shift toward Fonzie and away from Richie, Ron Howard told reporters that Henry Winkler's character was more important to the show as it brought attention to the series that would in turn raise its ratings. Howard was comfortable with the fact that Fonzie was as important as Richie. Ron Howard was a team player. Garry Marshall said that Howard learned that attitude from having worked with Andy Griffith for so many years. Griffith had never won an Emmy, while his popular co-star Don Knotts had won four. Yet even though Howard was all about the success of the show, he didn't like the network's suggestion that the show be renamed *Fonzie's Happy Days*. Neither did Garry Marshall, who said to Howard that he might have to quit if the name of the show was changed. Howard said he was inclined that way too. He could always go back to film school. The change hadn't appealed to Henry Winkler either. Winkler says that Fonzie did well because he was with that particular group of people. Winkler felt that a tighter focus on Fonzie would have been the death knell for the character. In the end, the possibility of losing Ron Howard was all the network needed to hear. The name-change issue was dropped.

Elsewhere on the lot, Paramount Television and ABC attempted to launch another comedy series on September 12, 1974. *Paper Moon* was a takeoff of the film of the same name, released the previous year. Tatum O'Neal's portrayal of Addie Loggins had earned her an Academy Award as Best Supporting Actress. Tatum's father, Ryan O'Neal, played Moses Pray in the film. *Paper Moon*, the television series, would follow the same story of the father and daughter con team as they traveled the country. This time the lead characters would be played by Christopher Connelly and a young actress named Jodie Foster. Connelly had become a teen heartthrob from his days on the prime-time soap *Peyton Place*. Foster was a child actor who had been seen in such films as *One Little Indian*, with James Garner, and *Kansas City Bomber*, with Raquel Welch. Foster had also been featured in the failed television series *Bob and Carol and Ted and Alice*, which aired in 1973. *Paper Moon*, the film, had been a moderate hit, but the television series never found an audience. *Paper Moon* aired only until January 1975.

Back at *Happy Days*, Garry Marshall and his staff were easier to work with than a lot of ABC's other producers. Paramount also liked various other aspects of the show. Set in the fifties, *Happy Days* could never go out of style. The setting of the show saved production costs as the producers didn't have the need to update the sets and costumes. (Although the era would change during the last shows as the fifties became the early sixties, only small "updates" were needed.) Paramount Television appreciated the fact that Marshall and his producers were willing to work with them to keep costs down. During an episode in which Fonzie serves on jury duty, the producers saved production money by not building a jury room set but having a painter come into the scene to say he had to paint the jury room so the jury would have to deliberate in the courtroom. This move saved the production $10,000 right there—what was not to like?

Why *Happy Days* was such a huge success is anybody's guess, but the characters and plotlines seemed to strike a positive note with the viewing public. By the end of the first season, the show was ranking sixteenth in the ratings and was ABC's second-highest-ranked series. Garry Marshall says the success of the show was due to a good 8:00 P.M. time slot on Tuesday nights, the high level of creativity, and just plain good timing. The return to the family-oriented days of earlier television productions was certainly part of the show's appeal. After the turbulence experienced by the American family in the sixties, viewing audiences were hungry for a show that could potentially restore good relations between teenagers and their parents. *Happy Days* seemed able to do that, employing likable characters on both sides of the parent/child relationship. While the parents often had a message, so did The Fonz, and the show explored the possibility that wisdom and positive guidance could be experienced and learned from people other than parents. "*Happy Days* is the ultimate family show," says Suzi Quatro. "We could all relate to the Cunninghams. And there was always one bad boy, one good boy and girl around. *Happy Days* captured the times perfectly, or should I say captured an ideal time when rock was young. There was an innocence that is missing now, a naïveté. Everyone loves a small town family with old values. It's the way we grew up . . . or should have."

Garry Marshall's belief in entertainment was simple and direct, and it worked. He said that with *Happy Days* he tried to do "feel good" scenes but was careful that the show didn't become too absorbed with sentiment. Marshall felt more than just an obligation to entertain. He encouraged the writers to disguise the message of any given episode with humor in order for it to be better and more readily received by the audience. Many of the scripts simply revolved around, as Donny Most would say, the normal dating patterns of teenage boys. Some episodes centered on family dynamics. Others reflected the pains, trials, and tribulations of growing up. In the end, most of the episodes focused on loving relationships. There was a little bit in the show for everyone.

As when the subject of a tough guy had arisen during the initial pitch for *Happy Days*, the network executives continued to have their doubts about the inclusion of a leather-jacketed "hoodlum." They didn't think such a character would be a good thing to bring to the family hour. Garry Marshall thought the powers that be had finally accepted that, although Fonzie rode a motorcycle and was certainly rougher than Richie Cunningham and his pals, his was a character with a heart of gold and he was far from a bad influence on the more wholesome teenagers. Marshall was surprised, then, when he left the shooting of the show early in the second season to go to Hawaii to shoot the pilot for a show titled *The Little People* and came back to find big changes in Arthur Fonzarelli. Gone was the brown leather jacket that Marshall's Fonzie had started to wear. Fonzie's wardrobe now once again consisted of a taupe gabardine windbreaker. Marshall wasn't pleased with the preppy jacket, and neither was anyone else on the show. Marshall thought Fonzie looked more like Potsie. Marshall fired off a memo to the ABC suits, explaining that the clothes Fonzie was wearing didn't work for the character. In his usual humorous style, Marshall explained that if Fonzie were to wear the clothes he was now wearing, the viewing audience might spend their time worrying about Fonzie freezing to death instead of enjoying the show or watching the commercials. ABC responded to the memo by allowing Fonzie to wear his leather jacket, but only when he was sitting, leaning on, or standing by his motorcycle. (Fonzie would be seen out of his leather jacket during one episode when he accompanied Marion Cunningham to a dance contest. In that show he wore a tuxedo!) Garry Marshall fired off another memo—this time to the writers, informing them that Fonzie was never to be written into a scene without his motorcycle. There was little that would sway the network executives away from their stance, so Fonzie was constantly shown with his bike, even to the point of once bringing the motorcycle into the Cunninghams' living room so that he could be featured in an indoor scene. Finally Marshall wore down the ABC executives, and Fonzie was allowed to appear in his leather jacket at all times. Henry Winkler and Garry Marshall helped counterbalance Fonzie's toughness by never having the character have a pack of cigarettes rolled up in the sleeve of his t-shirt, as was the custom in the fifties. Fonzie may have been a biker, but he was a wholesome biker.

The writers of *Happy Days* were top-notch. It was Marshall's practice to hire a mix of veteran and new-to-the-genre writers in order to keep the writing inspired. The younger writers would contribute their unbridled enthusiasm, and the older writers would provide the discipline necessary to successfully bring quality scripts to fruition. Garry Marshall said that the writers on the show ranged from college kids to people in their seventies. Writers William Bickley and Michael Warren invented a concept they dubbed "the six o'clock writers." The veteran writers would go home to their families at the end of a regular day, while the younger, mostly unmarried writers could stay on and brainstorm. All the writers would then fine-tune the show the next day. It cost the veteran writers a little money but was worth it to them. (One of the talented writers on the show was Fred Fox Jr., who was adored by the cast as he was often off the wall. He was the son of writer Fred Fox Sr., who had written for such shows as *The Red Skelton Show*, *The Andy Griffith Show*, *F Troop*, and *Here's Lucy*.) The writers had a great rapport with the cast, and only rarely did the actors disagree with the writers' instincts. One notable time was when Henry Winkler told Lowell Ganz he couldn't possibly deliver the line as written. Ganz responded that Winkler could . . . if he were taller. Radio personality Howard Stern once said that Marshall was a man who made a lot of unfunny people funny. The opportunities Marshall offered also made a lot of funny people even funnier.

Happy Days was about the tenderness of growing up. Yet the show was so much more. The messages wrapped in comic lines were effective. A Northwestern University history professor once wrote to Garry Marshall that when he asked his class when they first became aware of the potential for nuclear war, the majority of the students replied, "When the Cunninghams considered building a bomb shelter." When the National Library Association brought to Marshall's attention the fact that kids across the country didn't seem to be using their local libraries, the producers and writers reacted. After Fonzie got his library card, libraries all over the country experienced a huge rush by young people to get theirs. Another episode was inspired by a call Garry Marshall received from a group of advocates for abused children from Massachusetts. Marshall was told that the children didn't think it was okay to cry because Fonzie never cried and he was their hero. A *Happy Days* episode was written in which Richie is seriously injured and in the hospital, and Fonzie cries as he talks to God about saving his closest friend. The kids watched that episode and learned that it was cool to sometimes cry. Other episodes dealt with such subjects as women's lib: once Marion angrily told Howard to get his own dinner. There was also an episode in which Richie got drunk and suffered the consequences.

Misty Rowe feels the appeal of *Happy Days* lay in its simplicity. "It was fun, it was warm. It was sweet. And it was our heritage. It was how America grew up. The music, the clothes, that very sweet time when boys are noticing girls and wanting to go out with them. And wanting a mentor who is older and wiser but not your dad. Fonzie was like that. He just kept it cool. It was Americana. It was just such a wonderful family show, to be able to sit and watch with your kids or your parents. Everybody loved *Happy Days*."

The show received increasingly high ratings, and *Happy Days* was declared a hit. Garry Marshall would simplify the explanation for the show's success by calling the series a quiet moment to enjoy and love.

Chapter 4

**HELLO,
BLUE SKIES**

By the start of Season Two of *Happy Days* in September 1975, Paramount Television and ABC knew they had a strong hit series for the Tuesday, 8:00 P.M. time slot. After only a few glitches in the fine-tuning of the show, everyone seemed in agreement that the formula and the cast worked extremely well. If things continued as they had in the first episodes, *Happy Days* would be around for years to come.

By the second season the character Arnold had moved on to other things, and Big Al Delvecchio was the new owner of the drive-in. Big Al was portrayed by veteran comedy actor Al Molinaro. His character, bolstered by the actor's hangdog expression, was very popular and fit perfectly with what Marshall had in mind for Big Al. Born June 24, 1919, in Kenosha, Wisconsin, Al Molinaro was one of ten children. His brother Joseph was Kenosha County's longest-serving district attorney, and his brother George was a Wisconsin state representative. Molinaro started in television with small roles in *Get Smart*, *Bewitched*, and *Green Acres*, but became best known as Murray "The Nose" Greshler in Garry Marshall's *The Odd Couple*. Murray would enter a scene by poking his nose into the room, generating instant recognition. Molinaro would say that he spent twenty years in Hollywood before he "got lucky." He claims that success in the entertainment business is part luck and part being in the right place at the right time.

There were a lot of head-shaking moments for both characters, Arnold and Al, as they tried to mentor the *Happy Days* teenagers. Even though Arnold and Al were oddball types, they were treated with respect by the younger characters. Big Al was not really developed as a guru; he was more inclined to simply sigh as he tried to make sense of the mind-sets of the youngsters. Arnold would just look at them and shake his head.

Ron Howard was settling in and happy that he had chosen to attach himself to another quality television series. His time on *Happy Days* was well spent. Howard made lifelong friends with some of the members of the cast. He learned financial matters from Tom Bosley. He learned directing, including the art of physical comedy, from Jerry Paris. He learned to relate to a live audience and, from the producers and cast, how to work as an ensemble. The other actors, in turn, learned much from the seasoned teenager. Once when Henry Winkler was dissatisfied with the script, he pounded the actual script for emphasis. Howard reminded Winkler that the script was the result of writers working many hours and suggested he might want to show it a little more respect. Winkler agreed.

Garry Marshall was confident that his regular cast could deliver the goods every week, and they did. He liked having such seasoned actors as Tom Bosley and Marion Ross to act as "authority" figures and teachers for the younger, less experienced actors. While the stars of *Happy Days* were enjoying their rising fame, guest stars were brought in to help with the workload and the laughs. *Happy Days* was doing very well in the ratings, but Marshall felt that additional, more transient characters were needed to keep the show interesting.

Marshall's cast was secure enough to welcome an abundance of guest stars who once had been cast members of legendary television shows. They included Phil Silvers, Danny Thomas, Jack Dodson (who had appeared with Ron Howard on *The Andy Griffith Show*), Elinor Donahue (*Father Knows Best*), Linda Kaye Henning (*Petticoat Junction*), Clint Howard (*The Cowboys*), Diana Hyland (*Eight Is Enough*), Christopher Knight (*The Brady Bunch*), June Lockhart (*Lassie*), Dave Madden (*The Partridge Family*), Maureen McCormick (*The Brady Bunch*), Ken Osmond (*Leave It to Beaver*), Susan Richardson (*Eight Is Enough*), Ronnie Schell (*Gomer Pyle*), Dick Van Patten (*Eight Is Enough*), Lyle Waggoner (*The Carol Burnett Show*), Lorne Greene (*Bonanza*), and even Howdy Doody's friend "Buffalo Bob" Smith. Others would become famous for future television series, including Cheryl Ladd (*Charlie's Angels*), Peter Scolari (*The Bob Newhart Show*), Adam Arkin (*Chicago Hope*), Didi Conn (*Benson*), Janine Turner (*Northern Exposure*), Ed Begley Jr. (*St. Elsewhere*), Crystal Bernard (*Wings*), Jeff Conaway (*Taxi*), Conrad Janis (*Mork & Mindy*), Audrey

Landers (*Dallas*), J. Eddie Peck (*Dynasty*), Rhonda Shear (*Cheers*), Meeno Peluce (*The Bad News Bears*), Eddie Mekka (*Laverne & Shirley*), Richard Moll (*Night Court*), Charlene Tilton (*Dallas*), Ellen Travolta (*Charles in Charge*), and Morgan Fairchild (*Falcon Crest*). Legendary actors, including Pat O'Brien, Janis Page, Jesse White, and Nancy Walker, made appearances on the show, and some guest stars, such as Tom Hanks, Amy Irving, Crispin Glover, and Rita Wilson, were future major talents. *Happy Days* would sometimes feature celebrities like Hank Aaron, Frankie Avalon, Cassandra "Elvira" Petersen, Dr. Joyce Brothers, and Flash Cadillac. The set of *Happy Days* was a fashionable place to be, and Garry Marshall and his excellent casting director, Bobby Hoffman, were happy to have as many fine actors appear on the show as they could get.

"Bobby Hoffman . . ." muses director Howard Storm. "He did almost every show there [at Paramount Television]. He was amazing. With his little [trademark] hat? He was a very good man. A lovely man." In regard to guest-casting, Storm thinks Hoffman was excellent as a casting director. "I don't ever remember having to replace anybody. Lots of times on shows you bring a guest in and they're just not cutting it. You have no choice but to replace them, take them off and bring somebody else in. And that never happened [with Hoffman's choices]."

Garry Marshall says that a series has to be secure in order to have good experiences with guest stars, and *Happy Days* was certainly that. The guest stars were welcomed by the regular cast with open arms. Marshall calls it the "cocktail theory" of the hosts making the guest feel welcome. The guest stars would sometimes even appear in the *Happy Days* promos. Marshall said stars Ron Howard and Henry Winkler gave the guests confidence. The cast of *Happy Days* was like an extended family, with egos held in check. All the cast regulars had the same size dressing room, and there wasn't a prima donna among them. Rocker Suzi Quatro found the actors easy to work with. "The interaction helped all of us," Quatro believes. "There were no selfish actors on the set. We all worked as a family. I think that single point was the most important to the success of *Happy Days*." Quatro liked the camaraderie among the cast members when they weren't involved in a scene. "I thought the interaction was great, much like being on a small record label or on tour with other bands," she says. "It's fun. It relieves the tension, not to say the boredom between shooting, and there is always something to learn from other actors."

Another guest star was Ron Howard's younger brother Clint, who had been a child actor on dozens of other television shows, with solid roles in such series as *Gentle Ben* and *The Cowboys*. Howard appeared on so many shows that his memories of the set of *Happy Days* are somewhat vague at this stage in his life. "I personally was not really comfortable in front of a live audience," Howard remembers. "I hadn't had a lot of opportunity doing three-camera sitcoms. I felt like it was a fun thing to do and [eventually] relaxed. Working on a sitcom is the kind of gig a person might enjoy doing because it's really only two days of working [in a guest role]. The other days are relaxed. But for an actor, you really gear up and kinda kick ass for a couple of days . . . It seemed like everybody on *Happy Days* was getting along. There was kind of an excitement and a camaraderie around *Happy Days* that was fun, and it was exciting. Fun and exciting wouldn't necessarily breed success. Garry Marshall seemingly ran a pretty good ship. I knew these guys more from the softball team."

To Marshall the cast was a dream cast. He was often charmed at how mature the young actors were. By the time the show was off and running, the teenagers were making pretty good money. They enjoyed some of the perks young people new to wealth usually do. Henry Winkler bought a BMW, and Anson Williams purchased a Mercedes. Ron Howard, on the other hand, continued to drive his old Volkswagen van. The young people were also interested in long-term investments. One day Marshall came on the set and found them discussing their escrows.

There were some drawbacks involved in the success of the show. Ron Howard wasn't delighted with the added attention playing Richie brought him away from the studio as it made it difficult for him to live a normal life. Yet Howard had been in the entertainment industry long enough to know that public scrutiny was one of the prices a successful actor paid.

The young actors were quick to learn from the more seasoned actors, producers, and writers. They listened to suggestions and criticisms for the most part without attitude. Garry Marshall remembers only one disagreement with Henry Winkler. Winkler is the consummate professional, and outbursts of any kind rarely occurred involving him. After the wrapping of one show, Winkler was anxious about catching a flight. Jerry Paris asked him to stay a little longer to do some pick-ups. Winkler blew up at Paris and stalked offstage. Marshall followed him off and told him never to have a tantrum in front of an audience. Winkler agreed that Marshall was right and apologized. If that was the extent of set disturbances, *Happy Days* was doing pretty damn well.

Suzi Quatro remembers fondly the time when she was brought in as a romantic interest for Fonzie. Her time playing Leather Tuscadaro was an exciting change from her life as a musician. "The first episode I did was the first time I acted in my life," remembers Quatro. "[There I am] in front of a live audience, all psyched up and raring to go and just

Happy Days' Leather Tuscadero, rocker Suzi Quatro. Photo courtesy of Suzi Quatro; photo copyright David Lean.

a little nervous. I was waiting behind the set in Arnold's with my script, ready for my first big entrance. Henry wanders over and says, 'How ya doin', Suzi, you ready to do this? Great, now go out and kill 'em." So out I went, sauntering suggestively, rock chick attitude in abundance. I got to my spot and before I could speak, the director, Jerry Paris, who I absolutely grew to adore, says, 'Excuse me, Miss Quatro, what are you doing out here?' 'That's my cue,' I stammered. 'No,' he replied, 'you've got another page yet!' When I got backstage again, Henry was on the floor laughing. He had done it on purpose to take my nerves away. What can be worse than entering at the wrong time? 'Now, go out and really kill 'em,' he said. I then made my second entrance to thunderous applause. Thanks, Henry!"

Leather Tuscadero was a popular *Happy Days* character. Even though it was Quatro's first acting role, she acclimated quickly, and the audience loved her. Born Susan Kay Quatrocchio on June 3, 1950, in Detroit, Michigan, Quatro was the daughter of jazz bandleader Art Quatrocchio and his wife, Helen. Suzi had been very successful in England and Europe, with several hit singles, including "Can the Can" and "Devil Gate Drive." She was ready to take America by storm. ("*Stumblin' In*" would be a major hit in the U.S. in 1979.) Appearing on *Happy Days* as Leather helped Quatro become better known in the United States. According to

Quatro, Bobby Hoffman's daughter had a copy of *Rolling Stone* magazine with Suzi's picture on the cover, and when Hoffman saw it he knew he had found the edgy personality he wanted for Leather Tuscadero. Henry Winkler liked playing opposite Quatro: he thought she was a hard worker who fit into the *Happy Days* ensemble. Leather wrote and sang a number called "Do the Fonzie" in one episode.

The cast was not intimidated by the addition of characters: they felt that it was just so much fodder for their creativity. Misty Rowe was one of those brought in during the second season. As Wendy the Carhop, Misty was happy to associate with the Marshall/Paramount team. "I started my career in 1972, and it was just boom, boom, boom, one sitcom after another," Misty remembers. "I got *Happy Days* about a year and a half after I got *Hee Haw*. I loved [casting director] Bobby [Hoffman]. He called me in for *Happy Days*. I had actually been seen for *American Graffiti*, but I was considered too young. Suzanne Somers got the part and we're very close in age, so . . . But they called me up for *Happy Days* and I read, and they kept me there and then I read again. Then, Bill Bickley drove me in his car across the lot to wardrobe and said, 'You're saving my hide' because they had actually cast the carhop. The girl had done one show, and then she went to do *Apocalypse Now* and just left them. I can understand that; it was quite a big film. So this was my big chance, and I got Wendy the Carhop."

Other recurring characters would join the *Happy Days* cast over the years. Fifteen-year-old actor Scott Baio was brought in as Fonzie's cousin Charles "Chachi" Arcola. Chachi was somewhat of a ruffian and ran with a gang called The Lords. He was basically a younger, coarser, version of Fonzie. Fast-talking and less sensitive than his cousin, Chachi was a good-looking boy who quickly adapted to being taught the ropes by Fonzie and was soon welcomed into the extended Cunningham "family." It didn't take long for Chachi to begin his ultimately successful pursuit of Joanie. Joanie had had crushes before Chachi—notably Potsie, who sang to her in one episode. But the teenager had never experienced a serious love interest. Chachi affectionately called Joanie "Blue Eyes." (Fonzie always called her "Shortcake.") Chachi was not the first of Fonzie's cousins to be introduced. During earlier episodes, Fonzie had a cousin named Spike, but that character wasn't as appealing as the handsome young Baio.

Scott Baio says that during his first appearance on the show he was frightened out of his mind. He has jokingly said that if he'd had a gun, he'd have killed himself. He simply didn't want to go on the stage. The charismatic actor Scott Vincent James Baio was born in Brooklyn, New York, on September 22, 1961, to Italian parents Rose and Mario Baio.

Scott was the youngest of three children (his brother Steven and his cousins Jimmy and Joey would later become regularly working actors). At the age of nine, Baio told his mother he wanted to be an actor. He was taken for interviews in Manhattan and landed a few television commercials, the most notable being for Ovaltine. He soon was cast in the lead for Richard Marquand's television movie *Luke Was There*. Baio made his feature film debut as the lead in the kid gangster movie *Bugsy Malone*, opposite Jodie Foster. The film allowed Baio solid footing on his way to an acting career.

Baio was tapped by Garry Marshall to play Fonzie's cousin Chachi in a 1977 episode of *Happy Days* after Marshall saw and liked his performance in *Bugsy Malone*. The actor and the character were so popular that Marshall made Chachi a recurring character, and Baio soon became a member of the regular cast. The Baio family relocated to Los Angeles. Baio enjoyed appearing on *Happy Days* and soon had a tremendous female following. His catchphrase "wa, wa, wa, wa," although seemingly meaningless, was soon being repeated by teenage girls all over the country. Baio told *Entertainment Weekly* that it was party time every day. Erin Moran was happy to have Baio on the show because he was her age. She says that Baio was fun to work with, and the two quickly became friends. The viewing audience loved Chachi. Once he started appearing regularly on *Happy Days*, Scott Baio sometimes received 5,000 fan letters a week.

Misty Rowe remembers that each member of the cast would go out of their way to make recurring characters and guest actors comfortable. They also were available for guidance that can come only from experience. "Henry Winkler actually gave me a great piece of advice," recalls Rowe. "He said, you rush everything. You have maybe two or three lines a show and you rush right through them. You really should take your time and command that presence. I remember that being a very good piece of advice."

Rowe also remembers that the cast members would reach out personally. "I went away to do *Hee Haw*, and it was Henry's birthday or something and I sent him a birthday card," she remembers. "And he was so nice. He wrote me back and wrote me a poem. I wouldn't say it was romantic, but it was lovely. He titled it "Mist," which is part of my name. I think I still have that poem. People said, 'Oh, you should frame that,' and I said, 'I can't. It's too personal.' He was a great guy. I understand he married his publicist (Stacey Weitzman). They had a very long-term marriage and children. I mean these guys are really substantial. I was part of that family and happy to be so."

Wendy wasn't the only carhop on the show. In the early episodes the character of carhop Marsha Simms was played by Beatrice Cohen. Cohen was the granddaughter of Pulitzer Prize–winning author George S. Kaufman. She was another *Odd Couple* alum and had also done many other shows, including *Ellery Queen*, *The Rockford Files*, *All in the Family*, and *Barney Miller*. (Cohen died in 1999 of lung cancer at the age of fifty-one.)

Roz Kelly played Fonzie's girlfriend Pinky Tuscadero in several episodes. Kelly had a background in television and films, including *The Owl and the Pussycat* and *You've Got to Walk It Like You Talk It or You'll Lose That Beat*. There were rumors that Kelly alienated the cast and crew by doing unkind Fonzie impressions. (Regardless of Henry Winkler's personal feelings, he asked Kelly to appear in the *Happy Days Reunion Special*. Kelly would later have personal trouble when she was arrested for shooting up her neighbor's house with a 12-gauge shotgun.)

Garry Marshall did occasionally have problems with the writers regarding the guest stars or continuing characters. At one point the writers had written for the regular characters for so long that they started writing better lines for the guest stars. Marshall put a chart on the wall that listed the salaries of the stars of the show and told the writers he had to pay those salaries regardless of the number of lines they delivered. The writers got the point.

As the producers were adding characters to the hit show, its popularity stayed steady. *Happy Days* continued to be a viewer favorite and remained at the top of the ratings. Fonzie was still perceived as the epitome of cool. People all over the country were continuing to say "aaayyyy" while giving Fonzie's signature thumbs-up. Winkler says that a character can't be cool using a lot of words. The producers wanted to develop a Fonzie catchphrase, and it was Bob Brunner who suggested the phrase "Sit on it." After Fonzie said these memorable words, they too were heard all over the media and used by viewers across the country. Ron Howard said that the writers seemed to be in overdrive when it came to thinking up catchphrases that might attach themselves to common usage. They sent Garry Marshall a list of the phrases every week, hoping one or more of them would seize the imagination of viewers. Another pop-culture claim to fame that *Happy Days* enjoys is the use of the term "nerd." Although Dr. Seuss used the word in a book, it didn't have quite the same meaning there that it does today. Erin Moran says that she was the first to use the term on television during an episode of *Happy Days*. The cast was in on the game too. Anson Williams started referring to the Cunningham parents as "Mr. and Mrs. C." Donny Most developed

Ralph's signature line "I've still got it" after hearing director Jerry Paris use the phrase. Other things were tried, such as having Chachi wear a bandana around his leg, hoping the kids in the viewing audience would like it and start wearing one themselves. That didn't quite pan out.

Fonzie was on posters, t-shirts, even lunch boxes. Winkler says he was afraid to leave his apartment because of the fans. In the beginning, Winkler thought the reaction to Fonzie was unnatural, and he says he didn't know how to act in the presence of people who were impressed by his character. All in all, Winkler enjoyed his character's popularity, as did Ron Howard, who later said that he didn't feel any envy whatsoever over Fonzie's appeal to the masses. Howard says that Winkler earned every accolade, every fan.

As Anson Williams would say, people want heroes, and Fonzie was that. Especially fun was Fonzie's ability to make things happen with the snap of his fingers. He seemingly had some special powers, or as Fonzie said himself during an episode, it was "a gift." (Henry Winkler was rewarded for his efforts to create a believable character when he was nominated for an Emmy for Outstanding Lead Actor in a Comedy Series in 1976, 1977, and 1978, and when he won two Golden Globes for Best Performance by an Actor in a Comedy Series in 1976 and 1977.)

In September 1975 Paramount Television and ABC tried launching another comedy series. *When Things Were Rotten* was a thirty-minute show written by Mel Brooks, John Boni, and Norman Stiles and executive-produced by Brooks and Norman Steinberg. The show was about Robin Hood, but instead of the usual heroic depiction of the character, this Robin Hood is a bumbling fool. Richard Gautier (from the film *Ensign Pulver*) played Robin, and Dick Van Patten portrayed his sidekick, Friar Tuck. Van Patten had made several appearances on *Happy Days* but would become best known as Tom Bradford, the father on the hit series *Eight Is Enough*.

Brought in to play Maid Marian was *Happy Days*' Misty Rowe. "Mel Brooks saw a picture of me in *People* magazine, and they called me for another sitcom," remembers Rowe. "*When Things Were Rotten* didn't run as long as *Happy Days*. It was about Robin Hood, and I was Maid Marian. So I was very big on the Paramount lot."

Guest stars were invited for some of the episodes. The comedic talent included Sid Caesar, John Byner, Lainie Kazan, and Dudley Moore. The episode with Moore was directed by Brooks cohort Marty Feldman. The viewing audience seemed to expect a laugh a minute from Brooks, and that can't always happen with a sitcom. The show, which first aired on September 3, lasted only through December 3.

Another failed series for the studio and the network was *The Cop and the Kid*, which also first aired in September 1975. Cy Chermak, who had written for *Bonanza*, *The Virginian*, and *Ironside*, executive-produced the series, which starred Charles Durning as a white cop who adopts a black orphan played by Eric Laneuville. Television actor Durning had appeared in such films as *The Sting* and *Dog Day Afternoon*. Eric Laneuville would later make his mark as an actor in series such as *St. Elsewhere* and as a television director (*Gilmore Girls*, *My Wife and Kids*, and *ER*). The series also starred Tony Award–winning actress Patsy Kelly. This series didn't click either. By January 1976 *The Cop and the Kid* was history.

Gary Nardino, now the head of television production at Paramount, was solidly behind *Happy Days*. Nardino was respected as a businessman and television entertainment expert. Born on August 26, 1935, in Garfield, New Jersey, and with a business degree from Seton Hall University, he entered the television industry as an agent and was soon Senior Vice President with ICM's New York television department, representing important clients such as Arthur Godfrey, David Frost, David Suskind, Allan Funt, and Dick Clark, along with television production companies, including Filmways. Nardino moved to the William Morris Agency, where he packaged television specials for such legendary performers as Perry Como, Bing Crosby, and Andy Williams. He would serve as President of Paramount Television from 1977 to 1983. He enjoyed working with *Happy Days*, writing in a column for *Daily Variety* that the show "took us to an innocent time and brought us in touch with our adolescence."

Garry Marshall, in turn, liked working with Gary Nardino and Paramount Television. He said that Nardino, Doug Cramer (Executive Vice President of Production at Paramount Television when Marshall was doing *The Odd Couple*), and Emmett Lavery (who headed Paramount Television's Business Affairs) did whatever they could do to make him comfortable. Marshall and his staff were even allocated a basketball court on the Paramount lot. Marshall said that he remained associated with Paramount rather than form his own production company because Paramount was comfortable to work with and he didn't want to take on the responsibilities of running his own company.

Marshall and his colleagues knew that one of the keys to their shows' success was to keep things as light as possible. During the 1970s, Marshall would have 400 people under the age of thirty working on his shows. He created Camp Marshallmount, an off-set getaway that allowed the casts and crews to socialize. They performed skits, sang songs, and got to know each other better.

Garry Marshall's basic formula was working well for *Happy Days*. Marshall said that a producer basically has twenty-two minutes to introduce the characters, develop a plotline that is funny, satisfy the needs of the network, and make people want to tune in the following week. This was something that Marshall and his associates did well. The first thirty-nine episodes of *Happy Days* were shot with only a single camera. (The successful series *M*A*S*H* was also shot with a single camera.) Garry Marshall believed that each of the *Happy Days* episodes was like a self-contained little movie. For Episode #40, as the show experienced something of a sophomore slump, Marshall tried using three cameras and a live audience. It was a formula that worked, and Marshall would continue to use this approach.

Marshall felt taping in front of a live audience was very important. That technique had started with *The Danny Thomas Show*, and Marshall had noted its success. He felt it encouraged the actors to give their best effort. Non-industry people were better judges of what was funny to the viewing audience. Ron Howard was initially uncomfortable with the idea of using a live audience. He said that it scared the hell out of him. Howard had never performed in front of a live audience and wasn't relaxed at all. After he heard the laughs, he says it was exciting. Marshall remembered that in the movies of his childhood there was usually a hero and the audience would cheer when the hero arrived. He wanted that for Fonzie. Lowell Ganz says that Fonzie was the guy we were afraid of when we were growing up. *Happy Days* changed that image and instead made the tough character the protector. Henry Winkler himself said he wished he was more like The Fonz. He felt the character was his alter ego. Now the audience who watched the taping of *Happy Days* was indeed cheering for Fonzie—and Winkler—whenever he walked on the set.

Marshall himself got involved with the studio audiences. The shows would take about three hours to shoot, and Marshall would entertain the audience before taping began and between set-ups. He would tell jokes, introduce the cast, talk about the show, and throw candy. Director Howard Storm recalls that Marshall's warm-ups were fun. "Garry is a comedy writer who is extremely funny, and he probably would have been a marvelous stand-up if he'd stayed with it," says Storm. "He still continues to emcee things, and he's hilarious." When Marshall wasn't there, some of the writers and the producers would do the warm-ups. Later, professional comedians were brought in to entertain.

One of the ways Garry Marshall and the writers and producers kept the show fun for the actors was by inserting inside jokes and pop culture references to amuse them. During one episode, Marion and Howard come out of the movie *The Music Man* discussing whether the little boy in the movie looks like their son Richie. Ron Howard, of course, is the actor who played the boy in the movie.

Humor was a key element for the Cunninghams, and the Cunningham parents knew how to have fun. *Happy Days* was one of the first shows to feature parents who were still clearly involved in a sexual relationship. Although they were never seen together in bed, there were constant hints that the parents enjoyed intimacy. Especially endearing was Marion's catchphrase that Howard was "getting frisky."

The cast was always playing jokes on one another. Scott Baio would shoot spitballs at Henry Winkler while the cameras were rolling. The boys at Arnold's greeted Fonzie by pushing pies in his face. Winkler chased Marion Ross around the set with a can of whipped cream. Ross came down from Fonzie's apartment buttoning her blouse, or Winkler and Ross kissed during an otherwise family-oriented scene. Henry Winkler took many home movies during the run of *Happy Days* because he didn't want to forget what the experience was like. The cast really enjoyed their work.

Something else the cast and crew did for fun was play softball. Participation in the *Happy Days* softball team wasn't mandatory, but almost everyone participated. Garry Marshall said that he felt the cast needed a hobby to keep them grounded. They were young people, after all, and many young actors their age were getting involved with drugs at that time. The team played on weekends in an entertainment league and sometimes before major league games at Dodger Stadium, Shea Stadium, or Wrigley Field. Over the course of a few years they were playing games in two or three major league parks a year. Baseball fan Donny Most says those games were a huge thrill. The team also played against soldiers through the USO in Germany, where they were flown from base to base in a Black Hawk helicopter, and in Okinawa. Even Marion Ross became a good player. Erin Moran says that while playing was fun, it was all about winning. The *Happy Days* team—Cunningham Hardware—took their softball seriously. The games, like the show, were a team effort. Ron Howard loved to play and would play all out. He once slid into home, and his black eye had to be worked into the following week's story. Howard tutored Henry Winkler on how to be a dynamite pitcher, as Winkler had never really played the game before. Winkler says that he just couldn't catch the ball, but he found that he could really throw it. Ron Howard bought Winkler a mitt, and Anson Williams bought him a bat. Together they taught Winkler the game of softball. (Future star Tom Hanks played in the league when he was on the Paramount lot doing

Bosom Buddies, as did Penny Marshall from *Laverne & Shirley*, Robin Williams from *Mork & Mindy*, and Tony Danza from *Taxi*.)

Changes for the character Fonzie came about during the 1976–1977 season of *Happy Days*. Fonzie moved into the Cunninghams' garage apartment. By the end of that season, Richie, Potsie, and Ralph had graduated from high school. Not one to be left out of something so momentous, Fonzie revealed that he had been attending night school, and even he received his diploma. All of the boys except mechanic Fonzie enrolled at the University of Wisconsin at Milwaukee. Richie majored in journalism and Potsie in psychology, and Ralph followed in his father's footsteps and studied optometry. The boys weren't all about their education. Richie met a cute co-ed named Lori Beth, and their romance began.

Lynda Goodfriend was brought in to play Lori Beth Allen. Goodfriend had appeared briefly in an earlier episode in which she played Ralph's un-named girlfriend. She was now re-cast as a fellow college student of Richie's. Goodfriend was an aspiring actress born in Miami, Florida, who had yet to be cast in anything at the time of *Happy Days*.

The 1977 season of *Happy Days* received critical acclaim in the form of Emmy and Golden Globe nominations. Henry Winkler received an Emmy nomination for Outstanding Lead Actor in a Television Comedy and won a Golden Globe for Best Actor in a Comedy Series. Ron Howard also won a Golden Globe for Best Actor in a Comedy Series, and the show itself was nominated for Best Television Comedy Series.

Paramount Television produced another sitcom in 1977, but instead of airing on ABC, *Busting Loose* was sold to CBS. The series, about a college graduate who goes to work for a shoe store, was developed by *Happy Days*' Lowell Ganz and Mark Rothman. The series was Lowell Ganz's debut in the executive producer chair. He would later produce films such as *Mr. Saturday Night*, with Billy Crystal (he also co-wrote it). The series starred Adam Arkin, son of comedian Alan, who had yet to become known as *Chicago Hope*'s Dr. Aaron Shutt. Arkin had appeared in minor television roles on shows such as *Happy Days*, *Barney Miller*, and *Harry-O*. The episodes were directed by the likes of James L. Brooks, Mel Farber, and Howard Storm, but *Busting Loose* ran only from January to November.

Mulligan's Stew was produced by Paramount Television and was placed on the NBC schedule to air that year also. The show starred Lawrence Pressman, who appeared on the series *Man from Atlantis*, which starred Patrick Duffy. *Father Knows Best*'s Elinor Donahue and *Family Affair*'s Johnny Whitaker rounded out the cast. The premise this time was the life of a high school football coach and his wife and three children after the coach's sister and brother-in-law are killed in a plane crash. The family of five becomes a family of nine after the four children of the dead couple move in. Though it was an interesting premise for a comedy, the show aired only from October until December 1977.

In 1978 *Happy Days* again received entertainment industry recognition. Ed Cotter won an Emmy Award for Film Editing. Henry Winkler was nominated for Outstanding Actor in a Comedy Series, Jerry Paris for Directing, and Tom Bosley for Supporting Actor.

The *Happy Days'* sets were important to the cast and crew of the show. Arnold's, a constant in the life of the characters since Richie and Potsie first entered the hang-out as high school sophomores, caught on fire during one 1979 episode when Chachi leaves the drive-in with Joanie instead of checking the stove and closing up properly. The cast was forbidden to go near the set until their characters entered to see the interior burned. The set was so central to the show that the actors were visibly moved to see it ruined.

Scott Baio, with Lynda Goodfriend, who played Lori Beth on *Happy Days*, was selected to head the cast of another Garry Marshall–produced show called *Who's Watching the Kids* in September 1978. The plot centered on two Las Vegas showgirls (Goodfriend and Caren Kaye) who lived with their younger siblings (Baio and Tammy Lauren). The show also featured Lorrie Mahaffey, who had been playing Potsie Weber's girlfriend, Jennifer. (Mahaffey and Anson Williams married but later divorced.) The show lasted only a few episodes before being canceled.

In 1979 Marion Ross won an Emmy nomination in the Supporting Actress in a Comedy Series category. The show was still viable, and the television industry recognized that fact. *Happy Days* was now a television institution.

Ron Howard had learned a lot from director Jerry Paris and had been delighted when the producers offered him a chance to direct episodes of *Happy Days*. As Howard learned the craft of directing, the other actors found him not only a good director but one who was easy to work with. Misty Rowe remembers an incident from Howard's first time out. "Ron Howard directed the show where I came on as the carhop," remembers Rowe. "It was a political campaign and I had to wear a fifties' one-piece bathing suit. I had to jump on the platform and go 'Vote for [Stevenson].' Jerry Paris knocked on my dressing room door and I had a trench coat over the fifties swimsuit [while I] waited to go on. Ron Howard was there and he was like so embarrassed, 'cause he was directing the show that day: Jerry Paris was teaching him how to direct. Jerry said to Ron, 'Come on, you gotta see the suit. You gotta make sure it's the right color for the camera. You gotta okay it.' Ron was like, 'I don't know . . .' Jerry Paris said, 'Open the coat. Show him the suit.' So I opened the coat and Ron said, 'Yeah, it's fine.' And he just walked away. He was such a sweet guy."

Suzi Quatro remembers Howard directing one of Leather Tuscadero's scenes. "Ron directed me in a scene, telling me when to raise and lower my vocal tones." She has other nice memories about working with Howard. "We also shared a wonderful moment when we did 'Johnny B. Goode,'" Quatro recalls. "I had the idea to send him off stage into a snow-storm and back again, all the while doing the Chuck Berry shuffle. Wonderful moments."

Henry Winkler says that Ron Howard was born to direct. Starting in the days when he would capture his family and friends on 8mm film, he had shown an interest in the craft. Howard had already directed a few low-budget movies, such as *Old Paint*, a western that featured his family as the actors, *Cards, Cads, Guns, Gore and Death*, with his brother Clint in the lead, and *Grand Theft Auto*, with himself as the star. The rest of the *Happy Days* cast was very supportive of Howard's desire to make directing a career.

Ron Howard's *Happy Days* contract came up for renewal in 1979. Paramount was planning to double Howard's salary after the actor began making appearances in films once again. Actor Bruce Kimmel had appeared on *Happy Days* and during his visit had talked to Howard about a film he was making titled *The First Nudie Musical*. Kimmel recruited Howard for a cameo role as an auditioning actor. Howard also took the lead in a Roger Corman movie called *Eat My Dust*. But he began to real-ize that his heart was set on directing. Howard told *TV Guide* that if he ever got so busy with directing that he wouldn't have time to act, that would be okay with him.

The executives at NBC, ABC's rival, decided to offer Howard acting, directing, and producing opportunities if he would commit to an exclu-sive contract with their network. Some in the industry believed that Fred Silverman, now at NBC, made the deal to sabotage *Happy Days* and have it removed from the competition. It's more likely Silverman knew what a talented young man Ron Howard was and believed that those talents would greatly benefit NBC. It was an offer Howard couldn't refuse. Howard told Garry Marshall that he wouldn't be returning to star on *Happy Days* and accepted Silverman's offer. Marshall gave Howard his blessing and good wishes. The first of the projects that Howard directed for NBC was the 1980 television movie *Skyward*. It starred screen legend Bette Davis and Howard Hesseman. Marion Ross had a role, and Anson Williams was an executive producer.

Donny Most, who now goes by the name Don, also decided to leave the show to pursue a career outside *Happy Days*. He was soon doing voice-overs for the animated series *Dungeons and Dragons* and making guest appearances on *CHiPs, Fantasy Island,* and *Murder, She Wrote.* Most also tried his luck in theater and successfully landed parts in touring company productions such as *Barefoot in the Park,* with Maureen O'Sullivan, and *Damn Yankees,* with Dick Van Dyke. He would eventually also become a director.

The departure of Ron Howard and Don Most from *Happy Days* was a major blow to the show. Anson Williams later said that when they left, all the magic went out of the show. Although it was in NBC's offer that Howard not be allowed to appear on *Happy Days* at all, someone evidently talked the network into allowing the actor to make a couple of guest-starring appearances. Richie appeared in 1983 in the two-part "Welcome Home" episodes and again when he came back for Joanie and Chachi's wedding in 1984.

In 1980 the writers of *Happy Days* needed to decide how best to write out the characters Ron Howard and Donny Most played. This was accomplished by having Richie and Ralph join the Army, to be stationed in Greenland. Lori Beth would marry Richie over the phone, with Fonzie standing in for the groom. Fonzie would later even help Lori Beth deliver Richie's baby, Richie Jr.

Another show featuring Fonzie had been created, this time an animated version called *Fonz and the Happy Days Gang* that aired on Saturday mornings from November 1980 until November 1981. The plot featured the characters Fonzie, Richie, Ralph, Fonzie's dog Mr. Cool, and a time traveler named Cupcake. The premise of the show centered on the *Happy Days* gang getting accidentally stuck in Cupcake's time machine and their adventures as they try to find their way back to 1957. Ron Howard, Henry Winkler, and Donny Most voiced their characters while Didi Conn voiced Cupcake and Frank Welker was the voice of Mr. Cool.

When stars depart a continuing series often new characters are introduced. Such was the case at *Happy Days.* Joanie Cunningham's best friend, Jenny Piccolo, had been mentioned from the very start of *Happy Days* but was never seen. In 1980 actress Cathy Silvers, one half of a set of twin daughters born to legendary television actor Phil Silvers, was brought in to finally give the viewers a look at Jenny. Silvers, born on May 27, 1961, in New York City, was an entertaining addition to the cast. *Happy Days* was her first television appearance. Silvers said that the show couldn't have been a better initiation into the entertainment business as the cast was very warm and supportive and immediately took her into their *Happy Days* family. Cathy's real-life father was brought in during an episode in late 1981 to play Jenny's father. That experience was "magic" for Cathy. She had always heard how exciting it was to work with her father, and she had her first, and only, chance on *Happy Days*. Phil Silvers died in 1985. Cathy says that playing Jenny Piccolo was a riot. She says it was no less than frightening to play the role of a character who had been talked about for years but had never been seen. Silvers seemed to bring to the character exactly the nuances that the unseen Jenny possessed.

In 1981 Fonzie's work ethic was in overdrive. That was probably okay with Henry Winkler as by that time he had opted for less money and a percentage of the show's syndication profits. Winkler knew that screen time for Fonzie was golden. Fonzie became the co-owner of Arnold's, taught shop at the vocational school, and continued to operate Bronco's Garage. Even without Richie and Ralph, the show's momentum continued. Jerry Paris was nominated for an Emmy in the Outstanding Director in a Comedy Series category that year.

In 1982 Fonzie fell in love with divorcee/single mother Ashley Pfister, played by Linda Purl. Ashley's daughter was played by the lovely little actress Heather O'Rourke, who made famous the line "They're heeeere . . ." from the movie *Poltergeist* and who died from an intestinal obstruction at the age of twelve. The casting of Purl was noteworthy as she was an accomplished theater actress. Born in Greenwich, Connecticut, on September 2, 1955, Purl was raised in Japan, where she was the only foreign-born actor in her class to train at the Toho Geino Academy. She made several appearances at Tokyo's Imperial Theater, and then relocated to England to study under Marguerite Beale. Purl returned to the United States to study at the Lee Strasberg Institute. She has appeared in productions both on Broadway and at the Globe Theater. Purl's first television series was as a regular on the soap opera *The Secret Storm*. She first appeared on *Happy Days* in 1974–1975 in the role of Richie's girlfriend Gloria.

The *Happy Days* characters and actors continued to be popular. In 1983 the cast visited Milwaukee, where Tom Bosley, as head of the television family, was given the key to the city. More than 100,000 people participated in the *Happy Days* parade. In 1983 the show stayed on Tuesdays nights but moved to the 8:30 P.M. time slot.

With most of the male cast members away at college, the show needed a young, clean-cut character to play off Fonzie. Ted McGinley was brought in as Marion Cunningham's nephew, Roger Phillips. Roger had been a teacher at Jefferson High but was now the new principal at George S. Patton Vocational School, where Fonzie was the Dean of Boys. (Potsie, by the way, remained on the show as a perennial college student who worked for Howard at Cunningham Hardware.)

Ted McGinley was a young, good-looking actor who began his long and lucrative television career on *Happy Days*. McGinley was born in Newport Beach, California, on May 30, 1958. He was the captain of his water polo team in college as well as a member of Sigma Chi fraternity. The handsome and popular McGinley escorted sixteen-year-old Brooke Shields to her senior prom. McGinley first appeared on television in the made-for-television movie *Valentine*, with Mary Martin.

Fonzie's romance with Ashley didn't work out, but The Fonz didn't let that get him down. When Marion's nephew, Roger Phillips, arrived in 1983, Fonzie was very involved with his work as Dean of Boys. By now, Arthur Fonzarelli was going head to head with Mr. T from the increasingly popular new NBC show *The A-Team*.

The fifties had turned to the sixties in the land of *Happy Days*, and a lot of the episodes centered on the romance between Joanie and Chachi. The two characters had previously sung on the show, and decided to try their luck with careers in music; they moved to Chicago to live with Chachi's mother Louisa (played by Ellen Travolta). This became the opportunity for the spin-off series *Joanie Loves Chachi*, which, while created by Garry Marshall and Lowell Ganz, was developed by Tom Miller and Bob Boyett. Scott Baio said that when he was first asked to sing on *Happy Days* he was against it. The actor told the writers that he "didn't sing" and asked them to please not have him do that. Yet when Baio thought about the fame and attention other pop singers received, he decided that maybe it wasn't a bad thing.

Erin Moran has said that *Joanie Loves Chachi* was intended only as a limited run. "I don't know whether the show was a workable show," laments Howard Storm, who directed *Joanie Loves Chachi* episodes. "They thought the show would hinge on Scott's following." Evidently that following wasn't strong enough to sustain characters away from the comfort of their *Happy Days* friends and families. (Finding no success as professional singers, Joanie and Chachi would return to Milwaukee and *Happy Days*. Joanie enrolled in college and became a teacher's assistant at the vocational school. Chachi continued to dream about becoming a rock star.)

Joanie Loves Chachi was an opportunity for Erin Moran and Scott Baio that in retrospect they probably wish they hadn't had. Moran and Baio had such good chemistry as Joanie and Chachi that the real-life actors dated frequently during their time on *Happy Days*. Baio claims that their on-off personal relationship was tumultuous. By the time they started to film *Joanie Loves Chachi* the romance was gone, and appearing on the show together was difficult.

One of *Happy Days'* notable firsts was not necessarily a good thing. In Season Five, the three-part opening show featured Fonzie wearing a bathing suit but still dressed in his leather jacket, socks, and boots as he water-skied with Richie. Fonzie attempts to jump a shark encased in an ocean cage. This event would find a permanent place in Hollywood pop culture—it would forever be used as an example of a stunt used to bring attention to a flagging show that only signaled a severe drop in the show's quality. "Jumping the Shark" is used to describe this failing even today. (*Happy Days'* Ted McGinley later became the "patron saint" of the Jump the Shark Internet site. Several shows that brought in McGinley to play a character, including *Married . . . With Children*, *Dynasty*, and *Sports Night*, went off the air shortly after his appearance.) Ironically, Fonzie jumping the shark was not a portent for the end of the show. One hundred episodes aired after the one with the shark. Anson Williams, in fact, was nominated for a Golden Globe for Best Supporting Actor in a Comedy Series in 1982.

With Chachi gone to Chicago with Joanie, a young character was needed to take his place, even if temporarily, and the character of Roger's brother Flip was created. Billy Warlock read for the role, as did two young actors named Michael J. Fox and John Stamos. Warlock had once been employed as a stunt man for Robin Williams in an episode of *Mork & Mindy* and had appeared on the soap opera *General Hospital*. A charismatic actor, Billy Warlock was born in Gardena, California, on March 26, 1961, the son of a stunt man. *Happy Days* was Warlock's first television series, but he would go on to star in the hit series *Baywatch* as Eddie Kramer and on *Days of Our Lives* as Frankie Brady. Billy Warlock won the role of Flip, and Fox would later that year land a role on *Family Ties*, the sitcom that launched his career. Stamos played the role of Blackie on *General Hospital* and would later co-star in the hit series *Full House* and then *Jake in Progress*.

Actress Crystal Bernard also was added to the cast of *Happy Days*, first appearing as a new girl at the high school and later as Howard Cunningham's niece K.C. As a child, Bernard had sung with her father, Jerry Wayne Bernard, at revival meetings. She graduated from Westfield High School in Houston, Texas. Bernard appeared in a Pepsi commercial at the age of seventeen and then landed a role in the Garry Marshall–directed film *Young Doctors in Love*. *Happy Days* was Bernard's first television appearance.

There was another change to the show. This time *Happy Days* returned to its roots. Arnold (Pat Morita) came back to buy back Al's share of Arnold's Drive-In.

Happy Days was still revered by a certain sector of the viewing audience, but the show wasn't seeing the high ratings it once had received. To Garry Marshall "it just became time" for the show to end. *Happy Days* had been a top-20 series for eight of its eleven seasons. It became ABC's longest-running sitcom (from January 15, 1974, until May 8, 1984—a total of 255 original episodes). Henry Winkler agreed with Marshall, saying that it was time to move on, that the people involved in the show had done all that they had to do. The last episode of *Happy Days* aired on November 11, 1983. The final episode featured Richie and Lori Beth visiting Milwaukee with their son and informing the Cunninghams that not only was Lori Beth going to have another baby but Richie was going to take the plunge and try for his lifelong dream of becoming a screenwriter. They were moving to Hollywood, land of broken dreams and . . . hit television shows. For the final scene, Tom Bosley, with real tears in his eyes, stepped out of character to thank the viewing audience for their many years of loyal support. No bows, no curtain calls, just the end of the legendary hit television series.

The end of *Happy Days* was a bittersweet experience for those involved with the show. Tom Bosley believes that the final show wrapped up everything the cast and producers were trying to accomplish in the eleven years *Happy Days* was on the air. Marion Ross says that the eleven-year run of *Happy Days* was longer than college or a stint in the Army, so the cast had the opportunity to make lifelong friendships. (Ross would be nominated for an Emmy that final year for Outstanding Supporting Actress in a Comedy Series.) Producer Lowell Ganz remembers that the atmosphere behind the scenes of *Happy Days* was exactly what you wanted it to be. If anything, the cast and crew were family. Scott Baio says that *Happy Days* was as funny as it was because of Garry Marshall. Henry Winkler says that the cast really cared about helping the story. Winkler says he learned that there just can't be stardom or celebrities on a successful show. Everyone works together. Suzi Quatro also remembers *Happy Days* fondly. "Great cast, good stories, wonderful director, and, most important, beautiful memories."

Happy Days was quite a ride for everyone involved. Garry Marshall says that television can be powerful if you have the right characters and the right actors. With *Happy Days*, it was all that and a whole lot more.

Chapter 5

MAKING THEIR DREAMS COME TRUE

appy Days introduced and featured many guest stars. Three of those characters made a special impact on the viewing audience: Laverne, Shirley, and Mork from Ork. The two young ladies, introduced in *Happy Days* Episode #49: "A Date with Fonzie," immediately caught the eye of *Happy Days'* fans. On November 11, 1975, Laverne DeFazio and Shirley Feeney were initially introduced as "bimbo" friends of the girl-loving Fonzie when Fonzie attempted to set Richie up with a date after Richie ended the relationship with his girlfriend. Laverne and Shirley enter the episode walking into Arnold's while "Love Me Tender" is playing on the jukebox. With Laverne's yelled greeting "Hey, Fonzie!" a star was born—in fact, two stars. (Oddly, in this episode, Shirley seems to have as strong a Bronx accent as Laverne, which is a bit strange since the series takes place in Milwaukee.)

When the time came to cast the roles of Fonzie's female friends for Episode #49, Garry Marshall immediately thought of the comedic talent of his little sister Penny. Penny had experienced minor success as a regular on *The Odd Couple* in the role of ditzy secretary Myrna Turner. Penny seemed reluctant to seek work as a television comedian, but her brother had great faith in the fact that she was better than most actresses who performed in roles such as the one she had mastered on *The Odd*

Couple. Marshall thought Penny would be the perfect actress to play off Fonzie's character. But first, Marshall had to talk Penny into taking the role. Carole Penny Maschiarelli, named after her mother's film favorite, Carole Lombard, was born on October 15, 1942, in the Bronx, New York City, the third child of Tony and Marjorie. Brother Garry is eight years older than Penny, and Penny is six years younger than their sister, Ronny. Marshall says she was "pushed into" dancing at the age of three. She performed with The Marshallettes, a sixteen-person ensemble. Most little girls like performing, but Marshall says she hated it. When she complained to her mother, she was told that she had her choice: dancing with The Marshallettes or performing chores at home. Though strict, Marjorie Marshall was a proficient dance instructor. She landed The Marshallettes a booking on *Ted Mack & the Original Amateur Hour*, and they won their competition. At the age of fourteen Penny made a tap-dancing appearance on *The Jackie Gleason Show*.

Penny Marshall's teen years were awkward, and by her account not the best years of her life. Any thoughts she may have had about pursuing something in the entertainment world were tempered by the fact that she didn't view herself as attractive enough to be successful in that business. Marshall didn't even like people to take her photograph. She had a strong Bronx accent and felt uncomfortable in her own skin. She was sent to Jewish summer camps even though the family was Italian. She just never seemed to fit in, or at least she felt that way. When the time came for college, Tony Marshall thought it might be good for his daughter to get away from her New York roots and maybe become less ethnic and regional. He thought if Penny attended school out west maybe she would lose some of that strong accent and feel more comfortable around people. Penny selected the University of New Mexico, which was about as far away from the Bronx as she could possibly get. Once there, she majored in math and psychology.

Marshall seemed to enjoy college life. In her junior year she met a young man named Michael Henry who was attending the University of New Mexico on a football scholarship. After a whirlwind romance Penny and Henry were married. When their daughter Tracy was born, Penny dropped out of college in order to earn money to raise their little girl. Penny found work in Albuquerque as a Kelly Girl. (Marshall would later say that after being involved with *Laverne & Shirley* there were days when being a secretary looked calm and peaceful.) Unfortunately, the marriage to Henry didn't work out, and within two years the couple was divorced. Now with a baby to support, Marshall reached back to her roots to teach dance. She stayed in New Mexico for six years and to pass the time

The cast of *Laverne & Shirley*, 1976. Top (left to right): Phil Foster (Frank), Michael McKean (Lenny), David L. Lander (Squiggy), Eddie Mekka (Carmine). Bottom (left to right): Penny Marshall (Laverne), Cindy Williams (Shirley), Betty Garrett (Edna). Photo courtesy of Globe Photos, Inc.

became involved with a drama group. Her community theater company mounted a production of *Oklahoma!*, and Marshall played the role of Ado Annie for two years in Durango, New Mexico. She eventually tired of life in a small, rural community and decided to join her brother, Garry, in California in 1967.

Penny had enjoyed acting with the theater group and thought maybe there would be something for her to do in Hollywood. Garry Marshall says that Penny was always hung up on her looks, but now she decided that if she couldn't be pretty, she'd at least be funny. Garry arranged for her to have a small role in a *Danny Thomas Anthology* episode titled "My Friend Tony" that starred Jack Klugman. Ever the self-critical, reluctant performer, Penny didn't particularly like her performance and thought that maybe acting was not going to work out for her. Her brother *did* see her potential and encouraged her to pursue a show business career. Drawn to stunt work, she started getting work in movies such as *Free Grass* and *The Pink Garter Gang*. Her first speaking role was as an Indian girl who is a member of a motorcycle gang in the movie *The Savage Seven*. The roles were nothing to write home about. Even so, Garry Marshall continued to believe that his sister had great timing as a comedian and thought she would do just fine in the role of Myrna, Jack Klugman's goofy secretary in *The Odd Couple*. Penny had already demonstrated a certain chemistry with Klugman. Her blossoming career wasn't all about family connections. She was considered for the role of Gloria Stivic, the daughter of Edith and Archie Bunker, for a new television show called *All in the Family*. While Penny's comedic talents impressed the casting director, the producers thought that she wasn't "child-like enough" and that she was too old to play opposite Rob Reiner, who was cast to play Gloria's husband, Michael. The irony of that greatly amused both Penny and Reiner.

Penny Marshall and Rob Reiner had met through mutual friends during an outing to Barney's Beanery in Hollywood, and the attraction was almost immediate. Rob is the son of legendary comedian Carl Reiner, who was a regular on Sid Caesar's *Your Show of Shows* and developed into a major force in television comedy. Rob Reiner was also a native of the Bronx and had actually grown up in the same neighborhood as Penny and her family. Marshall remembers trick or treating at the Reiners' house, where she once gathered her courage to ask Carl for his autograph. The two young people didn't meet until years later, a long way from the Bronx. Marshall and Reiner decided to get married in December 1970, but Reiner was cast for the show that Penny had been denied. Because Reiner had to be on hand to shoot the first thirteen episodes of *All in the Family* and would be quite busy, the wedding was delayed until April 1971, when the couple married in the backyard of Reiner's parents' house in Beverly Hills. Reiner adopted Marshall's daughter, Tracy, and Penny set her sights on her new family life and her career.

Penny Marshall had successfully brought the ditzy Myrna to life, and through her efforts the secretary became a small but important character on *The Odd Couple*. Even so, Marshall's thoughts of inadequacy would rise to the surface. She was insecure during her time on the show, thinking that her casting and continued employment had less to do with any talent she might have and more to do with the fact that her brother was the producer. Garry tried to encourage Penny, stating that she indeed had real talent and should remain in the game beyond *The Odd Couple*.

Marshall was next cast in the role of Janice Dreyfuss for the television show *Paul Sand in Friends and Lovers*. Unfortunately, the show lasted only a half season before it was canceled. During this time Penny made several guest-starring appearances on shows such as *The Bob Newhart Show*, *The Mary Tyler Moore Show*, *Chico and the Man*, and others, mostly comedies. She also did a television movie titled *Let's Switch*, with Barbara Eden and Barbara Feldon. At that point, brother Garry got the idea for the characters of Laverne and Shirley on *Happy Days*, which he needed to cast quickly.

Penny Marshall wasn't that keen on her brother's casting idea. Garry thought his kid sister could use the money, but Penny wasn't sure she wanted to do the role. *Happy Days* was a big show by this time. For some reason, maybe only to make Penny feel guilty enough to accept the offer, Garry asked Penny to take the role as a favor to their father, Tony. Penny finally agreed, but only if she was given her choice of which of the girls she would play. She decided on Laverne DeFazio. Now they only had to cast Laverne's buddy, Shirley Feeney.

Several years before, Penny Marshall had met another young actress named Cindy Williams on the set of *The Christian Licorice Store*, a movie starring Beau Bridges and Maud Adams. Ironically, the premise of the film—a tennis player is overcome by the Hollywood lifestyle—would be one to which the actresses could later relate. It was filmed in the late sixties but not released until 1971. Marshall and Williams had very small parts, and both ended up on the cutting-room floor. Continuing with their kismet relationship, the two young women were hired as writers for a bicentennial spoof of American history that Francis Ford Coppola's company was doing. The girls liked each other and became friends.

Cindy had been thinking of making acting her career since high school. She was born Cynthia Williams on August 22, 1948, in Van Nuys, California, to electronic technician Beachard Williams and his Sicilian-American wife, Francesca Bellini, a waitress. Soon after Cindy was born, the family moved to Texas with Cindy's stepbrother, Jim, and sister, Carol. Williams says she enjoyed her time in Texas even though the family didn't have much money. Williams's parents both had a great sense of humor. Her father was known for his impressions of celebrities such as Jackie Gleason and Milton Berle, and her mother was a singer. When Cindy was nine, the family moved back to Van Nuys. Prior to attending Birmingham High School, Cindy entertained thoughts of becoming a nurse, but when she entered high school, she discovered that the drama department was a place where she could indulge her creative thoughts and take part in artistic activities. As a child, Williams had performed skits she wrote herself in the backyard of her family's home. She attended church camps and enjoyed putting on plays at the camp and the church. While at Birmingham High, Williams found that she not only enjoyed writing plays but also directing and acting in them. Williams made appearances in the school's productions, including *Our Town* and *The Diary of Anne Frank*. After graduating from high school, she attended Los Angeles City College, where she majored in drama. During the next few years, a time that would include the death of her father when she was twenty-two years old, Williams worked as a receptionist, switchboard operator, and telephone solicitor, and as a waitress for the International House of Pancakes.

Williams was devastated when her father died, but she didn't give up her dream of becoming involved in the entertainment world. She applied for a job through a government-sponsored theater program for low-income actors with an ethnic background. Garry Marshall's old Army pal Bud Freeman happened to be the one who interviewed Williams for the program. Although she wouldn't get the grant, Freeman liked Williams enough to send her along to meet with Marshall and his partner Fred Ross. Garry Marshall would later say that Cindy reminded him of stage actress Barbara Harris when he first met her. Marshall was impressed with Williams and recommended her to a management company. Soon the young actress was appearing on shows such as *Room 222*, *Barefoot in the Park*, *Nanny and the Professor*, *The Funny Side*, and other series. One of Williams's friends was a receptionist for budget film-maker Roger Corman, and Cindy auditioned for a Corman film titled *Gas-s-s-s* (the subtitle was the wordy *It May Become Necessary to Destroy the World in Order to Save It*). She was cast in the role of Marissa and made her feature film debut in 1971. Williams's next role was in *Drive, He Said*, Jack Nicholson's directing debut. Other movies followed, including *Beware the Blob*, the George Cukor–directed *Travels with My Aunt*, with Maggie Smith, and *The Conversation*, with Gene Hackman.

The roles were small, and Williams supplemented her income acting in commercials for TWA, United California Bank, and Foster Grant. (She took a stand regarding commercials that she honors to this day: she won't be a spokesman for any product in which she does not believe.) Finally, Williams landed a role in which she could catch the public's attention. She was cast as Laurie Henderson opposite Ron Howard and Richard Dreyfuss in *American Graffiti*. Williams was thrilled that the film career as a co-starring actress that she had long sought was at last a reality. When Garry Marshall, who had been so helpful in launching her Hollywood career, suggested that Williams appear with his sister on *Happy Days*, Cindy was reluctant to return to television and was inclined to say no. She says she turned down other television offers at this time as well. Penny Marshall and Cindy Williams were writing partners, so Garry Marshall figured the two women must have some chemistry. Garry thought that Cindy, like Penny, could probably use the money that appearing as a guest star on a hit television show could offer. Anyway, it was only a one-shot deal, so what was the problem? Okay, but Cindy Williams had a second objection to doing the role. Having just appeared in *American Graffiti*, with its early-sixties setting, she didn't want to be typecast. But *Happy*

Days was a hit show. The actress reconsidered her self-imposed television ban and agreed that doing the role of Shirley on *Happy Days* as a guest appearance would give her additional exposure in Hollywood. Besides, Williams had dated Henry Winkler and considered him a dear friend. Working with Henry—and Penny—would be fun, and she had already worked with Ron Howard on *American Graffiti*. Still, Williams played hard to get in the negotiations. She asked for a high salary and was surprised when the producers agreed to it. She also wanted to see the script. Finally, it was agreed. Marshall and Williams would do the appearance, with Williams billed as a guest star and Marshall as a special guest star. The first call Williams made to announce that she would be playing Shirley Feeney was to her friend Henry Winkler.

During the filming of that *Happy Days* episode, cameraman Stan Rosen called Garry Marshall over to the camera to look at the two actresses through the lens. They agreed: no one could have anticipated that kind of chemistry. The girls from Milwaukee were a smash.

Garry Marshall's colleague, Michael Eisner, had made some career moves of his own. He left ABC and by 1976 was the head of Paramount. Eisner had believed in Garry Marshall's ability to bring a hit show to ABC and Paramount Television, and Marshall had delivered. What could be better than to get Marshall involved with another show with which the network and studio could extend the success it was enjoying with *Happy Days*? And where better to look than within the extended Cunningham family itself?

Fred Silverman was the head honcho at ABC at this time. One day Silverman had lunch with Garry Marshall to see what else Marshall might have up his sleeve that could keep the *Happy Days* momentum going. Always quick on his feet, Marshall thought of Penny and Cindy's appearance on *Happy Days* and recalled how well they worked together. He realized that putting his sister in a show of her own would be great work for Penny. Before Silverman had arrived at ABC, Marshall had proposed a pilot titled "Wives" that had featured her. The network wasn't interested. Now, improvising and expanding the characters Laverne and Shirley, Marshall described to Silverman a show revolving around two blue-collar women who worked in a beer factory. Silverman knew that any idea of Garry Marshall's would likely be better than most other producers' and he liked what he was hearing. Fine, he agreed. Let's do it. But let's do it *now*. For Garry Marshall, who had been that route with the *Happy Days* pilot, it was déjà vu.

The pilot for what would become *Laverne & Shirley* turned out to be easy to produce. It was filmed on the standing set of *Happy Days* and took only ten minutes to shoot one night after *Happy Days* was finished taping. The premise was the same as Garry Marshall had suggested to Fred Silverman in his off-the-cuff pitch. Two young girls from Milwaukee who worked in the bottle-capping division of the Schlotz Brewery shared an apartment, and the stories would revolve around the idiosyncrasies of their single lives. (An interesting side note is that neither of the actresses who took the roles of Laverne and Shirley actually liked beer.) The time would be 1959, just like *Happy Days*. There would be a slight change in the characters. When Laverne and Shirley appeared on *Happy Days* they were more aggressive and promiscuous. Now the characters were upgraded to "fun," with a warmth that made them more personally appealing. The interactions of Laverne and Shirley harked back to television's real fifties because the young women had a Lucy–Ethel appeal. Laverne DeFazio was presented as tough, cynical, and street-wise. She doesn't take any guff from anybody. Penny Marshall would call Laverne a realist, just like she herself was. Shirley Feeney has more of a Pollyanna attitude toward life and has stronger ethics. As for Shirley's approach to men, her nickname is "Wait for the Wedding Night Feeney." Laverne is matter of fact and often becomes frustrated with Shirley's naïveté.

Garry Marshall felt it was important that Laverne and Shirley be self-sufficient. After *The Mary Tyler Moore Show*, it just wasn't politically correct for a young woman to have to rely on a man. The girls were perfect foils for one another, but also the fact that they were very close, almost sisters, was strongly evident. These were women the audience would know were committed to each other and would stick with one another through thick and thin, doing it *their* way.

In the mid-seventies, despite the success of *Happy Days*, ABC was third in the network ratings. Fred Silverman and his colleagues knew that one of the ways to address this problem was to air shows that would appeal to young, female viewers. The network needed to sell programming to advertisers, and that was the demographic that bought the majority of advertised products at that particular airtime. Teens and females were better demographics for the advertisers because they had more disposable income. The network was interested in Garry Marshall's proposed show from several standpoints. The viewers would be of the demographic the network needed, the show could be placed in a position where the *Happy Days* momentum would carry it forward, and Penny Marshall was already under a holding contract with ABC based on the "Wives" pilot. This made a series by Garry Marshall with an actress already under contract with the network even more appealing. The presentation of the show that was shot on Friday night after *Happy Days* was edited on Saturday. The ABC executives viewed it on Sunday, and the green light was given on Monday to put the show on the air. Stage 20 at Paramount was reserved, and the girls' apartment set was created. (Penny Marshall and Cindy Williams at first objected to the design of the apartment set: they thought it might be too upscale for working-class girls. Garry Marshall explained that the apartment had to be appealing and not a shabby apartment where people would feel sorry for them. Penny and Cindy ended up bringing things from their own homes and decorating the set a little more to their liking.)

The powers that be at the network and production companies figured it couldn't hurt to have Laverne and Shirley make another appearance on *Happy Days* in order to re-introduce them to the viewing audience. For *Happy Days* Episode #57: "Football Frolics," the two girls are involved with a baby-sitting enterprise that Richie sets up to raise money to attend a football game. Laverne and Shirley return in the following week's episode, "Fonzie the Superstar." This time they have more to do. Calling themselves "The Arnoldettes," Laverne and Shirley back up Pat Morita as the character Arnold sings "By the Light of the Silvery Moon." The pair provides some good physical comedy as they dance clumsily behind Arnold.

Dropped into ABC's line-up as a mid-season replacement series on Tuesday, January 27, 1976, *Laverne & Shirley* debuted following *Happy Days*. The first show was written by Bob Brunner and directed by Garry Marshall. A full-time director like Jerry Paris was hard to come by (although Paris directed the second show), so a series of directors were employed, including Alan Myerson, Jay Sandrich, Howard Storm, and James Burrows.

Part of *Laverne & Shirley*'s initial appeal was the appearance of Fonzie on the first two episodes. In Episode #1 he accompanies Laverne and Shirley to a swanky dinner party that was thrown by their boss. When the working-class girls aren't treated respectfully, Fonzie tells off the snobs who are looking down their noses at them, and the three leave the event with their heads held high. Fonzie comes back the following week to convince the girls to let him throw a bachelor party at Laverne's father's Pizza Bowl while her father is away. Drawing on the popularity of Fonzie was a great move to re-introduce the girls and get the show on its feet. Whether or not Henry Winkler's appearance was the critical element, that first show did well. *Real* well.

Laverne & Shirley began with the now-famous phrase "Schlemiel, Schlimazel, Hasenpfeffer Incorporated," followed by the infectious theme song "Making Our Dreams Come True," written by Norman Gimble and

Charles Fox and sung by Cyndi Grecco. The opening line had its genesis in Penny Marshall's Bronx neighborhood, where it was used as a jump-rope rhyme. A schlemiel is someone who is unlucky, and a schlimazel is a klutz. (Garry Marshall's wife hand-printed the *Laverne & Shirley* sign that appears on the opening credits of the first show while she was waiting for him to finish the pilot so that they and their kids could go on vacation to Palm Springs. Marshall says that if you listen closely to the "Schlemiel/Schlimazel" chant in the pilot you can hear one of his kids saying, "Hurry up, Dad!")

Done along vaudeville lines, with physical comedy and shtick, the show was a truly a throwback to fifties television. The peculiar fashion of that decade caused Penny Marshall to groan that she had to dress in those "horrible clothes" again. The fashion wasn't the focus of the show. The focus was the girls. Garry Marshall was of the opinion that the feminist role models being offered in 1976 were unrealistic. He thought it was important to offer female characters who could take care of themselves but were working-class, like the majority of the viewing audience. The producers and writers felt that a huge portion of the female audience could relate to Laverne and Shirley. They didn't wear designer clothes or live in high-end apartments like most of the other women portrayed on television.

Laverne & Shirley was filmed with three cameras. Film had a crisper quality than videotape and was easier to edit. With all the physical comedy—which could be sometimes intricate and nuanced—planned for the show, film was the preferred way to go as it is better suited for catching the little details. The apartment set of Garry Marshall's series *The Odd Couple* was adapted to use as the girls' apartment set.

Daily Variety reviewed the premiere show in its January 27, 1976, issue. They called it "a zippy idea which might catch on." The *Hollywood Reporter* thought it had potential but was "straining too hard for laughs." Still, they pointed out, it was on after the successful *Happy Days*, so it should get attention. *Weekly Variety* called it "proletarian comedy."

With hopes for at least some small measure of success, the producers looked down the list of the previous night's ratings to see if *Laverne & Shirley* might somehow have snuck in at the very bottom. Garry Marshall couldn't find it and was a little disappointed. But there was a reason he couldn't find it on the list. He was looking at the bottom ratings, not the top. To the amazement of all involved, *Laverne & Shirley* came in at number 1. The show even knocked off the ever-popular *All in the Family*, on which Penny Marshall's husband Rob Reiner was starring. In fact, the premier episode of *Laverne & Shirley* scored the highest share of any program on any network in the past ten years. The first two episodes garnered more than 50 million viewers. So much for Cindy Williams's thought that it was going to be a thirteen-week job, if that.

Laverne & Shirley was a go and could now establish its routine. Wednesday through Friday were for rehearsals, weekends were for rewriting, Monday was blocking, Tuesday morning was a quick run-through, Tuesday afternoon the cast did a dress rehearsal before a live audience, and filming took place Tuesday nights before another 300-person live audience. Garry Marshall warmed up the audience as he had done for *Happy Days*. It looked like *Laverne & Shirley* could be a major hit. But there was one little problem.

Although Cindy Williams knew from the get-go that she would be working for a production entity headed by Penny Marshall's brother, she was never comfortable with that fact. Marshall family involvement in the show grew when Garry Marshall appointed his father, Tony, as one of *Laverne & Shirley*'s producers. *Mork & Mindy* director Howard Storm, who directed several episodes of *Laverne & Shirley*, says that Tony Marshall was "kinda like the father figure." "There was great respect because he was Garry's dad," says Storm. "When Tony showed up [on the *Mork & Mindy* set] Robin [Williams] would kid about how he was 'The Godfather.' Tony didn't like that. Robin would always carry on. He'd drop to his knees and do all kinds of stuff around him, which was so typical Robin. It made Tony uncomfortable." One time during the run of *Laverne & Shirley* it came to Garry Marshall's attention that Tony Marshall had withheld daughter Penny's paycheck because she had mouthed off to him. (The paychecks could sometimes be a problem. During the first year of production Garry Marshall was told by the Paramount business office that Cindy Williams wasn't cashing her checks. When Marshall asked Williams about it she said she was hiding them in her sock drawer, uncashed. She was having a hard time realizing that she actually had earned checks in those large amounts.) Cindy Williams was uneasy with the Marshall dynasty as it related to *Laverne & Shirley* and continuously questioned if she was receiving the same treatment on-screen as Penny. It was a problem Cindy would continue to have.

Although the focus of *Laverne & Shirley* would always remain on the two girls, other actors had been brought in to fill out the cast and contribute to the comedy. First to be introduced was Carmine "The Big Ragoo" Ragusa, who danced across the screen as Shirley's boyfriend in the second episode, "The Bachelor Party." The inspiration for "The Big Ragoo" came from a kid that Garry Marshall knew in the Bronx who used to pull an ice truck with his teeth and a rope.

Carmine was played by Eddie Mekka, an Armenian-American actor born Edward Mekjian on June 14, 1952, in Worcester, Massachusetts. Mekka got his start in show business as a teenager through musical theater. He also trained as a gymnast and loved to dance. Mekka's first role was as a member of the chorus of *Fiddler on the Roof* with the Worcester County Light Opera Company in 1969. He studied with choreographer Phil Black and was involved with the Boston Conservatory. In 1974 Mekka appeared in the Broadway production of *The Lieutenant* and received a Drama Desk nomination and also a Tony nomination for Best Actor. He then appeared in other Broadway productions, including *Damn Yankees*, with Gwen Verdon and Ray Walston. "The Big Ragoo" was a fun character, full of life and a love of dancing. A good singer, Mekka, in character as Carmine, would often sing songs like "Rags to Riches" and "Because of You."

Every show needs an anchor, and Garry Marshall knew right where to look for the actor to play Laverne's father, Frank. Marshall had met Phil Foster when the two were doing the NBC radio show *Monitor*. Marshall later called Foster his mentor. Foster was a fellow New Yorker, born Fivel Feldman on March 29, 1914, in Brooklyn. He and his friends took to entertainment early, singing in front of movie theaters. Foster loved talent shows and sometimes worked with his friend Jackie Gleason. A stint in Chicago in the thirties doing stand-up introduced Foster to a broader audience. He eventually became a regular on the *Four Star Revue*, with Tallulah Bankhead. Billed as Arthur Cohen, Foster had written, directed, and appeared in a series of shorts during the early fifties. One was "Brooklyn Goes to Beantown," which featured Foster's character, Brooklyn, visiting cities all over the United States. Known as first Phil Brooks, then finally as Phil Foster, the accomplished comedian appeared in films such as *The Patsy*, with Jerry Lewis, *Hail*, with Richard Schull and Gary Sandy, *Every Little Crook and Nanny*, with Lynn Redgrave and Victor Mature, and *Bang the Drum Slowly*, with Robert De Niro. Foster also frequently appeared on *Toast of the Town*, *The Joey Bishop Show*, and *The Tonight Show Starring Johnny Carson* to perform his stand-up comedy. Garry Marshall found a slot for the actor on *The Odd Couple* and liked working with someone so reliable and funny. Foster was perfect for the role of Frank DeFazio, who, as Foster would relate, was a typical Italian father of the fifties. Frank was written as a loving father who was having a very difficult time letting his little girl grow up. He would weigh in on Laverne's dates and examine her sometimes questionable decisions. Foster was happy to work with Garry Marshall and delighted to have the role. He said that for the first three weeks that he appeared on *Laverne &*

Shirley he didn't know he was getting paid—obviously a joke, as Garry Marshall was known to take good care of his friends and casts.

Later cast to play opposite Phil Foster as Frank's girlfriend, Edna Babish, was veteran actress Betty Garrett. Edna acted as a buffer between the determined Laverne and the equally stubborn Frank. After Edna and Frank got married, Edna served as a mother figure to Laverne. Betty Garrett was an actress/dancer born in St. Joseph, Missouri, on May 23, 1919. Under contract as an ingenue in the heyday of MGM contract players, Garrett appeared in such all-star films as *Words and Music, Take Me Out to the Ballgame, On the Town*, with Frank Sinatra and Gene Kelly, and *My Sister Eileen*, with Janet Leigh and Jack Lemmon. Her career was seriously affected during the McCarthy hearings in the fifties when her husband, *The Jolson Story*'s lead actor, Larry Parks, was blacklisted by Senator Joseph McCarthy's House Un-American Activities Committee. Because of her association with Parks, the talented Garrett didn't work much until she was cast in *All in the Family* as Irene Lorenzo.

Phil Foster was pleased to be working on the show with Penny Marshall and Cindy Williams. He said that as he would watch Marshall and Williams act, his mouth would hang open because the two young women were so instinctive. He compared them to television great Phil Silvers. Another veteran television genius, Carl Reiner, was also impressed with Penny, claiming his daughter-in-law had "all the tools."

The cost of *Laverne & Shirley* was running about $250,000 per episode. Garry Marshall had assembled his usual staff of extremely talented writers, such as Bob Brunner, Lowell Ganz, Dale McRaven, and Arthur Silver. The weekly script for the show was usually written by one writer, than rewritten by several others. (Interestingly, many of the scripts from the failed series *Hey, Landlord* were said to have been adapted for use on *Laverne & Shirley*, where they were much more enthusiastically received.) Different scenes were assigned to different writers. Then Garry Marshall would put everything together. The next day the actors would read the script in the morning and tighten it with the writers in the afternoon. After that, there would be a rehearsal with the writers watching and rewriting. There would be a final run-through with the writers and producers, and then the show would be filmed.

"The gift of *Laverne & Shirley* was the two girls," says director James Burrows, who would later experience great success with future Paramount Television hit series *Taxi* and *Cheers*. "That was what really made that show. Their ability to have a rapport with one another and to do shtick comedy. Penny was one of the greatest physical comics I ever worked with, hands down. It was a sillier show [than others], a more juvenile show, I think. The girls were not the most advanced when it came to relationships with guys. They worked at the beer brewery. It was more of a lower-class comedy than *Taxi* was. I think the gift of that show was the two girls."

The cast was anchored by veteran writers, producers, and Phil Foster, but it was thrown on its ear by two other regular cast members, the tremendously hilarious David L. Lander and Michael McKean. Lander and McKean had become friends while members of the comedy troupe called the Credibility Gap. The two comedians created characters they named Lenny and Anthony, based on people they knew from their New York neighborhoods. Lenny was a Polish guy from Long Island, and Anthony was an Italian guy from the Bronx. Little did Lander and McKean know that those two characters would become comedic icons.

David L. Lander was born David Landau on June 22, 1947, in Brooklyn, New York, to Saul and Stella, two New York City teachers. Lander grew up in the Bronx and knew by the age of ten that what he wanted most out of life was to be an actor. His parents evidently supported his dream because Lander was allowed to enroll at the High School for the Performing Arts in Manhattan. (His brother Robert would become an opera singer.) Lander graduated and continued studying at Carnegie Tech and New York University. He moved to Los Angeles in 1967, where he and friend and roommate Rob Reiner were soon writing for a television variety show called *Romp!* starring Ryan O'Neal and Michelle Lee. The show never really got off the ground, and Reiner and Lander turned their attention to a one-act play called "The Exposure of Raymond Splotros," starring Lander and directed by Reiner.

While hanging out with Rob Reiner, Albert Brooks, and other friends, Lander found a job working for the Sunset Dial telephone answering service. Lander had such a knack for funny voice impressions that he came to the attention of actress Sally Smaller, who periodically worked with the rock and roll station KRLA's "Credibility Gap." Every day the station featured "the Gap," ten-minute sketches based on news events. Lander auditioned on-air with a sketch co-written by Harry Sherer and was so well received that he ended up being hired. One of the people with whom Lander would work was Michael McKean, a friend he had met at Carnegie Tech.

Michael McKean was born in New York City on October 17, 1947, to account executive Gilbert McKean and his high school librarian wife, Ruth. Michael was raised in Sea Cliff, Long Island, and started acting when he was fifteen years old. Like David Lander, McKean also attended Carnegie Tech in Pittsburgh and New York University. He was involved with the Eugene O'Neill's Playwrights Conference during college and decided to try his luck in Hollywood, to which he moved in 1970. McKean had a small role in *The Adventures of Robin Hood*, but he realized his talent writing the hilarious bits he brought to the Credibility Gap. His friendship with David Lander would be highly rewarding. By this time Lander was getting small parts in shows such as *Barney Miller*, *The Bob Newhart Show*, and *Maude*. Lander was also considered for a role as a lady killer when *Laverne & Shirley* was first being cast.

Lander and McKean had worked up their dim-witted characters Lenny and Anthony to perform with the Credibility Gap, and the characters were so popular the comedians' friends asked to see them whenever there was a group gathering. One Thanksgiving weekend when Lander and McKean were appearing with the Gap at the Improv, Rob Reiner called Lander to invite him to a party at his Studio City home that his wife, Penny Marshall, was throwing to celebrate her new television series *Laverne & Shirley*. Lander dropped by, and Marshall asked if he would return after his Gap appearance. She wanted him to bring McKean and do the Lenny and Anthony bit for her friends at the party. Marshall was familiar with the act and thought the two crazy characters would be terrific as friends of Laverne and Shirley. Her brother, Garry, producer of the show, was at the party. When Lander spoke to McKean about returning to the party, McKean didn't know if he felt comfortable as he didn't know the Reiners or their friends. Lander pointed out that if they could land a one-shot on the new series they would qualify for the maximum amount of unemployment insurance. McKean reluctantly agreed to go with Lander.

On the way to the Reiners', Lander and McKean agreed that they would do the characters only if they were specifically asked. As soon as Rob Reiner saw the two comedians arrive at the party, he asked them to perform Lenny and Anthony. The crowd watched with great amusement as Lander and McKean did a bit where Lenny and Anthony try to learn to be butlers at a domestic trade school. They had never really done that specific routine before and improvised their way through it. The Lenny and Anthony characters routinely used foul language, and such was the case that night. The day after the party, Garry Marshall called David Lander and asked if the characters Lenny and Anthony could be done "clean." Lander said he didn't know as they had never done the act that way. Marshall wanted to think about that but offered Lander and McKean jobs as apprentice writers on *Laverne & Shirley* for $300 a week, but no credit. Marshall told them at the end of the season they could write a script, which would enable them to join the Writers Guild.

When Garry Marshall told *Laverne & Shirley* executive producer Tom Miller that he had hired the two actor/comedians, Miller wasn't thrilled. Miller thought there should be a constitutional amendment barring television executives from hiring people at parties. He thought the characters were idiots, which Marshall insisted was the point. Miller changed his mind after he saw Lander and McKean work.

The first thing David Lander and Michael McKean worked on for *Laverne & Shirley* was a rewriting of a scene with the two girls. Lander and McKean found this a little difficult as they had never before written dialogue for women. When Garry Marshall saw the rewritten scene, he told Lander and McKean that they had misunderstood. He had wanted them to write a scene with their two characters, Lenny and Anthony—with one change: Marshall didn't want Lander's character to be named Anthony because there were already too many Italians on the show. Lander and McKean decided that since the show was set in Milwaukee and that city had a large German population they would re-name the character Andrew Squiggman and call him Squiggy for short, while McKean's character was named Lenny Kosnowski. Marshall told Lander and McKean to write the characters into the second act, which took place in the girls' apartment. They tried to think of a good entrance for Lenny and Squiggy and were coming up empty. Finally, McKean came up with the idea that Shirley would be talking to Laverne about the problems involved in finding an acceptable boyfriend. Laverne says to Shirley, "Don't worry, Shirl. One day your Prince Charming will walk right through that door." The door opens, and Squiggy (with Lenny beside him) pops in with what would become his trademark entrance: the nasal "Hell-o."

Lenny and Squiggy were unique characters. Squiggy, with the worm curl over his forehead, was deeply involved with the art of collecting moths. A forerunner of President George W. Bush, he would make up words that meant little but sounded good. Lenny, with his oddly worn hat, had a prize possession: his favorite shirt, which was kept in a mayonnaise jar in the refrigerator. The two characters worked as truck drivers for the company Laverne and Shirley worked for. Penny Marshall told *TV Guide* for the April 29, 1976, issue that Lenny and Squiggy were a pair of disgusting idiots that kept people wondering, "Who let them in?" Cindy Williams said that she felt the boys made Laverne and Shirley "look classy." Lander told *TV Guide* that he didn't know if anybody really believed Lenny and Squiggy, but they laughed at them anyway. McKean said he thought the younger people enjoyed the characters because Lenny and Squiggy got away with things and were shaking up the system. Whatever the reason, Lenny and Squiggy were a major hit.

Six weeks after Lenny and Squiggy's first appearance on *Laverne & Shirley*, ABC President Fred Silverman said that he liked the characters and felt they had the potential to anchor their own sitcom. McKean and Lander liked the idea and, with Garry Marshall, developed a show titled *Lenny and Squiggy in the Army*. Paramount Television supported the possibility of the show, but ABC couldn't get behind the premise. A week after the network viewed and rejected the pilot, Lenny and Squiggy were back on *Laverne & Shirley* to stay. Cindy Williams was glad the Army show didn't get picked up because she felt that Lenny and Squiggy leaving *Laverne & Shirley* would weaken the show. She was likely right. The characters were so popular that while Penny Marshall and Cindy Williams were appearing in the Macy's Thanksgiving Day Parade, David Lander and Michael McKean were getting steady offers to appear at auto shows, and on telethons and talk shows.

While the show was getting a lot of positive attention, the stars of *Laverne & Shirley* were also experiencing fame. Penny Marshall was at a party one night right after *Laverne & Shirley* hit the airwaves. Also in attendance was actress Louise Lasser, who was experiencing success of her own with *Mary Hartman, Mary Hartman*. Marshall and Lasser, who were friends, coolly walked into the bathroom at the party. Once in private, they jumped up and down, yelling, "We're famous!"

Chapter 6

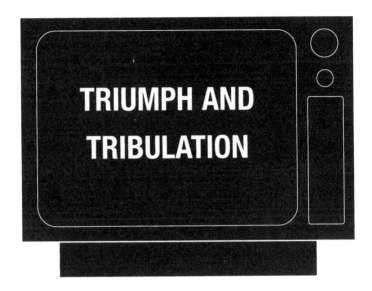

TRIUMPH AND TRIBULATION

Yes, *Laverne & Shirley* was a hit, but with fame came something else. There had been a problem between Penny Marshall and Cindy Williams from the beginning. Williams was still uncomfortable with the fact that Penny's family was so actively involved in the show and feared it would cost her professionally. The first situation arose immediately. It had to do with the actresses' billing in the credits. Each wanted top billing. It was finally agreed that the billing would be rotated, with one of the actresses receiving top billing one week and the other the next week. To appease the two actresses, it was additionally decided to have both names appear on the screen at exactly the same time. Penny Marshall's name appeared on the left side, but Cindy Williams' name was higher up on the right. A perfect balance. But not for long

The high-strung Cindy Williams developed an ulcer and a spastic bowel. She felt dominated by Marshall people. Even Penny's daughter, Tracy, appeared on the show. The tension on the set began to escalate as Marshall and Williams argued with the writers. The writers and the actors frequently didn't see eye to eye. One Christmas the writers even handed out dart boards to the crew with Marshall and William's faces on them. Often the writers would jokingly brainstorm different ways they could run down cast members with their cars.

Less than two months into the fall season of 1976 Williams walked off the *Laverne & Shirley* set. Production was suspended until the producers could figure out what to do about the situation. Williams complained that Penny Marshall was getting all of the show's attention. Williams told *TV Guide* for the June 18, 1977, issue that she had signed on to do a terrific part, but the show was thrown together so quickly that the terrific part got washed away. She said she asked the writers to get back on track, but they never did. Williams claimed that the issue was that the cynical Laverne was easier to write for than the idealistic Shirley. Williams said that she got unhappy when the writing began to favor Laverne.

The *Happy Days* and *Laverne & Shirley* sound stages were back to back on the Paramount lot. Garry Marshall said it wasn't uncommon for the cast of *Happy Days* to overhear the fighting that occurred on the next stage. It was probably a good thing the *Happy Days* cast was too involved in their own work to pay much attention to the screaming and yelling they heard next door. "Just to be really blunt," says Clint Howard, "I don't think anyone on *Happy Days* gave a shit who was working next door. It wasn't as if it was an arrogant sort of thing. I don't think anybody really cared. [They were] like, 'Oh, we have another show working down here. Anybody that can play softball? Do you wanna play softball?' My experience working on a television show, sitcom or otherwise, is that you were so wrapped up and involved with trying to get your job accomplished, trying to get your piece of product manufactured, that there wasn't a lot of time for outside focus even if the outside focus was literally on the next sound stage. As a child actor I was in a lot of situations where there was a lot of really interesting, crazy stuff going on on other soundstages but you never went over there—you didn't have time. If you weren't directly working at the moment on your thing you kind of didn't want to be involved in anybody else's thing. You know, grab a sports page and go lie down and take a nap, something like that."

Yet the *Happy Days* cast was friendly with the actors working on *Laverne & Shirley*. They often saw each other in the Paramount commissary and at other places on the lot. And they respected each other as actors. Sometimes they would run into each other in unlikely places. Misty Rowe remembers once sharing a table with Penny Marshall off the lot. "Penny Marshall's mother and [my mother] were in this thing called the Motion Picture Mothers Club," remembers Rowe. "They had this big Christmas thing and my mom wanted to go. You couldn't be a member unless your child was in motion pictures or a big TV star or something. So I went with my mom and sat at the table with Penny Marshall and her mom. I told my mother, 'I will go with you but you can absolutely not ask anyone for their autograph. I would be mortified.' We go in, and we're sitting at the table with Penny Marshall and her mom, and I see my mom pushing the cocktail napkin over. I'm like stomping on my mother's foot underneath the table and trying to look like nothing's going on. Penny looks over me and she goes, 'It's okay, miss. I have a mother too.'"

Garry Marshall experienced all sides of the situation. It wasn't a simple issue for him. Marshall called *Laverne & Shirley* "a producer's nightmare." Even so, the show was a hit with the viewing audience and the television industry. *Laverne & Shirley* was nominated for a Golden Globe for Outstanding Production, Musical or Comedy Series, in 1976.

Director Jim Burrows's experience with *Laverne & Shirley* wasn't as troublesome as that of some of the other people associated with the show. "I had a great time on that show," Burrows remembers. "I was there when it went crazy, when it blew up. I was around then, and I had no dog in the fight. I was just trying to every week do a show. I loved working with Penny and Cindy. They played so well off one another. I loved Lenny and Squiggy. It was early in my career, but I did have a good time."

There were good days as well as bad on the set of *Laverne & Shirley*. "The crew was wonderful, the writing staff was great," says director Howard Storm. "Garry ran the whole thing with a wonderful kind of fun attitude. Garry was amazing. When Garry was around there was hardly any tension.

Laverne, Mork, and Fonzie in one perfect universe: Penny Marshall, Robin Williams, and Henry Winkler share a laugh during the taping of a historic episode of *Happy Days*, 1978. Photo courtesy of Motion Picture & Television Photo Archive; photo by David Sutton.

There'd be tension, a lot of tension, then Garry would appear and he just would soften everything. He's an amazing guy. A guy who just loves his work and has a great need to have people around him that he likes. That he wants around him. And he's opened up the door for loads of writers. Guys that have gone on to bigger and better things due to the fact that Garry gave them their start. He was very, very good that way. He really understood the genre. He really knew sitcoms and what worked. There was a memorial recently for Tony Randall that Garry put together. Jack Klugman got up, and he spoke about Garry running [*The Odd Couple*], controlling it and being smart enough as a young man to keep everything going."

Cindy Williams told *TV Guide* for an August 1982 issue that the way she perceived the problem was that all the writers knew Penny Marshall personally and knew Marshall could do physical humor. Williams claimed that they didn't really know her and thought she was the one who did "the sweet stuff." Williams says she was disappointed with the writing and kept telling the writers that, but that they didn't hear her. She said that one day "with my knees knocking and shaking all over, I slithered off the lot and came home." Williams said she thought they might arrest her. "When a woman stands up for herself they call her a bitch and worse," she told the magazine. "I went through hell, and so did everyone else." The walk-out lasted two days. Williams demanded a change in the writ-

Making their dreams come true.
Penny Marshall (Laverne) and
Cindy Williams (Shirley), circa 1979.
Photo courtesy of Globe Photos, Inc.

ing staff if she was to return to the show, and Garry Marshall made some changes. Some of the writers were let go, and after a three-week halt in production, filming resumed.

Pam Dawber, who was later on the lot co-starring in *Mork & Mindy*, remembers the problems emanating from the *Laverne & Shirley* stage. "We all shared a lot of the crews," remembers Dawber. "And there was always a lot of gossip going back and forth. Cindy and Penny were just wonderful [acting] together, and I admired them so much. They treated me like I should not have been allowed to be on [*Mork & Mindy*], probably because they all knew Robin. Everybody was anticipating the show, and I was really not very good, although I got better and better. But in the beginning I didn't know what the hell I was doing. Being the young one, I just admired everyone. I had watched them on television for years and years before I ended up on the same lot. Ron and Henry [from *Happy Days*] were always darling and wonderful and sweet. Cindy and Penny to this day talk about how miserable they were on that show. It was not a good time for them. What a shame. They were making so much money and to ruin that experience. Being on a hit show is like catching lightning in a bottle. It's about magic casting, it's about the right words, and it's about your placement in time and space. Whether what you're doing is what the audience is in the mood for at the time. Seventy-five percent of being a success in this business is timing. And the rest is luck and brains, if you can keep it going. Not even luck, but the brains to keep the momentum going for yourself and make the right decisions. Actors that create problems for themselves, they are just miserable or they think they're going to be movie stars or they want to get off their show. Oh my God, you are so lucky if you are in the success line in the first place. So many people shoot themselves in the foot. It's so silly. And you see it over and over and over. You're in your prime usually when you're on a hit show and you're usually too young to realize that once that train pulls up to your depot, you think it's always coming to your depot. You think it's always going to be there, and it's not. If you're lucky enough to have gotten on the success train in the first place, enjoy the ride. It's such a waste. That's the way I always looked at the *Laverne & Shirley* experience. It's such a happy show, a happy to watch show. And to hear they were miserable and competitive, it was just so stupid. What a waste of time. They were such a good team, they just so complemented each other. They were great."

In 1973 a Christmas an album was released on Atlantic Records to capitalize on Laverne and Shirley's popularity. The album, of course, was oldies and was titled *Laverne & Shirley Sing*. (It would be re-issued years later to fairly good fan reception.)

The characters Laverne and Shirley remained as they were initially written but grew as individuals, as young women would hopefully do. Together they became involved in social causes, such as worker's rights at the bottling plant and animal rights at the pound. The storylines were light but interesting. Meanwhile, the actors continued to have problems. Now David Lander and Michael McKean were often upset with the writing. The characters Lenny and Squiggy were so out-there that they were difficult for the writers to understand, let alone write for. Lander says that the characters were hard to write for because they weren't "ordinary stupid, but busy stupid." The only actors who seemed not to complain were Phil Foster and, later, Betty Garrett. The younger actors felt they weren't getting respect from the writers or even other actors. It was a common complaint that people couldn't respect what they were doing on *Laverne & Shirley* because people didn't understand physical comedy. Sometimes the cast would throw the script into a trash container to humiliate the writers.

Michael McKean told *TV Guide* that while the show was high in the ratings, no one connected with the show felt secure and that the "people in charge" were panicking. McKean claimed that the cast was being yelled at and says that it became "messiah time." He said that every day the producers would bring some new guy around the set and say that he was the messiah who was going to save the show. "New day, new messiah." Executive producer Tom Miller was quoted in the issue as saying that they were all shocked by the success of the show and that the first year was a difficult year all around and one that none of them wanted to go through again. Miller and his partner, Eddie Milkis, tried to have an intervention. They had decided that they would rather have no show than one in which the cast and crew were so unhappy. With the network's approval, they called the cast in one by one and told them that they loved them, but everyone was so uncomfortable that anyone who didn't at least try to get along might be replaced.

As they began the third season of *Laverne & Shirley* things looked liked they might be just a little better. The show was nominated in 1977 for three Golden Globes: one apiece for Penny Marshall and Cindy Williams for Best Performance by an Actress in a Comedy Series, and one for *Laverne & Shirley* as Best Television Comedy.

Even with the tension between them, Cindy Williams and Penny Marshall bonded together to demand a pay raise. They were soon making about $75,000 an episode. Despite all of the problems with the actors, real or imagined, the crew Garry Marshall and the producers had brought together worked efficiently. One time when they were doing a musical number on the show, director Steven Spielberg came by to watch. He was surprised that the show was shot as quickly as it was. He was probably also impressed that neither Cindy Williams nor Penny Marshall was afraid of trying something new for the sake of the show. (Laverne and Shirley frequently sang on the show and their stunts were inspired.)

In the hearts of longtime sitcom audiences, *Laverne & Shirley* was heir apparent to the classic female buddy duo of Lucy and Ethel from *I Love Lucy*. Garry Marshall told the *Unicorn Times* in May 1978 that before *Laverne & Shirley* came along, no one was doing early Lucy. Marshall said that the other ladies on sitcoms were classy, smart, and dressed well. But Laverne, Marshall claimed, could "knock the stuffing out of Mary Richards and Rhoda and for good measure wipe the floor with Phyllis." Marshall said he took what he learned from Lucille Ball's broad comedy and taught it to Penny Marshall and Cindy Williams, and they, in turn, re-invented physical comedy. Marshall told journalist Rip Rense years later that while everybody seemed to want feminist leads on television, he thought that women would appreciate characters like themselves who were struggling but had strong friendships. It appeared Marshall was right. *Laverne & Shirley* wasn't really tackling any important social issues, as *Happy Days* had tried to do, but it was great entertainment.

Regardless of what was going on behind the scenes at *Laverne & Shirley*, in its first four years the show finished in either first or second place in the ratings. On January 10, 1978, two years after the show started airing, *Daily Variety* reported that it had the highest number of viewers in television history to that date. Penny Marshall was nominated for a Golden Globe in the category of Best Actress in a Comedy Series. Alfred E. Lehman was nominated in the Costume Design category. The hardworking producers were pleased with the show's continued success. Producers Lowell Ganz and Mark Rothman remained fully involved with the show. The two men provided a comfortable balance. While Rothman was usually reserved, Ganz was intense with comedic passion.

Cindy Williams was undoubtedly happy with the success of the show, but she still wasn't comfortable with the writers, who were challenged every week by having to make sure that the lines between Williams and Marshall were equal. Williams and Marshall would argue with each other and the writers when they thought one of them had more to do or say than the other. One time Williams's manager came in with a stopwatch to time her lines and compare them with the time allotted to Marshall. The nepotism issue continued to rear its ugly head. After all, one of the reasons that Penny Marshall had taken on the role of Laverne in the first place was as a favor to her father. She would say later that one good thing about working with your family is that you know they've got your back.

In 1979 Lenny and Squiggy made an appearance on *Happy Days* in the episode "Fonzie's Funeral." Each show gained from the success of the other. ABC continued to benefit from the appeal of both *Happy Days* and *Laverne & Shirley*, and naturally the thoughts of the network executives turned to spin-offs. There was the proposal that had Lenny and Squiggy joining the Army, which was an idea that never got off the ground. Another spin-off was considered that involved Fonzie being the father of a younger version of himself. That idea never gelled and also was discarded.

Laverne and Shirley remained close, while the actresses who played them many times weren't even talking. However, when Penny Marshall was separating from husband Rob Reiner in 1979 the actresses called a truce. Marshall told *TV Guide* in August 1982 that Williams was there for her when she needed support. Marshall said that her life off the set of *Laverne & Shirley* was in turmoil, and on some days she would have anxiety attacks and Williams would guide her through the script. Marshall claimed there were days when she didn't feel she could be funny, so Williams would try extra hard to entertain. Marshall said that she and Williams had been through a lot together, and Williams understood how hard it was for Marshall to keep going.

In mid-1979 *Laverne & Shirley* was sold into syndication. The price per episode broke the previous syndication record. Some observers estimate that the price stations paid for the opportunity to air the show was more than $50,000 per episode. An attempt to keep the series fresh for first run and future syndication was made in *Laverne & Shirley*'s fourth season by having the fifties setting of the show changed to the sixties. Penny Marshall was once again nominated for a Golden Globe for Best Performance by an Actress in a Comedy Series.

In 1981 the idea of putting Lenny and Squiggy in the Army was revisited. This time out the show was animated and featured Laverne and Shirley. *Laverne & Shirley in the Army* aired on ABC and featured all four characters. Laverne and Shirley were voiced by Marshall and Williams, but Lenny and Squiggy were voiced by actor Ron Palillo. The plot revolved around the girls in boot camp after they were drafted into service during the Cold War. The idea was lame, and the thirty-minute show didn't last longer than thirteen episodes.

For the sixth season of *Laverne & Shirley* the setting changed from Milwaukee to California, and the girls went to work for Bradburn's Department Store. *Daily Variety* said on October 15, 1981, that the series was beginning to show its age. There were only so many scraps and situations the girls could find their way into. Even so, *Laverne & Shirley* received high ratings in the 1982–1983 season.

Then all hell broke loose. Cindy Williams became pregnant by husband Bill Hudson. (Williams had dated *Taxi*'s Andy Kaufman and co-star David L. Lander, among others, before her marriage to Hudson.) In August 1982 Williams again walked off the set. Williams claimed that the producers said that they would write her pregnancy into the show but changed their minds. According to Garry Marshall, the plan was for Williams to shoot several shows before her pregnancy showed and then be out of the show for ten episodes. That wasn't how Williams saw it. Williams claimed that the producers said they would change her work hours and pay her salary even if she missed work days because of her pregnancy, and she wanted to be paid for any episodes she was written out of. She started to argue with Paramount and the production staff over her work schedule. One day when Garry Marshall wasn't there to diffuse the situation, there was a blow-up on the set. The next day Williams filed a $20 million lawsuit against the show's producers. Williams told *TV Guide* that she did not ask for more money. She claimed all she asked for was a commitment outlining her hours in writing. Williams said the producers refused to do that and then charged that she was unable to do her job because she was pregnant. The actress took great offense at the producers' claim that she couldn't work because she was pregnant. Williams said that what they really wanted to do was ace her out of the show and finally "give it all" to Penny Marshall. The producers claimed that no formal contract had been written on these matters.

The lawsuit was settled out of court, but Cindy Williams never returned to the show. Garry Marshall felt betrayed because he had known Williams for so long and had tried to help her with her career when the actress was first starting out. But there was no turning back. The producers simply had Shirley Feeney marry an Army medic named Walter Meaney (Shirley was now Shirley Feeney-Meaney!) and join him on overseas duty. Shirley, and Williams, was history.

It was a different show having Laverne alone and on her own without her best friend, Shirley. Penny Marshall invited friends such as Angelica Huston, Hugh Hefner, and Carrie Fisher to appear on the show. The show had used guest stars before, but only occasionally. In Season Three fifties pop idol Fabian had made an appearance. Laverne was also made over to be more glamorous, and the character now had a boyfriend who was a fashion designer, played by Ed Marinero. But no matter how much they loved Laverne, audiences had a hard time getting behind the transformation. The appeal of the show wasn't the same, and Laverne without

Shirley wasn't as well received. Even so, despite the changes and the fact that Cindy Williams appeared in only two episodes that year, the show maintained a high rating.

In addition to Cindy Williams leaving the show, Penny Marshall suffered another blow during the 1983 season. Marshall had been dating actor Larry Breeding. Breeding, who had been seen on a number of sitcoms and had also made several appearances on *Laverne & Shirley*, was killed in a car accident on October 1, 1982.

Although Cindy Williams and Penny Marshall had once been named Women of the Year by the Hollywood Radio and Television Society, the show had never received an Emmy Award. Penny Marshall *did* have those Hollywood Foreign Press Golden Globe nominations for her role as Laverne, although the departure of Cindy Williams had proved that Laverne wasn't all she could be without her sidekick.

The producers were tired of the hoopla surrounding *Laverne & Shirley*. For the creative forces behind the hit series, the magic had gone out of the show. It was time to let *Laverne & Shirley* ride off into the sunset. In an ironic twist to the behind-the-scenes story of *Laverne & Shirley* and Cindy Williams's charges of nepotism, the last episode revolved around Laverne's father, Frank, running for office against a councilman whose family ties guarantee him the job. The final episode of *Laverne & Shirley* aired on May 10, 1983.

Tom Trbovich was the primary director of *Laverne & Shirley* for the final two years, but both Penny Marshall and Cindy Williams had tried their hand at directing episodes of the show. Marshall said that she learned a lot about how production worked by observing the various professionals at work on the set of *Laverne & Shirley*. Marshall decided that she was more comfortable behind the camera than in front of it and directed an episode of the very short-lived series (three weeks!) *Working Stiffs*, with Jim Belushi and Michael Keaton, in 1979. Marshall directed her first feature, *Jumpin' Jack Flash*, starring Whoopi Goldberg, in 1986. Cindy Williams decided to continue to act in television and films after the birth of her daughter, Emily.

Lenny and Squiggy were characters the television viewing audience would never forget. The actors who played the popular characters moved on as well. Michael McKean continued to be involved in quality comedy, most notably *This Is Spinal Tap*, in which he played aging rocker David St. Hubbins, and *Best in Show* as the kooky character Stefan Vanderhoof. David L. Lander, diagnosed with multiple sclerosis when he was thirty-six, hid the symptoms of the disease during the years 1984–1999 and continued to work as an actor. Lander kept active doing voice-overs for films and cartoons, appearing in films such as *1941*, *Used Cars*, and *The Man with One Red Shoe*, and in guest-starring roles on such television series as *Twin Peaks*, *Pacific Blue*, and *On the Air*.

Interestingly, despite the harsh ending of their association on the television series, the story wasn't over for Penny Marshall and Cindy Williams with the end of *Laverne & Shirley*. In 1988 the actresses put their differences aside, and Williams attended the premier of *Big*, which Marshall directed and which starred Tom Hanks. There would be *The Laverne & Shirley Reunion* in 1995, which reunited the cast, and *Entertainment Tonight Presents: Laverne & Shirley Together Again*, which aired in 2002.

One of the unique dynamics—and successes—of *Happy Days* and *Laverne & Shirley* was the constant cross-over of characters from one show to the other. *Happy Days* viewers were familiar with Laverne and Shirley from their many adventures with Fonzie and Richie, and vice versa. The characters of *Happy Days* and *Laverne & Shirley*, although they appeared on two different television shows, were one big family. The shows gave the viewing audience many delightful moments, and each series would leave an indelible mark on television history. *Laverne & Shirley* may have been a successor to *The Odd Couple* and Lucy and Ethel, but the influence of the characters and the show itself went far beyond that. *Laverne & Shirley* was a cultural phenomenon. Academy Award–winning actress Julia Roberts once told Garry Marshall that when she was a little girl she would dress up and play Laverne and Shirley with her sister. Penny Marshall, always direct and pragmatic, summed up her years on *Laverne & Shirley* by saying that after the show went off the air she often wished that she and Cindy Williams had had more confidence in themselves so that they could have avoided the fights and enjoyed the success of the show more.

Garry Marshall once said that the success of *Laverne & Shirley* was owed to its solid premise, the fact that it aired following *Happy Days*, and the presence of blue-collar women. Marshall says the show was about survival. *Laverne & Shirley* made a significant contribution to television history and created a legacy of which all those associated with the show would eventually be very proud.

Chapter 7

MORK CALLING PARAMOUNT

The success of *Laverne & Shirley* made spin-offs look easy. With that in mind, Garry Marshall and the creative forces behind *Happy Days* began to see there was even more that could be accomplished. Garry Marshall, Bob Brunner, and ABC realized they had a great commodity with the tremendous popularity of Scott Baio from *Happy Days* and the handsome and talented Eddie Mekka from *Laverne & Shirley*. They decided to put together a show they titled *Blansky's Beauties*. Nick D'Abo was brought in as producer. The show starred Tony Award–wining veteran actress Nancy Walker, who had portrayed Mildred on the popular series *McMillan and Wife*, with Rock Hudson, and had played Rhoda's mother, Ida Morgenstern, on *The Mary Tyler Moore Show* and *Rhoda*. For *Blansky's Beauties*, Walker portrayed Nancy Blansky, an employee of the Oasis Hotel in Las Vegas. The hotel also employs her nephew as choreographer for the floor shows. Nancy acts as the mother hen to a group of showgirls, headed by actresses Caren Kaye, Lynda Goodfriend (Richie's girlfriend from *Happy Days*), and Rhonda Bates. The girls live with Blansky in a rather large apartment, along with her two nephews Joey (Mekka) and Anthony (Baio) DeLuca. Also living in the apartment is a big dog named Black Jack. Pat Morita was brought in to play Arnold (again), the manager of the coffee shop in the Oasis. Johnny

Desmond, an actor-singer who in years past was the vocalist for the Glenn Miller, Gene Krupa, and Bob Crosby Orchestras, played Emilio, Nancy's boyfriend. And, oh yeah, Nancy Blansky was the cousin of . . . Howard Cunningham. Nancy Blansky, it turns out, was the person who introduced Howard to Marion, which was revealed on an episode of *Happy Days* that aired the week before the premiere of *Blansky's Beauties*. Reference is also made on *Blansky's Beauties* to one of Nancy's former acquaintances, Laverne DeFazio, who Nancy says wanted to be a dancer. The show was a jiggle show with minimum jiggle, and it was rather unbelievable in its premise of all those people living under one roof. Paramount Television, ABC, and Garry Marshall seemed to be reaching too far for a spin-off this time. The show aired only thirteen episodes, from February 12, 1977, to May 21, 1977.

Despite the lack of success of *Blansky's Beauties*, Garry Marshall's abilities to create hit television shows still existed. For his next show Marshall would be inspired by an idea from his young son, Scott. Just a boy with no knowledge of the decade of the fifties, Scott wasn't a big *Happy Days* fan. Like most children his age, he was more enamored with the characters of the current huge hit movie, George Lucas's *Star Wars*. Marshall asked Scott what would make him watch *Happy Days*. Scott replied he would watch if it had a space alien in it. Marshall tried to explain that, given the nature of the show, a space alien wasn't feasible. Scott suggested that Richie could have a dream about a space alien. Garry Marshall considered the idea. If having Richie experience a space alien in a dream would make Scott watch *Happy Days*, perhaps other young people would tune in to the show too.

Giving life to a fantasy alien character was something the talented writers of *Happy Days* could easily accomplish. Garry Marshall would have been delighted to write the script himself but instead asked Joe Glauberg to do the honors. Casting that alien to fit in with the immense talent on the show was harder than the producers expected. Director Jerry Paris thought the appearance of an alien, which certainly had the potential to be hilarious, was a delicate casting issue that should have his input. Paris decided to work with casting director Bobby Hoffman for the casting of this very special character. Howard Storm, who would later become *Mork & Mindy's* director, says that comedian John Byner was supposed to play the alien, Mork, for the *Happy Days* episode. Whatever happened, Byner didn't appear in the part. There was an open call, and about twenty actors showed up at the studio. Actors came to read, but none of them seem to fit the role. The cast rehearsed until Tuesday without their Mork, while Paris and Hoffman continued to have more actors read for the role. One was a young stand-up comic named Robin Williams. Trying to find something unique among the actors who auditioned, Paris asked Williams if he could give him an idea of how an extraterrestrial might sit down. Williams went over to the set's sofa and sat on his head. Robin Williams had Jerry Paris's attention. Garry Marshall said that Williams was the only alien who auditioned for the role. All agreed that Williams would be great as Mork, and he was cast for the February 28, 1978, *Happy Days* Episode #110: "My Favorite Orkean."

The premise of the episode remained Richie's dream, but the audience doesn't know that until the end of the episode. The show begins as Richie runs into Arnold's exclaiming he has just seen a flying saucer. When no one believes him, he returns home. Richie is watching television when a man in a red space suit walks in the door (an inside joke has Richie watching an episode of *The Andy Griffith Show*). The strange man remarks that he really likes the show, especially Opie, and then blows up the television with his finger. He introduces himself as Mork from Ork. Richie is fascinated as Mork tells Richie that he knows all about him and has been assigned to come to Earth to learn more about its people. Mork wants to take Richie back to Ork with him because Richie is everything that is ordinary about earthlings. Various members of the family come home, and Mork stays focused on Richie by "freezing" them with his finger. When Richie tells Mork he doesn't want to go to Ork, Mork issues a challenge, a "holly tacker." Mork tells Richie if Fonzie can beat him in the challenge, a challenge he has won on 200 other planets, Richie won't have to accompany Mork to Ork. Fonzie, having been frozen by Mork during this exchange, is still The Fonz. While frozen, Fonzie's thumb slowly rises in his "aaayyyy" gesture. Mork is impressed but is not ready to give up. Mork offers other dares to Fonzie, and Fonzie rises to the challenge. Finally, in exasperation, Mork tells Richie and Fonzie that he can collapse Arnold's by holding his fingers together. The shocked Fonzie says that Mork won't have to do that. Fonzie declares Mork the winner. Mork, who claims to know nothing of human emotions, is touched by Fonzie's action. Mork says he considers Fonzie a worthy competitor and tells Richie he will take Fonzie to Ork instead of Richie. At this point, Richie awakens from a dream as his family comes home. Howard tells Richie that the alleged flying saucer was in fact a weather balloon. Richie is relived to learn it was all a dream until there is a knock on the door. A man, who looks like Mork sans the red outfit, asks for directions.

The executives at ABC thought the episode was silly at first. Eventually they decided to bow to Marshall's wishes as he had, after all, delivered the successful *Happy Days* and *Laverne & Shirley*. They didn't like the episode, but decided that it was Marshall's show, so he had a right to try to sell the idea of an alien to viewers. So it was that, with Robin Williams playing Mork from Ork, it was time to film the episode. The cast, and the producers, didn't know what they were in for. Henry Winkler says that Robin Williams just exploded in his first scene. Winkler says, "You knew you were in the presence of greatness" and that the main job the other actors faced was not falling apart with laughter. Scott Baio says Williams came in and just "went insane." When Robin Williams took his curtain call after filming the episode, the 300 people in the studio audience gave him a standing ovation.

The question around the set, then on the Paramount lot, and finally in audiences across America was, *Who is this guy?* Until his appearance on *Happy Days*, Williams was primarily a stand-up comedian who appeared at the various comedy clubs around Los Angeles. He had landed a gig on *The Richard Pryor Show* and a bit part on the television series *Eight Is Enough* and had been a cast member of the failed revitalization of the classic comedy show *Laugh-In*. While several people in network television may have heard a small buzz about the comic, television executives for the most part weren't really aware of Robin Williams.

Robin McLaurin Williams was born in Chicago, Illinois, on July 21, 1952, to Robert and Laurie Williams (although when he was starting out, Williams told reporters he was born in Scotland). Two half-brothers, Todd Williams and McLaurin Smith, were much older and already out of the household by the time Robin was born. He was raised virtually as an only child. Robert Williams was Vice President and Midwestern Regional Manager of the Lincoln–Mercury division of the Ford Motor Company, and the family was quite well off. Williams describes his father as an elegant man whom he called "Sir." Formality aside, Williams says his father was a wonderful, ethical gentleman. It was Robin's mother, Laurie, who was the wild card. She was from the South and full of life, with a wonderful sense of humor. Williams says that while his father was the disciplinarian, his mother was his pal. He calls her a crazy southern belle. Laurie once attended a country club dinner dressed elegantly, but with her front teeth blacked out. It was from Laurie that Robin would get his outrageous sense of humor.

Despite her affection for Robin, Laurie Williams was frequently out of the house, and Williams was raised in a thirty-room mansion with mostly a nanny as his companion. To overcome loneliness, Williams turned to the 2,000 soldiers he had set up on a battlefield in the basement of the house. The young boy invented personalities for each of the soldiers, and they all had different voices. Williams told *Time* magazine that his imagination was his friend. His interactions with his toy soldiers taught Williams the power of fantasy. While the boy was finding comfort with his fantasy friends, he says that he was fat and spoiled and different from the other children he knew. He got beat up a lot and was called "dwarf" and "leprechaun" while attending an all-boys prep school in Birmingham, Michigan.

Robert Williams decided to leave the Ford organization, and the family moved to Tiburon in Marin County near San Francisco in 1969. Robin attended Redwood High School, which he enjoyed. He would later joke that he was suddenly at a gestalt high school where students graduated if the energy was right. Williams went on a diet and dropped thirty pounds. He took up wrestling, cross-country, and tennis. He was voted "Most Humorous" in his senior class, but also "Least Likely to Succeed." After graduating from high school, Williams talked to his father about his future and decided to study political science at Claremont Men's College in Claremont, California. While attending Claremont, Williams played soccer and enrolled in a theater improvisation class. While he had been doing comedy "covertly," the young man now decided to go public with his obvious gift. He enjoyed learning his craft, but he was having so much fun that he was failing his other classes. As he studied improvisation, it became clear to Williams that comedy was where he should be devoting his professional energy. Williams's father realized his son's conviction and commitment to comedy and wasn't too upset with his failure at Claremont. Robert encouraged Robin to follow his dream, but maybe have a back-up plan as well. Williams enrolled at Marin College in Kentfield, California, to study Shakespeare.

Williams attended Marin College for a year before trying out for the Julliard School of Drama in New York City. He was delighted to be accepted. Williams thrived in the theater. Christopher Reeve, who was Robin's roommate at Julliard, said that Robin "simply defied description." Legendary actor John Houseman, who had founded the Mercury Theater with Orson Welles, was one of Williams's teachers at Julliard. The astute Houseman appreciated Robin's unique abilities but thought he would do better moving away from theater and Julliard and into improvisational, stand-up comedy.

On weekends while at Julliard, Williams and another student performed mime for spare change in front of the Metropolitan Museum of Art. Williams was good at mime but didn't like it as much as stimulating comedy. Performing as a mime he wasn't able to use what he considered his greatest instrument, his voice. The other students were talking about comedy club appearances, and Williams decided to try that out. He was soon making appearances at local clubs, though for little or no money.

While Williams was a junior at Julliard, he fell in love. When the girl he was interested in moved to San Francisco, Robin quit school and followed her. Unfortunately, the romance didn't work out, but Williams started to do better in his professional life. He auditioned at comedy clubs in the San Francisco area and found there were people who would pay to listen to him. He did sets at the Boarding House and the Holy City Zoo, as well as other clubs. He auditioned for parts in theatrical productions but struck out. Stand-up simply worked better for him, as it had for his comedic heroes: Jonathan Winters, Woody Allen, and Peter Sellers. He decided to further explore comedy and joined a comedy workshop.

Needing to support himself, Williams got a job as a bartender at a club that featured comedians. He was a riot behind the bar, entertaining and personable. Valerie Velardi, a grad student who was working as a cocktail waitress, noticed how hilarious Williams was. She thought he was funnier than the comedians who were on stage. A month after they met, Robin and Valerie moved in together. Velardi believed in Williams's talent and did everything she could to encourage him to advance his career. In the summer of 1976, Valerie talked Williams into trying his luck in Los Angeles. He and Valerie Velardi were married in June 1978.

Williams was able to get on the stage at the Comedy Club on the Sunset Strip during Open Mic Night. He later told *TV Guide* that the experience was a terrifying combination of the Roman arena and *The Gong Show*. He was well received and was soon was appearing at the Comedy Club on a regular basis. One night producer George Schlatter dropped in. Schlatter knew funny and he knew talent. He had been the producer of *The Judy Garland Show* back in the sixties and of *Rowan and Martin's Laugh-In* and the *Cher* show as well. Schlatter caught Williams's act and found him hilarious. Schlatter told Williams backstage that if he would shave his beard and cut his long hair he would give him a part in the new version of *Laugh-In* he was casting. Williams thought the show just might be the break he was looking for.

Dan Rowan and Dick Martin didn't play any part in the new *Laugh-In*. The "stars" this time were Bill Rafferty (who would go on to host the game show *Card Shark*) and Ben Powers (who would find more success on *Good Times* and in *Cheech and Chong's Next Movie*). The show ran along the lines of the original *Rowan and Martin's Laugh-In* but for some reason this time out fell flat. At least Robin Williams got some benefit from the endeavor. He was allowed to develop his own characters and exhibit some of the manic energy for which he would become known. With a cast of characters as diverse as Marcel Marceau and Marjoe Gortner, it's hard to imagine where the show was headed. The only value of watching *Laugh-In* seemed to be the small peek at newcomer Robin Williams's talent. His appearance on the show enabled him to land an appearance on *The Richard Pryor Show*, then on *America 2-Night* with his friend Martin Mull. Nothing much came of the appearances, but at least Williams was starting to get noticed.

The *Happy Days* episode introducing Mork from Ork aired on February 28, 1978. Mail poured into the studio regarding Mork and the actor who portrayed the character. Director Howard Storm believes that the "best kind of comedy is character-driven," and Mork was a character who certainly captured the viewing audience's attention. Robin Williams must have been thrilled with his reception. In the meantime, Williams returned to the Comedy Club the next week.

Michael Eisner had arrived from ABC Television to assume the position of second in command to Barry Diller at Paramount, and in the spring of 1978 Garry Marshall received a call from Eisner asking Marshall to help out Paramount Television. They were short new programs to show the ABC network heads in New York. Since *Happy Days* and *Laverne & Shirley* were such big shows for the network, Paramount could easily get behind another Garry Marshall–produced show. Marshall suggested to Eisner that the Mork character that had appeared on *Happy Days* might make for a good spin-off. Marshall, Dale McRaven, and Joe Glauberg had already been talking about the possibility. The television show *My Favorite Martian*, starring Ray Walston, had been a big hit in the sixties, but Robin Williams could take the idea of an alien living on Earth so much further with Mork. People all over the country had already picked up on Mork's "Na-nu, na-nu" and were doing Mork's hand signals. McRaven initially had a slight hesitation about a Mork show as he was concerned that a regular sitcom with Robin would be a waste of his unique talent. That being said . . .

Eisner liked the idea of a series featuring those unique talents and put Marshall on a conference call to the studio executives in New York. Marshall pitched the idea to Paramount's Marcy Carsey, explaining that the premise of the show could be that of an alien coming to Earth who reports back to his planet on the nature and experiences of those he meets. Marshall suggested the show be called *The Mork Chronicles*. One of the executives replied that no one would know what "chronicles" meant. The show needed to be titled after something people could name their kids or their animals. He explained that when people did that, it meant the show was a hit. They also needed to have a female character who could interact with Mork. Marshall suggested *Mork & Melissa* or *Mork & Marlo* or *Mork & Mindy*. They liked *Mork & Mindy*, thought it was catchy. The next question was where to base the series. Garry Marshall's niece was going to school in Boulder, Colorado, so off the top of his head he suggested Boulder as Mindy's home base. Okay, that was fine. They liked Robin Williams for the role of Mork, but who could they get to play Mindy? Garry Marshall remembered an actress named Pam Dawber and a pilot she had made called "Sister Terri." Marcy Carsey also knew Dawber's work, and since Marshall was under pressure to name an actress to play the pivotal title role, he suggested Dawber.

Marcy Carsey and Gary Nardino, head of television at Paramount, took some silent footage from the "Sister Terri" pilot and spliced it together with some footage of Mork's appearance on *Happy Days* to show the network. Instead of the usual $400,000, the pilot ended up costing $63. Pam Dawber remembers it a little differently. "I think what made *Mork & Mindy* so unique was that there wasn't a pilot," says Dawber. "They found Robin from *Happy Days* when Garry wrote an episode for his son. They'd had so many *Happy Days* episodes then. They were always sort of hung for what to do, and Garry's son said, 'What about doing one about a space man?' Garry presented the idea, and they came up with this idea and they cast this guy named Robin Williams. I guess they received so much fan mail and Robin was so outrageously funny that the network said, 'We want this guy and we want him on this fall.' What happened was they were in a desperate casting mode to find a show for this guy, find the girl to go with this guy, and I guess they had auditions. They were looking around California and they didn't find anybody. I already had an outstanding development deal with ABC at the time that was about ready to expire. They were flying me out every now and then to audition for various things during the course of that year. I was emphatic that I didn't want to get involved in some dumb show. I wanted it to be a little more special. So when this *Mork & Mindy* idea came around, I thought it was just the most stupid thing I'd heard. But it didn't [just] come along. What happened, unbeknownst to me, I had done a pilot for ABC called 'Sister Terri' where I played a nun who used to be a gang leader but she found God, so she's there to fix up the neighborhood. I remember when I was filming it, Garry Marshall walked through a couple of times. It flipped me out, because Garry was so huge. So I did the pilot really praying it didn't sell. But the year was going by, and they had given me a load of money and I hadn't done anything for ABC. So I was pretty much just taking the money and running. The casting director at the time had told my agent,

'Look, this pilot is probably not going to sell, but we need her on film. We can pay her that money and not have her even do a pilot, so tell her to do this but it's not going to sell.' I did the pilot thinking, good, it won't sell. I had done a Robert Altman film (*A Wedding*) prior to that, and I thought I was going to become a movie star."

The next thing Garry Marshall heard about the mini-pilot was when he was on vacation on St. John and Gary Nardino called him to tell him that *Mork & Mindy* had been sold to ABC and would air on Thursday nights. When Garry Marshall's wife, Barbara, asked him what the show was about, Marshall had to tell her he really didn't know.

Pam Dawber was cast in the role of Mindy, though without her knowledge. "I got back to New York and my agent called me and said, 'You're not going to believe what I'm going to read to you.' And there it was announced in *Variety*, the fall line-up. 'On Monday night,' it was announced, 'Garry Marshall presents *Mork & Mindy* starring Robin Williams and Pam Dawber; space alien lives in girlfriend's apartment.' I hadn't auditioned, I hadn't met, and I knew nothing. I remember going, 'And who the hell is Robin Williams?' I guess ABC said, 'Look, we've got this girl, we like her.' They showed the pilot to Garry. What they did, they cut segments out of 'Sister Terri' of me reacting and segments of [Robin on] *Happy Days* and cut together a presentation thing, showed it to the

Mork & Mindy co-star Pam Dawber.
Photo courtesy of Pam Dawber.

affiliates, [who] bought it without any pilot, without anything. So pretty much they bought two people and they didn't have a show. And we started doing publicity immediately. I remember flying in from New York to do all the ABC publicity. And that was the first day that Robin and I ever met. I thought he was so cute. The minute I met him I went, 'Oh, he's so cute. And he's so odd and so funny and boy, oh boy, am I lucky!' And so it went from there."

Pam Dawber grew up in Farmington, near Detroit, Michigan, where she was born on October 18, 1951. Her mother operated a stock photo company, and her father was a commercial artist. Young Pam took flute lessons, played guitar, and danced. After graduation from high school, she attended Oakland Community College. At the same time, Dawber discovered an interest in modeling. She found work as a model and singer for automobile trade shows. Pam's life was good, with the exception of a personal tragedy. Her younger sister, Leslie, died during open heart surgery. Evidently realizing that life is unpredictable, Dawber decided to invest in her modeling career and left college to move to New York City to become a model full-time. She was signed by a top agency and was soon doing television commercials and appearing in magazines. Dawber realized that she was also interested in acting and began to take acting lessons. She soon landed a job in a production of *Sweet Adeline* at the Goodspeed Opera House in East Haddam, Connecticut, and was asked to audition for a role in the new television series *Tabitha*. Dawber didn't get the role, but in 1977 she was cast in Robert Altman's *A Wedding*. The film starred the usual eclectic group that Altman was known for casting: Desi Arnaz Jr., Carol Burnett, Geraldine Chaplin, Mia Farrow, Lillian Gish, and a dozen other name actors. Dawber played the role of Tracey Farrell. ABC liked what they saw of Pam on-screen, and soon after signed her to a holding contract.

The first episode of *Mork & Mindy*, which aired on September 14, 1978, has Mork arriving in Boulder, Colorado, via his egg transport. Mork has been temporarily exiled from his home planet of Ork because the leader of that planet (Orson) finds Mork's sense of humor offensive. Mork is sent to Earth to observe that "primitive society" and report his findings back to Orson telepathically. He is befriended by Mindy McConnell, a college girl who has just broken off with a boyfriend. Mork explains to Mindy that he is from another planet, which he proves by various "tricks" and displays of Orkean customs. The first episode, which aired in two parts, has Mork reuniting with Fonzie via flashback when Mork tells Mindy about the first time he visited Earth. In an effort to help Mork learn to date, Fonzie sets Mork up with Laverne. In the meantime,

Mindy's father, Frederick, a musician who operates a music store, thinks Mork is crazy and attempts to convince Mindy that Mork should not be staying with her in her apartment. (The house used for the exterior of Mindy's house was located at 1619 Pine Street in Boulder, and Fred's music store was a real bookstore, also located in Boulder.)

Howard Storm was brought in to direct the *Mork & Mindy* series. Storm had previously directed the television shows *Rhoda*, with Valerie Harper, and *Doc*, with Barnard Hughes. He had also been called in to do a few episodes of *Laverne & Shirley*. Storm was a respected director, and Garry Marshall thought he would be a perfect fit for the unique talents of Robin Williams.

"Robin has an overwhelming personality," says Storm. "It's intimidating. He's so powerful. Luckily I was older than those guys, and I had been a stand-up comic for a while. I was an actor and an improvisational actor. I worked with The Committee for a couple of years, so I was pretty seasoned. So he didn't intimidate me. As a matter of fact, Robin always talks about how he would come in exhausted because he was partying all night. And when I'd give him notes after a run-through, we'd go to the green room and he would lie down and his eyes were closed. I didn't know if he was awake or asleep. I'd be giving notes, and I'd have a note for Robin and he wouldn't respond. I'd give him the note a second time and he wouldn't respond. So I'd kick him in the arm, up near the shoulder, and say, 'Robin!' And he'd go, 'Yeah, yeah.' I'd say, "Did you hear me? I need you to do so and so.' Every time I see him and there are people there he tells about how I would kick him to give him notes."

Howard Storm was not only an experienced director, but his background made him perfect in dealing with the improvisational nature of Robin Williams's comedy. "Basically that's why I was brought in," says Storm. "Because of my background. They gave me two shows and they gave two shows to another director, a very good director, Joel Zwick. We both did two, and then they asked me to do the series. I don't mean to say that I was better than Joel, but I think the reason I [was selected] was because I connected with Robin because of my background. There was that stand-up and improv actor, and I understood him very well."

Producer Dale McRaven would head the writers. McRaven was well-grounded in comedic television. He had been a writer on *The Dick Van Dyke Show*, *Gomer Pyle*, *U.S.M.C.*, *Get Smart*, *The Odd Couple*, *The Partridge Family*, and *Laverne & Shirley*. "Dale McRaven was really the genius," says Pam Dawber. "He was the guy. He was really the creator, because Dale was definitely out there. [Producer] Bruce Johnson was more the financial guy. Dale captured the essence, the wackiness of the show." The writers who worked on *Mork & Mindy* had a special challenge in working with Robin Williams, but they were at the top of their game and excited about the possibilities.

"There was a terrible falsehood going around that the writers didn't write," says Howard Storm. "That they would just say 'Robin does his thing,' which wasn't true at all. They wrote great stuff for the show. As a group. Dale McRaven created the show along with Garry [Marshall]. Dale was the executive producer and writer, so I think of Dale immediately. He was very powerful. Then April [Kelly] did some great shows. Ed Scharlach and Tom [Tenowich] were teamed. Bruce Johnson and Dale McRaven were the execs who wrote together most of the time. There was just good stuff. Really good stuff."

Pam Dawber sees it that way too. "We had lots and lots of writers who came and went," she recalls. "A lot of people thought that Robin improvised the whole show, and he certainly did not. There were areas where he wouldn't be satisfied with what they wrote and then he would go off, something would come flying out."

As physical as Robin Williams was on the set, wordplay was equally important to his acting. While Williams would stick to the basic premise of the script written by some very talented writers who understood Robin's need to be unconventional, filming each week's episode was still a sticky situation. Marshall says that Williams was hip and topical, and the writers wrote to his uniqueness as a comedian. Yes, he ad-libbed, but he ad-libbed in character, and many of the lines were already developed in the script. After the story was published stating that basically Robin Williams did his "own thing," the writers gave Williams a script of blank pages with the words "Robin does his own thing." Robin laughed at the joke but assured the writers that he never told the press that he was simply doing his own improvised material.

The writing of *Mork & Mindy* was truly a team effort by the writers, director, and stars. "We would work," says Storm. "The example I always give is that they wrote a scene once in which Robin plays poker and he was all five characters at the table. Which was a wonderful idea except that within the two- or three-minute span of the scene I felt the audience would have difficulty keeping up with the characters. There was just too much going on. So I suggested to Robin that we try to do an old Jew and an old WASP playing chess, as opposed to five guys. And he played both characters. We played with it a little bit at rehearsal. Then we called up to the office and asked the writers to come down and look at it. They did. They came down and looked and said okay and went back up and rewrote the scene and it worked very well. That was the kind of thing that we did.

The input I had, I would go to a lot of writing sessions when they were re-writing or punching up and they would ask me whether I thought this would work or would Robin do this. It was a wonderful collaboration. What happens today, if you notice, is that on most shows, every week there's another director. I think the reason for that is they don't want the director to build a relationship so that he has the power. I did [have a relationship]. Robin and I got along very well. I'd get calls from the writers at eleven o'clock at night, saying, 'Do you think you can get Robin to do this?' I'd say, 'Yes.' 'How's this working? Did that work?' I was able to call up and say, 'We're having a problem here.' And they would come down and look at it. And it was never like, 'Why are you having a problem?' They were very open to the fact that if we thought there was a problem, there was a problem. And they would look at it and help it. I always maintained that if I'm blocking a scene and I'm having difficulty blocking it, somewhere in the writing there's a problem. Because when it's right, when it's there, it just flows. It was a great crew. Garry [Marshall] was marvelous [at putting together a crew]."

The episodes of the show remained true to what was pitched to the network: Mork, a misfit in his own society, is sent to Earth to study the people of Earth, which is a civilization the people from Ork could never understand. As punishment for his many jokes and perceived lack of respect for all things Orkan, Mork experiences emotions, something Orkans do not. Garry Marshall would say that the show was about the harsh realities of our life and society as seen through the eyes of an innocent.

The magic of Garry Marshall was working again. "Garry has an eye, I guess," says Pam Dawber. "Garry Marshall is one of those guys; I always see them as a handful of guys, like Carl Reiner, Garry Marshall, Mel Brooks. The kind of guys you go, 'Boy, they don't make them like that anymore.' Garry is one of those guys in that crowd. They were guys who came out of theater, they came out of live television, and they came out of true live television comedy. So they really knew what was funny. That was really the high point of the sitcom in the late seventies, early eighties. I think it was because of the kind of people who were running it at the time. Of course, you always have your stupid shows, but you still had great writers out there. You had great theater out there. Original ideas were still coming around. Now so much is recycled. The same-old same-old. But you had those kinds of guys at the helm who had such great experience under their belt. Garry really knew what was funny. I think so many of them came from 'Noo Yawk' and they just had that Catskill comedy, think on your feet. The Milton Berles and the George Burnses, they all knew each other and they all wrote together at different times and in different configurations. It was just a different time, but it was a different kind of producer too. Garry just recognized talent. I'm not saying that for the fact that I was cast. [That was more like] 'Ah, she's cute, he likes her . . .'"

Being hastily assembled certainly didn't hurt the show. By week two *Mork & Mindy* was number 1 in the ratings. "It was the Gary Nardino regime at the time," says director Howard Storm. "It was amazing. Gary Nardino oversaw a period that was just fantastic at Paramount. I think he was smart enough to buy those shows (*Mork & Mindy*, *Laverne & Shirley*). He agreed to the shows, and Garry Marshall had great power, of course. He could get almost anything he wanted done. I knew Gary [Nardino] way back in New York when he was an agent. Gary was able to control the business. When people didn't want to come back next season, that kind of thing. They're holding out for money and all those fights and things. Gary knew how to meet with them, give them gifts and get them back."

"I had a very funny incident with [Nardino]," remembers Storm. "He made a deal with me in the second season [of *Mork & Mindy*]. It was an all-around deal whereby I would give them a first look at ideas I had and so forth, which they never looked at. They paid me a flat fee and it was very, very nice. It was really great. It didn't start until July. My agent called me and said, 'They want you to do some tests for a show called *Taxi*.' I did the tests for that show and for [the future Paramount Television show] *Angie*. At that time I was getting a thousand dollars a test, for the day. They wanted me to apply it to my overall deal. I said to my agent, 'The deal doesn't start 'til July. I'm doing this in May. They have to pay me.' So I get a call from Gary. He calls me to his office. He had a pedal under his desk [whereby] he could close the door. So as soon as I walked in, *shoosh*. Now I knew Gary from when he was an agent; now all of a sudden he's the head of the studio and he's sitting behind this big desk. He says to me, 'What the hell's goin' on, you little son-of-a-bitch?' I said, 'Nothing's going on, Gary. I'm just asking to be paid for my work.' He says, 'Well, you're getting paid. I gave you a great deal. You got the whole thing.' I said, 'I know, but it doesn't start 'til July. You're asking me to do some work before then and I don't have a contract for then. You have to pay me.' He said, 'Tell your agent that you're getting a gift.' I said, 'What am I getting?' He said, 'Nothing! Just tell your agent that.' I said, 'No, now you're asking me to lie on top of all of this.' So he said, 'Okay, what do you want?' I said, 'A Blaupunkt for my Mercedes.' I had an old Mercedes 450. I wanted a radio and cassette player. He said, 'You got it.' Two days later I get a call from him. He said, 'Do you know how much those things cost?" I said, 'No.' He said, 'Eight hundred and fifty dollars! I might as well pay you the thousand rather than buy you a gift!' I said, 'Okay.' He said, 'No gift!'" But he paid me for the show."

Robin Williams was a complete novice to situation comedy, and during the first weeks of filming *Mork & Mindy*, the cast and crew were exhausted. Williams's approach to comedy was unlike anything anyone involved had ever experienced. The cameramen were exhausted from following Williams, who rarely, if ever, hit his mark. He moved so fast that during those first few weeks some of Williams's improvisation, which was brilliant, had to be cut because the scenes were simply too blurry. A fourth camera was added to the set-up, which gave the cameramen better coverage of Williams. Garry Marshall also showed the dailies to Williams, something he didn't ordinarily do, so that Williams could see his performance—where he hit and where he missed.

Randall Carver, who co-starred on the Paramount Television hit *Taxi*, remembers Williams as being a bit insecure in those early days of the show. "I knew Robin Williams from the Harvey Lembeck Studio for about a year or so before *Mork & Mindy*," remembers Carver. "We started rehearsing *Taxi* about the same time they started rehearsing *Mork & Mindy*. Partway through their rehearsal they replaced Graham Jarvis with Conrad Janis [as Mindy's father]. Robin and I had lunch together, and we were visiting and he was bemoaning the fact that 'I got this great break and now they're having trouble with the casting thing.' He was kind of real concerned about it because he was the star of the thing, the leading character. I said to him, 'Don't worry about it, Robin. If they cancel this thing you'll have some nice film on yourself and you maybe can get something else.'" Carver laughs. "I was trying to reassure him that his career wasn't over. I didn't know how they were going to bottle him because I saw him at Harvey Lembeck's. Incredible, but as far as working well with others? He learned how to be more of an ensemble player, I think, with *Mork & Mindy*."

"I was working with a genius," remembers Howard Storm. "I knew it almost immediately. There are very few people like Robin . . . Sid Caesar, Jonathan Winters, Charlie Chaplin. There are a handful of those kinds of talents. On the second or third day I just kept saying to everybody, 'This is amazing. This kid is a genius. It's just overwhelming to watch.' The feeling that I was doing that show was marvelous. There wasn't anything he couldn't do. He's so well read that he's got a brain full of stuff that's available to him at any time. He just calls on it. There are few people who have that kind of ability. Number one, he has an amazing power to remember things. The point I make is that the first week I was panicked because he didn't seem to know a line of the show. He was ad-libbing and fooling, bouncing around, and it was all his nervous energy. And then came the Friday shoot day. He knew the script word for word and knew every blocking movement, knew exactly where he had to be, where the cameras were. I was just amazed by that."

Williams would start on Monday, playing with the props and seeing what developed. He'd pitch ideas with the writers. When there were disagreements as to what was really funny, the reaction of the live audience would decide if the joke remained in the show. The live audience was critical for Robin Williams. He would frequently grab the microphone during the audience warm-up and climb into the seats and interview the audience, do bits of improvisational comedy or impressions. Sometimes in the course of the filming, he would slip in foreign profanity to see what he could get past the censors. Writing for Williams was sometimes difficult as he would frequently get tired of a joke by the end of the week, and the writers would become frustrated. It affected some of the writers so much that they decided that they couldn't work that way. No offense to the genius of Robin Williams, but it was just too frustrating to make their jobs fun.

Howard Storm saw things in perspective. "I think it was because I wasn't intimidated. I had great respect for him. You can't not respect that kind of ability. But also I have a feeling that it is God-given, if there is such a thing, if there is a God or whatever. You're born with that. So I'm not impressed. It's like if someone is good-looking. You know, you're born with good looks or you're not. And that kind of ability, you've just got it. I think I would respect it more if somebody could not do it and learned to do it and became that. But I think Robin and people like that, it's there from the beginning. It's like great songwriters and composers. They can go to school and all, but you can't teach that. I see that they have stand-up comedy classes and things like that. To me that's idiotic. You can't teach anybody to be a stand-up comic anymore than you can teach someone to be an opera singer. Either you have that kind of vocal ability, and yes, you can train it and control it. You teach a technique, but if someone doesn't have that voice and is unable to reach those kinds of notes, there's no way. And as an actor, I think you've got it or you don't have it."

Co-star Pam Dawber remains in awe of Robin Williams's talent. "It was just a marvel to watch Robin percolate," says Dawber. "I always felt like I would watch Robin almost be his own audience to his own genius. I could see Robin sometimes looking for something, looking for something, in an area where he wasn't happy with the script. I could see him. It'd be like he could see what was coming up in his own brain. I'd watch his eyes and I could see him see it. I always viewed it as a bubble that kind of came from the depths of his unconscious mind. And as it was coming into his conscious mind he was reviewing it, he was like reading it and going, 'Ooooh, this is going to be good.' Then it would come out. It was almost like he stood witness to his own genius. You can see it happening, especially if you look at [his performance in a film like] *Good Morning, Vietnam*. I got to know Robin so well. I know when Robin's on and when he's off and when he's nervous and when he's not and when they just let him go. There's an area in [that film] where he's just on a riff and you can see him. That's exactly what I'm talking about. He knows what's coming up next, he can feel it. He can see what's coming up in his brain and he's about to say it, 'cause he starts enjoying what he's about to say. And it's so endearing."

Howard Storm was said to be the only one who could keep Robin in check. "I was lucky enough to have done a Broadway play as an actor with a brilliant talent, a guy named Gabe Dell," says Storm. "Gabe Dell was one of the Dead End Kids originally, and then he was an actor on *The Steve Allen Show*—he was one of the men on the street. Gabe was a brilliant actor who was so undisciplined and so problemed that he never, never got the respect that he was due. He did a lot of marvelous things. The industry was aware of him and loved him. He did Broadway plays and was just a marvelous character. We did a play together, and it was with a director who was directing for the first time. Gabe was one of those actors like Robin who, if given a note, found eight hundred things more to do. He was bigger than life on stage. He would do everything possible. I watched the director sit on him, stopping him each time, saying, 'No, no, no, no, you can't do that.' And I watched Gabe's frustration until he almost exploded. He never got past it when we got to do the shows. He still was climbing the walls. I was doing a series called *Doc* with Barnard Hughes, who was just a brilliant actor. I had just done my first show, *Rhoda*, and then someone recommended me to *Doc*. At any rate, I was doing *Doc*, and I requested Gabe Dell to play a character who came in to buy the clinic. The producers were very concerned, knowing Gabe and how undisciplined he was. And I said, 'No, no, I can deal with him.' What I found, and I used it with Robin, I allowed him during rehearsals to do whatever he wanted to do. Until a certain point, and then I would say to him, 'Gabe, you can jump on the table, but you can't knock the vase off. You can read the book, but don't throw it, just drop it.' Those kinds of things. And the beauty was that [Gabe and Robin] brought ten things more to it. I'd say, 'Why don't we try taking the glass and throwing it up in the air.' Well, guys like Robin would then go ten times more than that, throw it up in the air, spin around, tumble, and then catch it. You just had to peel the onion. Luckily I was ready for that [with Robin] because of Gabe. When Robin would take off with a note and go ten times further I allowed it. I didn't say, 'No, no, no, you can't do that.' I allowed it and allowed it until a certain point, and then I'd say to him, 'Robin, we've got to lock this in. We can't do this, do this, do that.' He called me Papa, by the way, which made me feel very old. I loved the idea that he called me Papa. At the same time it was like I'm not that old! I don't know if I taught him anything. I just think that he was brilliant and Pam was brilliant."

In addition to the outstanding talents of Robin Williams and Pam Dawber, *Mork & Mindy* had an excellent supporting cast. Actor Conrad Janis was signed to play Mindy's father, Fred McConnell. The son of art dealer Sidney Janis, Conrad was born on February 11, 1928, in New York City. Janis appeared on Broadway in the forties and was a Theater World Award winner for his role in *The Brass Ring*. He appeared in many Broadway productions and also on television, including the shows *Suspense, Kraft Television Theater, The U.S. Steel Hour*, and *Armstrong Circle Theater*. The well-respected actor landed roles in such early television sitcoms as *Get Smart, My Favorite Martian*, and *The Jeffersons*, and accumulated a host of other television and film roles. Janis was also known for being a renowned jazz trombone player. He was perfect as Mindy's caring father, who was naturally suspicious of Mork and his odd ways. Fred McConnell didn't like the fact that Mork was living in Mindy's attic. "Conrad Janis was wonderful as the father," says Howard Storm.

Playing Fred's mother-in-law and Mindy's grandmother was the talented Elizabeth Kerr. Born on August 12, 1912, Kerr had appeared often on television in such shows as *Adam 12, The Betty White Show*, and *The Bob Newhart Show*, and in films including *Messenger of Peace*, with John Beal, and *Six Bridges to Cross*, with Tony Curtis. Kerr's Cora Hudson was a swinging senior who wasn't afraid to speak her mind and who loved to give her son a hard time about his being so straight-laced. "[She] was just delicious and sweet," says Storm.

Also in the first year of the series was Jeffrey Jacquet, who played Mork's friend Eugene. The talented little boy had been seen in the film *Return from Witch Mountain*, with Bette Davis and Christopher Lee, and was fairly new to the business when he was selected to play the only child on *Mork & Mindy*. The show was one of only a handful of television series that featured a young black character during that time.

Ralph James was the voice of Mork's boss, Orson. James was a veteran actor who had appeared in television series such as *Bonanza, Gunsmoke*,

Kojak, and *Barretta*. He also was a voice actor who had done voices in *The Jetsons*, the short Mel Brooks animation *The Unmentionables*, and the film *The Nine Lives of Fritz the Cat*.

Beefing up the on-screen cast was Tom Poston, who appeared in the role of Franklin Delano Bickley, a grumpy man who lived in Mindy's apartment building. The often contentious neighbor was a good foil for both Mork and Mindy. Poston's gruff delivery and excellent comedic timing brought an added element of humor to the show. Poston was born on October 17, 1921, in Columbus, Ohio. At the age of nine he was performing with an acrobatic troupe. While attending Bethany College in West Virginia, Poston enlisted in the Air Corps, and he served during World War II in North Africa, Italy, France, and England. He was discharged as a captain. Poston won an Air Medal for his participation in D-Day as well as two Oak Leaf Medals. After the war he enrolled in and graduated from the American Academy of Dramatic Arts in New York City, where he worked with legendary acting teacher Sanford Meisner. Poston was soon appearing on television on *Studio One*, *Robert Montgomery Presents*, *The Phil Silvers Show*, and other dramatic and episodic shows. Poston won an Emmy Award for his work on *The Steve Allen Show* as The Man Who Can't Remember His Name. He also appeared in several films as well as on many game shows, where his droll wit made him a hot commodity. Poston fit nicely into the show. "Tom was just always solid," says Howard Storm. "Tom is always Tom. He's so strong. Robin was in awe of Tom and everybody who was there because he was this young kid around all these people. He saw Poston on *The Steve Allen Show*. And there was Tom. It was just special. Robin had great respect for all of them."

Garry Marshall calls Robin Williams a master of single-person comedy. Yet *Mork & Mindy* was an ensemble cast. Marshall says that the other actors had a hard time because they rarely got the agreed-upon cue but that they learned to adapt because they loved Williams and his special talent. Williams's improvisation kept the other actors stimulated. So too did Williams's practical jokes, which abounded on the set. Many times the jokes were on co-star Pam Dawber. "We had a scene where [Mork] stepped into the armoire to shower because he didn't know," remembers Howard Storm. "He had a shower cap on. Mindy opens it, and he was supposed to have a towel wrapped around and the shower cap on 'cause he thought he was in the shower. [Mindy] hears a noise and opens the armoire. Well, he didn't have the towel on."

"Robin was always naked somewhere, behind some corner," says Pam Dawber. "I think the very first time he got me . . . I remember what show it was because it's forever etched in my memory bank. It was the first Morgan Fairchild show. It was called 'Mork's First Date.' I remember standing behind the counter and I had a line. The audience was there and we were filming. [Mork] was busy getting changed in the bedroom, not in the attic, in the bedroom, and my line was 'Mork, you'd better hurry up, you're going to be late. Susan's going to be here any minute. What are you doing in there?' His line was—twenty-five years later and I can remember this—'Taking the worry out of being close.' And [Mindy says], 'Well, you'd better take the worry out of being late because Susan's going to be here any minute.' I was supposed to cross around. He flung open the door. I'd say one-third of the audience could see him because of that door. When he said, 'Taking the worry out of being close,' he was standing behind that door stark raving nude. He had pulled all of his genitalia to the back and did it in a fey voice. I'm tellin' ya, it literally dropped me to my knees. To my knees! I had not seen anything like that in my entire life. I didn't know it could be done. Oh my God."

It wouldn't be the last time that Williams would tease Dawber in this manner. "There was another time where [Mindy] had to go to a baby shower and [Mork] thinks he's coming with me. He comes down in a shower cap and a towel. And sure enough. Just as I get to the door he's standing there with his little towel on. I turn around and say, 'Put on some clothes' and I leave. Of course as I'm standing there and just for me he opens up his towel, and there he is, naked again. With the Robin face on. But I'm telling you, it was so much fun."

Sometimes Howard Storm would join in the crazy, impromptu banter on the set and become a character himself. People loved to go on the set of *Mork & Mindy*. "We were the hottest show on television," says Storm. "People [would love to] come and watch the show itself. We just had a lot of fun, and the runs we had constantly while the audience was there [were fun]. I'd run onto the set and take a pillow and hit Robin in the head with it and just beat him for goofing and lousing up a scene. He would have a great run and then decide that he didn't like it as much. I realized that he learned that trick after a while. He'd make a mistake on purpose. He'd do something to throw it off so he could get another run at it. Actors learn that after a while. They'll purposely go off so they can get one more run because they didn't like the way it started or whatever. There were things like that that were a constant throughout the show because you never knew what he was going to do. It was all set by Friday. But you didn't know where he was going to go with it. If he got bored with the run or what was happening he'd purposely do something that was crazy. He'd grab Pam's behind or goose her or whatever. And she would just look at him. There was no reaction like 'That's terrible.' He was able to get away with an awful lot. I was always amazed at that. I guess because it was innocent in a way. There was something about him that didn't make it ugly."

Pam Dawber wasn't the only one who was the victim of Robin's teasing. "I remember when he played the old man, with the old woman," recalls Storm. "[Elizabeth Kerr] was around seventy at the time. She's walking away from him in the rehearsal and he took the cane and goosed her! And I thought, if I did that all the grips in the place would come down from all over the set and beat the hell out of me. He did it and there was nothing ugly about it. She looked at him and said, 'Oh, Robin.'"

Some of the people who came to visit the set were friends of the cast and crew. "Robin and Chris Reeve were roommates when they were at Julliard," recalls Storm. "Chris hadn't done *Superman* yet. I think he was up for it. He'd done some Broadway stuff. Chris used to come to the set once in a while and visit with Robin. That's where I met him. Next thing you know, there was Chris, this major star. Both those guys did extremely well."

Garry Marshall says that the success of *Mork & Mindy* was due to the fact that kids picked up on the show and started emulating Mork. Parents tuned in to see what all the fuss was about. But back when the show first aired, parents had a more hands-on approach to what their children were watching on television. It's possible that the parents were watching and the kids picked up on the show and the crazy antics of Mork from passing through the living room.

The success of the show was terrific for Pam Dawber. "*Mork & Mindy* completely launched me," says Pam. "It allowed me to suddenly walk through the front door. I didn't have to stand in line anymore like anyone who wants to be an actor does. I was getting things without having to audition, which for me was one of the greatest gifts of all time because I have always been terrified of auditioning and I never thought I was very good at it. So it was an enormous gift."

Chapter 8

**NANU NANU
MEANS SUCCESS**

Mork & Mindy was a smash success. Out of the gate, Robin Williams won a Golden Globe in 1978 for Best Actor in a Comedy Series. Everybody throughout the entertainment industry and in households across America was talking about Williams and how crazy funny he was. Yet while Williams was attracting vast amounts of attention, Pam Dawber was still overlooked as an accomplished actress. "I don't know why any of the reviewers or people who would see the show didn't see [what a talent Pam was]," says Howard Storm. "They were so busy talking about Robin that they kind of ignored her. She was so solid. In order to do [what Robin did], you need grounding."

Storm looks back on previous comedy teams to illustrate that a comic is sometimes not as good without a reliable straight man or woman. "Proof of that is when Martin and Lewis broke up. Everybody thought that Jerry would just take off and poor Dean would disappear. And the reality was that Dean was as strong as Jerry was. Except that Jerry, being the comic, always gets the attention. On a comedy team the comic is always the one people pay attention to and think that if they split up the comic will just go on and this other poor guy is just lost. Look at Gracie Allen and George Burns. Without George Gracie couldn't function. And vice versa. The proof is that George did function on his own. And so did

Dean. As a matter of fact, if you go back over the years [there's] Bud Abbott and Lou Costello. Costello intimidated Bud so much that he literally got more money than Bud. He took sixty percent or something. Bud accepted that. It's too bad, but I guess he thought he had no other place to go. I believe he probably would have been working with another comic and done as well."

Randall Carver, who dated Pam Dawber, agrees that she was a solid force on *Mork & Mindy*. "She's a very talented lady," says Carver. "Pam was really nice. I really liked her. She's quite talented. There's lots of ways [Pam's talent] has not been explored all that well. She's a wonderful singer, for example."

Pam Dawber says that while working with Robin Williams was a special challenge, it wasn't necessarily intimidating. "It was because Robin is such a darling human," says Dawber. "Robin is such a deep soul; he's such an old soul. He's so sweet and nuts and funny and every-thing. And *he* was new too! We were all brand-new. It was the seventies, and we were in our twenties, and boy, were we having fun. It was like paid playtime. Robin could have, if he wanted to, chewed me up and spit me out. But he didn't. He liked me. Robin and I just love each other to this day. We know what we've been through together. There's always going to be a deep connection between the two of us. But it wasn't intimidating, just because he was nice to me. Now if he had thrown that kind of energy *at* me, of course I would have unraveled. I was always ready to unravel. I felt like I was personally hanging on by my fingernails just to try to pretend that I deserved to be there. But he was wonderful and became one of my closest friends."

The chemistry between Mork and Mindy was so solid that another interesting character was brought into the show. Exidor is a schizophrenic homeless man who befriends Mork. Robert Donner did an excellent job of portraying a character who acts even crazier than Mork. Donner had already made a name for himself in films such as *Rio Bravo*, *The Man Who Shot Liberty Valance*, *Cool Hand Luke*, and *Rio Lobo*. He had also done episodic television, with appearances on *The Waltons* and *Columbo* and in television movies such as *How the West Was Won*.

Robert Donner was born on April 27, 1931, in New York City. He moved from state to state as a young man and lived in New Jersey, Michigan, and Texas. After graduating from high school, Donner joined the Navy for a four-year enlistment. After his discharge he moved to Los Angeles, where he attended San Fernando Valley State College at night, studying speech, psychology, and art history. During the day Donner held various jobs—bartender, salesman, commercial artist, insurance investigator, gardener. Donner befriended a young actor who lived in his apartment building named Clint Eastwood. Eastwood encouraged Donner to study acting, as Eastwood thought Donner had a good face for the business. Soon Donner was appearing in *Rio Bravo*, with John Wayne, Dean Martin, Walter Brennan, and Ward Bond, and his acting career was well on its way. By the time he came to *Mork & Mindy* Donner was an excellent addition to the cast. The character Exidor was very entertaining, and the writers liked to write for him.

Other guest stars were brought in as well. "What was really cool about our show was that every comedian who was performing at the Comedy Store at the time wound up on our show," says Pam Dawber. "[John] Laroquette came up to me years later and [recalled that] he did a small role on our show. Of course, we had Dave Letterman, who was such a strange guy. People came on our show and just loved it, had the time of their lives. It was fun and we'd all hang out. We had these dressing rooms on the second stage, and we'd just hang out, lying on the floor and talking. It was a blast. Letterman was the only guy who would do his role, he was on for two weeks in a row, and he'd do his lines and then he'd climb to the top of the bleachers and just be all by himself. Whereas everybody else was just hanging out. He was sort of an odd duck. It was great, it was just great."

Robin Williams made another visit to the Cunninghams in a *Happy Days* appearance titled "Mork Returns" on March 6, 1979. The viewing audience—and the television industry—couldn't get enough of Mork. Both Robin Williams and Pam Dawber won People's Choice Awards for their work on *Mork & Mindy*, and Williams won a Golden Globe for Best Television Actor—Musical/Comedy in 1979. (Williams also won a Grammy that year for his album *Reality . . . What a Concept!*) *TV Guide* would later name a 1979 episode, "Mork's Mixed Emotions," in which Mindy kisses Mork and unleashes emotions never before experienced by the alien, as one of the 100 greatest television episodes of all time. "You know, when you're filming those shows you're just every day locked up in the big barn and you're doing your shows," remembers Dawber. "But all I knew was, we were having a blast. Paramount at the time was just an incredible place. It was so hot and happening. Especially for someone like me. I had been a model, and I had done commercials, and I had done a Robert Altman film and the pilot. So it was like, Oh my God, suddenly you're on the A-team. But we weren't sure. All I knew was there's Penny Marshall and Cindy Williams [doing *Laverne & Shirley*] and they were doing *Taxi* right next door. ABC at the time thought *Taxi* was going to be the big hit show. I remember you'd hear little rumblings from the net-

Another uproarious moment on the set of *Mork & Mindy* with Pam Dawber and Robin Williams, circa 1980. Photo courtesy of Globe Photos, Inc.

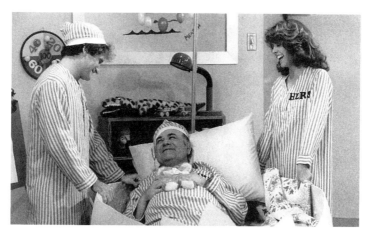

Mork's happy family, 1978. Robin Williams (Mork), Jonathan Winters (Mearth), and Pam Dawber (Mindy). Photo courtesy of Globe Photos, Inc.

work because the network would come and sit in, and they would go to this one and that one, and pretty soon we're hearing that *Mork & Mindy* is the hit. And it *was* a hit."

"Very close by [the Paramount lot] there was a restaurant called Nickodells, and Lucy's Adobe was across the street," remembers Howard Storm. "It was kind of our own little world. We'd eat in those places, and we knew we were doing well." (Nickodells was a restaurant and watering hole for industry insiders for decades. It was located on Melrose Avenue near the gates of the Paramount and RKO studios, and it was common for actors, directors, writers, and producers of film and television to gather for lunch or at the end of the day for drinks and companionship. The public was seemingly unaware of the potential the restaurant provided for star-spotting, and the casts and crews viewed the establishment almost as a home away from home. At one time there were even telephones that connected to the Paramount switchboard at the booths. The restaurant has since closed—a major loss to Hollywood history and lore.) "We had a softball team that was for muscular dystrophy. We went out to play our first game. I remember Henry Winkler was pitching on the team before us. We were waiting to take the field. They were just finishing their game. All the kids in the stands were yelling, 'Fonzie! Fonzie!' He finished, and they announced *Mork & Mindy*, and we went out to the field. Robin went out to right field. And everybody in the stands went out to right field. It was frightening. Robin just panicked. He didn't know what was happening. All of a sudden all these people were running at him. They were all lined up along the right field line because we asked them to please let him play the game. But they were talking to him, stepping over the line and all. Finally the game was over, and we had to make a wedge around him to get him back to his car. It was the first time we realized the power of that show. At the time he had a beat-up old Triumph. It was our first season. I don't think he was ready to invest in a new car yet. He wasn't sure whether he had a hit or not."

Mork & Mindy was certainly a hit. Robin Williams was now a household name. Still, while everyone seemed to know who Mindy was, Pam Dawber wasn't necessarily receiving the critical acclaim she deserved. "I was such a novice they hired an acting coach for me," remembers Dawber. "Thank God they didn't fire me. They could have easily replaced me, but they didn't, thank God. I didn't quite realize they'd hired an acting coach until I got smarter, years later. I was so out of my realm. I quite didn't know where I fit into the show because Robin was such a big performer, and I felt that I had to try to kind of equal that energy. It wasn't until I saw the show that I realized, 'Oh, oh, oh, I need to be real. I'm the one who's gotta be real and anchor this show.' It took me a while to catch on. I'm just happy it was still there [for me] to do it."

Some of the more seasoned people on the set disagree with Dawber's assessment of her talent. Playing against the unpredictable Robin Williams was a challenge unlike what most sitcom actor's face. "I don't think Pam ever got the credit she deserved," says Howard Storm. "She was a brilliant straight woman. She was the strength of the show. As important as Robin was to that show, to me Pam was as important. Had it been someone else, they would not have been able to handle it. Very few actresses could have stood there and waited. I mean she didn't know where her cue was. Half the time he'd go off, do his little run. She would have to hold and be in character and stay with it until he'd come up with her cue line. She would set him up, and to me she was as brilliant as he was in her own way. I think she did grow, but I think she had natural ability. She had a great sense of timing. To me she's a female Bud Abbott in terms of knowing where the joke is and holding for the laugh. She never got in the way of Robin, which was amazing because sometimes he wouldn't give you the cue you expected, and it's very easy to kind of go to the next line. She knew how to hold for laughs when there was a laugh, she never stepped on it. As an actress I guess she grew just being there and doing it each week and realizing what her job was. The pity is I thought she never, never was given the credit for it."

In 1979 *Mork & Mindy* received an Emmy nomination as Outstanding Comedy Series. Robin Williams was nominated for Outstanding Lead Actor in a Comedy Series. Williams was also nominated for a Golden Globe as Best Actor in a Comedy Series.

Mork made an appearance on another television sitcom that year. Garry Marshall attempted yet another spin-off from *Happy Days* titled *Out of the Blue*. The main character of the proposed new series was first introduced when Chachi sold his soul to the devil's nephew and turned to his guardian angel, Random. This time the show would be set in contemporary times as Random comes to Earth to help a woman raise her five orphaned nieces and nephews. Random pretends to be a human and rents a room in the woman's house to be close to the action. The kids in the show know Random is an angel and turn to him for advice and solutions to their problems.

Out of the Blue starred stand-up comedian Jimmy Brogan as Random, with actress Dixie Carter, who would later make it big on television but at the time was primarily known for her roles in the soap operas *The Doctors* and *The Edge of Night*, co-starring as Aunt Marion. The children were played by Clark Brandon (*The Fitzpatricks*), Tammy

Lauren (*Who's Watching the Kids*), Olivia Barash (*Secret Storm, A World Apart*), and newcomers Jason and Shane Keller. Eileen Heckart played the "Boss Angel." Heckart was a noted film and television actress who had appeared on multiple drama series, as well as such episodic television as *The Mary Tyler Moore Show*, *Barnaby Jones*, and *The Streets of San Francisco*. She also enjoyed a film career, appearing in films such as *Somebody Up There Likes Me*, *Bus Stop*, and *Butterflies Are Free*. The show was primarily directed by Peter Baldwin and Jeff Chambers, who had been involved with *Happy Days*.

Robin Williams appeared as Mork on the September 9, 1979, episode "Random's Arrival." The problem was that the *Happy Days* episode featuring Random had not yet aired at the time the series was ordered into production. ABC didn't know how the character or the premise would be received by the viewing audience. Evidently not well. *Out of the Blue* lasted only four months.

In the beginning of *Mork & Mindy*'s run the show was more slapstick and driven by the Mork-is-crazy idea. Garry Marshall enjoyed the comedy of Robin Williams and felt that Williams was one of the funniest, wittiest, quickest comedians he'd ever seen. Marshall says he is also one of the "better human beings." Williams enjoyed playing Mork. The character wasn't jaded in the way those in sitcoms can be. Williams said it wasn't unusual for Mork to discuss matters with a moose head or his space suit because he wasn't sure if they were real and he didn't want to risk offending anything. This kind of innocence and sincerity made Mork a very lovable character.

The viewing audience continued to receive *Mork & Mindy* with very open arms. "We were on the cover of everything and just busy and doing our little thing and not realizing how big we were," remembers Pam Dawber. "We didn't quite realize [how big the show was] because you're just making them and they're putting them on the air. You hear your ratings are good, and that's about all you know. Then suddenly you're starting to get press requests and this and that, but you're not out there in the Midwest. Until we were we didn't realize that we were like The Beatles for five minutes."

Mork & Mindy had been airing on Thursday nights at 8:00 P.M., a perfect time slot for the show. Then something very strange happened. Garry Marshall went to New York to do a play titled *The Roast*. While he was gone, ABC decided to move *Mork & Mindy* from its time slot on Thursday nights to Sunday night at 8:00 P.M. Believing that the move was motivated by greed and power, Marshall, Dale McRaven, Bruce Johnson, and the executives of Paramount Television protested. Their opinion wasn't entertained. The change was a done deal. As of August 1979, *Mork & Mindy* would air on Sundays.

In order to compete in the new time slot, Garry Marshall says, the show was forced to introduce new, younger characters. For various reasons, ranging from appeal to salaries, ABC wanted to weed out forty-five actors from the network's prime-time line-up. Among those who were selected to be let go were Conrad Janis and Elizabeth Kerr. The disappearance of Mindy's father from the show was explained as Frederick's pursuit of his lifelong dream of becoming an orchestra leader and going on tour.

"I was in shock," says Howard Storm. "I thought it was a major mistake. They didn't talk to anybody about it. I came back, and the little black boy was gone, the grandmother was gone. Conrad, the father, was gone. And the set was gone. For the first time in television there was a set that just wasn't a living room and the usual luncheonette or whatever. They went back to the luncheonette."

Pam Dawber was equally disturbed by the changes. "They had a show that was based around this real family," says Dawber, "with one crazy guy and his crazy friend, Exidor. The way I always saw the show, Robin was the strangest person you should ever have on that show, so that your audience had a platform. The audience viewed Mork through Mindy's eyes. In other words, Mindy was the real girl, and she had a real dad, who had his concerns, and the grandma, who was kind of funny. Exidor was [Mork's] one and only friend, and he was a crazy bag person."

The network executives weren't happy just sitting back and continuing to let that dynamic work for the show. "What happened is, they tested the show," says Dawber. "They decided, 'Oh, we should test it now.' We've got the number one show in the country. The test showed that the audience liked Mork first, Mindy second, and then Dad and Grandma fell way off. So what did they do? They take the number one show and they fire half of a five-person cast. Then they decide they need to bring more young people in and change that. So they bring in more zanies."

Jay Thomas was brought in to play one of the younger characters on the show, Remo DeVinci, who is the owner of a neighborhood deli that Mork and Mindy frequent. Remo's sister Jean was played by Gina Hecht. Now Mork and Mindy have characters their own age with whom to interact. Remo and Jean are transplants to Boulder from the Bronx, which allows for some regional humor. Jean is working at the deli so that she can attend medical school, and she and her brother become immediate friends with both Mork and Mindy.

"They brought in Jay Thomas and Gina Hecht, who were wonderful," says Howard Storm. "They were marvelous, but I thought that the music store set was a great thing. Somewhere they got this idea that they needed younger people on the show, so they got rid of the grandmother and the father. I came back and they were gone. And I was furious. That was it. It was a fait acompli. I'm sure they talked to Garry about it. I thought it was a major mistake. I said so when I talked to everybody I could about it. That was a crazy move."

One of the reasons ABC decided to change things on *Mork & Mindy* is because the network executives believed they needed to schedule a successful show against CBS's hit series *All in the Family*, which by now had morphed into *Archie Bunker's Place*. "I remember discussing that and saying, '*All in the Family* has its own audience,'" says Storm. "They are not an audience that's going to watch our show. It's a very adult audience, and we're not going to pull away their audience, and they're not going to pull our audience away. That show is already locked in. Sure enough, the people who watched that show watched *it*. Our people didn't know where the hell we were, what happened to Thursday night. [The audience] went and looked for us and didn't know where to find us. We were on Sunday. And we got killed. [*Mork & Mindy*] was a show that could have run for seven, eight years. I think they destroyed it by making those changes. I think it was the network. And I think Paramount went along with it. I don't think they had any choice. But I'm not sure because I never knew where it came from. I can't imagine Garry [Marshall] would make the change. [*Mork & Mindy*] was working. We had a year that was just unbelievable. We were first almost every week. Then all of a sudden, bing. It was gone. It was strange."

Pam Dawber agrees with Storm. "You had the number one show," says Dawber. "This show was such a hip show, so cutting edge at the time because of Robin and all his funny little comments that worked real well for children. They also were very avant garde and timely and politically charged, and there was a lot of undercurrent there that the college kids liked. It was a mid-week show. I have always felt that every day of the week has a flavor for your audience. How people feel on Monday, how they feel on Tuesday, where they are by the time they get to Friday, what Saturday and Sunday are about. With *Mork & Mindy* they never put us on Monday night, which they said they were going to, they put us on Thursday night, and we were in a perfect spot for us. So we were the number one show.

"So now they bring in other characters that make it a little more cartoony and then they *move* it," continues Dawber. "We went from being number one to somewhere in the thirties. They were wanting to gun down Archie Bunker, that's all. They were wanting to go up against

Carroll O'Connor and see if they could kill that show, so they moved us to Sunday night. Now *Mork & Mindy* is clearly not a Sunday night show. It's war games. It's not really about just entertaining people. They wanted to gun down *All in the Family* or *Archie Bunker's Place* or whatever the heck that show was called by that time. What they did was split the difference, so Carroll O'Connor was down there in the thirties and we were in the thirties. He was doing better than we were. He might've been thirty-one and we were thirty-four, or something like that."

The audience's problem had nothing to do with the actors who were brought into the show. Jay Thomas was a very good actor, even if the character Remo didn't have much to really do. He was born Jon Thomas Terrell on July 12, 1948, in Kermit, Texas, to T. Harry and Katherine Guzzino Terrell. Thomas graduated from Jesuit High School in New Orleans and found his calling serving as an emcee for the school's talent show. He developed an interest in radio-announcing at Gulf Coast Junior College and went on to graduate from the University of North Carolina. Thomas's first professional job was as a disc jockey in Jacksonville, Florida. He decided to also pursue a career in acting, and his first television role was when he was cast as Remo on *Mork & Mindy*. Gina Hecht, born on December 6, 1953, in Winter Park, Florida, was also new to acting. *Mork & Mindy* was her first role as well.

Jim Staahl was brought on the show to play Mindy's cousin, Nelson Flavor. While Nelson was close to Mindy's age, the character was quite different. Where Mindy was sweet and down-to-earth, Nelson was a social climber with political ambitions. In other words, Nelson was totally obnoxious. Mork enjoyed baiting the smug Nelson Flavor.

Jim Staahl was born in Evanston, Illinois, birthplace of actors Charlton Heston and John Cusack. At the beginning of his comedy career, Staahl was a part of Canada's famed Second City improvisational group. He appeared on the troupe's television series *Second City TV*, with John Candy, Eugene Levy, Rick Moranis, and Dave Thomas. Staahl had appeared in the film *Cracking Up*, with Fred Willard, Michael McKean, and David L. Lander.

Mindy McConnell, who had been a student at the University of Colorado, took a job at the local television station. Her boss was Mr. Sternhagen, played by veteran comedian and Garry Marshall friend Foster Brooks. While Brooks also didn't seem to have much to do, he was a prestigious addition to the cast. Foster Brooks was born on May 11, 1912, in Louisville, Kentucky, and had had a long-standing career in television comedy. One of eight sons of a county sheriff, Brooks wasn't well educated, having dropped out of school after the sixth grade, but he found a niche for himself in radio. He became a disc jockey and newscaster in Louisville and then Buffalo, New York, then decided to try his luck in television broadcasting. After moving to Los Angeles when he was in his forties, Brooks began finding work in such notable television series as *Gunsmoke*, *I Dream of Jeannie*, *Bewitched*, and *The Beverly Hillbillies*. Brooks also worked as a stand-up comedian, and developed an act he called "The Lovable Lush." Perry Como was in the audience at one of Brook's appearances—a celebrity golf tournament—and liked what he saw. Como asked Brooks to be his opening act at the new Hilton Hotel in Las Vegas. The hotel wasn't sure the untested Brooks was right for the spot, but Como told them that Brooks would open or Como would not appear. After his Las Vegas appearance, Brooks made his television debut in 1962 on *The Tonight Show Starring Johnny Carson*. He then became a regular on *The Dean Martin Show* roasts. Brooks's "Lovable Lush" was a popular act. (Despite his alcoholic persona, Brooks gave up alcohol himself in the sixties and didn't drink at all. He would later become a national spokesman for Mothers Against Drunk Drivers.)

Seeing that the Sunday night time slot was not working for the show and that *Mork & Mindy* was going down in the ratings rather than maintaining its number 1 spot, in December 1979 the executives at ABC finally decided to move the show back to Thursday night at 8:00. "So then [they] said, 'Oh, we made a big mistake, we've made a terrible mistake,'" says Pam Dawber. "So they decided to move us back the next year. By that time [television executives] had discovered someone named Tom Selleck on CBS and put him on *Magnum, P.I.*, opposite [our] 8:00 time slot on Thursday night. He was now up there in the top ten or five, and we never recovered. We never, ever regained [our status]. I don't think we ever got back to top ten status. We always hovered somewhere in the twenties for the rest of the four years we were on."

When the producers prevailed upon the network to re-hire Conrad Janis and the network agreed, they were lucky that the actor was available. Despite the shake-up of the show, the stories on *Mork & Mindy* remained interesting, if different from their original content. The show, likely through the influence of Robin Williams and because of the success with such episodes over at *Happy Days*, took on a more serious tone. Complicated stories about good and evil, Bickley's blind son Tom, and Mork getting a face-lift were written. Some of the episodes addressed specific, much-debated social issues but were made fresh as seen through the innocent eyes of Mork.

"I remember when we did a show which in those days was shocking," remembers Howard Storm, "where Mork comes home and tells

Mindy that he met these wonderful people who invited him to help clean up Boulder. They are going to get rid of the Polacks and the Kikes and that kind of thing. That [kind of storyline] was a big step in those days. It was shocking. Mindy says, 'Mork, do you understand what this is about?' And he doesn't. When she explains it to him, we had a wonderful scene that I remember so well because we had to figure out how to do it, where Mork decides he's going to zap all the KKK members and turn them into blacks and Jews and Indians, Indians from India, American Indians, every color you can think of. We had to figure out a way to do that. I remember they come in and we see all these white people and they put their hoods on and the grand marshal or whatever is speaking to them. We had Robin make a mistake on purpose so that we had to cut. I actually choreographed it more or less. We had people in the background with hoods, waiting. There were blacks and Jews and all, all in back. These people kept strolling in and out until the whole white group was out. The Caucasians went backstage, and they were replaced while we were trying to re-set the light or whatever that went wrong from Robin goofing. Then we said okay, let's roll. We did it and then he zapped them and they took off their hoods, and the audience went nuts. They were shocked. It was so simple when you think about it. They just strolled around and other people strolled in, and before you knew it there was a whole new group on stage. [Mork] zaps them because he's told what they're doing is wrong and turns them all into blacks and there are all these white racists. It was wonderful stuff. We did a lot of things like that."

Another very poignant show dealt with growing old. "There was a wonderful show called 'Old Fears' where Mindy's grandmother is very lonesome because all of her friends are dying off," recalls Storm. "Mork decides when he hears about this, that he is going to make himself old so that he can be her friend. He zaps himself and becomes an old man. He comes in and flirts with her and so forth, and she falls in love with him. It's this wonderful scene where he confesses that's he's really not old, [but] she knew a while back. Mindy was very upset with him because he tells her what he's done and she says, 'What happens when she finds out?' 'Cause she's told Mindy that she's met this wonderful man. So it was very sweet. Lovely show."

Robin Williams was demonstrating that not only was he great at comedy and improvisation, but he was developing as a dramatic actor as well. "Robin realizes when he needs to snap in shape," says Pam Dawber. "He knows when to push it, but then when it's time to get serious. He definitely could pull it together and get serious."

Fearing "jumping the shark" episodes, the series started to look to stunt-casting, like having diva Raquel Welch come on the show in a two-part episode titled "Mork vs. the Necrotons." The experience with Welch was not a pleasant one for many of those associated with the show. She looked great but brought new meaning to the word "diva." The Welch episodes were also done to appease the network, which had suggested "sexing up" the show. "Garry [Marshall] doesn't remember this, but I know this happened; it was probably no big deal to him, but it was to me," says Pam Dawber. "When *Mork & Mindy* first started, it was back when people weren't wearing bras. I was not wearing a bra. I had been a model, and I was not endowed, and the network wanted me to wear a padded bra. They wanted to put sex into the show. Me, with my no experience, said, 'No, I'm not wearing a padded bra! It's not that kind of a show.' I just flatly refused. Garry came up to me after one of the shows and said, 'The network wants me to talk to you and nee nah nah . . .' I just wouldn't do it. That was somewhere around the end of the first year. That next year is when they fired half the cast, they changed the time slot, and they also changed the whole gist of the show. It got sexier. They brought in Raquel Welch, remember that nightmare? Then they brought in the Bronco Cheerleaders. They wanted to make Morgan Fairchild a semi-regular because they had brought her in midway through the first year as Mindy's friend. [The character] was always trying to steal Mork from Mindy. It was actually very cute. She was really good on the show with it. It was a fun thing. [Then] they wanted to make it sexier." (Garry Marshall says that the episode with the Cheerleaders—"Hold That Mork"—was the only time he ever saw Robin Williams uncomfortable. This was when Williams rode the Denver Broncos' pony in his cheerleading outfit. Marshall says the show didn't work because it wasn't up to *Mork & Mindy's* usually high standards.)

Robin Williams and the writers now wanted Mork to become more hip rather than stick to his alien innocence. "Mork went from being this innocent observer to someone a little hipper," remembers Dawber. "They put him in situations where [Mork] was becoming a little more of what Robin did in his club act than the purer character that people liked. I think they actually took away the black box which was the 'Mork to Orson' thing. And that was so charming with his oddball truisms. He would report back and make some wonderful little social statement in a very wacky way. That changed it a bit too. They should have just left it alone."

Like any young actor, Robin Williams was enjoying his fame. Unfortunately, like many young successful actors at the time, that often meant staying out late and partying with alcohol and drugs. "We had our tough times when he was going through his partying, and there were problems there, as everybody knew," recalls Howard Storm. "He's perfectly clean now but at the time . . . He was a kid, and all of a sudden there was all this success. I remember going to meet him at his apartment [when the show first started], and there was hardly any furniture. There was a mattress on the floor. 'Cause this kid had done nothing to make money. He just about got around doing the clubs around town. That paid very little, if anything, all the Comedy Stores and the Improvs. This was the first real money he ever saw [as an actor]. I think it was overwhelming. Drugs get in the way. For anybody, whether it's Robin or anybody else. He was just so talented that he got through it. He'd come in exhausted in the morning. I remember him taking little naps and we had to look for him. He'd sleep anyway he could to catch up."

"It was a very weird time, and Robin's talked about it," says Pam Dawber. "You had many people [realizing success] at the time; you had *Saturday Night Live* and that whole crowd. So many people were young and famous all of a sudden, and when you're young and famous in Hollywood, especially in those days, it was the big cocaine time. It was very interesting to be there when John Belushi died. That was huge for everybody. Especially because Robin had been with Belushi the night before. Robin admitted to having drug problems. I was like Robin's daytime wife. 'You're stoned!' 'No, I am not stoned, I'm nuts!' 'Yes, you are!' He'd lie to me and I'd believe him. Later he finally admitted to it. But there was all this success, and when you're a comedian and you're out late and there's someone there with a spoon up your nose to say, 'Hey, I blew coke with Robin Williams . . .' I always felt that John Belushi's death, in a way, was a sacrifice—it saved so many other people. Because they were all being investigated 'cause they hung out together. It forced Robin to have to take a really hard look, good look, at his life. And he really did straighten up his act. But those were the days, my friend . . ."

Williams himself has said that you're only given a little spark of madness and you must not lose it. He called cocaine "God's way of telling you you are making too much money." Luckily, Williams was smart and driven enough to allow those he loved and respected to point out that drugs and partying were getting in the way of a successful future. "He never didn't do the show," says Storm. "There was a period once where I felt for a couple of weeks that he was so good that he was just kind of floating through the show. He was just kind of doing it by rote. I remember having a conversation with him, saying to him, 'Listen. You're much better than what you're doing. What's happening is you're doing mediocre work, which means my work is becoming mediocre. And I don't want that.' We talked about it, and he said, 'Okay, okay.' He turned around. I think that happens [when someone does drugs]. You just get so exhausted and then the mind has to be fed, and the energy has to come from somewhere, and when it's drained then you're not doing [the work]. You can't work at your top level."

Regardless of who was on the show or what was going on behind the scenes, the crew of *Mork & Mindy* had a pretty entertaining working environment. "The crew adored [Robin]," says Storm. "They couldn't wait. They loved doing that show. It was so much fun on the set. It was just such a great atmosphere, even with the difficulties when he was going through his craziness. The show was always bizarre. You never knew what was going to happen. I remember rehearsing for one or two days, and then Robin would say to me, 'Papa, it's not working.' I'd say, 'Robin, you've been doing it for two days and it's getting stale. When the crew comes in they'll not have heard it and you'll see the difference.' They'd come in on Thursday, and we'd do camera blocking, and then Friday we did the show. And there were the laughs again. By the end of the day Friday, the laughs were not coming so much because the camera guys had seen it five, six times. Robin also knew the names of the crew. He's one of those guys who knew everybody. He wasn't a star who just went off and did his thing and disappeared. He took the time to know the names of the operators and the guys on the set. And there was a relationship. And it was lovely. It was fun."

The set of *Mork & Mindy* was much different than what was going on over at *Laverne & Shirley*. Rather than avoid going near the set, people would often stop by the stage to watch rehearsals. "One of my favorite visuals is when Robin was the toast of the town," remembers Pam Dawber. "I remember Tom Hanks and Peter Scolari coming over in full drag because they were right next door doing *Bosom Buddies*. They were coming over in full drag just to sit and watch rehearsal for a while. It was definitely the place to be. I remember Drew Barrymore coming over with little Melissa Gilbert from *Little House on the Prairie*. [Our set] was the place to be. It was just great. I remember sitting on top of the bleachers the time Ginger Rogers came over. She was telling me that our sound stage was where she did that big dance scene with Fred Astaire where she had the gown on with all the feathers and he was so mad—he hated it because the feathers kept flying off in his mouth. But suddenly, because *Mork & Mindy* was a hit show, the world just opened up. The people you got to meet. And the people who wanted to meet you. I think we were all so thrilled when Jerry Mathers came on the set. I'm tellin' ya, because we all grew up with him. Jerry Mathers came on the set and everything just stopped. *The Beav!* Robin had fun with *that*. It was just an incredible experience."

The cast of *Mork & Mindy*, like that of *Happy Days* and sometimes *Laverne & Shirley*, eased whatever tension there was in grinding out a show per week by blowing off steam however they could. "Remember when suddenly roller-skating became the big thing in the seventies?" asks Pam Dawber. "Some roller-skating company had sent us roller-skates the first year of *Mork & Mindy*. So Robin and I started rehearsing on roller-skates. We started doing *everything* on roller-skates. Paramount actually passed some sort of a rule because of us. We'd roller-skate over to *Taxi* and we'd roller-skate to the commissary. Boy, roller-skating around on those big sound stages was really fun. I think they finally went, 'Enough already!'"

Sometimes visitors to the set got in on the fun. "Christopher Reeve was good friends with Robin, and I was dating Christopher at the end of *Mork & Mindy*," remembers Dawber. "At the first-year cast party, everybody was drinking and having fun. It was back when [Paramount] had the *Little House on the Prairie* set. We all stole a golf cart, a whole bunch of us, and we were racing all around the *Little House on the Prairie* streets at twelve at night. I remember Christopher, six foot four, came running out, and there were about five of us piled on this golf cart. We're racing down the street, and Christopher leaps on the back of it, 'Wait for me!' And the entire thing lifted off the ground on two wheels. It was so funny because it was such a 'Superman' moment."

The studio audiences loved to be present for the tapings of *Mork & Mindy*. "Robin did so much improvisation, especially when we were filming," Dawber remembers. "Once the audience came in, Robin just came to life. Things would fly out of his mouth that I would be hearing for the first time. I would find myself saying, 'Okay, okay, he didn't say, "Mindy, we've got to go, go to the closet and get my coat."' It taught me improvisation. I hadn't had a tremendous number of acting classes. Certainly it helped me to just have to think on my feet."

But changing the airing of the show back to Tuesday nights was too little too late. The wonderful momentum that *Mork & Mindy* had first enjoyed had been too seriously disrupted. "We had such fun doing [the show]," says Pam Dawber. "There was a lot of frustration in having one of the biggest hit shows to come along in a long time and watching the network and the studio screw it up so incredibly." The ratings were never the same. Something had to be done to save the show.

Robin Williams thought the solution might be to have the character Mork personally evolve. Mork had been on Earth a while now and had seen and experienced a lot. Mork was very intelligent and perceptive, and maybe it was time to have Mork look at things with the benefit of those past experiences. Director Howard Storm didn't necessarily agree. "[Robin] and I would argue about this all the time," says Storm. "I would say to him, 'You can't have the character grow. If Archie Bunker grows and is no longer a racist, you don't have a show.' I said to him, 'Robin, I'll give you this much. Let the character grow *somewhat*. But it's like a guy whose first language is Italian. When he gets upset or he is thrown, he goes back to what he knows—he speaks Italian.' He didn't want to do nanu, nanu and all of that stuff after a while. It was tough to get him to do those things. So I said, 'So when you're upset you can go back to that, and with Mindy you can go to that because Mindy knows who you are. So you can relax there.' No one wanted to deal with that. It was strange."

Mork and Mindy were married in the fall of 1981. That alone would not be enough. A strange twist was about to be revealed.

Robin Williams had always been in awe of comedian Jonathan Winters. Williams wondered if Winters might be persuaded to join the show on a regular basis. He must have been astounded when he said that he would. Winters had appeared on *Mork & Mindy* once before. "He appeared as [Mindy's] uncle, the brother of Conrad Janis," remembers Howard Storm. "[His character] was an obnoxious multi-millionaire. Robin was in awe of Jonathan. He was like a kid around Jonny. Robin and [Jonathan] worked together on that show for the first time. Robin just couldn't believe that Jonny was there and doing it. It was just lovely to see. Jon was just so sweet with him. They both were. There was such affection. And such respect for each other."

There are few people in the universe like Jonathan Winters, and certainly the actor is a comedic icon. Born in Dayton, Ohio, on November 11, 1925, to banker Jonathan Winters, who would lose his fortune in the Great Depression and become an alcoholic, Jonathan would be the son of divorced parents. Winters moved to Springfield, Ohio, to be raised by his mother and grandmother. His mother remarried and took up a career as a radio personality. During World War II, Winters quit high school in his senior year to enlist in the Marines. Upon returning home, he attended Kenyon College and later enrolled in the Dayton Art Institute. Winters is an accomplished artist and writer. He won a talent contest that resulted in his being signed to do a children's television show in Dayton. Winters was soon the host of a local game show and a talk show. When he asked for and was denied a raise, Winters and his wife, Eileen, moved to New York so that he could try his luck in the big time. He soon was a popular comedian on the nightclub circuit. By 1956 he was headlining on television in *The Jonathan Winters Show* and was soon making appearances in films such as *It's a Mad, Mad, Mad, Mad World* and *The Russians Are Coming, the Russians Are Coming*. Winters continued to host his own television shows, *The Jonathan Winters Show*, which ran from 1967 to 1969, and *The Wacky World of Jonathan Winters*, which appeared from 1972 to 1974. A true improvisational genius, Jonathan Winters suffered through two nervous breakdowns, in 1959 and in 1961. Rather than let the breakdowns hinder his career, he often joked about them in his act. Winters stayed employed as an actor, personality, and recording artist: he was a ten-time-nominated Grammy honoree, at least one for each of his comedy recordings.

Soon after Mork and Mindy were married, Mork, as was the custom on Ork, gave birth to their child by ejecting a small egg—and a full-size baby—from his naval (talk about jumping the shark!). Things were backward on Ork. Instead of aging, Orkans gradually grew younger. Mork and Mindy's baby would be Mearth, played by . . . the 225-pound Jonathan Winters. "Then they came up with the idea of having Jonathan as the baby," winces Storm. "I never [directed] any of those. I escaped." Garry Marshall and Dale McRaven thought that Winters would not only inspire Robin Williams but also boost the ratings. However, according to Garry Marshall, the filmed material wasn't as funny as it might have been. The two comics used too much X-rated material that had to be left on the cutting room floor, and so the casting didn't work as well as it might have.

Once Winters joined the cast of *Mork & Mindy*, the set was a place unlike any other. "Quite honestly, the two of them together were like two bad children," remembers Pam Dawber. "You can work with one bad child, but when you get two bad children in the room, I must say that was really hard. If they were following lines, Robin would go off in another direction and do some wild, hysterical improvisation. But he knew how to come back. He could go off and wind it up and come back and continue on. If Jonathan would go off, he'd be past the moon, he'd be on Mars. He didn't know where he was. Jonathan was more nuts than Robin by far. That was very difficult because Jonathan would just go off and not come back. Robin was very protective of him. You'd have these two comedic geniuses wandering off. Robin would be climbing up in the bleachers, and Jonathan would be talking to the guy with the broom in the corner. So when it came to doing the show, it was really tough. Robin helped a lot with Jonathan. Jonathan truly, at that point, couldn't remember where he had to stand. I'd hang on to him and pull him. What was hardest was the whole rehearsal process, especially with comedians like those guys. If somebody came up with a great joke on Tuesday they'd go,

'Oh, that's great. Remember that.' The script supervisor would write it down, and Robin would remember it. Jonathan would never be able to revisit it, much less remember what the character was."

While everyone was delighted to have the legendary comedian as a part of the show, it indeed sometimes made their work harder. "There was a show where Mindy was taking Mearth to the park," recalls Dawber. "Mearth was all excited to go to the park. That was how the scene evolved. [Mindy] loses Mearth. Either [Mork] was with him or I was with him . . . he gets lost. The whole thing is that Jonathan [as Mearth] is supposed to be very, very happy. So all week we rehearsed it the way the character was supposed to be. Well, come the day of the shooting Jonathan doesn't want to be happy. Jonathan decides that Mearth is going to come down the stairs and go, 'No!' No matter what we did, he's fully in character as this three year old; he wouldn't do one single thing that we were supposed to do. Jonathan was just out there that day. Robin did this brilliant improvisation that got him out of the room. They ended up using it in the show even though it had nothing to do with what was supposed to happen. We had to do it three or four times just to get Jonathan to behave properly, and he wouldn't. Robin goes and becomes a drill sergeant, and he starts doing this drill sergeant thing. Jonathan is now improvising with Robin and pretending he is in rank. Robin gets him to march out the door. That was nothing that was ever written or intended in that particular show. We'd often be thinking, 'Oh my God, we're going to be here until two in the morning.'

"There was so much comedic genius that had nothing to do with *Mork & Mindy* but that happened while we were supposed to be rehearsing *Mork & Mindy*, that went on between Jonathan and Robin, that I actually got this idea of getting a documentary film crew in just to be there to put this on film, to document these two geniuses together," recalls Dawber. "Everybody agreed to do it. Paramount agreed to do it, we all wrote it off as yes, you can do that, we agree. And wouldn't you know it, Robin's damn management said no. In retrospect, what a wonderful thing that would have been to have. The two of those guys were so nuts, so wonderfully nuts together and so funny. Oh my God, it was funny."

By this time Robin Williams was becoming bored with the Mork character. He had been doing Mork for four years and began to feel the character was a dead end. He starred in the movie *Popeye* for director Robert Altman, but Altman evidently didn't want him to improvise or change the dialogue. It was a hard film for Williams. Looking to the future, the actor now needed to decide where he wanted to take his career.

In what was to become *Mork & Mindy*'s final season, Bob Claver was brought in to direct the show. Claver was another television veteran, having directed episodic series such as *The Partridge Family*, *The Bob Newhart Show*, *Rhoda*, *Welcome Back, Kotter*, and other successful shows. Howard Storm had directed the show from its unexpected success through Season Three but felt it was time to move on. "What happened is I felt that I was getting burned out," says Storm. "I did three years of the show. It was great fun, but after a while my ideas started to run out. I felt like I was starting to imitate myself on the show. When I direct, I promise myself, when I'm doing a sitcom, that I'll bring or add at least two things that weren't there, that weren't in the script. Bring at least something to it rather than just direct the script. It was getting harder. It was getting tougher. Then I was offered *Taxi*, and I spoke to Garry about it. I said, 'I feel like I'm getting burned out,' and he said, 'I understand. Don't worry about it. Go do it. Good luck.'"

Actor Corey Feldman was brought in for an episode at about this time. "I did a character called Billy," Feldman remembers. "It was going to be Billy the Kid. It was when Mork started working for the orphanage and started bringing kids home with him. They talked about me being a character that was going to be a regular. They tried one episode, and the one episode went well. They wrote me into the very next episode. It was going to be a recurring role at that point. I don't remember what happened, but after the second episode I guess everybody decided not to go forward, not to bring my character back. Which was too bad because it was a great character. It was a great episode. It was called 'Gunfight at the Mor-kay Corral.' It was a showdown in the Wild West between me, Billy the Kid, and Mork. It had an old-style saloon, and we had an old-style saloon fight. Mork was shooting out the bottles with his fingers. It was great. It was lots of fun."

Even though he was a child, Feldman remembers working with Robin Williams. "He was amazing," Feldman says. "He was so great. He used to always tell me I looked like the Damien kid. Every time I walked down the set he'd start whistling *The Omen*. He'd go, 'Damien! Damien!' He was always very quiet. The thing people didn't realize about Robin Williams, because all you ever see is him on, is that when you're on the set with him he pretty much keeps to himself. He's a very quiet guy. The only time he actually turns on is when you're on-stage and doing stuff. He was always very nice to me. Very sweet. I like him very much. I've seen him since then, and he actually remembered doing [that episode], which was interesting. Obviously, it left a lasting impression in both of our minds. I just remember having a great experience overall."

The show was moved to the 8:30 P.M. time slot on ABC's Thursday night line-up for the months of April and May 1982, then back to 8:00 P.M. for May through June. By this time the viewing audience was so confused as to where to find the show that they were simply giving up and not watching it at all. Everyone was so frustrated it was decided to call it quits. The last episode of *Mork & Mindy* aired on May 20, 1982, with a non-consequential episode primarily written by Winifred Hervey and directed by Robin Williams.

The network was so frustrated with the number 1 show that they had ultimately destroyed that they seemed to just wash their hands of it. "The ultimate stupidity was canceling us," says Pam Dawber. "And Paramount not picking us up to make that five-year syndication package they could have made. That was really stupid. Now they syndicate shows in the second year, but in those days cable hadn't really taken off. They were just very shortsighted. The network set the pace, and I think there were some production problems as far as decisions that were made."

Regardless of the ending of the show, *Mork & Mindy* had established its place in television history. *Mork & Mindy* was unlike other television sitcoms and managed somehow to remain very special. Director Howard Storm sees the show's place in television history as distinctive. "It opened up sitcoms for stand-up comics," says Storm. "Well, there was *The Danny Thomas Show* before that, but for new, young stand-ups [there was *Mork & Mindy*]. It was an entirely different kind of show. It wasn't the usual *Dick Van Dyke*, which was brilliant, but was a living room, drawing room comedy kind of thing. A family. This [*Mork & Mindy*] was so bizarre, the approach. Mork was someone who takes things literally. I remember discussing this with Garry [Marshall] when we were doing the first one or two scripts. We talked about the fact that if you say to Mork 'zip it up,' he zips it up because that's what he hears. Like the opening show, with the egg. He just tells it to fly, which is so sweet and wonderful. They hold up, somehow. They do hold up because there's just such sweetness about some of the shows. Robin is just so powerful and fun. The relationship between Mork and Mindy is so lovely."

Pam Dawber remembers her time on *Mork & Mindy* fondly. "I always sort of saw myself as Mrs. Santa Claus," Dawber says. "[The audience] really wants to know what Santa Claus is about. I felt very honored that I was allowed to do *Mork & Mindy*. I had the best seat in the house. I thought that I was allowed to really be able to live a life for years, daily, with one of the greatest comedic geniuses of our time. I look back and go, how did my life turn out that way? It was serendipitous. I was not someone who thought that I would be a dyed-in-the-wool actress. I thought I would be a commercial artist. I didn't plan on any of this. It just sort of happened to me. These different opportunities, as they pop up in people's lives, I always see them as little crossroads. I always took an opportunity even though it was one that I didn't know I was interested in. I just see life as a great adventure. Every day might bring something positive, negative, an opportunity, you just don't know. But taking those chances is what makes a life interesting. I feel so blessed that I've lived such an interesting life. I see it in so many chunks, phases. Having grown up as a middle-class, midwestern girl in Michigan to going to college one year, dropping out, becoming a trade show model to somebody saying, 'Let's go to New York and we can be models!' Then having that work, to living in New York, becoming successful, and then going, 'Wow. Maybe I could do Broadway musicals,' and starting to study for that, and then getting that opportunity, and then, bam, getting this opportunity. It's really just kind of 'go for it' in your life, whatever it is."

Mork & Mindy earned high acclaim for innovative and exciting casting, an interesting premise, and extremely fascinating storylines. For Pam Dawber, *Mork & Mindy*'s contribution to television is more focused. "The discovery of Robin Williams," says the actress. "There hadn't been anything like that since the discovery of Jonathan Winters."

Chapter 9

As *Mork & Mindy* was gearing up at Paramount Television, another potential hit series was in the making. It wasn't a Garry Marshall show, but it certainly wasn't lacking in creative brilliance. This time the talent was coming from MTM Productions. For Paramount Television's other new comedy show, the key elements would be James L. Brooks, Stan Daniels, David Davis, and Ed. Weinberger. Creative producers and directors, exemplary writers, and an outstanding ensemble cast would come together for an innovative approach to the television sitcom. It was called *Taxi*.

James L. Brooks knew quality television. Born in Brooklyn, New York on May 9, 1940, Brooks attended New York University and began his television career working at CBS Television Sports. He also worked as a free-lance writer at this time and wrote for the series *My Three Sons* and *The Andy Griffith Show*. Brooks found a career in television intriguing and decided to stay in the field and explore his options. He transferred to CBS News, where he worked from 1964 to 1966. In 1967 Brooks relocated to Los Angeles to become a documentary writer and producer for David L. Wolper.

By 1968 Brooks had formed a partnership with Allan Burns. Burns was born in Baltimore, Maryland, and attended the University of

Oregon. He moved to Los Angeles in 1956 to pursue a career as a commercial artist and cartoonist. By 1962 Burns was working on the cartoon series *Rocky and His Friends* and *The Bullwinkle Show*. His partnership with Chris Hayward resulted in the creation of the hit series *The Munsters*. Burns was also working as head writer on *Get Smart* and the series *He and She*, which starred Richard Benjamin and Paula Prentiss.

Jim Brooks developed an idea for an atypical type of television series, and Allan Burns liked the pilot Brooks had outlined. Soon Brooks and Burns were receiving well-earned attention for their creation of the new television drama *Room 222*, which focused on a black high school teacher. *Room 222* addressed social issues with a convincing cast in stars Lloyd Haynes, Denise Nichols, and Michael Constantine. In 1969 the show won an Emmy as Outstanding New Series, and James L. Brooks was on the map.

Grant Tinker enjoyed a career as an executive with NBC in radio and programming, and he was married to the talented Mary Tyler Moore, who had co-starred on television's popular *The Dick Van Dyke Show*. Moore and Tinker received a thirteen-week commitment from CBS for a show that would display Moore's talent and exhibit the appeal she had demonstrated through her role as Van Dyke's wife, Laurie Petrie. Tinker formed MTM Productions with the idea that, in addition to Moore, he would hire and encourage other stellar creative talent. It was a perfect home for Brooks and Burns. Tinker asked them to develop a series they would call *The Mary Tyler Moore Show*.

Brooks and Burns's first thought was to make the Mary Richards character a recently divorced working woman. The network executives wanted no part of that idea. They didn't think the television audience would accept a divorcee. Mary Richards's martial status was changed to that of a single girl coming off a failed dating relationship. The premise worked, and the rest, as they say, is history. *The Mary Tyler Moore Show* was a legendary hit series.

Jim Brooks and Allan Burns developed a host of successful shows out of MTM Productions, including spin-offs from *The Mary Tyler Moore Show* that included *Rhoda* and *Lou Grant*. The talented duo was not alone in their creativity. There was a new breed of television writers and producers, called the "auteur producers," who were developing their ideas at MTM. The series that MTM produced were not created, then left to their own devices by the producers. The shows were nurtured by the creative involvement of the minds that had conceived them. These programs were character-driven, rather than focusing on the usual domestic or situation background. Brooks's approach to television included the belief that the writers of the show are just as important as the actors. Brooks excelled at presenting ensemble comedy. The characters he featured were friends and co-workers developing as individuals in the real world. While the premise was similar to *Laverne & Shirley,* the comedies created at MTM took the buddy system a step further by adding to the mix individuals with very different backgrounds. This new approach to comedy was as issue-driven as other shows of the time, but motivated by human foibles.

With so many different types of characters, along with the intricacies of their back stories, several writers were needed to guide character development. Chief among the writers and producers nurtured by MTM was Ed. Weinberger, who had a solid background in comedy, having written for nightclub performers. Specializing in monologues, he wrote for comedians Johnny Carson and Bob Hope and for *The Dean Martin Show.* Brooks and Allen Burns became familiar with Weinberger's work when they were exposed to a film script Weinberger had written that was

Members of the cast celebrate the 100th episode of *Taxi.* Top (left to right): J. Alan Thomas (Jeff), Marilu Henner (Elaine), Tony Danza (Tony), Judd Hirsch (Alex). Bottom (left to right): Christopher Lloyd (Jim), Danny DeVito (Louie). Photo courtesy of Globe Photos, Inc.

similar in tone to *The Mary Tyler Moore Show*. After *The Dick Van Dyke Show* writer Jerry Belson left *The Mary Tyler Moore Show* to become involved in film, Brooks and Burns hired Weinberger as a writer during the second year of the show. While working on *The Dean Martin Show*, Ed. Weinberger partnered with another creative force in writer Stan Daniels. Weinberger and Daniels together created and produced the MTM series *Phyllis*, *Doc*, and *The Betty White Show*.

David Davis was another innovative writer who also wrote for *The Mary Tyler Moore Show*. Davis created the hit MTM series *The Bob Newhart Show* and also wrote for *Rhoda*. Davis was the son of comedy writer Paul Davis and attended UCLA with thoughts of becoming an editor or director. He served as apprentice on *The Many Loves of Dobie Gillis* and wrote scripts for *The Glen Campbell Goodtime Hour* and *Love, American Style*. Jim Brooks liked Davis's work and brought him onboard as a MTM producer.

James L. Brooks, executive producer of *Taxi*, 1983. Photo courtesy of Globe Photos, Inc.

By 1977 Paramount Television was looking in the direction of Jim Brooks, Ed. Weinberger, Stan Daniels, and David Davis. Paramount was anxious for more hit series but wanted to expand beyond the offerings of Garry Marshall and company. Brooks had tried his luck at film-writing with *Thursday's Game*, starring Bob Newhart, Gene Wilder, Cloris Leachman, and Ellen Burstyn. The film ended up as a television movie. Brooks was keeping an eye out for new adventures in television and film.

Along with Jim Brooks, Weinberger, Davis, and Daniels agreed that their creative talents might be better served if they were to leave MTM to form their own, smaller production company. It was time to confront new challenges. The quartet was having a hard time coming up with a name for their new company when Weinberger saw a sign from an English pub in a Los Angeles antique shop. The pub was called the Charles Walters. The name sounded good to the producers as a tag for their new company, but there was already a director working in Hollywood named Charles Walters (he had directed *High Society*, *Gigi*, *The Unsinkable Molly Brown*, and other hit movies). They added the name John and formed the John Charles Walters Company.

Jim Brooks was a client of Gary Nardino's talent agency back when Nardino was involved in that business. Nardino knew Weinberger from *The Tonight Show Starring Johnny Carson*. When Michael Eisner resigned as head of programming for ABC to become president of Paramount and appointed Nardino president of Paramount Television, the two men discussed the talents of Brooks and Weinberger. Eisner told Nardino that one of the first things he wanted to do in his new position was bring the guys from MTM, especially Jim Brooks, to Paramount Television.

The first venture of the John Charles Walters Company was a television musical titled *Cindy* that aired on March 24, 1978. The setting was Harlem during World War II, and the movie starred Clifton Davis and Charlayne Woodard. Written and produced by Brooks, Weinberger, Daniels, and Davis, the plot featured the Cinderella story but modernized the fairy tale by the use of a contemporary setting and a cast that was black. Even though the movie didn't receive sizable ratings, ABC gave the John Charles Walters Company an on-air commitment of thirteen episodes for whatever series the producers wanted to do. Neither a pilot nor a look at the script was required by the network.

Jerry Belson had previously mentioned to Jim Brooks an article he had seen in *New York* magazine about a group of cabdrivers employed by a New York cab company. The drivers were pursuing other careers while they drove cabs for the money they needed to get by. The article, "Night-

Shifting for the Hip Fleet," written by Mark Jacobson, was published in the September 22, 1975, issue of the magazine and featured the Dover Taxi Garage #2 at Hudson and Charles Streets in Greenwich Village. Based in that garage, actors, writers, college professors, and others worked as cabdrivers while they pursued their dream occupations.

Belson, Brooks, and Davis optioned the story for possible use by MTM. When Belson left MTM and Brooks and Davis formed the John Charles Walters Company with Weinberger and Daniels, the producers approached MTM head Grant Tinker about buying the option for the story for the original price paid. (Tinker later said that the option had run out, and Brooks took the project and never paid Tinker. Brooks and Davis remember it otherwise. Either way, there appears to be no hard feelings.) Mark Jacobson believes the original option paid was around $500. When Brooks left MTM, he and Davis called Jacobsen to re-option the piece. When Jacobson balked at the original number now that the story was going to be the basis for a television series, Ed. Weinberger agreed to give Jacobson $350 for each airing of a new episode and a script-writing arrangement. Jacobson agreed.

Things were now in place with the John Charles Walters Company and ABC, and Paramount Television was delighted to join the new venture. The new series would be called *Taxi*. When the story was with MTM, the series had been envisioned as a one-camera, videotaped show. With Paramount now involved with John Charles Walters, it became a four-camera shoot on film.

In early 1978, the producers scouted both the Dover Taxi Garage and another cab company called Ding-a-Ling, which was also located in New York City. During the visit, fictional characters started to form in the heads of the writers as they observed the comings and goings of the various employees. As Jim Brooks watched the company operations, one of the cabbies tried to bribe the dispatcher in order to be assigned to a certain cab. The dispatcher saw Brooks watching and waved the money away. Brooks said later that was when the character Louie De Palma was born. The writers were also told about one particular driver who was extremely well-liked and hardworking. All the drivers wanted to be friends with this individual. This guy was unique because, while the other drivers were constantly talking about what they wanted to do with their lives other than drive a cab, he was heard to often state that he was "just a cabbie." Enter Alex Reiger. Reiger would be *Taxi*'s main character, a man who was a career cabdriver. Along with the devious dispatcher, the other characters would be those who aspired to other careers.

The face of the fictional taxi garage was in place. Brooks, Weinberger, and Daniels pitched *Taxi* to ABC President of Entertainment Tony Thomopolus, and they were given the green light. The deal actually called for three series that would later include *The Associates* and *Best of the West*, but in the meantime *Taxi* was the focus.

While *Taxi* centered on a working-class profession, the characters were almost sophisticated in their different approaches to life. The study of each individual's dreams and personality made for intricate character exploration, but at the same time simple comedy. The storylines that would be developed would not be yuk-based but rather an opportunity for the viewing audience to identify and sympathize with the characters as they developed their life plans and interacted with one another. There was much work to be done to launch the series, and the extended production team and cast would reflect the high standards of those who founded the John Charles Walters Company.

Glen and Les Charles were brothers pursuing their own dream. Born to Mormon parents and raised near Las Vegas, Nevada, the Charleses knew how to relate to complexities such as those the *Taxi* stories would explore. Glen and Les both received liberal arts degrees at the University of Redlands near Los Angeles. Glen used his education to become a schoolteacher, while Les attended law school and earned his living as an advertising copywriter. The brothers loved television and wrote a script for *The Mary Tyler Moore Show*. They submitted it to MTM but didn't receive a reply. Undaunted, they wrote episodes of several other of their favorite television shows and submitted the scripts to the various producers. The Charles brothers both quit their jobs to pursue careers in screenwriting, although they had yet to sell a script. They were confident that realizing their dream was just a matter of time. Les and his wife were living out of their van when word came that the brothers had sold a script to the producers of *M*A*S*H*. They were excited that someone finally agreed they had talent, but the Charles brothers went another couple of years without selling another script. Then the day they had been waiting for arrived. The MTM producers had uncovered Les and Glen's original *Mary Tyler Moore Show* script and wanted to know if they would like to come to work for the show *Phyllis*. The brothers worked first as story editors on *Phyllis* but were so talented that they were soon writing and producing for *The Bob Newhart Show*. While at MTM, they formed a friendship with James Brooks, and when Brooks and his friends left to create John Charles Walters, Les and Glen were asked to join the *Taxi* team as writers and co-producers.

Another person who became an important part of the *Taxi* creative ensemble was director James Burrows. Entertainment was in his blood. Burrows was born on December 30, 1940, in Los Angeles to legendary writer Abe Burrows. Although the senior Burrows had written for *The Milton Berle Show* and radio's *Duffy's Tavern*, he was best known for writing the books for the Broadway productions *Guys and Dolls*, *Can Can*, and *How to Succeed in Business Without Really Trying*, for which he won a Pulitzer Prize, with Frank Loesser. James Burrows was more interested in television and film, and he received a B.A. from Oberlin College and an M.F.A. from Yale. In 1966 Burrows was the assistant stage manager on his father's musical *Holly Golightly*, starring Mary Tyler Moore. Through Moore, Burrows met Grant Tinker. When Burrows asked Tinker for a job in 1974, Tinker thought that the younger Burrows likely had talent. Burrows was told to observe the directors on MTM's shows and see what he could pick up. Burrows was a constant on the set of *The Bob Newhart Show*, and Tinker soon teamed him with director Jay Sandrich so that he could further study the craft. Burrows directed episodes of not only *The Bob Newhart Show* but also *The Mary Tyler Moore Show*, *Rhoda*, *Phyllis*, and *Lou Grant*.

Brooks, Weinberger, Davis, and Daniels thought that Jim Burrows had the perfect sensibility to direct their new series. He was also familiar with the Paramount lot as he had directed several episodes of *Laverne & Shirley*. Burrows was happy to direct *Taxi*—he knew the writing would be top-notch. (Danny DeVito would nickname Burrows "Beads" because he would look upon the set with beady-eyed intensity. By the end of Burrow's tenure on *Taxi* most of the cast members were calling him by that name.)

Jim Burrows would be one of the first television directors to use four cameras simultaneously as he directed the complicated *Taxi* ensemble. Before that entry into television history could be made, though, he needed a cast to direct. Casting the perfect actors to bring the *Taxi* ensemble to life was tricky. The producers began their casting process with the man they envisioned as their lead. The character Alex Reiger anchored the rest of the drivers in the garage and was an important element to the plotline. The producers thought immediately of an actor named Judd Hirsch to fill the role.

Judd Hirsch had been appearing in Neil Simon's play *Chapter Two* on Broadway when the *Taxi* producers first thought of him as a possibility for the role of Alex. He had starred in the Emmy-winning movie *The Law*, which was the first made-for-television lawyer movie. Hirsch appeared in a handful of movies and television shows and, likely on the basis of his appearance in *The Law*, was awarded the lead in the series *Delvecchio*. *Delvecchio* wasn't a rousing success, and Hirsch really wasn't thrilled to be doing episodic television. Hirsch's work had impressed Brooks, Weinberger, Davis, and Daniels, and they believed the somber actor would make a perfect career cabbie for their new show. ABC didn't think casting Hirsch in the role of Alex would work. They felt the actor was too solemn in appearance. The network suggested that actor Cliff Gorman might be better cast. (Ironically, Gorman was currently appearing with Judd Hirsch in *Chapter Two*. Regardless of what the network thought, Gorman wasn't interested in taking the role.)

Taxi's casting director, Joel Thurm, had his work cut out for him. Several actors were called in to read for the role of Alex—including Barry Newman, Jeffrey Tambor, and Hector Elizondo—but the producers balked at hiring any of them, thinking that they didn't radiate the complexity of their anchor character. John Charles Walters continued to push for the casting of Judd Hirsch, and finally the network relented and agreed. Before the producers could breathe a sigh of relief, Judd Hirsch had second thoughts about taking the role he was now offered. Hirsch felt that after the disappointment of *Delvecchio* it was too soon for him to return to a television series. He apparently started to change his mind when all three of his co-stars in *Chapter Two* were nominated for a Tony Award and he was not. Yet Hirsch continued to have reservations about signing on to *Taxi*. He instructed his agent to give the producers a monetary figure they wouldn't be likely to accept. Brooks and Weinberger were sold on Hirsch and asked for additional money from both ABC and Paramount Television to make the deal happen. Eventually both entities kicked in the money needed, and John Charles Walters could meet Hirsch's offer. He was hired.

Judd Hirsch is as complex a person as his character Alex Reiger. A native of the Bronx, New York City, Hirsch was born on March 15, 1935, to Joseph Stanley and Sally Hirsch. Because Hirsch is notoriously private, dislikes the Hollywood publicity machine, and is a bit suspect about people's intentions, not much is known about the early years of his life. Hirsch attended DeWitt Clinton High School, then City College of New York, where he studied engineering and physics. He soon transferred to Cooper Union College to study architecture. Hirsch developed an interest in theater and decided to study acting at the American Academy of Dramatic Arts. While attending the AADA, Hirsch worked as a driver, busboy, and law office clerk. During this time he answered an ad looking for someone to drive a New York taxicab to Colorado. Once there, he decided he liked the area and joined a Colorado stock company. Hirsch was soon back in New York, however, where he made his 1966 Broadway debut in *Barefoot in the Park*. He also worked with New York's Circle Repertory Theater. After *Barefoot in the Park* the actor worked off-Broadway and was soon employed to work in television commercials for Listerine and American Airlines. Then came *The Law*, which had failed to launch as an ongoing series. In 1976 Hirsch signed to play the lead character on *Delvecchio*. After the cancellation of that series, he returned to Broadway, taking a role in Jules Feiffer's *Knock Knock*, for which he won a Drama Desk Award.

Because of all the hoopla, Judd Hirsch was actually not the first person to be cast for *Taxi*. That honor would go to a relatively unknown actor named Danny DeVito. Joel Thurm had met DeVito when Thurm was casting the series *Starsky & Hutch*. Thurm didn't cast DeVito in that series and was initially hesitant to cast the actor for *Taxi*. James Brooks was not as indecisive. Brooks later said that Danny DeVito had the part from the minute he came into the casting room. DeVito attracted the attention of the producers in a unique way. He entered the room where the producers were meeting actors and made some initial small talk. When given the script and asked to read, DeVito looked at the script and then back to the producers. "One thing I wanna know before we start is," said DeVito, "who wrote this shit?!" There was silence in the room, and then the producers began to laugh, uproariously. Danny DeVito was the Louie De Palma they had envisioned. DeVito was cast. Joel Thurm later said that DeVito doing the reading in character was really taking a gamble, as most actors who do so can't make it work. DeVito was the exception. Thurm later said that when he first saw the dailies with DeVito, all of his earlier reservations vanished, and he thought DeVito was "simply wonderful."

Danny DeVito was one of the few actors associated with Paramount Television sitcoms at this time who was not a native New Yorker, but he was close: he grew up in Asbury Park, New Jersey. Daniel Michael DeVito was born on November 17, 1944, in Neptune, New Jersey, to Chet and Julia DeVito. As a young man DeVito served as an altar boy at Our Lady of Mount Carmel. He attended Asbury Park High School and graduated from Oratory Prep School. DeVito always liked to have fun and engaged in pranks with his schoolmates. He loved jokes and all the various forms of comedy. While at Oratory Prep, DeVito decided to try his luck at drama. He was cast as Saint Francis of Assisi in one of the school's plays. Young Danny had found his calling. DeVito's father, Chet, was an entrepreneur who operated a pool hall and a luncheonette. Chet supported his son when Danny announced that he'd like to pursue acting as a career.

Chet told Danny that, if that was what he thought would make him happy, it was worth taking a shot. DeVito entered the American Academy of Dramatic Arts in Manhattan.

While attending the 1966 Playwrights Conference in Connecticut, Danny DeVito became friendly with Michael Douglas, the son of actor Kirk Douglas. Douglas was working as a carpenter as he waited to appear in some of the conference's plays. The two young actors found they had a lot in common. They both loved acting, motorcycles, and New York City nightlife. After his summer in Connecticut, DeVito decided to try his luck in Hollywood. He read for one of the lead roles in the film *In Cold Blood* but lost out to actor Robert Blake. By 1969 he was back in New York, rooming with Michael Douglas as they pursued their acting careers. Another roommate at this time was fledgling actress Rhea Perlman. Perlman and DeVito became romantically involved while they were appearing in Joseph Papp–produced Shakespeare productions.

DeVito, who continued to do regional theater, appeared with Judd Hirsch in a Philadelphia production of *The Line of Least Existence*. In 1971 DeVito took the role of Anthony Martini in the off-Broadway production of *One Flew Over the Cuckoo's Nest* and began to receive some notice. When DeVito's friend Michael Douglas decided to produce the play as a film, DeVito was again cast in the role of Martini. In 1976 DeVito and Rhea Perlman relocated to Los Angeles, where DeVito received roles in such films as *Hurry Up, or I'll Be 30* and *Lady Liberty*. DeVito also appeared in the Kirk Douglas movie *Scalawag*, with Michael Douglas. Then came the *Taxi* casting call.

The next character the producers were able to cast was that of the sole female driver at the garage. Elaine Nardo was first written as a thirty-three-year-old, Italian, single mother with a twelve-year-old daughter. More than three dozen actresses read for the role, including Shelley Long, who would later figure prominently in the future of Paramount Television. The producers liked Long, but casting director Joel Thurm thought her perhaps too docile to play the role of the feisty Nardo. None of the actresses who read was jumping out at the producers as suitable for their needs. Red-headed Marilu Henner had been working on Broadway and in television. The producers liked the fact that when Henner came in to read she gave off the feeling of being one of the guys. That was the type of personality they were looking for in the Nardo character. Yet still they were unsure. Henner read three times before telling the producers that they had better make up their minds one way or another because she was running out of outfits to wear to the auditions. Thurm thought Henner would do an excellent job, but the others continued to waver. Thurm finally told the producers that they had better commit to casting Henner if they thought they wanted her; he was afraid they would lose her to another role if they didn't make up their minds. Henner had done a pilot of a potential television series called *The Paper Chase* that looked like it was going to be green-lighted by CBS. Henner's striking, red-haired good looks might have influenced the *Taxi* executives to hire her for the role of Nardo, but it was her talent to easily roll with the punches among actors as flexible as DeVito that sold them on her talent. The producers finally agreed that Marilu Henner was their Nardo. Elaine Nardo's ethnicity was changed to Irish.

Although Marilu Henner's hair color would imply she is Irish, she is in fact Polish-Greek. Henner was born on April 6, 1952, in Chicago to Joseph and Loretta Henner. Her mother owned a dancing school located at the back of the family's home, and Marilu began dance lessons when she was only two and a half years old. While attending parochial school, she won a scholarship as Illinois' Outstanding Teenager, presented by the Outstanding American Youth Foundation. Henner used the scholarship to attend the University of Chicago, where she studied political science. During college she served as a choreographer for the Center Stage Group and also appeared in college and community theater productions.

When Jim Jacobs wrote and produced the musical *Grease* in Chicago, Henner was cast in the role of Marty. When the play relocated to New York City, Henner stayed behind to continue her studies at the University of Chicago. Jacobs was a huge fan of Marilu's work in *Grease* and finally convinced Henner to join the touring company of the play. After a year with *Grease*, Henner was cast in the Broadway production of *Over There*, with the Andrews Sisters. She relocated to New York City to continue her work in the theater. She was soon cast in *Pal Joey* and eventually went back to her role of Marty in the Broadway production of *Grease*. Henner also found work doing television commercials for products such as Fruit of the Loom, Samsonite, Schlitz Beer, and other national brands. She received a Clio nomination for an Exxon Bicentennial Moment. Henner made her film debut in *Between the Lines* as a topless dancer and then did *Bloodbrothers*, with Richard Gere. She relocated to Los Angeles and landed a panelist position on the game show *The Match Game*.

Joel Thurm liked Marilu Henner's energy, and the producers of *Taxi* had no problem adjusting the role of Elaine Nardo to better fit the actress. Although she says that comedy is hard for her as an actor, the character Nardo as performed by Henner was everything the producers had hoped it would be. Marilu comfortably fit right in with the male cast members and made the role her own.

The development of the character Phil Ryan wasn't as easy. Phil Ryan had originally been envisioned as an Irish boxer who knew little about anything outside the ring. Actor Charles Haid, who would later become known for his excellent work on *Hill Street Blues* and as a director, was one of those who read for the part. The role of Ryan had yet to be filled when producer Stuart Sheslow brought a young man by the name of Tony Danza to the attention of *Taxi*'s producers. Danza was a middle-weight boxer who had been recruited by Sheslow from the Gramercy Gym in Manhattan to appear in a boxing movie he had planned. The movie never came to fruition, but when Sheslow moved to a position with ABC-TV he signed Danza for a pilot called "Fast Lane Blues." The pilot didn't sell, so Danza auditioned for a role in the feature film *The Warriors*. Around this same time Sheslow suggested Tony Danza for the Phil Ryan role. Jim Brooks went to New York to screen-test the young boxer. Brooks and the other *Taxi* producers decided they liked Danza's puppy-dog quality. They changed Phil Ryan to Phil Banta to make the Irish character Italian and better suited to Tony Danza. Elaine Nardo and Phil Ryan would simply switch ethnic identities. In a move to further identify the character with the actor, the character's name was changed to Tony Banta.

Antonio Salvatore Iadanza was a Brooklyn native, born on April 21, 1951, to parents Matty and Ann Iadanza. His father was a sanitation worker, and Danza learned the value of hard work and family support early in his life. Danza was an all-American boy who enjoyed baseball, football, and wrestling. He was *very* good at wrestling and managed to win a wrestling scholarship to attend the University of Dubuque. Danza met a young woman named Rhonda Yeoman while at college and was married by the time he was eighteen years old. The couple soon had a son named Marc Anthony (who would appear on *Taxi* a few times himself as a child).

Danza earned a degree in education and social studies at Dubuque but found himself missing life in New York City. After returning to his hometown, he worked as a bartender and even bought a carwash with a group of friends. His parents talked him out of taking a job as a cab-driver as they thought it was too dangerous. Danza wasn't content with his life as it was, but he really didn't have a direction. Then one day some friends talked Danza into entering a Golden Gloves competition. He won seven out of the nine fights he entered in 1975. Danza would later say he was never a serious boxer despite winning most of the matches in which he competed.

While Danza was working out in the Gramercy Gym in Manhattan, producer Stuart Sheslow asked him if he would like to do a screen test for a boxing movie he was involved with called "Augie." The movie never came to fruition, but Sheslow liked the young man and was able to help him obtain a role in the television pilot "Fast Lane Blues," which was being shot in Los Angeles. After the pilot failed to sell, Danza again returned to New York City, and Sheslow sponsored Danza to read for Walter Hill's *The Warriors*. Danza was intimidated by the director and didn't feel confident about his acting skills. He invited Hill to attend one of his fights in order to show the director who Tony Danza really was. Hill was present on a night when Danza knocked out his opponent and told Danza he could have the role of Cowboy in the film. During this time Jim Brooks was looking at the young actor for the role of Phil Ryan on *Taxi*. Danza was offered the Ryan role while he was on the Paramount lot for costume fittings for his role in *The Warriors*. The role of Cowboy was eventually brought to the screen by Tom McKitterick, as Danza decided to go with the series.

Two final roles of the ensemble were left to be cast: Bobby Taylor and John Burns. (Alex Reiger was first called Alex Taylor. Bobby Taylor was changed to Bobby Wheeler, and *none* of the characters ended up with the name Taylor. Some of the names of the *Taxi* characters were the names of real people who were associated with the show. Elaine Nardo was named after assistant Patricia Nardo, Tony Banta after writer Gloria Banta, and Bobby Wheeler after assistant Donna Wheeler.)

An actor named Jeff Conaway read for the role of John Burns, as did Brian Kerwin. The producers didn't like Conaway for the role of Burns, but they *did* like him for the role of aspiring actor Bobby Wheeler. Conaway had worked as a child actor and model, and he played the lead role of Danny Zuko in *Grease* on Broadway. In the meantime, he had appeared in a *Mary Tyler Moore* episode and was quite taken by the creative people behind the hit series. He wanted to work with them again. Conaway heard about the formation of the John Charles Walters Company and the company's first production. He asked his agent to set up a meeting with them to see if he could land a role on *Taxi*. Thinking that his reputation as a good actor had preceded him, Conaway was surprised when he showed up for the meeting and Jim Brooks stuck his head out the door to ask him to be patient. Brooks said that the part Conaway was to read for was being written on the spot. Conaway didn't know he was going to actually *read* for a role. He thought he was just meeting the producers to *talk* about a role.

After he read for the character John Burns, Conaway got his hands on the entire script. He then decided that he would be better suited to the role of Bobby. The producers were thinking in a different direction at that point. When Conaway talked to Joel Thurm about the possibility of being hired for Bobby, Thurm told him that they were considering making the character Bobby a black man and were now seeing some black actors. Cleavon Little was being considered for the role. Finally the producers decided that Jeff Conaway would be better in the role, after all, and so he was cast.

Jeff Conaway had come to Los Angeles also via New York City. He was born there on October 5, 1950, the youngest of three children. His father was an actor and producer and his mother an actress. Conaway's parents were divorced by the time he was three years old, and his mother taught at New York's Brook Conservatory. As a child, Conaway wanted to be an astronaut. That all changed when he was ten years old and accompanied his mother to a reading for *All the Way Home*, a play being produced by Arthur Penn. There were roles for little boys in the play, and Conaway was awarded one. He was with the play for a year. The next step in the development of the young actor's career was joining the national touring company of *Critic's Choice*. He also worked as a child model while attending the Quantico School for Young Professionals. When he was fifteen, Conaway formed a rock band with friends called $3^1/_2$, and the band opened for local shows, including one headlined by Chuck Berry. Continuing his education, Conaway entered North Carolina School for the Arts but soon transferred to New York University so he could study with Martha Graham, among others. He continued to do plays and commercials and eventually landed the role in *Grease*. (John Travolta, who would go on to play the Danny Zuko role in the movie *Grease* while Conaway moved to the role of Kenickie for the film, was also in the Broadway production. Travolta appeared in the chorus as Doodie. The talent of another Paramount Television show is connected to the movie. Henry Winkler was offered the role of Danny Zuko but turned it down because he didn't want to be typecast.) Conaway made his feature-film debut in 1971 in *Jennifer on My Mind*, with Tippy Walker. He appeared in *The Eagle Has Landed*, *I Never Promised You a Rose Garden*, and several other films prior to the movie version of *Grease* in 1978.

The role of John Burns would not go to Jeff Conaway, but rather to a young actor named Randall Carver. Carver would be the only actor in the *Taxi* cast besides Judd Hirsch who had been in a television series. At first look, Joel Thurm didn't think Carver was right for the role. Carver's agents pursued the possibility, and Thurm agreed to let the actor read. It was about a month and a half before Carver finally got the part. "I auditioned and auditioned, and it finally got to the point where, gosh, if these people don't make up their minds soon, I'm going to go crazy," says

Carver. "Eventually they did make up their mind, and everything worked out real well."

The character John Burns is not a native of New York City but rather has re-located to the Big Apple. Randy Carver isn't from New York City either. He was born in Fort Worth, Texas, on May 25, 1948, and adopted by Russell and Virginia Carver, who lived in Canadian, Texas. Carver's father owned an International Harvester dealership and later went into banking. Exposure to the theater came early for Carver. He learned to read while helping his mother run lines for dramatic productions. Carver's first experience in acting was a community theater production of *Rest Assured*. After graduating from the Missouri Military Academy, where he was a member of the Dramateers, Carver was signed for a one-line role in the John Schlesinger film *Midnight Cowboy*. He continued his studies at West Texas State University, where he received a degree in theater. Carver joined the Army and was stationed first at Fort Knox, and then Fort Hood; finally he was stationed for two years in the DMZ in Korea, where he was a tank platoon leader. When he was discharged from the Army, Carver was accepted for graduate studies in the Theater Arts program at UCLA. Resuming his acting career, Carver was cast as the lead in the feature film *Time to Run*, with Ed Nelson. His first television role was in the series *Room 222*. Carver hit pay dirt when he was cast in the oddball hit television series *Mary Hartman, Mary Hartman* as Jeffrey DeVito.

"I played a nice guy," Carver remembers. "He was a member of a Mafia family and he tried to go straight. They kept pulling him back in. I was eventually killed off by Vincent Schiavelli. He injected me in the neck and killed me, then sold me for body parts. That's how they got rid of me. I was the only guy Cathy (played by Debralee Scott) had married, so they had to think of a big finish for me."

Now Randy Carver was playing John Burns, who had just moved to the big city. "*Taxi* gave me invaluable experience," says Carver. "I got to work with the best in the business at that time." Some of the cast had solid experience, and others were new to the game, but all were unique individuals, much the same as the characters they would play.

Speaking of unique individuals, the final cast member to be signed to *Taxi* was someone upon whom a role was based, rather than casting an actor to fit a role that was already written. Andy Kaufman was a performance artist working the comedy club circuit. His character "Foreign Man" was a routine Kaufman performed to rope the audience into dramatic reactions. Those watching Kaufman's character would squirm in embarrassment as the man with the foreign accent, who was obviously an amateur comedian who didn't understand American humor, would tell jokes that weren't funny and would grow increasingly upset when he delivered bomb after bomb. "Foreign Man" would start to apologize for his clueless lack of entertainment. He would start to cry, causing the audience to become even more uncomfortable. Then Kaufman would start banging on conga drums until he had a rhythm going and the act turned into a completely different performance that the audience could get behind.

Someone told James Brooks and Ed. Weinberger about Andy Kaufman's strange act, and they went down to the Comedy Club on the Sunset Strip to see it for themselves. Tony Clifton, Andy Kaufman's alter ego, was the opening act. Clifton was the stereotypical smarmy Vegas lounge act of the fifties, but with a crusty and offensive manner. Brooks and Weinberger, as was the case with most if not all of the audience, didn't realize that Clifton and Kaufman were one and the same until someone told them that was the case. The two producers thought they were pretty sophisticated when it came to comedy, and when they heard that Kaufman had fooled them they were excited. The *Taxi* producers loved Kaufman's "Foreign Man" and eagerly wrote a character named Latka Gravas based on "Foreign Man." But before Latka could come to life there was the matter of signing Kaufman to a contract.

Andy Kaufman was hesitant to do series television but finally agreed only if a couple of conditions could be met. One was that the *Taxi* producers also sign Tony Clifton, whom Kaufman presented as a completely different entity, to a contract to appear on the show as well. Kaufman insisted that he and Clifton were not the same person. Finding the ruse amusing, Brooks and Weinberger agreed to a contract whereby Clifton would appear in one or two episodes. The agreements for Tony Clifton and Andy Kaufman were two separate contracts. Kaufman's was more complicated. Kaufman agreed to sign on to the show only if it was agreed that he would appear in just thirteen episodes a season. Further, he would rehearse only two days a week during those episodes and could use a stand-in the other days of the week. The producers agreed. "Foreign Man" was just too funny to lose to particulars and strange demands. Brooks figured that what the producers at John Charles Walters had in mind appealed to Kaufman's artistry. The fact that they were willing to sign both actors (Kaufman and Clifton) was probably the reason Kaufman agreed to come to the series. The creators made room on *Taxi* and rounded out the character Latka in a way that was specifically suited to Kaufman's humor.

Andrew Geoffrey Kaufman was the oldest of three children born to wealthy parents, Janice and Stanley Kaufman, on January 17, 1949. While growing up in Great Neck, Long Island, Kaufman realized that his approach to humor was certainly different from others'. As a young boy, Andy was constantly telling jokes and performing tricks. He began entertaining at other children's parties for free at the age of eight, and by the age of fourteen he was being hired as a paid performer. When he was fourteen, Kaufman, his father, and brother went to see the championship wrestling match between Nature Boy Rogers and Bruno Sammartino, and Andy was so impressed he started to consider a career as a professional wrestler. Kaufman wrote poetry and by the age of sixteen had completed a novel titled "The Hollering Mangoo." After graduation from high school, Kaufman was adrift. He would later say that he was labeled 4-F after scoring 0 on the Selective Service Psychology test and that he received a deferment that kept him from having to serve in Vietnam. Kaufman started using drugs, drinking, and hanging out with unmotivated losers. He eventually enrolled at Graham Junior College in Boston to study radio and television. While there he wrote, produced, and starred in the campus television production *Uncle Andy's Funhouse*. (The "funhouse" would later be revisited by Kaufman for a 1979 ABC special.)

In 1969 the ever-adventurous Kaufman decided that he *had* to meet his hero, Elvis Presley. He hitchhiked to Las Vegas, where he hid in a walk-in cupboard in the kitchen of the Hilton to await Presley's pass-through on his way to the stage. Kaufman surprised Elvis and attempted to give him a copy of a novel he had written about him titled "The King." Elvis patted Andy's shoulder, gave him his blessing, and moved on. While visiting Vegas, Kaufman claimed he met Tony Clifton, a lounge performer. "Clifton" would later play a major role in Andy Kaufman's life. Back in New York, Kaufman graduated from Graham College with an associates degree in applied science.

In the meantime, Kaufman was getting noticed as a performance artist/comedian, most importantly by Improv owner Bud Friedman, who took in his act while Kaufman was performing at My Father's Place on Long Island. Kaufman's approach to "performances" was certainly different from most people's definition of the word. Sometimes he would offer to wrestle women; other times he would crawl into a sleeping bag and "sleep" during his time on-stage. It wasn't unusual for him to go on-stage with a book and read it to the audience. He appeared at comedy clubs in the New York area in the early seventies, and in 1974 a trip to California resulted in an appearance on *The Dean Martin Comedy World*.

In 1975 Andy Kaufman caught the attention of NBC executive Dick Ebersol and was asked to audition for a new television show called *Saturday Night*. That first appearance on what would come to be known as *Saturday Night Live* featured Kaufman's conga act and a very strange rendering of the theme from the cartoon series *Mighty Mouse*. Kaufman returned to *Saturday Night Live* to do "Foreign Man" and a fantastic Elvis impression. He would appear on the show fourteen times. Many other television appearances followed, including *The Merv Griffin Show*, *The Tonight Show Starring Johnny Carson*, and even *Hollywood Squares*, which featured a week-long "Foreign Man" appearance. And then, *Taxi*.

Andy Kaufman joined the *Taxi* cast, along with his "friend" Tony Clifton. (Clifton would play Louie's brother in Episode #10). "I remember that whenever Tony Clifton was going to come on the show, Ed. called the cast together without Andy and said, 'Okay, next week Andy's not going to be on the show,'" says Randy Carver. "'There will be a character cast, but it won't be Andy. You might think it's Andy, but it's not Andy. The name of that person is Tony Clifton. We have a separate contract with Tony Clifton from the one we have with Andy Kaufman, so he is to be treated as Tony.' But he wasn't that specific, he was vaguer than that. So when we got there on Monday morning, [Tony] was there. We had a read-through, and it was okay. He was blustery and kind of a foolish man. Not a very good actor, really. His script reading wasn't very good. That night when I went home I sent a telegram to Tony Clifton at Paramount [to welcome him to the show]. He gets there the next morning and says, 'Who is this Randy Carver here?' I said, 'I am.' He said, 'Did you send me this?' I said. 'I sure did.' He said, 'Thank ya. You're all right.'" Tony Clifton and Andy Kaufman would be a trip.

There had initially been another character considered for the show. This character was written as a black, feisty female driver named Nell. Nell Carter had been one of the actors on *Cindy*, and the role in *Taxi* had been written with her in mind. The casting of Carter didn't come to pass, however, as she was under contract to 20th Century Fox by this time, so the role was written out. The producers did cast a black character in the person of assistant dispatcher Jeff Bennett, who was played by J. Alan Thomas. Also hired was T. J. Castronova, who would play the bartender at Mario's, the cabby's hangout. (Castronova would go on to appear in other television series and to produce the television anthology *Tales from the Dark Side*.)

The vast television experience of the producers and writers made the creation of *Taxi* exciting. "I think the producers did a real good job in casting," says Randy Carver. "They got people they wanted to work with, who could fit the script. I see them as the nucleus of whatever happened with the actors. It was their success as writers, seeing it on the stage and being able to rewrite, see what the little problem was, or, if it's not a problem, just how it can go over better. They were able to see what the actors did when they got on-stage for the rehearsal, and they could see what worked and what didn't work. How things were. It was just their background in television sitcoms. They could just look at something and automatically tell you this, this, and this. If this guy did this, this'll happen. They had that real good overall idea of what was going on."

The actors were very comfortable working with Jim Burrows as director. "Burrows worked with a lot of producers," says Carver. "His directing was so effortless that it seemed like he wasn't really directing. He was just encouraging us. Telling us what's good, how this could be more effective. It didn't seem like he was directorial in attitude. He was more a buddy."

Jim Burrows found the job remarkable, but also a challenge. "I think it was the hardest show I ever had to do because it was the most eclectic bunch of actors I've ever worked with," remembers Burrows. "Definitely not all of them playing in the same field or playing on the same stage or playing the same colors. You had Andy Kaufman, you had Chris Lloyd (who would play Reverend Jim), you had Danny and Judd, and you had Tony, who was green to the acting trade. You had all these different people coming at the center in a different way. Those were difficult times. The set was so big, and the show was so all over the place on the set. Because at that point Ed. and Jim, who created the show, [weren't always around]. Jim was off doing a movie, so Ed. ran the show for a while, then Jim would come back periodically. There was a lot of stuff to put up with. It's amazing that those shows are as good as they are. I don't think I worked harder on a show in my life. And it's a funny show still. I saw it the other night in syndication. It's an amazingly funny show."

Paramount's Stage 25 would be home to *Taxi* that first year, and the final elements of the show were discussed and set. Dave Davis had created the successful opening for *The Bob Newhart Show*, and he was called on to handle the main music and titles. The original idea was to intersperse shots of the cabdrivers talking about what it was like to drive a cab, and those shots would run over and under the opening credits. That idea was dismissed when the producers agreed that the approach was too long and distracting. Instead, the opening would be a shot of Tony Danza driving a cab over the Queensboro Bridge that had been originally shot for the opening of Episode #2. (Tony Danza recounted the opening shot during an interview with *Entertainment Weekly*. He said that as he waited underneath the bridge for his cue, a man got in his cab. When Danza tried to explain that it wasn't a real taxi, the man refused to leave the cab and had to be dragged out by the show's security personnel.)

A mellow Bob James instrumental composition called "Angela" was also to be used for Episode #2, but when James's song "Touchdown" proved to be too inharmonious for the opening shot, "Angela" was chosen to be the *Taxi* theme. Everyone agreed that not only was "Angela" special but it was distinctive and would receive notice from viewers.

Like the Garry Marshall shows that preceded it at Paramount Television, *Taxi* would be shot in front of a live audience. The shoots were mainly on one large set that served as the garage, but also would include the cabdrivers' hangout, Mario's, and occasionally one of the cabby's apartments. The fact that the cabdrivers who would be portrayed on the show worked on the night shift made it easier and cheaper to do moving shots involving the cabs. All that was needed was the shell of the cab without the windshield for filming the cab interiors.

The stage was set. Monday morning was the first read-through of the script. After lunch the writers would bring in their line changes, and the first scene would be blocked. Tuesday morning was reserved for the blocking of the second act. That afternoon would be a complete run-through of that week's story. Wednesday would bring changes in blocking and lines. Thursday would be the final run-through with blocking and cameras. Friday morning would be a complete run-through, with a final run-through in the afternoon. The producers and writers stayed on hand at the run-throughs to offer their suggestions. Jim Burrows told *Entertainment Weekly* in 2004 that the producers would either laugh at the scenes or ask, "What the fuck was that?" At 7:30 P.M. it would be show time. After the audience left, pick-ups were done by the actors, and the cast was usually finished with their work by midnight.

The premiere episode of *Taxi* was titled "Like Father, Like Daughter." The story focused on Alex Reiger reuniting with his long-lost daughter in Florida. The other cabbies were along for the drive to Florida, so the audience met all the characters. The show was written by James Brooks, Stan Daniels, David Davis, and Ed. Weinberger. It was directed by Jim Burrows.

Taxi debuted on September 12, 1978, and was well-received for a new entry into Tuesday night television viewing. It followed ABC's popular show *Three's Company*, which provided a high viewership ripe for the picking. The number of characters featured in *Taxi* and the different tone of the series necessitated that the viewing audience watch more than just the first night to form an educated opinion of the show, so it was strange that the show opened with an episode that focused on the complex emotions of a character the audience had never met. This element made the premiere episode a bit confusing.

The week of *Taxi*'s debut, *Variety* agreed that the show was a flavor that required exposure and time to be appreciated. The review read: "Both the script and the direction in this initial show had a hurried feeling about them as though the producers were afraid that the audience would be bored if the show slowed down." Since Alex was the featured character in that first show, Judd Hirsch was singled out by *Variety* as the star, but the other characters certainly couldn't be ignored. "Hirsch is gruffly sentimental and appealing but the others are such oddballs as to frustrate the audience identification." The review went on to note the "safe berth" provided the new show after *Three's Company* and to suggest that the show was good enough to take the time to develop the other characters.

The *New York Daily News* expected more from the show's producers. They wanted to see more episodes before they would pass judgment. James Wolcott of the *Village Voice* called it "laugh track Eugene O'Neill." *TV Guide* stated, "As a driver, he's unruffled, but as a man, Judd Hirsch looks keenly driven." James Brooks himself didn't think that first show realized *Taxi*'s potential. He feared that if the first episode had been a pilot it might not have been picked up. There was some work to be done to make *Taxi* a stronger show, and the producers, writers, and cast were up for the challenge.

Taxi was more than just a television sitcom. It was more of a morality play. The stories sometimes centered on trivial occurrences either within the garage or as experienced by one of the drivers, and the characters were very real. There was something in Alex, Bobby, Tony, Elaine, John, Latka, and even Louie to which we all could relate. Alex could be self-righteous. Elaine sometimes lost her temper, and John was an eternal optimist. Tony was impulsive, and Bobby was alternately self-centered and needy. Louie, while mostly just plain mean and devious, had a deep-rooted need for acceptance. Latka let it all hang out. All of the characters were capable of making mistakes, but they all went about their lives doing the best they thought they could do. The writers approached their job as writing for the exploration of each individual character and for the group dynamic as a whole.

Many of the episodes written for *Taxi* were based on real-life experiences. One featured Alex having a heart-to-heart conversation with his estranged father in a hospital bed, only to discover that he is talking to the wrong man. Hirsch says that incident came from the real life of producer Jim Brooks. Hirsch told *Entertainment Weekly* that Brooks would think of the most embarrassing scenarios and dare to write them into a *Taxi* episode.

"One of the things I liked about *Taxi* was that it was like an original, very well written one-act play every week with the same characters," remembers Randy Carver. "I really enjoyed that idea a lot, of doing an original piece. It was performed like a play with different scenes. One act was always twenty-five and half minutes long. Friday night was opening night. You would rehearse the piece and then [do it] one time with the audience. Each of those scripts was so well written. If you changed the name and called it something else, you could put in on Broadway as a one-act play."

Gary Nardino continued in his role as head of television production at Paramount. He later wrote in a column for *Daily Variety* that *Taxi* took an ensemble of different characters with conflicting viewpoints and contradictory experiences and placed them in "a microcosm of stark reality." Nardino called *Taxi* weekly human drama.

Taxi began to develop a viewing audience and was well on its way to becoming a hit series. The show's second episode, "Blind Date," which dealt with the handsome, hip Bobby dating an overweight woman, won a Humanitas Prize for its attention to social issues. The episode also received an Emmy nomination for writer Michael Leeson.

"There were a lot of sitcoms on when *Taxi* came on," says Jim Burrows. "You had *Laverne & Shirley* and *Happy Days*, all the Garry Marshall stuff. And *Three's Company*. It was just after *All in the Family*. *Taxi*'s gift was the eclectic bunch of characters gathered in this garage. It was more of a weird ensemble than just a name ensemble like *Cheers* [would be]. You had your Sam Malones [on *Cheers*] and your Alex Reigers, who were kind of the people who tethered everybody. But Alex's group of cabdrivers was much weirder than the group of layabouts in *Cheers*. *Taxi*'s gift was the ability to kind of tell these strange stories and make them real."

During their off hours the *Taxi* cast got along better than many expected. They were actors who had come from a variety of experiences, just like their characters on the show. Because of his character or because those in the know were influenced by his resume, Judd Hirsch seemed to be the star of the show. At least Hirsch was the most recognized by television viewers. Jeff Conaway, on the other hand, had starred in the recent hit movie *Grease*. Conaway was under the impression that *he* was the star of the show or was at the least on an equal footing with Hirsch. If there was resentment against Hirsch's position other than from Conaway, from whom the posturing was nothing against Hirsch personally, it didn't show. Marilu Henner said that Hirsch never pulled rank on anyone in the cast nor ever acted the star. Hirsch seemed comfortable in the role of star of the show, although he seemed a bit uneasy in that role around the other cast members.

"Judd's a theater guy," says Randy Carver. "Everything is figured out, thought out, in the theater. It has to be done that way. In TV or movies you're more in touch with spontaneity. You're more in touch with being instinctive. It's more an art than a craft. I know he had that theater background. I like Judd a lot, but he never really felt secure, I don't think. Maybe Judd had an idea [about] the way the words would flow, the way words should come out. He would offer little suggestions to make his dialogue flow go a little easier, not have too many transitions in one [set of lines]. He helped the writers focus on what the story was about, because they'd all get involved with a lot of other things because they're producers as well. His idea was to focus and [see] how he could best do his part."

The cast shenanigans on and off the set were to be expected from a relatively young group of actors. The approach to the show was never viewed as anything other than serious business, but the cast also managed to have fun with one another and ease the tension of long work days with jokes, pranks, and a certain brotherhood. Marilu Henner had proved the producer's right in their assessment that she could be "one of the boys." Henner fit right in. She would joke with the other actors and the crew, and sometimes provide a shoulder to cry on. She seemed to love her work, and everybody involved was happy to have her involved with the show.

"Marilu and I first met each other in Harvey Lembeck's [comedy] class," remembers Randy Carver. "She mentioned to me that she was reading for a pilot, and I said I was too. She said, 'It's called *Taxi*.' I said, 'Me too!' When we both got it we were really happy. I liked working with Marilu. She brought a really fun, feminist image to the process that was really needed with a bunch of guys. She seemed like she could be a good guy pal. So sweet. She's always real solid as an actress. She put up with a lot of stuff from the guys."

Tony Danza said he felt a little strange to be on a show such as *Taxi*. Danza said that, with his inexperience in acting, he might have been better suited to light comedy. Danza was a tremendous practical joker, and the other actors were often his targets. Sometimes Danza would borrow a golf cart from the legendary Paramount Security guard everyone called "Fritz" and run all over the Paramount lot. Other times he would shoot a fire extinguisher over the backstage area. The other cast members would retaliate by writing graffiti on the back of the set that said, "Tony is gay." (Danza was far from homosexual. He dated a variety of women while on the show, including Marilu Henner and *Taxi*'s talent coordinator Robin

Chambers.) James Brooks fondly recalls Tony Danza as being a kid in a grown-up's body.

"Tony is a very bright and talented fella," says Randy Carver. "I always felt that he was able to bring his talent in a way that would manifest into a fella who had two real long-term series, *Taxi* and [later] *Who's the Boss?*, and could be on Broadway with George C. Scott and do the things that he [later] did. He was a really good student of what was going on. He was paying a whole lot of attention. He was very good."

Danza did have some anger-control issues, as might be expected with someone of Tony's fun-loving but intense personality. "He gets steamed over certain things and people," says Carver. "On a couple of occasions I had to say, 'Now Tony, come on. You don't want to do this. This could be really bad.' I remember one time Danny [DeVito] and I were leaving the lot, and Tony had gotten this brand-new, mid-sixties Corvette. He was driving off the lot, and they were shooting something, and this guy was holding up traffic. When it was clear to go, the guy waved him on and said, 'Get that pile of junk out of here.' Tony got all bent out of shape about it. I had to stop my car. I was behind him, and I saw what he was fixing to do. Danny was behind me. So we went over there and talked to him a little bit so he wouldn't get into it with this fella. But he's a really nice guy."

Danny DeVito took his acting seriously, but he also found ways to amuse himself. Since Louie, as dispatcher, calls out the names of the drivers on the show, DeVito was in a position to make some money from the venture. DeVito was constantly approached by the cast and crew to use their friends' names during these announcements so that they would be heard on national television. DeVito would find ways to fit them in . . . for a price. While DeVito laughs and says he charged a dollar a call, Tony Danza says that he remembers DeVito charging $100.

DeVito also placed several of his own props in Louie De Palma's "cage." In the cage was a photo of Robert De Niro and Martin Scorsese standing by a cab on the set of *Taxi Driver*. Written on the photo was "To Louie. Love, Bobby and Marty." When the character Jeff Bennett shared the cage with Louie, DeVito assigned the character real dispatcher chores, such as tallying receipts and looking over logs.

Danny DeVito was appreciated by the other cast members. "He was very giving," remembers Randy Carver. "All you had to do to do your part was just memorize your lines and look in his face. That was it. That was all you needed because he was there. He did a lot of research and study and that sort of thing. Working with Danny was really exciting. He was a real joy to work with. A lot of fun. He brought so much to the table that you just really had to be there in the moment and everything would work out fine."

Danny DeVito and Randall Carver started a tradition that would be long remembered by those associated with *Taxi*: the *Taxi* after-party. "*Taxi* was famous for having a big Friday night party after every show," says Carver. "We had been rehearsing for about a month before we got to do the first show. It got to be that Wednesday before [the first show], and Danny and I got together. I said, 'Danny, I don't think we have any kind of a wrap party [planned]. We've been working on the thing for so long. I'd like to get some champagne. He said we could go to Greenblatt's [Deli] and get some cold cuts, like a deli platter kind of thing. So he and I set that up. He got the cold cuts and I got the champagne, which was just primarily for the cast. But of course everybody trickled in, then there was more champagne, and then more, and it just kind of grew. Then it was the same thing, the next week, the next week. We had a party every Friday night." The actors would continue to kick in with the producers to fund the parties and enjoy the after-show camaraderie.

Mork & Mindy's Pam Dawber was at one of the *Taxi* Friday-night parties when she first met Andy Kaufman. "What a wacko," Dawber laughs. "Yeah, he was really nuts. I only had one interaction with Andy Kaufman, and it was really odd. It was the end of the first year of *Mork & Mindy* and *Taxi*, and we were going from our cast party to their cast party. It was on the *Taxi* set. Marilu and I were sort of friendly, [although] we were never girlfriends. I went over there to visit, and I had some friends with me. Andy Kaufman was sitting on the set with a couple of people, maybe Marilu, I don't quite remember, but he was sitting with a couple of people I knew. I knew Danny DeVito and Rhea Perlman just a little bit. I walked over, and he was conversing with someone. He didn't quite notice that I was there. There were about three people there and Andy. He was being a normal guy. I threw a comment into what was being discussed. He looked up at me, and his eyes got very big and round. It was like suddenly he realized that I was a stranger that he didn't know or wasn't a normal character on that set. He completely went into the 'Thank you vedy much,' completely retreated into someone that was speaking with the wacko accent—the Latka character. It was really odd to see. I thought, 'Oh my God.' In my opinion, I'd been around so many comedians I thought, 'I don't have time for that craziness.' I thought he was nuts. But everybody knew that he was definitely way out there and rolled their eyes about him."

Andy Kaufman would continue to be an enigma. "Some of the other cast members weren't so warm to him" says Randy Carver. "They thought he was stealing their moment in the sun." Judd Hirsch wasn't always amused by Kaufman. "Andy's actions kind of upset him," says Carver.

Meanwhile during Episode #10, "A Full House for Christmas," a problem developed with Tony Clifton. Clifton had been "hired" to play Louie's Las Vegas gambler brother Nicky. Clifton was so overbearing, demanding, and rude that Ed. Weinberger and the other producers felt they had no choice but to fire Clifton from the episode and the show. (Andy Kaufman was conveniently "away doing a college appearance.") Clifton came in two hours late the day Weinberger had chosen to fire him. Everybody by this time had heard that Clifton was to be fired, so the audience stands were full of both people associated with the show and others from the Paramount lot. As Clifton ranted, Judd Hirsch became enraged with the "actor." Clifton and Hirsch argued heatedly and eventually started wrestling. Finally, studio security arrived to physically drag Clifton off the set. As he left, he yelled at Judd Hirsch, "You'll never work in Vegas again!" Tony Danza was prepared for the firing and the expected scene and managed to record the entire event on his 8mm movie camera. The next week the cast gathered to watch the firing in one of the set's anterooms. As they whooped and laughed at the events unfolding before them on the makeshift screen, in walked Andy Kaufman. "Who's that asshole?" remarked Kaufman. Then he left the room.

"When [Clifton] got fired I was really disappointed," says Randy Carver. "'Cause I was thinking it would be so great if [Andy] could actually come on as an actor doing another character and be successful. I didn't know any other show [where] he would have [been able to] work that way. I was really intrigued by the idea."

There was a prop room/kitchenette backstage where the cast relaxed when they weren't needed elsewhere. While Marilu Henner might prepare something macrobiotic, Andy Kaufman was busy stuffing his face with various forms of sugar. Kaufman's complexity had him addicted to something as bad for his body as sugar while at the same time he used the breaks to meditate.

In Episode #8 Latka discovers that his visa has expired. In an effort to help his friend remain in the United States, Alex hires a call girl to become Latka's American bride. The couple is married by Reverend Jim Ignatowsky, one of *Taxi*'s strangest characters yet. Reverend Jim, who changed his name from James Caldwell to Ignatowski thinking that it was Star Child spelled backward, is a hippy who was ordained by the Church of the Peaceful. Jim is drug-addled, has a paranoid personality, and is enamored with Louie, Alan Alda, and the cabdrivers. The *Taxi* producers wanted a character based on a sixties drug casualty but hadn't found a way to work one in as a regular. The opportunity to have such a character for Latka's wedding was perfect. When the time came to cast someone offbeat to marry Latka and the call girl, Joel Thurm thought immediately of an actor named Christopher Lloyd. Thurm had met Lloyd when Thurm had served as the stage manager in a production of *Once Upon a Mattress*, in which Lloyd acted. The role of Reverend Jim was supposed to be a guest-starring appearance for Lloyd, but the character was so well received the role was expanded during the second season.

Writing for the character Jim was a delight. Jim's reactions were always off the wall, and he was prone to outrageous statements. Once when Elaine was looking for an apartment, Jim asked her if she had looked in Brooklyn because that's where his usually turned up. Jim, and Lloyd, became a welcome addition to the show.

Christopher Lloyd was a serious actor who primarily was involved in drama. He had done Shakespeare at Lincoln Center and had won Obie and Drama Desk Awards for his appearance in the one-man presentation *Kaspar*. Lloyd had previously said he would never get involved in television sitcoms. He didn't think Hollywood was the place for an earnest actor. When he read the part of Jim Ignatowski, he changed his mind. He decided to give the role a try.

Christopher Allen Lloyd was born on October 22, 1938, in Stamford, Connecticut. He grew up in New Canaan and attended Staples High School in Westport. Lloyd was one of seven children in a wealthy family. He decided to pursue his aspirations to become an actor and began his acting career at the Neighborhood Playhouse. He also performed off-Broadway and in summer stock. Lloyd worked at the Yale Repertory Theater with aspiring actress Meryl Streep and landed a small role in the Broadway production of *Red, White and Maddox*. Then came his role in *Kaspar* and his Obie and Drama Desk Awards. Lloyd made his screen debut as Taber in *One Flew Over the Cuckoo's Nest*, with Danny DeVito and Jack Nicholson. He also had roles in *Goin' South*, *The Onion Field*, and *The Lady in Red*.

Though Chris Lloyd immediately immersed himself in the role of the whacked-out Reverend Jim, he was actually quite different from the character he played. Where Jim was loud and had to search for words, Lloyd was quiet and well-spoken. That didn't stop him from going to the audition for the role in character. The secretary who greeted Lloyd at John Charles Walters didn't know whether he was there to read or he had wandered in off the street. For the audition Lloyd threw together some old clothes that became the actual wardrobe of Jim Ignatowski. He based the character on derelicts he had seen on the streets of New York City.

Lloyd says he tried to bring an authentic presence to the character Jim but basically delivered what the writers wrote.

"I was in the show the first time he showed up," remembers Randy Carver. "I was amazed at him. I was so intrigued by him. When the writers originally wrote the thing they had a character named Phil Ryan. That was Tony Danza's character. The other character was a punch-drunk palooka who would come up with these observations which were hilarious. They were from a mind that had been confused in the past, befuddled. He'd taken too many hits in the head. When Tony came in, he didn't really play that. [John Burns] was kind of young and unsophisticated and naïve, and [Tony and I] were kind of playing the same note. So they changed [Phil's] name to Tony, and [Danza] kind of made it his own. When Reverend Jim came in, *that* character was the befuddled guy. They wanted to write befuddled stuff, a guy with a thick head. They got that in Reverend Jim, probably much better than they would have in a punch-drunk palooka. He had a whole other hippy background and series of life events."

Lloyd says he enjoyed doing the character Jim because he didn't have to worry about his appearance. He says it was an once-in-a-lifetime role. Jim was different from the other cabbies as he didn't take offense at Louie's abrasiveness. Lloyd says because he was new to sitcoms he just soaked it all in. Lloyd's Reverend Jim was exactly what the *Taxi* producers wanted it to be—and then some.

"I would start watching him and forget I was in the scene," says Carver. "I was just really paying attention to him and one or two times got so involved with what he was doing and how he was appearing that I just momentarily forgot. 'Oh, I'm on stage and not just observing some fella that's trying to marry these people.'"

The *Taxi* characters and the assorted talents of the individual actors made *Taxi* must-see television. It was hard for the viewing audience to become invested in just one or two of the characters. *All* of the characters had something to offer and were equally fascinating. *Taxi* was certainly one of a kind.

Chapter 10

A NEW KIND
OF FAMILY

The cast of *Taxi* enjoyed their success and their professional association with each other. "The people who worked on *Taxi* were very, very close," says Randy Carver. "The cast and crew kind of became a family to me. Just kind of a *Taxi* family. Which is kind of a misnomer. It was really a *Taxi* gang. If it was a family it's more like the Sopranos. It wasn't the Waltons, it was the Sopranos. It was a real thing. Everybody was just so professional. Also so personable. We had a good time together."

As with the other Paramount sitcoms, the *Taxi* cast and crew sometimes got together on Sundays to play softball. Marilu Henner served as scorekeeper. The only one who didn't participate was Andy Kaufman. Kaufman rarely, if ever socialized with the cast off the lot.

The average production cost of the show was working out to be about $260,000 per episode. ABC had contracted for $275,000, so the show was a good deal for them and they were happy. The network was even more delighted when *Taxi* ended up in the top-10 ratings that first season. "I think the high ratings of the show were primarily from urban areas," reflects Randy Carver. "I think that's because living in a large city, just getting around and being on time for places is kind of difficult, taxi-wise. I think the audience was familiar with people they knew [who were like the cabbies]. Former athletes like Tony, young men who thought they could be involved in the professional sport of their choice. Single working moms [like Elaine]. The life of an urban environment. [Latka], a fish out of water. People could relate to that. Trying to get along in a new place with new people. Reverend Jim appealed to people who really explored the sixties social life. People who are in positions of management identified with Louie. I felt people could identify with my character [John] because it was a guy who moved from the Midwest to the city. [There are] so many factors involved with that. That was one of the things I felt they didn't explore enough."

The show received Emmy nominations that first year for Outstanding Comedy Writing, Comedy Lead Actor (Judd Hirsch), and Comedy Supporting Actor (Danny DeVito). Ruth Gordon, who had appeared in Episode #8: "Sugar Mama," won an Emmy for Outstanding Lead Actress in a Comedy Series, and M. Pam Blumenthal won the Emmy for Outstanding Film Editing for a Series. Best of all, *Taxi* received the Emmy for Outstanding Comedy Series. There were other awards, such as Bob James's Grammy for the *Taxi* theme, "Angela," and the Hollywood Foreign Press liked the show too. Judd Hirsch was nominated for a Golden Globe for Best Performance by an Actor in a Television Series, Musical or Comedy; Jeff Conaway, Danny DeVito, and Andy Kaufman were nominated in the Supporting Actor category, and Marilu Henner was nominated for Supporting Actress. Although none of the actors won the award that year, the show was awarded a Golden Globe for Best Television Series—Musical or Comedy.

"The work was superior," says Randy Carver. "I think the acting was superior. The writing was superior. There wasn't one weak link in the whole deal. Some shows have a weak link, but I felt like [with *Taxi*] everything was pretty well covered."

Season Two in 1979 brought some changes to *Taxi*. The sets were moved to Sound Stage 23 on the Paramount lot as there was an audio problem within the cavernous former stage. There was too much feedback, and moving to a smaller stage worked better for the audio technicians.

One of the major changes that year was the elimination of the character John Burns. The writers were having a difficult time writing for the character. Randall Carver, who had been successfully portraying the character, asked if there was anything he could have done to help develop John Burns. Carver was told no, it was the character, not the actor. John Burns fell somewhere between the characters Bobby and Tony, and there was only so much that could be done with Burns to make him different. Although he was the only married cabdriver, that sub-plot wasn't working. "They were always trying to figure out what to do with this guy," says Carver. "It wasn't that much of a surprise to me [that the character was written out]. There were so many [characters]. Most of us were on the stage at the same time; so that it seemed liked everybody was kind of vying for their moment in the sun. Sometimes things needed to be straightened out. A couple of times Tony Danza and I changed lines at the director's or producers' request. Our characters were coming off as too much in one boat. I know they felt real responsible for Tony relocating to California and everything. They'd do tooling and restructuring, and while it was not always pleasant at times, you can sort of see from this distance that everything worked out for the best anyway. I was very happy to be on that show for a year. I showed people I can do what I can do and do it well. I was pleased with the outcome in that respect."

The *New York Times* received the second season of *Taxi* fairly well. The morning after the first show, the *Times* wrote, "Within its severely constricted borders the show manages to be inventive and surprising." *Taxi* was off to a better start this time with the critics, but the viewers remained what they had been—fans of the characters.

The character Zena Sherman was introduced as Louie's girlfriend in Episode #25. The actress hired to play Zena was a perfect fit: Rhea Perlman. Danny DeVito says even though she was an ideal girlfriend for

Taxi's Randall Carver (John Burns), 2004. Photo courtesy of Randall Carver; photo by Leslie Bohm.

Louie, Perlman wasn't guaranteed the part just because she was his real-life girlfriend. (Danny DeVito and Rhea Perlman were married during a *Taxi* lunch break in 1982.) Perlman earned the role through her talent. Although the character Zena was initially attracted to Louie because he was a man with a certain degree of power, Zena is something that Louie most certainly is not: a nice person.

Rhea Perlman is yet another New Yorker, this time from Brooklyn. She was born on March 31, 1948, in Coney Island and grew up in Bensonhurst, a Brooklyn neighborhood. Perlman's mother was a book-keeper, and her father worked at a company that produced doll parts. (Her father, Philip Perlman, would later appear on *Cheers*, and her sister Heide was an executive producer and writer for *The Tracey Ullman Show*.) Perlman worked off-Broadway while studying drama at Hunter College. To make ends meet, she at one time worked as an eraser at a company that recycled textbooks. At another time she was a waitress at New York's famous Rainbow Room. Her first role was in the play *Dracula Sabbat*. Perlman would bring believability to her portrayal of Zena. A certain poignancy was evoked by having the tough, boorish Louie have a sweet girlfriend, and Rhea Perlman fit the role perfectly.

The episode titled "Guess Who's Coming for Brefish?" brought another girlfriend into the show, but while Episode #40's Simka Dahblitz was also sweet, she was nothing like Zena. Simka came to the Sunshine Cab Company to apply for a job as secretary, and Latka was delighted when he heard Simka speaking his native language, whatever that was. A romance between Simka and Latka ensued, and the audience was in for a tremendous treat with actress Carol Kane.

Andy Kaufman was never happy working on television and didn't particularly like relinquishing his "Foreign Man" character to the show. *Laverne & Shirley*'s David L. Lander knew exactly how Kaufman felt; pointing out to Kaufman that Latka was the Lenny and Squiggy of *Taxi*. When Carol Kane came to *Taxi* to play Simka, Kaufman was thrilled to have such a talented and unique actress play opposite "Foreign Man."

Carol Kane was already an established actor when she arrived on the *Taxi* set. She made her film debut at the age of eighteen in the horror movie *Blood of the Iron Maiden* and was soon appearing in films that included *Carnal Knowledge*, *The Last Detail*, *Dog Day Afternoon*, and *Annie Hall*. In 1976 Kane won an Academy Award nomination for her role as Gitl in *Hester Street*.

Kane didn't bring a film diva attitude to the *Taxi* set. She jumped in with both feet as she and Kaufman developed the language they would use as Latka and Simka's native tongue. The pair's dialogue in the script was in English, and it was up to the actors to come up with their own interpretation. To prepare Kane for the challenge, Kaufman took her to a Chinese restaurant, where she was to speak only the invented language while he interpreted it for the waitress.

Carolyn Kane seems to have always known that she wanted to be in entertainment. She was born on June 18, 1952, in Cleveland, Ohio, to a father who was an architect and a mother who was a jazz singer and pianist. Kane saw the play *Alice in Wonderland* when she was seven and decided then and there that she was going to be an actress. Her family moved to New York when she was eight, but her parents were divorced by the time she was thirteen. Kane lived in Paris and Haiti during her youth and attended a boarding school in Connecticut. She eventually attended the Professional Children's School in New York City. When Kane was fourteen, she was cast in a touring company production of *The Prime of Miss Jean Brodie*. She was accepted by Bernard Baruch College but never attended, preferring instead to work off-Broadway and with tour companies. Kane appeared with Christopher Lloyd in a production of *Macbeth* and eventually co-starred with Shelley Winters in Broadway's *The Effect of Gamma Rays on Man-in-the-Moon Marigolds*.

Kane was initially interested in appearing on *Taxi* because of the quality of the writing. She thought appearing on the show would result in good growth for her career. (Simka would return in Season Four, and it was for that work that Carol Kane won an Emmy for her performance. By the final season of *Taxi*, Kane had become a cast member and won another Supporting Actress Emmy.)

Andy Kaufman was continuing his performance art while he was appearing on *Taxi*. Sometimes that included reading *The Great Gatsby* to his audiences. Back on the set, it took a while for the rest of the cast to warm up to Kaufman, if they all ever did. Opinions on Andy Kaufman were as diverse as the actor. Director Jim Burrows said that Kaufman was "one of the strangest, funniest comedians you'll ever see." Tony Danza says he hated Kaufman at first because Kaufman was always late and drove him crazy with his peculiar approach to acting. Danza notes that, even so, Kaufman never missed a line. Sometimes Danza would provoke Kaufman by shooting off the fire extinguisher at him. Kaufman would just stand there, not reacting to the assault. Marilu Henner got close to Kaufman and considered him a friend. Randy Carver says Kaufman was both giving and self-centered. You either loved him or hated him. Judd Hirsch didn't seem to like Kaufman. Jeff Conaway said that he and Kaufman had problems the first year but had a long talk and worked out their differences. Danny DeVito never liked to say anything negative about his fellow cast members and kept his feelings about Kaufman mainly to himself. DeVito was likely somewhat amused by the strange actor. Carol Kane was probably the closest person on the *Taxi* set to Andy Kaufman. Within their characters they were kindred spirits, and Kaufman no doubt related to that. Marilu Henner says that the *Taxi* experience was like that in a repertory company. When it came to acting, everyone worked together regardless of their personal feelings. Randy Carver feels the same way. "My philosophy is that one week you're a spear handler, the next week you're playing Hamlet," says Carver.

Taxi continued its relationship-driven episodes. "Instead of a policeman trying to catch a guy or something like that, it was 'How can we help one another?'" says Carver of the plotlines. "That to me seemed to be explored very fully in a way that had never been portrayed before in any previous series that I can recall. Some of that was done in the *Mary Tyler Moore* shows, but this was done where everybody was in transit. Everybody was moving from one place to another, and this was just a stop-off point. It was about people in that situation, when they're on kind of a solo mission and they don't have a group to relate to. How they bond immediately with their friends and fellow workers. A mixed bag of nuts. It was able to [appeal to] the American people. I know you had Lou Grant and Mary Tyler Moore, but those people were ensconced in their jobs. [In *Taxi*] these were people always one step away from the street. Elaine lost her job and couldn't get another one. The character had a tough time. Tony wanted to be a fighter. John wanted to be a forest ranger. Bobby wanted to be an actor. Alex just wanted to be a cabdriver. He was the only one who wanted to be there. Louie was looking to move up; he wanted to end up owning that place one day. The [premise] was a kind of fishes out of water, all tossed together, just passing through. But they end up realizing [their time at Sunshine Cab] is probably going to be a big part of their life. They will always have that experience to look back on."

Though the show slipped to number 13 by the end of the season, the second season was recognized again by the television industry through additional honors for *Taxi* and its cast and crew. Awards once again abounded for the show. For the second year *Taxi* won the Emmy for Outstanding Comedy Series. James Burrows won Outstanding Directing in a Comedy Series, and M. Pam Blumenthal again won for Film Editing for a Series. Judd Hirsch was again nominated for Outstanding Actor in a Comedy Series, and Glen and Les Charles were nominated for Outstanding Writing in a Comedy Series. The Hollywood Foreign Press' Golden Globes were good to *Taxi* also. Marilu Henner was nominated for Best Supporting Actress in a Television Musical and Comedy, and Jeff

Conaway and Tony Danza for Best Supporting Actor. Judd Hirsch was nominated for Best Actor in a Television Musical or Comedy. This year Danny DeVito would win the Golden Globe for Best Supporting Actor in a Television Musical or Comedy, and the show itself would win Best Television Series—Musical or Comedy.

There were some changes in the production crew for *Taxi*'s third year, which began airing on November 19, 1980. David Davis decided to retire. When First Associate Producer Budd Cherry decided to leave the show, Richard Sakai was tapped to replace him. Sakai had started out as an assistant and was well-liked. He quickly worked his way up the ladder. (After *Taxi*, Sakai would produce *The Tracey Ullman Show* and eventually become president of James Brooks's Gracie Films.)

Before reporting for work for the third season of *Taxi*, both Judd Hirsch and Danny DeVito asked for an increase in their salaries. When Hirsch failed to show up for work, Paramount filed a $1 million breach of contract suit against him. Danny DeVito missed one day of rehearsal, and then the producers adjusted his salary. The suit against Hirsch never landed in court, presumably because an agreement about salary was reached.

During the show's first two seasons, *Taxi* had been airing on Tuesday nights against *Three's Company*. Things changed when ABC decided to air a new series on that night called *Too Close for Comfort*, starring Ted Knight. *Taxi* was moved to Wednesday night. At mid-season *Taxi* was moved again, this time to Thursday night to follow the popular series *Barney Miller*. The lack of continuity definitely affected the audience. *Taxi* was considered an adult comedy geared to intellectuals, and the network thought the *Barney Miller* viewers would appreciate the show and stick around after it aired to watch *Taxi*. It didn't necessarily turn out that way. The ratings were unstable during and after the two moves.

Some of the moves for *Taxi*'s third season were positive. Zena returned, and other guest stars included Louise Lasser (formally of the cult series *Mary Hartman, Mary Hartman*), film actor Victor Buono, Eileen Brennan (who would receive an Emmy nomination for her appearance in the *Taxi* episode "The Boss's Wife"), *The Munsters*' Al Lewis, and future *Cheers* co-star George Wendt.

One very special guest was Danny DeVito's mother, Julia, who played the title role in the episode "Louie's Mother." As unharmonious and contentious as Louie De Palma might be, he loved his mother. Julia DeVito was terrific in the role. After her appearance, the cast went out to dinner at a French restaurant. Because Mrs. DeVito didn't like to eat anything but Italian, Ed. Weinberger had Italian food delivered to the restaurant. Julia DeVito would return in Season Four's episode "Louie's Mother Remarries."

Although the character Bobby Wheeler seemed to receive a lot of screen time that third season, Jeff Conaway wasn't happy with the show. Conaway says that he was ready to leave *Taxi* after six weeks. According to Conaway, he was promised star billing but never received that honor because Judd Hirsch wanted it. Even though Conaway was given first co-star billing, the fact that he wasn't given star billing always stuck in his craw. He was used to leading roles. Conaway was also interested in building the character of actor Bobby Wheeler and decided to try and develop the role himself. He says he became increasingly uncomfortable with the way the character was being written. To Conaway, Bobby was too self-centered, and Conaway didn't like the derogatory "actor jokes." Joel Thurm says that the characters Bobby and Tony were too similar and consequently got harder to write. Some of the writers and producers believed that Jeff Conaway was many times harder to deal with and Tony Danza easier. Conaway was unhappy with the fact that the writers wouldn't let him sit in on their meetings to give input to Bobby's character. He claimed that anyone could do the Bobby character as written, and he wanted a bigger challenge in the role. Conaway said that acting was important to him and he hated to see actors put down in any way. He seemed to lose sight of the fact that *Taxi* was a comedy.

Jeff Conaway said that he was offered a film role that offered to pay him twice as much as he was earning on *Taxi*, but the *Taxi* producers wouldn't release him to do the movie. He complained bitterly about all of this, and the producers decided it would be best for everyone if Bobby's character was written off the show. Conaway wasn't happy about that, and he didn't leave on good terms. The actor was suffering hard times all around. He was having problems with drug and alcohol abuse and in his marriage to actress Rona Newton-John. Conaway landed a recording contract with Columbia Records and recorded the album *Jeff Conaway*. He claimed that he got out of the contract when Columbia failed to properly promote the album. (In one of the *Taxi* episodes, the song "Summer Nights" from *Grease* is playing on the jukebox. Instead of John Travolta singing the lead, the vocals are by Jeff Conaway, who sang the song for the Broadway production of the play.)

The character Bobby Wheeler would leave the garage for a role in a touring company. Conaway would later return in a guest-starring role. (After leaving *Taxi* Jeff Conaway was involved in a driving incident involving a bicyclist. He entered rehab and was able to temporarily turn his life around. Conaway did some terrific work while on *Taxi*, and his contribution to the show will hopefully be remembered long after his meltdown on 2005's *Celebrity Fit Club* and subsequent re-entry into rehab.)

"Jeff was a real nice fella," says Randy Carver. "I met him before *Taxi* in seventy-three or seventy-four. He and I both auditioned for the movie *Time to Run*. He didn't get that. [Carver did.] They offered him another part, and I think he turned them down. He was a child actor on Broadway. When I got to work with him he was coming off of *Grease* and the whole Kenickie thing. He was getting thousands of letters a week between Kenickie and *Taxi*. He was fine to work with. I got along well with him. I don't think he ever had a problem with me. He's a real nice fella. He comes equipped with a lot of complicated background. We all have problems, but he's overcoming them."

The awards for Season Three poured in. The show won Emmys for Outstanding Comedy Series, Outstanding Achievement in Film Editing for a Series for M. Pam Blumenthal and Jack Michon, Outstanding Directing in a Comedy Series for James Burrows, Outstanding Lead Actor in a Comedy Series for Judd Hirsch, Outstanding Supporting Actor in a Comedy or Variety or Music Series for Danny DeVito, and Outstanding Writing in a Comedy Series for Michael Leeson. Additional nominations were earned by Eileen Brennan for Outstanding Lead Actress in a Comedy Series, and by Glen Charles and Les Charles and David Lloyd for Outstanding Writing in a Comedy Series. There were Golden Globe nominations of the show for Best Television Series—Musical or Comedy, of Judd Hirsch for Best Actor in a Comedy, of Marilu Henner for Best Actress in a Comedy, and of Carol Kane for Best Performance by an Actress in a Supporting Role.

Season Four began airing on October 15, 1981, and would be rather a strange season for *Taxi*. Some of the shows were daffy humor centered on Reverend Jim, Latka, and Simka. (Carol Kane was nominated for an Emmy that year for "Simka Returns.") Chris Lloyd wanted more focus on the "reverend" aspects of Jim as he felt that really was who Jim was, but the focus at this time was more on his druggy past. Jeff Conaway returned for an episode when Bobby landed a television pilot and returned to the garage to celebrate with his old friends. Jim Burrows was directing fewer episodes, as he was busy creating and producing a new comedy called *Cheers*, which he would also direct.

Andy Kaufman, always a reluctant *Taxi* cast member, continued his performance art. Kaufman and alter ego Tony Clifton appeared on stage and television throughout his time on the show. He also worked as a waiter at Jerry's Famous Deli in Studio City. Andy Kaufman had always wanted to be a wrestler and found a way to accomplish this by coupling the sport with his performance art. He began wrestling women during appearances in 1979. In 1981 Kaufman set up a World Intergender Wrestling Championship by wrestling Playboy playmate Susan Smith. On April 5, 1982, Kaufman received a huge amount of publicity for another "wrestling match."

Nashville recording artist Donna Frost was there the night Andy Kaufman once again made entertainment history. "To me Andy Kaufman was the best comedian to ever take the stage," remembers Frost. "I have always been a huge fan of his ever since the *Saturday Night Live* days. I don't think anyone since has come close to him either. He was always living on the edge, and I loved that. He had such a way of keeping us guessing whether he was serious or putting us on. I was one of the people to see Andy Kaufman wrestle professionally. There was a wrestling promotion based out of Memphis, Tennessee, which had a weekly Saturday morning TV show that aired here in Nashville. They also had their big matches in Nashville on Saturday nights and in Memphis on Mondays. The big star of the promotion was Jerry "The King" Lawler. Imagine everyone's surprise when Andy Kaufman shows up on the Saturday morning TV show and starts up this huge feud with Jerry Lawler and the good people of Memphis. He cut some of the funniest promos I have ever seen. He would make fun of "the stupid rednecks" in Memphis and Jerry Lawler. He would always say, "I'm smart, I'm from Hollywood!" Naturally the fans were coming out in droves to boo this guy. Lawler was very, very popular in Memphis and all over the mid-South. The fans hated Kaufman and wanted to see Lawler waste him. Lawler was defending the wrestling profession because up to that point Kaufman had only wrestled women, and Lawler challenged him to come wrestle a *real* wrestler. I was a bit surprised that a huge star like Andy Kaufman would get in the ring with Jerry Lawler. Lawler was a big guy and could hurt Kaufman in a bad way, whether the wrestling was real or not. This went on for weeks and ended up with Kaufman and Lawler in a huge match in Memphis. Lawler was disqualified for giving Kaufman a pile driver, and Kaufman left the ring on a stretcher. Kaufman threatened to sue Lawler, the City of Memphis, on and on. Then there was the famous Letterman appearance where Kaufman and Lawler got into it."

But Andy Kaufman wasn't through. "We all thought we'd seen the last of Andy Kaufman in the wrestling ring," recalls Frost. "Surely he wouldn't be crazy enough to do this again! But he was. He reappeared on the Saturday morning TV show. This time he was in a feud with [wrestling manager] Jimmy Hart. They booked a match in Nashville at the Fairgrounds. Needless to say, my brother Andy and I were there. We weren't about to miss this one. The place was packed. The fans really hated Andy Kaufman, but there were plenty of them who hated Jimmy Hart too. Neither one of these guys was very good at wrestling. They were smacking each other around for a while (like kids in a playground fight), and it was pretty funny. All of a sudden, one of Jimmy's wrestlers, a big seven-footer called "The Giant Rebel," came out of the dressing room and delivered a giant leg drop on Andy Kaufman, and that ended the match. Andy left the ring on a stretcher again, then later got on the mic and threatened to sue all of us in Nashville, Tennessee, plus Jimmy and "The Giant Rebel." Kaufman returned to the Saturday A.M. television show and some wrestling matches in Memphis, but he never did come back to Nashville. The whole feud with Hart was a ruse to trick Lawler, and they ran with it a little while longer before Andy gave up the wrestling gig. Years later it did come out that the whole Andy Kaufman/Jerry Lawler feud was a big set-up by Kaufman, Jimmy Hart, and Lawler. They had all been in this together. It remains one of the funniest things I have ever seen. We were had by Andy Kaufman once again!"

Meanwhile, back at *Taxi*, Paramount Television, the John Charles Walters Company, and ABC Television had a pretty good working relationship when it came to the show. This year, however, strange things started to occur. There was a heated discussion between the three entities over a proposed episode that included a scene in a gay bar. ABC didn't want anything to do with that, although the network executives had previously had no problem with one of the shows that dealt with a humorous bi-sexual encounter ("Elaine's Strange Triangle"). The executives at ABC wouldn't give Paramount's Gary Nardino a straight answer as to why they didn't want to air the show that featured the gay bar. When James Brooks heard about ABC's stance on the episode, he told Nardino that he thought that ABC didn't want to be in business with him anymore. Nardino told ABC that Brooks would leave the show rather than be censored, and ABC appeared to back down. But rumors began to circulate that ABC was going to cancel *Taxi*.

Paramount Television continued to back *Taxi*. At this time *Happy Days* was in its ninth year and *Laverne & Shirley* in its seventh. In April 1982 Gary Nardino sent a memo to Tony Thomopolus at ABC, asking Thomopolus to let the producers know if *Taxi* was going to be canceled. Nardino mentioned in the memo that several of the writers, as well as Ed. Weinberger, Chris Lloyd, and Danny DeVito, had received calls from various people wanting to hire them. Nardino said that the rumors were demoralizing and causing hard feelings. What was the deal?

When Thomopolus didn't really address the issue of the show being canceled in his reply, Gary Nardino didn't feel that the response from ABC to his memo was adequate. He felt the issue wasn't satisfactory resolved. Nardino started talking to Brandon Tartikoff at NBC about the possibility of that network taking over *Taxi*. Nardino pitched the show as a "landmark" series that, if aired on NBC, would lead other important producers and writers to the network.

ABC's bluff was called. The network was moving into nighttime soaps such as *Dynasty* and fluff like *The Love Boat*. On May 4, 1982, *Taxi* was canceled. Danny DeVito, Tony Danza, Marilu Henner, and others of the cast and crew threw a wake in James Brooks's office and got drunk on tequila. After leaving Brooks' office the group retired to Danza's house, where they continued the post-mortem party until dawn. Little did they know that *Taxi* had not breathed its last breath.

Upon hearing the news that ABC had ended the show, Tom Shales of the *Washington Post* wrote a column questioning ABC's intelligence for canceling what he called their "best comedy." There was a huge outcry from both the viewing public and the television industry. The Emmy nominations once again included several for *Taxi*. Ken Estin won for Outstanding Writing, Christopher Lloyd for Outstanding Supporting Actor, and Carol Kane for Outstanding Lead Actress. Additional nominations included Holly Holmberg Brooks and Barry Kemp for Writing, Danny DeVito for Supporting Actor, Judd Hirsch for Outstanding Actor, Jim Burrows for Directing, and the show itself for the Outstanding Comedy Series award.

James Brooks said that had ABC not canceled *Taxi* they would have been in line to air the future hit series *Cheers*. During an appearance on *Saturday Night Live* Danny DeVito brought cast members and many of the production staff from *Taxi* onto the stage at the end of the show. DeVito's mother, Julia, was there. To the amusement of the *Taxi* folks, Mrs. DeVito called ABC executives "stupid jackasses" . . . in Italian.

An offer to air *Taxi* was received by the John Charles Walters Company from Michael Fuchs, HBO's Vice President of Program Development. Fuchs offered Brooks almost total creative freedom if the show aired on the cable channel. Fuchs said the storylines could be taken further if they were on cable, something the producers and the cast found amusing. HBO offered good money for the series, but issues with syndication proved complicated.

Meanwhile, over at NBC, Brandon Tartikoff believed Michael Fuch's HBO negotiations to air the show to be a publicity stunt. That was okay. On May 21, 1982, NBC announced that *their* network would begin airing *Taxi*. Although the cast was delighted that the show would continue, Judd Hirsch decided that he wanted a higher salary and more perks. NBC's Grant Tinker had to call Hirsch to tell him that if he didn't back off on his demands, the show might not be able to continue, be it on NBC or anywhere else.

A problem arose with NBC almost immediately. NBC's Program Standards and Practices didn't like the fact that Jim Ignatowski was a doper. The producers of the show had to explain that Jim's mental state was a demonstration of the *bad* effects of drug use. Program Practices eventually accepted that explanation and gave Jim their blessing.

Taxi was put on the air immediately at NBC rather than as a mid-season replacement. It followed the new series *Cheers* and led into the hit series *Hill Street Blues*. It was now airing against ABC's *The Greatest American Hero*. Viewers were no doubt once again confused about the changes. The ratings, as they had done in the last year, continued to drop. The audience the show had been building either didn't know where to find *Taxi* or the series was now up against something else they had grown used to watching. *Taxi* finished the season in seventy-third place.

During the fifth and what would be final season of *Taxi*, the show took a more dramatic and downcast turn. Tony Danza says the show "got strange" in the last season. Jim Burrows had left to direct *Cheers*, and the cast of *Taxi* had begun to suffer from the loss of its beloved director. Burrows had been a guiding light for the actors. He knew them and their characters so well that it was hard for someone else to take over. The actors had loved acting with Burrows in the director's chair and found his direction of them instinctive and spot on.

"He would make comments rarely," says Randy Carver. "When he did they were always good ones. If you were smart you would take his suggestions. He was always very supportive. You could hear him laughing throughout the scene. You knew if you scored on that line or that joke or whatever."

Noam Pitlik, who had directed television shows including *Barney Miller* and *The Betty White Show*, came in to direct several episodes. Richard Sakai helmed several of the episodes, and others also came in to direct. Danny DeVito decided to give directing a try himself.

DeVito had learned the various aspects of television production through ardent observation. He enjoyed directing the *Taxi* episodes "Elaine and the Monk," "Sugar Ray Nardo," and "Jim's Mario's." DeVito says the cast made it easy because of their talent. DeVito had prospered as an actor on *Taxi* and remembers the *Taxi* producers being open to improvisation and not caring about sticking to the written script. They welcomed input on the characters from the actors. Everyone was ready and willing to learn from the others around them. DeVito applied that same tenet to directing.

Although the directors brought in to replace Jim Burrows were good in their own way, the show suffered from the change. But what was going on with the directors was small potatoes compared to what was going on at NBC in relation to *Taxi*. NBC placed *Taxi* on hiatus from December to January. When it resumed, the show was moved to Saturday night for three weeks. Then *Taxi* was again placed on hiatus. It was also frequently pre-empted. Finally *Taxi* was canceled for good. (Danny DeVito told *Friends* star Jennifer Aniston that as a successful series actor there wouldn't be a day you don't think about the ending of your hit show.) The last show aired on June 15, 1983. Danny DeVito shot an introduction to a retrospective two-part episode titled "A Taxi Celebration" and that was it.

Co-creator James L. Brooks told *Entertainment Weekly* in 2004 that *Taxi* was the right show at the right time with the right group of people. He called *Taxi* a labor of love. "It was a strange show," says Jim Burrows of the *Taxi* series. "But it turned out to be a wonderful show."

Chapter 11

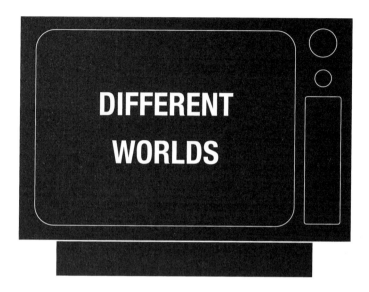

DIFFERENT WORLDS

B y the end of 1978 things were hopping on the Paramount lot. Paramount Television's presentations of *Happy Days*, *Laverne & Shirley*, *Mork & Mindy*, and *Taxi* were all up and running. The shows were all reaping awards, and the casts and crews were dynamite. Life was good at Paramount Television, but in the minds of the studio executives, it could always get better.

Garry Marshall and his team of producers and writers had yet another idea for a sitcom. This time Marshall took more of a background role as producer, and the production entity, along with Paramount Television, would be Miller-Milkis Productions. The show was titled *Angie*.

Tom Miller, who had been so instrumental in the creation of *Happy Days*, had by this time produced two television series, *Night Games*, with Barry Newman, and *Petrocelli*, which also starred Newman. He also was one of the producers on *Laverne & Shirley* and had produced the movies *Silver Streak*, with Gene Wilder, Jill Clayburgh, and Richard Pryor, and *Foul Play*, with Goldie Hawn and Chevy Chase. One of his producing partners for those films was Edward Milkis.

Edward Milkis had also been a producer on *Happy Days* and *Laverne & Shirley*. Starting out working with the television series *Star Trek*, *The Brady Bunch*, and *The Odd Couple*, Milkis had produced several made-for-television movies, such as *The Devil's Daughter*, with Shelley Winters, *Night of Terror*, starring Martin Balsam, and *Women in Chains*, with Ida Lupino, Lois Nettleton, and Jessica Walter.

The executive producer for this new show was Leonora Thuna. Thuna had written for *The Love Boat II* and *Lou Grant* and received acclaim for co-writing with Maya Angelou *I Know Why the Caged Bird Sings*, a television movie based on Angelou's book of the same name. The movie had a terrific cast, headlined by Diahann Carroll, Ruby Dee, Esther Rolle, and Paul Benjamin. Thuna had also been the co-executive producer on *Grandpa Goes to Washington*, a television series starring Jack Albertson and *M*A*S*H*'s Larry Linville.

Joining Thuna, Miller, and Milkis for the production chores was Robert Boyett, who had been a creative consultant for *Happy Days* and had developed *Joanie Loves Chachi*. He had also been a producer on *Laverne & Shirley*. The combined production forces promised a creative and exciting venture in a series they would title *Angie*.

The premise of *Angie* harked back to the days of *Cindy*, the show produced by those other Paramount Television guys Brooks, Weinberger, et al. *Angie* was a comedy about a pretty young waitress named Angie Falco who falls in love with, then marries, a handsome, rich young doctor named Brad Benson. The story is set in Philadelphia. The two families involved are very different, setting up a premise that, while almost expected these days, was not run of the mill for comedy viewers in the late seventies. The differences between the leading characters made *Angie* a forerunner to future successful comedy series such as *Dharma & Greg*.

Angie obviously needed a strong actress to play the title character. The producers found that in Donna Pescow, who had just two years before performed the poignant role of Annette in the hit film *Saturday Night Fever*. Donna Pescow was born on March 24, 1954, in Brooklyn, New York. She studied at the American Academy of the Dramatic Arts and with famed acting teacher Lee Strasberg. (She worked to lose her Brooklyn accent, only to resurrect it for her appearance in *Saturday Night Fever*.) Pescow began her acting career on the stage and appeared in *Promises Promises* and *Guys and Dolls*. She first came to the attention of filmgoers with her role in 1977's *Saturday Night Fever*, for which she earned a New York Film Critics Circle Award for Best Supporting Actress. Pescow appeared on *The Love Boat* and other television shows, such as *One Life to Live* and the television movie *Human Feelings*, with Billy Crystal and Nancy Walker. She also appeared in another made for television movie, *Rainbow*, a story about Judy Garland's early years in which she co-starred as Jinnie Gumm, Garland's sister.

When it came time to cast *Angie*, Garry Marshall knew just where to look for his star. "*Saturday Night Fever* was released several months prior [to *Angie*]," Pescow recalls. "Garry Marshall saw it and thought it would be a good match. He had me come to Paramount and told me all about it. Unfortunately, at that time I was under contract to do something else, so I couldn't do it right off. But I loved the idea of [*Angie*], so when it was still around and it came to me again, I jumped on it. I thought it was a wonderful idea, and working with Garry was obviously pretty terrific."

Cast opposite Donna Pescow as Brad Benson was actor Robert Hays, who also wasn't a novice to television or acting. Robert Hays was born in Bethesda, Maryland, on July 24, 1947. His father was in the Marines, and Hays lived with his family in locations as diverse as Turkey, India, England, and Nebraska, where he graduated from high school. While attending San Diego State University, he joined the Actors Guild of the Old Globe Theater. Hays appeared in the theater's productions for the next five years and won the Globe's Atlas Award for his appearance in *Say Who You Are*. He was also involved with theater in San Francisco. Hays's first television appearance was on the detective series *Harry O*, which starred David Janssen. He appeared in episodic television on *The Rockford Files*, *Marcus Welby, M.D.*, and *Cannon*. He also had a role in the horror movie *The Initiation of Sarah*, with Shelley Winters and Kay Lenz, and co-starred with Eva Gabor in the short-lived television series (only three

Angie star Donna Pescow. Photo courtesy of Globe Photos, Inc.

Esteemed director Howard Storm. Photo courtesy of Howard Storm.

episodes) *Almost Heaven*. (A new comic actor named Jay Leno portrayed the character Danny in that series.) Hays also co-starred in the *Young Pioneers* with *Happy Days'* Linda Purl and *Mork & Mindy's* Robert Donner. Hays crossed paths with other Paramount Television talent while he was coming up as an actor. The movie *Young Pioneers' Christmas*, made for television, was directed by Michael O'Herlihy, uncle of *Happy Days'* original Chuck Cunningham, and in the movie *Delta County, U.S.A.*, Hays co-starred with *Taxi's* Jeff Conaway. Hays also made an appearance on *Laverne & Shirley*.

Robert Hays and Donna Pescow had an immediate chemistry. The actors liked each other, and although Hays was more seasoned in television, the newness of it all was inspiring to both actors. "He's still today one of my closest friends," says Pescow. "He's my son's godfather, and I'm his son's godmother, which is kinda cute."

"*Angie* was a good show," recalls director Howard Storm. "Mark Harmon [who would later marry Pam Dawber of *Mork & Mindy*] did the test against Bob Hays, and Hays got the role. I thought Bob Hays would be a wonderful star. He was a Jimmy Stewart kind of guy."

Doris Roberts was cast to play Angie's Italian mother, Theresa Falco. Doris May Roberts was an acclaimed actress by the time she came to be cast in *Angie*. She was born on November 4, 1929, in St. Louis, Missouri, and was raised by her mother, Doris Meltzer. She moved to New York City, where she took a job as a clerk-typist to pay for acting lessons from acclaimed acting teachers Lee Strasberg and Sanford Meisner. Roberts's first television appearance was on *Studio One* in a production of *Jane Eyre*. She received notice in the stage productions of *Desk Set*, with Shirley Booth, and the original production of Edward Albee's *American Dream* in the role of Mommy. Roberts made her film debut in 1961's *Something Wild*, starring Carroll Baker. She appeared in several other films, including *The Honeymoon Killers, A New Leaf*, with Walter Matthau and Elaine May, and *Rabbit Test*, starring Billy Crystal. Prior to her casting in *Angie*, Roberts appeared on many television series, including *The Mary Tyler Moore Show, The Streets of San Francisco, All in the Family*, and *Barney Miller*.

Doris Roberts and Donna Pescow hit it off right from the start. "Doris is unbelievable," says Pescow. "Doris will always be the pro that you look toward to take as your lead. She's just so incredibly smart and inventive and talented. She loves what she does so much that it's contagious. For me, Doris was a friend who understood. I would occasionally need a little advice on the industry because I just didn't know the world that well. She was really wonderful about advising and also keeping things running on a normal level even when [*Angie*] got incredibly successful, and I would get kind of nervous about that. I had no learning time. My first film was *Saturday Night Fever*, and my first TV show [playing the lead] was *Angie*. I was new to being the lead or being in a big role. I understood the acting part of it all, but all of the surrounding elements were so overwhelming to me that it was also great to have some voice of reason, a calming effect, nearby. I learned a huge amount from her just by watching her work. I loved when we had scenes and we could play off each other because those were just gold."

Veteran actor John Randolph was hired to play Brad Benson's father, Randall. The actor came with quite a history. He had been involved with films and television for more than thirty years. He also was black-listed during the McCarthy era because of his union and social activism. John Randolph was born Emanuel Hirsch Cohen on June 1, 1915, in the Bronx, New York City. He was the son of Russian and Romanian immigrants. After the death of his father, his mother married Joseph Lippman, who renamed the boy Mortimer. After attending college and beginning his drama training with famed teacher Stella Adler, Cohen renamed himself yet again, this time as John Randolph. During World War II, Randolph served in the Army Air Force. After his discharge, he married actress Sarah Cunningham while the two were appearing in Orson Welles's 1945 stage production of *Native Son*. (Sarah Cunningham died during the telecast of the Academy Awards in 1986 of an asthma attack.)

John Randolph, one of the original members of the Actors Studio, made his film debut in the small role of a police dispatcher in 1948's *The Naked City*. Things were going along well professionally, but the actor was compelled to share his political philosophy and all hell broke loose. Randolph was quoted as saying that anyone who did not become radicalized during the Depression had to be an idiot. He and his wife were called before the House Un-American Activities Committee in 1955, and Randolph pled the Fifth Amendment. He was blacklisted from films and television for fifteen years. During this time, Randolph worked on the New York stage. In 1966 director John Frankenheimer broke the Hollywood blacklist by casting Randolph, Jeff Corey, and Will Geer in his production of *Seconds*, which starred Rock Hudson. His career back on track, Randolph went on to appear in roles in dozens of movies, including *Gaily, Gaily, Escape from the Planet of the Apes, Serpico, All the President's Men*, and *Heaven Can Wait*. During this time he also appeared in the television series *Lucas Tanner* and in such made-for-television movies as *Backstairs at the White House, The Winds of Kitty Hawk*, and *Kill Me If You Can*.

All of the actors involved in *Angie* had experience in both film and theater on which to draw. "[Robert Hays and I] both came out of theater," reflects Donna Pescow. "I think the majority of the cast did. We always enjoyed that rehearsal period prior to the filming of the show. We would all have great fun taking the script in various directions in order to find the right way to do it. I think generally that everybody really approached it the way you would a theater piece, with the rehearsal time. That's the beauty of a sitcom—the element of time that you don't have with features."

Angie's trouble-making sister Marie was played by Debralee Scott, who had earned good reviews for her portrayal of Cathy Shumway on *Mary Hartman, Mary Hartman* and *Forever Fernwood*. Scott was born on April 2, 1953, in Elizabeth, New Jersey, and appeared in several movies, including *American Graffiti* as Bob's girlfriend, *Dirty Harry* as the abducted girl, and *The Reincarnation of Peter Proud* as Suzy. She had also appeared on the television shows *Welcome Back, Kotter* and *The Love Boat*.

Donna Pescow remembers Scott fondly. "She was just a pistol," says Pescow. "She was just this perpetual motion of a person. She was very young as well and had done so much more; she had started so much younger. She was kind of the voice of show biz. I remember her saying, 'You have to go out to parties. You must.' I'd say, 'Why?' She'd say, 'You *have* to go.' I would say, 'Don't you go home after school?'"

ABC aired the first episode of *Angie* on Thursday, February 8, 1979, at 8:30 P.M. The show aired in that time slot from February through August 1979. Some of the shows were directed by *Mork & Mindy's* Howard Storm.

Storm brought to *Angie* much of the same energy he brought to *Mork & Mindy*. A skillful professional, he knew how to work well with younger actors. "He was fabulous," says Donna Pescow. "Even now I love working with him when I can. He's so funny and inventive, and he knows this [business] like the back of his hand. He's also one of those directors who let you find your way and who keeps you on course without telling you how he wants it done. He's very much into a group effort to find it, which is great. He's confident enough in his work to not strong-arm any of the direction. He's great for actors because he comes up with great ideas, and you know that you can trust him. If you need help, he's there."

Jeff Chambers directed many of the *Angie* episodes, as he had done for *Mork & Mindy* and *Taxi*. Lowell Ganz and John Tracy also directed episodes. *Angie's* writers included Alan Eisenstock, Larry Mintz, Emily Levine, and even Tom Miller himself.

The *Angie* theme song, "Different Worlds," was written by Charles Fox and sung by Maureen McGovern. When it was released as a single after the show aired, it hit the charts. The song rose to #1 on the Adult Contemporary chart and #18 on the Pop chart. (The show was originally going to be titled *Different Worlds*, but the network wanted to focus on Donna Pescow because of her success with *Saturday Night Fever* and chose to title the series after the main character.)

While the show was initially under Garry Marshall's umbrella, *Angie* was very much a Miller-Milkis production. The producers continued to bring quality to the shows they launched. They knew that a hit series is only as good as its cast, crew, writers, and producers. "The shows were managed so beautifully," says Donna Pescow. "The care was really above and beyond. They really, really, really hired the best people. The tone of a show is always set by those who run it. They had great love and respect for all their projects. They really cared and made us feel that way. We always felt appreciated. We always felt like we wanted to do our best. I felt in a funny way that we were kind of off on our own in this little show business world because everybody was there [at Paramount and at the set]. We never felt the corporate hand. You felt a very one-to-one tangibility; you could speak to whomever you needed to. Everybody was there for the same reason. For me it was especially great because I was so young and inexperienced that they really walked me through so much of it."

Marshall continued to care deeply about the Paramount sitcoms, whether or not he was directly involved. "He was hands-on, but he had just started to work in the feature world, so he was there, but I believe a lot of what was done with *Angie* was run by the Miller-Milkis team," recalls Pescow. "But I don't think Garry was ever unaware or not a part of something. We just didn't see him as often, but he certainly was a presence. He was always very accessible, and for me, being truly green at doing this, I just always loved to talk to Garry. I felt like it was a little piece of New York, something I could hang on to. He was just, 'Nah, don't worry, it's okay. That was fine, you were funny. It's a nice thing, you'll have fun.'"

Gary Nardino, as President of Paramount Television, wanted to see *Angie* succeed, and he was happy when it did. He had observed how Garry Marshall had fostered the family atmosphere of his shows. "I remember when I was on the cover of *People* magazine during one of the seasons," Pescow says. "Gary Nardino wouldn't let anyone tell me until he came to the sound stage and told me. When the thing came out he had [a copy] framed for my mother. It was kind of a homey, sweet, very unusual time."

In 1979 Donna Pescow was nominated for a Golden Globe for her performance as Angie, and she received a People's Choice nomination for Favorite Actress in a Comedy Series. "It was a very special time because it was my first television show," remembers Pescow. "I had never done anything [that is, a television lead] prior to that. I was learning as I was doing. I was pretty much in a state of being overwhelmed most of the time. But there was so much support. It was great fun."

The people involved with *Angie* on all levels, from the studio to the crew, delighted in the graceful presence the show provided. It was a good time. There was none of what was going on over at *Laverne & Shirley* on *this* set, but those involved with *Angie* weren't isolated from the other Paramount Television shows. "Most of the directors and producers on all of the shows knew each other," recalls Pescow. "I just ran into [*Taxi*'s] Jim Burrows recently. It's as if we all went to school together. It was a really extraordinary [time]. I look at it now and realize how unusual it was because I had nothing to base it on then. But I thought at the time, 'Wow. This is really amazing. This must be what it's like at every studio.' But I don't think it was. I think it was really unique to Paramount at that time."

During the week of January 28, 1979, four of the top five shows rated by Nielson were produced by Garry Marshall. *Laverne & Shirley*, *Happy Days*, and *Mork & Mindy* were one, two and three, and *Angie* was number five. Paramount Television and the actors involved in their shows were on a roll. "The amazing thing was, if you lined up the sound stages, there was *Mork & Mindy*, then *Angie*, then *Taxi*, then *Laverne & Shirley*, then *Happy Days*," recalls Pescow. "It was Sitcom College. We'd all meet in the commissary, and it'd be an *Animal House* kind thing but without the food fights. It was kind of a wonderful feeling of community in a sense. Even though they were the top ten shows, it [felt that way] because we were all working together in the same space. On the same lot. It felt like a community even though it was much bigger than that."

That community extended to the actors themselves. "I used to watch [*Taxi*'s] Tony Danza playing catch with his son," remembers Pescow. "Danny DeVito played Angie's Uncle Cheech. Everyone knew each other. We were all there and all so young. Playing basketball or being outside the sound stage even to talk on breaks was common. You didn't run to your dressing room and hide. You wanted to see everyone else. [*Mork & Mindy*'s Robin Williams] used to come running on the set and kill us all with his unbelievable comedy and humor. In the middle of a show he'd just come running in and do a bit and run out. [*Laverne & Shirley*'s] Cindy Williams and I would try to work it out so that we would have lunch on the same schedule. It just seemed natural. It sounds so naïve now, but we all had a good time. Everyone was so happy to be there. It's that joy of being twenty years old and thinking you can conquer the world and this is the way it should be."

Donna Pescow thinks the viewing audience related to *Angie* because of the Cinderella aspects. "The one side of the tracks meets the other," says Pescow. "The whole Cinderella story of marrying Prince Charming and suddenly living in a castle. I thought that it was very sweet because they focused on the relationships of the people. Even though the backgrounds were so different, they would still find common ground somewhere through the episode. It was that really sweet, old-fashioned-style relationship sitcom where you liked the people you were watching. You were interested in what happened to them that week. It was sweet and had an amazing cast, a really fabulous cast."

Angie was a hit and was renewed for a second season. The first show of that season aired on September 11, 1979, with the episode "Angie's Old Friends." Leonora Thuna decided to change one of the key elements of the show, and Angie and Brad sold the coffee shop where Angie worked and opened a hair salon that Angie would run. "[Thuna] put the show into a bit of a new stage," remembers Pescow. "She took us out of the coffee shop and gave us a beauty shop, which was kind of fun to bring both worlds together in a blue-collar sort of atmosphere."

After Angie opened the hair salon, Tim Thomerson was brought in to play a *Shampoo*-like hairdresser named Giovanni. Born on April 8, 1946, in Coronado, California, Thomerson had appeared in several films prior to *Angie*, including *Car Wash* and Robert Altman's *A Wedding*, with *Mork & Mindy*'s Pam Dawber and *Happy Days*' Gavan O'Herlihy.

The show's producers and writers tried to keep the series entertaining. Danny DeVito came in to play Angie's obnoxious, prank-playing Uncle Cheech. "How fabulous was that?" says Donna Pescow, referring to DeVito's turn on the show. "He played this really hysterical character who was a practical joker and drove [the other characters] crazy. It was free reign for Danny to go nuts. It was sort of that blue-collar, Italian, annoying uncle. Wonderful. I loved the ethnicity of it all. They played on the wonderful family connection that this big Italian family had. It was just great. It was so up his alley. He was great fun. He was doing both [*Angie* and *Taxi*] at one time, so he was running back and forth. I think he had a great time and had a lot of fun. Obviously, we all had a great time doing it."

Corey Feldman, who would come on the Paramount lot to co-star in *The Bad News Bears*, was a guest actor on *Angie*. "I remember how adorable he was," says Pescow. "The storyline that he was involved with was that his mom made a play for Brad. It was a very funny script. It was one of my favorite scripts. I remember that little face with those little bangs. That little cherubic look. It's so sweet to see the kids at that age and then watch them advance. Corey was very, very young, and he was cute. I remember him as being incredibly cute. It was a funny, funny script. It was one of those I remember."

Another episode had Angie and Brad's families faced off against one another on the popular television game show *Family Feud*. The writers, producers, and actors involved with the show knew how to have fun. The show was in for some problems, however. There were a couple of strange little things that occurred in the plotlines, such as Brad having a sister named Joyce, who disappeared from the show in a way that was similar to Chuck Cunningham's disappearance from *Happy Days*, but then came back. That was minor. Another major situation was about to unfold.

Angie's airdate and time was moved four times in just one and a half seasons, and the audience, as it had been with the changes in *Mork & Mindy* and *Taxi*, was confused about where and when to find the show. In September 1979 the show was moved to Tuesday nights at 8:30. In January 1980 *Angie* was moved to Monday nights at 8:30. In April of that year it was moved again, this time to Saturday nights at 8:00 and in July finally back to Thursdays at 8:30. *Angie* was thought to be a strong contender against NBC and CBS programming, but a show can suffer only so much movement before it loses its momentum.

The changes within the plot of the show must have been confusing as well. First Angie worked in a coffee shop, then she married the rich Brad, and he bought the coffee shop for Angie to manage. She convinced Brad to move out of his mansion, and then the newlyweds moved into a smaller, but upscale house. Brad moved his practice from across the street from the coffee shop to a suite in their home. Then Angie decided she wanted a beauty shop and opened that, employing her mother (who worked at a newsstand). All of this occurred during a fairly short period of time and had the audience jumping as they tried to keep track of occupations, residences, and characters. The initial good ratings of the series suffered greatly.

Angie was a great vehicle for both Donna Pescow and Robert Hays, but it simply couldn't survive the changes. *Angie* lasted only thirty-six episodes. ABC had done it again. What had been a potentially big series was lost in the ratings war.

"I think that unfortunately the show didn't run as long as it could have," says Pescow. "It's one of those top-ten shows that got canceled. At the time ABC had so many shows that they didn't know where to put it.

So they kept putting it on hold—not because it wasn't doing well but because they didn't know where to put it . . . Ultimately it just kind of fell. I think part of the problem was that [ABC] had, at that time, such a monopoly on comedy that it was really a game of where to put what on the schedule, and they had so much product that was so high-end there was never a concern about whether or not it would go, but it was about where. I think ultimately what happened [to *Angie*] was when Garry [Marshall] really involved himself more in features than in television, that's when things started to fall by the wayside because it wasn't necessarily run by Garry anymore."

Doris Roberts directed the last episode, "Angie and Joyce Go to Jail," which aired on October 2, 1980. "I think everyone was really sorry that the show ended," says Pescow. "Everyone liked everything about it. We were all disappointed when it was canceled because we were still ready to go. We all had a real affinity for the show and wanted it to carry on. We were all shocked when it did end. I remember that I was supposed to do a play on Broadway for Neil Simon, and ABC was pretty sure at that point in time that *Angie* was going to be picked up [for a third season]. I had to bail from [the play]. It would have run into a production problem, time-wise. So I don't think even [ABC] expected *Angie* not to be on the schedule until the last moment. It was surprising."

Angie may have been canceled before its time, but it left a lot of good memories for those involved with the show. "It was a really lovely, non-threatening show," says Pescow. "It was very sweet and funny. It was well written, and people just enjoyed the entertainment of it. *Angie* was great. It did just wonderful things for me all the way around. I look at it as great fun. I think it was a show people remember because it was something they could identify with in that Cinderella kind of world. It's great that Bob and I are still friends and Doris and I are still friends. I value that tremendously."

Paramount Television tried out several other sitcoms in 1979. *Brothers and Sisters* was brought to NBC by Bob Brunner and Arthur Silver and put on the air in January. Brunner was one of the primary writers on *Happy Days* and had also written for the series *Alice* and *Diff'rent Strokes*. Silver had also been a *Happy Days* writer. The show starred Larry Anderson and Randy Brooks. Anderson had played the lead in the television series *The Amazing Spider-Man*. Brooks came to the show via appearances on *One Day at a Time*. Mary Crosby, daughter of singer Bing, and Chris Lemmon, son of actor Jack, rounded out the cast. The plotline for *Brothers and Sisters* was an *Animal House* approach to college living, featuring two lead characters that lived in a fraternity house. By April 1979 the show was gone.

Struck by Lightning was a comedy that starred Jeffrey Kramer and veteran character actor Jack Elam. The show, produced by Michael Friedman, centered on a science teacher who moves into a creepy house and discovers that he is a descendant of Dr. Frankenstein. Elam is evidently descended from Frankenstein's monster. Kramer had appeared in the movies *Jaws* and *Jaws 2* as Deputy Hendricks. Elam had been in scores of film and television roles by this time, having begun his career in 1944 with the movie *Trailin' West*. He appeared in such films as *High Noon*, *Vera Cruz*, *Gunfight at the O.K. Corral*, and *Cat Ballou*. He had supporting roles in television series including *Rawhide*, *The Dakotas*, *Temple Houston*, and *The Texas Wheelers*. Michael Friedman had come from the television series *Project U.F.O.* and *Wally Brown*. The series was to be directed by Joel Zwick, who was a popular director at Paramount Television. Lightning failed to strike, and the show was canceled soon after it began.

Working Stiffs was a show that seemed to have promise, at least on the talent front. The premise was a thin one, focusing on two janitors who work at their uncle's office building and try to work their way up into other jobs. The series starred Jim Belushi and Michael Keaton, and was directed by Penny Marshall and Norman Abbott, who had directed episodes of *The Munsters*, *Get Smart*, and *Welcome Back, Kotter*. Belushi was new to acting and had done only a small role on *Who's Watching the Kids*. Keaton had appeared in small roles on the television shows *All's Fair*, *The Mary Tyler Moore Hour*, and *Studs Lonigan*. Unfortunately the show . . . stiffed. It lasted only three weeks. Paramount Television wanted another hit series. Soon, it was a wish granted.

Chapter 12

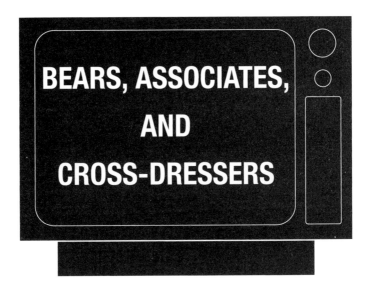

A Paramount Television series debuted on March 24, 1979, that would end the studio's short run of bad luck with new shows and that would find a place in the hearts of family viewers. *The Bad News Bears* was patterned after the 1976 movie of the same name, which starred Walter Matthau, Chris Barnes, Vic Morrow, and Tatum O'Neal. Two sequels to the popular movie had been released as features: *The Bad News Bears in Breaking Training*, with a totally different cast, this time starring William Devane, and *The Bad News Bears Go to Japan*, starring Tony Curtis as a promoter. The original story and plotline center the series as it follows swimming-pool cleaner Morris Buttermaker after he agrees to coach a Little League team to keep out of jail. It's not quite as bad as it sounds. Buttermaker was a former minor league baseball player, and the crime he had committed was driving a client's car into a swimming pool after the client refused to pay him. The team he is assigned is, of course, the worst in the league. Buttermaker teaches the kids baseball and learns lessons of his own pertaining to the heart over the course of the season. The show had a plot that was really nothing unique to television and the movies, but it starred such a terrific group of young actors that it managed to avoid the schmaltz (for the most part) and offer an endearing group of poignant characters. In addition to the gruff coach, *The Bad*

News Bears featured the usual "fish out of water" roles: the klutz (Corey Feldman), the overweight kid (J. Brennan Smith), the smart aleck (Meeno Peluce), the kid with the glasses (Sparky Marcus), the black kid (Kristoff St. John), the girl (Tricia Cast), and two additional kids with a lot of energy (Billy Jayne and Shane Butterworth). Cast as the coach was veteran actor Jack Warden. Buttermaker enjoyed the counsel of school principal Dr. Emily Rappant, played by Catherine Hicks.

The Bad News Bears possessed all the right producers, directors, and writers to become a hit. The show was executive-produced by Bob Brunner and Arthur Silver. Jeffrey Ganz, Ron Leavitt, and Brian Levant (all writers on Garry Marshall shows such as *Happy Days*) were the producers, along with Norman Stiles and John Boni (who had been involved with *When Things Were Rotten*). The writers were Paul Diamond from the less successful *Brothers and Sisters* and Bill Lancaster, who had developed the characters for the original *Bad News Bears* movie. The shows were directed by outstanding talent, including Lowell Ganz, Norman Abbott, Jeff Ganz (*Laverne & Shirley*), and veteran director William Asher (*I Love Lucy*, *Make Room for Daddy*, *The Patty Duke Show*, and *Bewitched*).

It's a show business adage to never work with kids or animals as they'll draw the focus away from the actor. While the serious Jack Warden didn't necessarily have the personality to immediately become enamored with the children of his cast, he certainly had the film and television experience to enable him not to worry about being upstaged. Warden had co-starred in such legendary films as *From Here to Eternity* as Captain Buckley, *Twelve Angry Men* as Juror #7, *Run Silent, Run Deep*, with Clark Gable and Burt Lancaster, and a multitude of other popular movies, including *The Man Who Loved Cat Dancing*, with Burt Reynolds and Sarah Miles, *The Apprenticeship of Duddy Kravitz*, with Richard Dreyfuss, *All the President's Men*, with Dustin Hoffman and Robert Redford, and *Heaven Can Wait*, with Warren Beatty and Julie Christie. Warden's television credits were almost as impressive as his film career, with roles in series such as *Bonanza*, *The Twilight Zone*, *The Untouchables*, *Naked City*, *Ben Casey*, and 1976's *Jigsaw John*, in which he starred as an Los Angeles Police Department investigator.

Warden's personal life was as fascinating as his professional accomplishments. He was born John Lebzelter on September 18, 1920, in Newark, New Jersey. He moved to Louisville, Kentucky, to live with his grandparents when he was a boy and eventually graduated from Du Pont Manuel High School. Warden fought as a welterweight boxer under the name Johnny Costello. He served in the U.S. Navy from 1938 to 1941, and then entered the Merchant Marines as a water tender in the engine room of a ship. Deciding he didn't like sea life, Warden joined the Army in 1942 and became a platoon sergeant and parachute jumpmaster in the 101st Airborne. He fought in World War II's Battle of the Bulge. After he injured his leg in a jump, Warden was hospitalized. While recovering from his injury, Warden read a play by Clifford Odets and decided to become an actor.

Warden experienced minor success on the stage and was cast in his first feature film (with a setting that was quite familiar to the actor), *You're in the Navy Now*, starring Gary Cooper and Jane Greer. Warden's career took off, and he became known as one of Hollywood's most successful utility players. Warden received an Emmy Award for his appearance as a football coach in the 1971 made-for-television movie *Brian's Song*, which starred James Caan. He was nominated for an Academy Award in the Supporting Actor category for his appearance in 1975's *Shampoo*, in which he played Lester, and again in 1978's *Heaven Can Wait*, in which he was cast as football coach Max Corkle.

"Jack Warden was great on the show," says Corey Feldman, who played Regi Tower on *The Bad News Bears*. "He wasn't a big 'kid guy.' He really fit his character. He was never rude or mean to the kids. He was really sweet, but he was never like the Big Poppa either. He wasn't somebody you could go cry on his shoulder. He was very stern, but he was also accommodating to the children. He put up with us well."

Corey Feldman (Regi) on the set of *The Bad News Bears*, 1979. Photo courtesy of Globe Photos, Inc.

Feldman, who had made appearances on *Mork & Mindy* and *Angie* and was already known to Paramount Television casting director Bobby Hoffman, was one of the first kids to be cast in the show. "I was always on the Paramount lot," remembers Feldman. "I was always working for them. When I met with Bobby Hoffman [for the role in *The Bad News Bears*], it wasn't the first time. It was a huge casting call for *The Bad News Bears*. They had a bunch of kids from all over the country. I remember when I went in; there was a huge group of kids waiting outside. It finally came down to me and one other kid. There was this big thing that my parents had to go in and have a meeting with Bobby and let him know that I was going to be a responsible kid, all that kind of stuff. Then I got the job."

Corey Scott Feldman was born on July 16, 1971, in Chatsworth, California, one of four children of Sheila and Bob Feldman. His father was a songwriter ("My Boyfriend's Back") and producer ("Hang On, Sloopy"). Bob was also a member of the pop band the Strangeloves, which had a hit record with "I Want Candy" in 1965. Corey made his professional debut at the age of three in a commercial for McDonald's and landed parts in the television series *Eight Is Enough*, *Alice*, and *The Love Boat*. He appeared in his first film in 1979's *Willa*, with Deborah Raffin and Diane Ladd. Feldman's casting in the role of *The Bad News Bears*' Regi would not come without its downside. "He was the shortstop on the baseball team," Feldman explains. "He was the one who always got hit with the ball. I got hit with a *lot* of balls. And it was sometimes painful."

Also appearing on the show were other talented young actors. Sparky Marcus portrayed Leslie Ogilvie. Born on December 6, 1967, in Hollywood, California, Marcus already had quite a few television and film credits under his belt. He appeared in *Starsky & Hutch*, *Eight Is Enough*, *The Bob Newhart Show*, *Maude*, *WKRP in Cincinnati*, and *What's Happening?* He played Jimmy Joe Jeeter on *Mary Hartman, Mary Hartman* and had a role in the film *Freaky Friday*, with Jodie Foster.

Meeno Peluce played Tanner Boyle. Peluce was the son of makeup artist (*Easy Rider*) and actor (*The Missouri Breaks*) Virgil Frye. (Meeno's brother Sean Frye would play the character Steve in *E.T.: The Extra Terrestrial*, and his sister Soleil Moon Frye would make her mark as Punky Brewster.) Meeno first appeared on *Starsky & Hutch* playing "The Crying Child" and advanced to roles on *Kojak*, *Eight Is Enough*, *The Incredible Hulk*, and *Lou Grant*.

Billy Jayne appeared in the role of Rudi Stein. (Jayne also used his real name, Billy Jacoby, throughout his career.) William Jacoby was born on April 10, 1969, in Flushing, New York. He is the grandson of actor Lou

Jacoby (Lou is noted for his appearances in the films *The Diary of Anne Frank*, in the role of Hans Van Daan, and *Irma La Douce*). Jayne was fairly new to television, having only appeared in *The Horrible Honchos* (an *After-School Special*) and *Little Lulu* (an *ABC Weekend Special*), Jayne played the role of James in Stanley Kramer's 1979 film *The Runner Stumbles*, with the all-star cast of Dick Van Dyke, Kathleen Quinlan, Maureen Stapleton, Ray Bolger, Tammy Grimes, and Beau Bridges.

Shane Butterworth was cast to play Timmy Lupus. Butterworth was born on October 3, 1969, in Sherman Oaks, California, and had appeared on *The Love Boat*, *The Dark Side of Innocence*, a made for television movie starring Anne Archer and Kim Hunter, and 1979's *The Cracker Factory*, which starred Natalie Wood and Perry King. He had also been seen in the film *Exorcist II: The Heretic*.

Kristoff St. John would become an award-winning soap actor, starring in *The Young and the Restless*. As a child he played Ahmad Abdul Rahim in *The Bad News Bears*. St. John was born on July 15, 1966, in New York City. His father, Christopher St. John, appeared in the 1971 film *Shaft*. Kristoff had appeared in *Wonder Woman*, in *The Richard Pryor Special* in 1977, and as the young Alex Haley in the mini-series *Roots: The Next Generation*. It was likely his appearance as Brooker Brown in the 1976 *Happy Days* episode "Football Frolics" that brought him to the attention of *Bad News Bears* casting director Bobby Hoffman.

J. Brennan Smith, the nephew of actor Jim Stacey (*Lancer*), was new to acting. He had appeared only in the short-lived series *The Cliffwood Avenue Kids*. Tricia Cast, who, like Kristoff St. John, would become a soap star on *The Young and the Restless*, would make her acting debut in *The Bad News Bears*.

Catherine Hicks had come from the soap *Ryan's Hope* to play Dr. Emily Rappant. Born on August 6, 1961, in Scottsdale, Arizona, Hicks was a cheerleader at Gerard High School in Phoenix, and she majored in theology and English literature at St. Mary's College, Notre Dame. She won an acting fellowship to Cornell University and earned a Master of Fine Arts degree. Playing Dr. Faith Colleridge on *Ryan's Hope* was her first dramatic role.

The Bad News Bears debuted on Saturday, March 24, 1979, on CBS at 8:00 P.M. "There weren't many prime-time children's shows at the time," remembers Corey Feldman. "We were one of the [few] children's prime-time shows. It was [also] one of the [few] prime-time shows that were developed out of a movie."

The episodes of *The Bad News Bears* were not just stories to which kids could relate but also incorporated good morals and ethics, which no doubt pleased parents. "It was a great show," says Feldman. "It was a great example for kids, I think. Now everything is so pre-packaged and shelf-fed, if you will, whereas then they were still being creative and innovative. They would come up with things that had a good, positive moral message. [We were] doing something that was quality. Nowadays even if they're trying to do quality, I don't think it is necessarily with the pretense that that's what children are looking for. I think it's more for adult drama. The morals and standards were so much different then. [*The Bad News Bears*] was the end of the hippy-dippy phase for everybody, at the end of the seventies. It was like people were trying to become socially aware, people were trying to become politically correct. It was a changing period in culture and in history. I think [*The Bad News Bears*] kind of epitomized that."

With so many children on the show, *The Bad News Bears* set was a unique experience for most of those involved. "I remember how much fun it was," says Feldman. "It was a great experience for me because when you're a kid working as an actor you don't have a lot of down time. You're not able to go play with the other kids and do normal kid stuff. It's really a great environment to be working with a group of other kids. It's kind of like you have a surrogate world, an outside life that's built inside. That's an amazing thing to have. Probably like the kids on *Our Gang* had. You're so secluded from the real world where there are other kids. You're not able to go play baseball; you're not able to do that stuff. One of the great things about the show was that, first of all, you're always outside. We were always on the baseball field. We were always getting to do what kids do."

The nature of the episodes also gave the children an opportunity to expand their horizons when it came to both work and play. "During one of the episodes we built some go-carts and we had this big go-cart race," remembers Feldman. "That was great fun. I think when I did the go-cart episode I burned out like three engines. I was seven years old trying to drive a go-cart, hitting the gas and the brake at the same time. There was another one where we did a triathlon on the grounds of the baseball diamond. They had all this really cool stuff, like water stuff, stuff to climb, stuff to jump down on. Stuff to make it adventurous for a kid. It was a great episode. There was one where we had a car wash, and we were washing people's cars. I remember having water fights. So it was great for me. It was a lot of fun. The episodes were great. There was a lot of joy in it all."

With so many kids involved, one would expect there would be arguments and posturing, but for the most part the children got along well. Several of them formed friendships that would endure into adulthood.

"It's very rare that you get that connection on any show or any film or any project you do," muses Feldman. "Especially for a group of kids to have that bond. If Meeno and I saw each other or if Billy Jacoby and I saw each other it would be like old home week. They were really close to me. We used to take family outings on days off. I used to sleep over at Meeno's house a lot. Maybe once in a while he would come sleep over at my house. J. Brennan Smith came over once and slept at the house. It wasn't very common that we were allowed to have sleep-overs because we were always working. At least if it was with other members of the cast it would some-times be a doable kind of thing. The one I see a lot [today] is Kristoff St. John. We still see each other probably once a year, every couple of years. We'll run into each other at a celebrity event or we'll get together for dinner or something. He's a great guy, a really nice guy."

As it was with the other shows filming at the time, working on the Paramount lot was an adventure for the cast of *The Bad News Bears*. "We used the sound stage that *The Brady Bunch* used to work on [from 1969 to1974]," remembers Feldman. "That was a big adventure for us. We'd be really excited about that. We would walk through the hallways, and we'd see like little love letters from Greg to Marsha. Or stuff scribbled on the walls or in the trailers. We'd say, "Are we getting the Bradys' trailer? Are we getting Peter's trailer?' That was like a big deal to us. I also remember they filmed *American Gigolo* on the Paramount lot around that time. I was never able to go on the set because it was always closed. They didn't want kids on the set. I remember walking by and going, 'What is this? Why are they always closed? Why can't we see it? What is it?'"

When the kids worked away from the lot they enjoyed meeting fans. "*The Bad News Bears* really was my introduction to becoming famous," says Feldman. "People would start gathering around to watch us work. We would be working out somewhere like a gas station or a freeway on-ramp, wherever it was that the story took us. People would gather round. That was the first time I remember fans coming to the set and actually asking for autographs. I think at seven years old is when I really learned how to sign my name professionally."

Even the seasoned members of the crew would be affected by the positive nature of the show and the kids who acted in *The Bad News Bears*. "The other great part about the experience was the camaraderie between not just the kids but a lot of the crew," recalls Feldman. "I remember at the wrap party when we were ending the show and saying good-bye. It was so sad, and I remember the director of photography because he was a very stern man. You couldn't get a lot out of him, but when you did it was meaningful. He was this very straight, kind of stodgy old man, into his own thing. At the cast and crew wrap party everybody was so sad. I went up to say good-bye to him, and I gave him a hug, and he started crying. He was just hugging me, going, 'I'm going to miss you kids so much.' It was just very moving. It really gave you the feeling that 'We've done something here and we've really had a close experience with people.' Very bittersweet."

Unfortunately, the same thing that was going on at rival ABC was going on at CBS. The show changed time slots once too often. First it aired at Saturday nights at 8:00. Then in September and October 1979 it was moved to Saturdays at 8:30. In June 1980 it was moved back to 8:00. Then in July back to 8:30. The audience couldn't keep track of it and was confused as to when to tune in. Corey Feldman thinks part of the problem was the night on which it aired. "It was a terrible night," recalls Feldman. "It's still a terrible night. Nobody wants to watch TV. You want to go out, you want to do stuff. I'm sure that at the end of the day [that] was the biggest deterrent to [the show's success]."

The Bad News Bears was only three episodes into its second season when it was canceled. The fans, especially the young ones and their parents, would miss the show. So would the cast, who had learned some important professional lessons during their time on the series. "It taught me first of all what it is to show up every day," says Feldman. "At that point I had really only been doing episodic and commercial work. I had done a couple of films, but they were bit parts. It was before *Gremlins*. I had done a TV movie called *Willa*, and I had done *Time After Time* and *The Fox and the Hound*. None of that stuff was like you had to be there every day. That was my first time having to show up to work every day, seven in the morning. I hated having to be up early in the morning, kind of like I still do now. I learned how to be a professional and how not to cry if somebody was mad at me or yelled at me or whatever. You learned how to just suit up and show up."

The last episode of *The Bad News Bears* aired in July 1980. Yet the series (and, of course, the movie that preceded it) inspired enough of a following that another movie of the same name was made in 2005. Richard Linklater, director of the film *Dazed and Confused*, would direct Billy Bob Thorton (as Buttermaker), Marcia Gay Harden (as the principal), and Greg Kinnear (as a character named Bullock) in the remake. Unfortunately, the film lacked the magic of the series or the original movie and had limited success.

On September 23, 1979, another Paramount Television show debuted on ABC. *The Associates* was a creation of the folks who brought us *Taxi*: James L. Brooks, Stan Daniels, and Ed. Weinberger. The show was created by Charlie Hauck, and the primary director was *Taxi*'s Jim Burrows. The new series centered on three young lawyers who are fresh out of law school and become associates at the New York City firm of Bass and Marshall. The show was based on the novel by John Jay Osborn Jr., who was also the author of *The Paper Chase*. Guitar legend B.B. King performed the theme song, "The Young Lawyer Blues."

The Associates had a wonderful cast. Veteran stage, film, and television actor Wilfrid Hyde-White headed the group of talented actors as the firm's scatterbrained but extraordinary managing partner, Emerson Marshall. Hyde-White had appeared in the films *The Third Man*, *Ten Little Indians*, and *My Fair Lady*, as Colonel Pickering. Hyde-White was born in Gloucestershire, England, on May 12, 1903. He attended Marlborough College and the Royal Academy of Dramatic Arts. (He was later quoted as saying that he learned two things at drama school: that he couldn't act and that it didn't matter.) Hyde-White made his stage debut in 1922 and was active in London theater until being "discovered" by film director George Cukor. He made his film debut in 1934's *Night Mail*, with Henry Oscar and Hope Davy. He worked steadily in films and continued to perform on stage, several times with Laurence Olivier and Vivien Leigh. Hyde-White was nominated for a Tony Award in 1957 for *The Reluctant Debutant* and in 1973 for *The Jockey Club Stakes*. He appeared on television in such shows as *Peyton Place*, *Columbo*, and *Battlestar Galactica*.

Canadian Martin Short played Tucker Kerwin, a midwesterner who is sometimes baffled by the viewpoints of his Ivy League co-workers. Short would later enjoy massive success with *Second City Television*, *Saturday Night Live*, and eventually his own vehicles, *The Martin Short Show* and *Primetime Glick*, but he was fairly new to acting at the time of *The Associates*. Martin Hayter Short was born on March 26, 1950, in Hamilton, Ontario, to Charles Patrick (an executive with a Canadian car company) and Olive Short (a musician). When he was twelve, his brother David was killed in a car accident. By the time Short was twenty, both of his parents were also dead. Short graduated from Westdale High School and then attended McMaster University in Hamilton, Ontario, where he was a pre-med major. He had a change of mind about the profession he'd like to pursue and switched to sociology to study for a career as a social worker. After acting in a Toronto production of *Godspell* with Gilda Radner, Paul Shaffer, and Eugene Levy, Short decided to become an actor. His first professional acting job was in a Visa commercial, playing a giant credit card. Prior to being cast in *The Associates*, Short had landed roles in the Canadian children's television show *Cucumber*, on *The David*

Steinberg Show, where he appeared with his friends Dave Thomas and John Candy, on *Cementhead*, and *Right On*, and in a small role in the film *Lost and Found*, with George Segal, Glenda Jackson, and Maureen Stapleton.

Several of the cast members came to *The Associates* even more bright and shiny than Martin Short. Joe Regalbuto was cast to play Eliot Streeter, a junior partner determined to one day take over the firm. He had appeared only in a small role in the film *The Goodbye Girl*, with Richard Dreyfuss and Marsha Mason. Regalbuto was born in New York City on August 24, 1949. Alley Mills was cast in the role of Leslie Dunn, a Columbia University graduate determined to save the world. Mills had only a few acting credits to her name. She was a Chicago native, born on May 9, 1951. and had appeared on *The Waltons* and *Kaz*. Another newcomer was Shelley Smith, in the role of Sara. Smith was a former print and runway model born on October 25, 1952, in Princeton, New Jersey. *The Associates* was also her first acting experience. *Angie*'s Tim Thomerson played the role of the lascivious mail boy Johnny Danko.

By this time Fred Silverman had left ABC for NBC, and Tony Thomopolus was the head of programming at ABC. For some strange reason *The Associates* was scheduled to air after *Mork & Mindy*. The two shows were quite different, and the chance of their finding the same audience was remote at best. *The Associates* had been on the air for only five shows when ABC put it on hiatus. Although the show was quality television, the viewing audience decided to switch channels at the end of *Mork & Mindy*. *The Associates* went back on the air in March 1980 on Thursday nights. Wonderful guest actors were brought in, including Danny DeVito, Cloris Leachman, John Ritter, Jack Gilford, and John Houseman. Yet the high level of talent couldn't sustain a show that was originally scheduled at the wrong time. This time, although more episodes were filmed, *The Associates* lasted only four weeks before ABC canceled the series for good.

"I don't think [*The Associates*] appealed to the people," says Jim Burrows, who directed the pilot. "I had a great time doing it. The set was fabulous. I thought the pilot was really good." Yet some shows have that magic and others just fall short of whatever ingredient it is that makes a show a hit. "Some shows work and some don't," continues Burrows. "I can't tell you why. I just don't think there was a guy [who was] a center of that show like there was on *Taxi* or there was on *Cheers*. I don't think there was anybody to hook into."

It was a shame that *The Associates* was never awarded a better time slot, as it was well written and beautifully acted. The show's talented cast would make their mark upon television at a later date. There *were* some rewards for those who had been involved in the series. In 1979 Wilfrid Hyde-White was nominated for a Golden Globe, and despite its short run, *The Associates* was nominated for Best Television Comedy. Stan Daniels, Ed. Weinberger, Charlie Hauck, and Michael Leeson were nominated for Emmys in 1980 for their writing. All for a show that had lasted only nine episodes.

Goodtime Girls allowed Paramount Television and Miller, Milkis, and Boyett another opportunity. The producers of *Angie* were back, with a premise that featured four young women who were forced to share an apartment during the housing shortage of World War II as they worked in Washington, D.C. Howard Storm, Joel Zwick, and Tony Mordente served as directors. (Mordente had portrayed Action in the film *West Side Story*, and then went on to direct episodes of series such as *M*A*S*H*, *Rhoda*, *Quincy*, and *Benson*.) The theme song was the catchy "Back in the Forties," sung by the Charles Fox Singers.

Once again the talent was exceptional. The show starred Georgia Engel in the role of "dumb blonde" and war bride Loretta Smoot. Engel had been a featured player on *The Mary Tyler Moore Show*, playing Ted Baxter's love interest, Georgette, and on the popular *Betty White Show* as Mitzi. Engel was a unique comedic talent. Georgia Bright Engel was born on July 28, 1948, in Washington, D.C. She attended the University of Hawaii at Manoa (her sister Robin was 1967's Miss Hawaii). Engel made her film debut playing Margot in the 1971 Milos Forman film *Taking Off*, with Buck Henry. *The Mary Tyler Moore Show* was her first series. The producers of that show liked her so much that they expanded her one-shot appearance into a recurring role. Engel won two Emmy Awards for her role as Georgette.

Playing the more sensible character Edith Bedelmeyer was actress Annie Potts. Potts had gained attention in the 1978 film *King of the Gypsies*, with Shelley Winters, Susan Sarandon, and Eric Roberts. (*Taxi's* Judd Hirsch also appeared in the film as Groffo.) Potts's first television role was a guest-starring stint in the series *Family*. She then went on to star in the television movie *Flatbed Annie & Sweetiepie: Lady Truckers*, with Harry Dean Stanton and Kim Darby (Ron Howard's dad, Rance, also had a role in the movie). Potts was born on October 28, 1952, in Franklin, Kentucky. Upon graduation from high school, she attended Stephens College in Missouri. Potts studied Theater Arts and participated in graduate studies in California. She married her college boyfriend, Steven Hartley, at the age of twenty. The couple was involved in a car accident soon after their marriage that resulted in the loss of Hartley's leg and multiple serious injuries for Potts. After her rehabilitation, the actress decided not to let the accident affect her future and continued on her career path.

Lorna Patterson appeared in the role of the wholesome Betty Crandall. Patterson had worked on the Paramount lot before, playing the role of Nikki in the ill-fated *Working Stiffs*. She was born on July 1, 1956, in Whittier, California. She attended Rio Hondo College in Whittier and became active in community theater. Patterson's first role was in Garry Marshall's 1979 made-for-television movie *Beanes of Boston*, a takeoff on the British television show *Are You Being Served?* The story involved the employees of a department store. Patterson played Miss Brahms and co-starred with Alan Sues, John Hillerman, and Charlotte Rae.

The fourth goodtime girl was society snob Camille Rittenhouse, played by Francine Tacker. Tacker had played the role of Elizabeth in the popular series *The Paper Chase*. Joining the "girls" were the characters Frankie Molardo, the 4-F cabdriver, and his roommate, Benny Lohman. Frankie was played by the personable Adrian Zmed. Zmed had appeared a couple of times on *Starsky & Hutch* and had made a guest appearance on *Angie*. He also appeared in the role of Socks Palermo in the 1979 Gary Adelson series *Flatbush*. Zmed was born to Romanian parents on March 4, 1954, in Chicago. A young actor named Peter Scolari was cast in the role of Frankie's buddy Benny, although Benny had little to say or do. Scolari had a small role in the 1978 film *Take Off* and played the role of Douglas Burdett in the short-lived series *Wally Brown*. Marcia Lewis played landlady Irma Coolidge. Lewis came to the show after earlier appearances in *Happy Days*, *Who's Watching the Kids*, and *The Bob Newhart Show*. Scott Baio from *Happy Days* popped up as Edith's brother in a *Goodtime Girls* guest appearance, and *Laverne & Shirley*'s Michael McKean played a wheelchair-bound vet.

Goodtime Girls debuted on January 22, 1980. The Vietnam War had ended just a few years earlier, and setting the series during World War II was a risk. Would viewers want to revisit that era? They didn't get much of a chance to make their choice known. The show unfortunately suffered the fate of *The Associates* because of its constant movement on ABC's schedule. Its first few episodes aired on Tuesday nights, although the show was pre-empted during its third episode. The series was pulled, only to air again, this time on Saturday nights from April 12 though April 26. It was pulled yet again and came back to life on August 1 on Friday nights. By August 29 *Goodtime Girls* was gone for good.

Miller-Milkis-Boyett had better luck on their next venture. Chris Thompson, who had written for *Laverne & Shirley*, joined forces with Tom

Miller, Bob Boyett, and Eddie Milkis to create a show they titled *Bosom Buddies*. Thompson brought along Leonard Ripps and David Chalmers, who had worked with him on *Goodtime Girls*, to help develop the concept.

Similarly themed to the 1959 movie *Some Like It Hot*, starring Tony Curtis and Jack Lemmon, *Bosom Buddies* involved the adventures of two advertising agency tyros from Ohio who lose the New York City apartment they share when the building is demolished. Kip Wilson is an illustrator who would rather pursue art, and Henry Desmond works as a copywriter but dreams of writing a novel. When the young men tell their co-worker Amy Cassidy about their need for housing, she offers to share her apartment with them. The catch is that Amy lives in the Susan B. Anthony Hotel, a women-only residence. When an apartment becomes available in the Susan B. Anthony, Kip and Henry invent feminine alter egos named Buffy and Hildegard. Buffy and Hildegard are Kip and Henry's "sisters," which allows visiting possibilities while ensuring that the two men can continue to live in the inexpensive residence (and, of course, be surrounded by women). Only Amy knows that Buffy and Hildegard are actually men. Henry decides to write a book about their experience, and Kip wants to score with Amy's roommate, Sonny Lumet. The premise was far-fetched but had interesting possibilities for comedy.

The right casting of the characters Kip and Henry was crucial if the comedy was to work. The producers' first choices were Bobby DiCicco for the role of Kip and Perry Lang for the character Henry. DiCicco had starred in Robert Zemeckis's film *I Wanna Hold Your Hand* and appeared as Wally Stephens in Steven Spielberg's *1941*. Lang had appeared in a slew of teen pics and also in *1941* as Dennis De Soto. (Lang would go on to become a successful director, helming episodes in such television series as *Gilmore Girls*, *Everwood*, *Las Vegas*, and *Jack & Bobby*.) Those two actors were not available for *Bosom Buddies*. With just a week to go before *Bosom Buddies* was set to shoot, Chris Thompson called in Peter Scolari, whom he knew as a talented actor who had been underused in *Goodtime Girls*. Scolari had already shown comic potential. Pairing him with another actor who could lose himself in the iffy foundation of the comedy was critical. The producers looked to a young actor named Tom Hanks. Hanks had appeared only in an episode of *The Love Boat* and in the horror flick *He Knows You're Alone*, but he showed definite promise in the eyes of the seasoned Miller, Milkis, and Boyett.

Future Academy Award–winning actor Thomas Jeffrey Hanks was born on July 9, 1956, in Concord, California. He was one of four children of Janet and Amos Hanks. Amos was a chef who was a descendant of Nancy Hanks, the mother of Abraham Lincoln. Hanks's parents divorced when he was a young boy, and the family was divided. Tom and his brother Larry and sister Sandra lived with their father, and younger brother Jim stayed with their mother. Life with Amos Hanks was nomadic and insecure. Tom experienced ten moves, five elementary schools, and two stepmothers by the age of ten. In 1966 the family settled in Oakland, California, where Tom eventually attended Skyline High School. The young man displayed an avid interest in sports and participated in soccer and track. Hanks joined the Thespian Club while in high school and discovered he had a strong interest in acting. He appeared in both dramatic and musical productions and was named Skyline High's Best Actor of 1974.

After graduation from high school, Hanks attended Chabot College in Hayward, California. In conjunction with a drama class, he attended a performance of *The Iceman Cometh* produced by the Berkeley Repertory Company. Hanks was impressed by the talent of actor Joe Spano, who appeared in the production, and decided to become a professional actor. He transferred to California State University, Sacramento. When he appeared in a local theater production of *The Cherry Orchard*, he impressed the director and was invited to play the role of Gremio in *The Taming of the Shrew* for the Great Lakes Shakespeare Festival in Cleveland, Ohio. When Hanks returned to Sacramento after the summer of 1977, he decided to not continue his college education but rather to work at the Sacramento Civic Theater, learning the trade of stage production. The following summer he returned to Cleveland to play Proteus in *Two Gentlemen of Verona*. He won the Cleveland Critics Circle award for Best Actor.

At the age of twenty-two, Hanks tried his luck as an actor in New York City. He took his college sweetheart, Samantha Lewes, with him, and the couple was blessed with their first child, their son Colin. (Colin would later also become an actor, appearing on the popular television series *Roswell* and *The O.C.* and in films. The couple would later part, and in 1985 Hanks would meet his future wife, Rita Wilson, on the set of the movie *Volunteers*.) Having no luck in New York, Hanks returned to Cleveland for the summer, but in the fall he was cast in *The Mandrake* at the Riverside Shakespeare Theater. He finally got an agent and was cast in the slasher movie *He Knows You're Alone*.

About the time Tom Hanks was looking to develop an acting career, ABC Television was actively pursuing young talent. The network launched a talent-development program, and Hanks auditioned. A series of in-depth auditions led the talent scouts to include Hanks in their program, and he was shortly thereafter cast as Kip on *Bosom Buddies*.

Henry and Kip's alter egos, Hildegard (Peter Scolari) and Buffy (Tom Hanks). *Bosom Buddies*, 1980. Photo courtesy of Globe Photos, Inc.

The cast of *Bosom Buddies*, 1980. Top (left to right): Telma Hopkins (Isabelle), Holland Taylor (Ruth), Lucille Benson (Lilly). Bottom (left to right): Peter Scolari (Henry), Wendie Jo Sperber (Amy), Tom Hanks (Kip), Donna Dixon (Sonny). Photo courtesy of Globe Photos, Inc.

Peter Scolari was happy to come aboard the production as Henry Desmond. Born on September 12, 1954, in New Rochelle, New York, Scolari discovered his love of acting while appearing in a high school production of *How to Succeed in Business Without Really Trying*. Pursuing a career in acting wasn't his first choice. Scolari wanted to be a professional baseball player, but those dreams were dashed when he injured his elbow. While attending the City College of New York, he began to audition and appear in off-Broadway plays, and was one of the founding members of New York's Colonnades Theater Lab. Scolari's appearances in the movie *Take Off* and in two short-lived series, *Wally Brown* and *Goodtime Girls*, would precede his being cast on *Bosom Buddies*.

Hired to play Kip and Henry's pal Amy was Wendie Jo Sperber. Sperber was better known as a film actress, having just come off the film *Used Cars*, with Kurt Russell and *The Bad News Bears'* Jack Warden. She was born in Hollywood on September 15, 1958. While still in high school, Sperber attended a summer drama workshop at California State University, Northridge, and decided she wanted to be an actress. At the age of fifteen, she was cast in the small role of Kuchinsky in the movie *Corvette Summer*, with Mark Hamill and Annie Potts. A role in the film *I Wanna Hold Your Hand* followed, as well as appearances in the Steven Spielberg film *1941*, in which she played Maxine and co-starred with Dan Ackroyd and John Belushi, and then in *Used Cars*, as Nervous Nona alongside Kurt Russell and *Laverne & Shirley's* David L. Lander and Michael McKean. Sperber also landed the tile role in the made for television movie *Dinky Hocker*, with *Lassie's* mom, June Lockhart. Sperber's brother would later say that she "dedicated her life to making people feel good." Sperber was a good choice for the role and very believable as *Bosom Buddies'* good pal with the heart of gold and two insane male friends who just happen to masquerade as women.

Donna Dixon was the perfect choice for Sonny Lumet. Dixon was working as a model while attending college when she came to the attention of the show's producers. *Bosom Buddies* was her first acting role. Dixon was born on July 20, 1957, in Alexandria, Virginia. Her father owned the club Hillbilly Heaven in nearby Lorton, where Donna was raised. Dixon was anointed Miss District of Columbia 1977 and was the first runner-up as Miss U.S.A. that year. Most everyone found Dixon very much like the sweet and beautiful character she would play.

Tony Orlando and Dawn's Telma Hopkins played Isabelle, who was a much bolder sexpot who also lived in the hotel. Hopkins was born on October 28, 1948, in Louisville, Kentucky, and had appeared in a couple of episodes of *The Love Boat*. She also played Daisy in *Roots: The Next*

Generation and appeared for a few weeks in the series *A New Kind of Family*, with Eileen Brennan.

Holland Taylor was cast in the role of Ruth Dunbar, Henry and Kip's unscrupulous boss. Taylor had begun her career in the television movie *J.T.* She was born on January 14, 1943, in Philadelphia to Virginia and C. Tracy Taylor, an attorney. Taylor attended Quaker schools while growing up in Allentown and enrolled in Bennington College to major in drama. She moved to New York City, where she became an acting student of Stella Adler and studied dance at the Joffrey. In 1973 she was cast as Ruth Winter in the television soap *Somerset*. She went on to appear in such television series as *Beacon Hill* and *The Edge of Night* (as Denise Norwood Cavanaugh) and in the film *The Next Man*, which starred Sean Connery. (Holland would become very successful as an actress and is known also for her roles in *The Naked Truth*, *The Practice*, and *The L Word*, as well as dozens of other television shows and movies.)

Rounding out the *Bosom Buddies* cast was veteran Hollywood actress Lucille Benson, who played landlord Lilly Sinclair. Benson, born on July 17, 1914, in Scottsboro, Alabama, was seen often in early television programming. Her first role was in a 1952 episode of the *Armstrong Circle Theater*, and she was a regular on episodic television productions through her work on *Cannon*, *Bonanza*, *Petrocelli*, *Police Woman*, *Little House on the Prairie*, and dozens of other series. Her first feature role was as Beulah Binnings in the 1959 film *The Fugitive Kind*, with Marlon Brando and Joanne Woodward. She appeared often in films, with roles in *Little Fauss and Big Halsy*, *Slaughterhouse-Five*, and *Mame*. (Miss Benson died of cancer on February 17, 1984, in her hometown of Scottsboro.)

To the tune of its theme song, "My Life," written and sung by Billy Joel, *Bosom Buddies* debuted on November 27, 1980. The show was placed between *Mork & Mindy* and *Barney Miller*, which practically guaranteed a good start. To the delight of the cast and producers, it placed seventh in that week's ratings.

The first episode was shot on film, but the decision to switch to videotape was made for Episode #2. The dialogue was hip and finely honed, and the jokes were continuous and well-delivered. The stars of the show were extremely talented, and the rest of the cast added to the excellence of the acting. The cast was tight, and the humor outside of the cross-dressing premise flowed easily.

Tom Hanks and Peter Scolari had chemistry to spare. Although they were fairly new to television, they both hit the ground running. Hanks later said that it was his goal to "deliver the goods" as best he could. He said there was no time to be lazy since they did so much of the show in such a short period of time. Scolari says that he and Hanks started "winging the script" from the very beginning, ad-libbing and adding to the dialogue. Scolari was pleased that he and Hanks became fast friends from the first day of production.

Although they would acknowledge the talent of the actors, the critics were mixed in their reviews of *Bosom Buddies*. A review in the *Los Angeles Times* claimed that "if ever there was a turkey, this is it." Yet that newspaper's Howard Rosenberg wrote, several episodes later, that although the show was too "scattershot and uneven," *Bosom Buddies* was on the "edge of something." *TV Guide* said that while they were not fooled by the female impersonations, they were willing to "make the effort" due to the talent of the lead actors. *Time* magazine found the premise a bit stale but thought the show had promise nonetheless.

The show continued to get high ratings, but then ABC once again began to tinker with the time slot. After a few weeks the network put the show on a short hiatus. The high numbers never returned for *Bosom Buddies*. The viewing audience likely thought the show had gone off the air.

The second season of *Bosom Buddies* debuted on October 8, 1981, on ABC, which renewed the show but was not wholly committed to seeing it through. Changes to *Bosom Buddies* seemed to sound its death knell. Henry and Kip left the ad agency to take over the firm of Henry's Uncle Mort. Their former boss, who continued to be played by Holland Taylor, went with them. The character Lilly left the show, and Isabelle became the manager of the hotel. Kip proclaimed his love for Sonny, who pursued her dream of becoming a nurse.

Hanks and Scolari were so good together that the premise of cross-dressing was almost completely abandoned. That foundation was iffy at best to sustain a long run, although in the first few episodes it was very funny. It was also difficult, time-wise, to have the actors change in and out of their clothes while filming before an audience. Once the boys were "found out" by the people with whom they lived at the Susan B. Anthony, the show took a definite turn south. Even the hilarious exchanges between Hanks and Scolari couldn't hold the audiences' attention. Without the emphasis on the deception, the show had an almost split personality. Was it a show about crossing-dressing and its intricate problems and situations, or was it more about the trials and tribulations of two young ad men and their friends? The viewing audience was confused, and despite the show's strong start, the ratings fell. *Bosom Buddies* was not renewed for a third season. (The network received more than 35,000 letters from viewers protesting that decision.) The last episode aired on May 27, 1981. Even so, *Bosom Buddies* wasn't quite dead yet. After Tom Hanks began to gain popularity in films, NBC purchased the series and re-ran a handful of episodes in the summer of 1984.

As *Goodtime Girls* was struggling to locate its audience and as *Bosom Buddies* was taking off, Paramount Pictures producer A. C. Lyles executive-produced a series titled *Here's Boomer*. Lyles, who to this day is a popular producer on the Paramount lot, began his career as a producer with 1957's *Short Cut to Hell*, directed by legendary actor James Cagney. Lyles was born in Jacksonville, Florida, on May 17, 1918, and has been employed by Paramount Pictures since 1928. His first film was *Raymie*, starring David Ladd (son of actor Alan) and John Agar. Lyle's pictures include *The Young and the Brave*, with Rory Calhoun, *Town Tamer*, *Johnny Reno*, and *Apache Uprising*, with Dana Andrews and Pat O'Brien, *Waco*, starring Howard Keel and Jane Russell, and many other notable westerns.

Here's Boomer was written by Lowell Ganz and Arthur Silver. The series was not exactly a sitcom, but rather a poignant show about Boomer, an adorable mutt who wanders the countryside bringing happiness into the lives of the people he encounters. The series was developed from a one-hour holiday special that aired on NBC in December 1979 and starred *M*A*S*H*'s Larry Linville, Joyce Van Patten, Harriett Nelson, and *Happy Days*' Al Molinaro. The show was cute and family-friendly. Boomer even appeared on *The Tonight Show Starring Johnny Carson* and *The David Letterman Show*. The series ran on NBC from March 1980 until August 1, 1982. (*Here's Boomer* was picked up years later to air on the Disney Channel.) A Boomer movie titled *Boomer in Hollywood* also aired in 1980 and starred a young Michael J. Fox, who was about to bring a welcome presence to Paramount Television.

Chapter 13

A NEW FAMILY
IN TOWN

By 1982 Paramount Television had enjoyed a tremendously successful television comedy run of more than eight years, thanks to Garry Marshall and his associates and the team from John Charles Walters. Gary Nardino continued as President of Paramount Television, and he decided to inject some new production energy into the studio's strong command of the television sitcom. As in the past, Paramount looked to someone already well tested in the genre to produce their next entry. Nardino was well aware of the talent that rose from the ranks of MTM Productions, and it was there that he found his next executive producer.

Gary David Goldberg was a successful writer on such mega-hits as *The Bob Newhart Show*, *M*A*S*H*, *Alice*, *The Tony Randall Show*, and *Lou Grant*. Goldberg's talent and creativity had been responsible for his ascent to the position of producer of the Randall show. Goldberg also produced *Lou Grant*, for which he won an Emmy for Outstanding Comedy Series in 1979. Goldberg was ready to produce episodic television on his own and formed Ubu Productions. (The dog that is featured in the opening of Goldberg's shows was the dog Goldberg had treasured during his college years. Although Ubu has long-since passed from this world, his likeness remains a constant on Ubu Productions credits.)

Goldberg's first production was the CBS series *Making the Grade*, starring Graham Jarvis, James Houghton, Alley Mills, and George Wendt. Another show he attempted to launch was 1979's *The Last Resort*, which starred Larry Breeding and Stephanie Faracy. Breeding was the actor who appeared on *Laverne & Shirley* and who was killed on October 1, 1982, in a Los Angeles car accident. He also appeared in *Who's Watching the Kids*. Faracy had also been seen on *Laverne & Shirley* and in the film *Heaven Can Wait*, with Warren Beatty. Airing on CBS, *The Last Resort* lasted only six months. Goldberg said that the new show that he had in mind for Paramount Television would be his last attempt at a series.

Gary David Goldberg was yet another New Yorker, born in Brooklyn on June 24, 1944. He had his introduction to the television industry when he landed a position as writer on *The Bob Newhart Show*. By the early eighties Goldberg had in mind a television series that would perfectly match the times. The "Reagan Era" was thriving, and the show Goldberg suggested would focus on the differing cultural values of America's most current decades. The premise was an attempt to appeal to the social and political awareness of the sixties and early seventies, as well as the self-centered and ambition-driven nature of the late seventies and early eighties. It was risky television at a time when the viewing audience was very particular in making choices that were age- and interest-driven. To appeal to both flower children and those who viewed themselves as warriors on the track of financial success and wealth, the show would need to tread a fine line. Goldberg was up to the challenge. He struck a deal with Paramount Television whereby he would retain partial ownership of his future shows, and Paramount's money would help launch and maintain those shows, should they be well received by viewers. In exchange, Paramount Television would retain the rights to distribution and syndication.

Family Ties featured the Keaton family, who lived in Columbus, Ohio. Semi-autobiographically based on producer Goldberg and his wife Diane's experiences, the family was a fusion of social ideals. Steven and Elyse, the family's mother and father, are former Vietnam War protesters and Peace Corps volunteers. Steven and Elyse remain entrenched in their liberal and ideological approach to life and society. Steven works as a station manager for the local PBS station, and Elyse is an independent architect. The Keatons have three children: Alex, Mallory, and Jennifer. While Mallory is an underachieving teenager whose main interests are boys and shopping, eldest child Alex is the epitome of everything his parents are against. Alex claims he's . . . gasp . . . a Republican and throws himself into the pursuit of great personal accomplishment and wealth (a portrait of William F. Buckley hangs over his bed). Alex's long-suffering parents try to impose their values of charity and selfless service on their angst-ridden, over-achieving son. Little Jennifer, the youngest child, sees both the good and the not-so-good in her siblings' beliefs and conduct and is quick to comment. The elements were firmly in place to explore the mind-sets and differences of the times and of the family's viewpoints and aspirations. *Family Ties* was presented as a sitcom, but it was to be much more than that as it traversed the rocky terrain of individual family values. *Family Ties* was initially developed for CBS as an hour-long show. But CBS decided that they didn't want to invest in the show, and it was then sold to NBC as a half-hour series.

"It's my understanding that when we began the show in 1982, there were few, if any, intact nuclear families on prime time, and few sitcoms that viewers felt they could watch together, as a family," says Michael Gross, who would play the patriarch of the Keaton family. "I think we helped to make the family sitcom popular again. *The Cosby Show*, for all its acclaim, actually followed us by a year or two."

Gary David Goldberg looked to Susan Borowitz, Lloyd Garver, and Michael J. Weithorn to be the producers of his new show. Garver had been a writer for episodes of *Love, American Style*, *Alice*, and *Happy Days*, among others. Weithorn had written for the Goldberg-produced series *Making the Grade*. It was the first television-producing appointment for all three writers. The show didn't have just one director, but rather drew on the talents of various directors, including Peter Baldwin, Tony Mordente, Debbie Allen, Michael Zinberg, Sam Weisman, and Will MacKenzie. The first show was directed by Asaad Kalada (*Rhoda*, *WKRP in Cincinnati*, *Benson*) and was written by Goldberg himself.

The key to the casting and to the success of the show would lie with the central character Alex Keaton. Goldberg had an actor named Matthew Broderick in mind for the role. The teenage Broderick, son of actor James Broderick, was appearing on Broadway in Neil Simon's *Brighton Beach Memoirs*. Broderick listened to Goldberg's pitch but decided that he didn't want to leave New York or commit to a long-term television project. Actor Michael J. Fox had earlier auditioned for the role of Flip on *Happy Days*. Although that role had gone to Billy Warlock, Fox was at least known on the Paramount lot, and Goldberg had likely met Fox when Fox made an appearance on *Lou Grant* in 1979.

Michael Andrew Fox was born in Edmonton, Alberta, Canada, on June 9, 1961, one of four children of Bill and Phyllis Fox, an actress. (The J. that Fox adopted for his screen name was a tribute to character actor Michael J. Pollard.) When Fox was ten, his father retired as a sergeant in the Canadian Army Signal Corps, and the family settled outside Vancouver. Michael made his acting debut in the 1976 Canadian sitcom *Leo and Me*, starring as Jamie (the "Me" of the title) alongside Canadian actor Brent Carver. The series was short-lived, but the acting bug had bitten Fox. He quit high school and appeared in local stage productions (Fox received his G.E.D. in 1995). When he was eighteen, Fox moved to Los Angeles to pursue his acting career. Small roles in the television movies *Letters from Frank*, with Lew Ayers and Art Carney, and *Trouble in High Timber Country*, starring Eddie Albert, in the films *Midnight Madness*, with James Naughton, and 1982's *Class of 1984*, with Perry King, and on the series *Palmerstown, USA* as Willy-Joe Hall didn't do too much for Fox's career other than look good on his resume.

When Fox first auditioned for the role of Alex P. Keaton, producer Goldberg wasn't too impressed. Goldberg thought that Fox played the role as too much of a smart aleck. Casting director Judith Weiner thought the young actor was perfect for the role and prevailed on Goldberg to allow Fox another reading. Weiner advised Fox to try a different approach, and this time Goldberg liked what he saw. Fox left word with the casting director that he could be reached at home only between the hours of four and five and that if they needed to call him that was the time he'd be available. It seems audacious for a struggling actor to dictate the time of a call-back, but Fox had a good reason: He didn't have a telephone. The phone number he left with Wiener was that of a nearby Pioneer Chicken store. Fox was there to take the call and was delighted when he was cast as Alex. (When the show was sold to NBC, network president Brandon Tartikoff also had reservations about Fox. He at first thought the actor was too short and thus unbelievable as the child of Gross and Meredith Baxter Birney. Second, Tartikoff couldn't see Fox's face on lunchboxes. That point was moot as Fox refused to have his likeness used in that manner.) Like the actor who was cast to play him, the character Alex would feature an initial for his middle name. Fox ad-libbed the initial J., as in Michael J. Pollard, for his own name during his audition, but it was never disclosed what the P. in Alex P. Keaton represented.

Equally important as the character Alex were the two people cast to play the boy's parents. Steve and Elyse Keaton served as the moral compass of the show. As in life, the *Family Ties* mother was central to the interactions of the other family members. The first person cast was Meredith Baxter Birney, in the role of Elyse. Baxter Birney had already appeared in several films and dozens of television shows, and had co-starred in two popular series, *Bridget Loves Bernie* and *Family* (as daughter Nancy).

Meredith Ann Baxter was born in Pasadena, California, on June 21, 1947, the daughter of Tom Baxter, who worked in radio, and actress Whitney Blake. Blake had worked often in episodic television and became best known playing Dorothy Baxter in Shirley Booth's hit series *Hazel*. Meredith Baxter graduated from Hollywood High School and set her eyes on an acting career herself. In 1971 she made her dramatic debut on the television series *The Young Lawyers*, which starred Lee J. Cobb. Other roles in television followed, with appearances on *The Partridge Family*, *Owen Marshall*, *Barnaby Jones*, *Medical Center*, *The Streets of San Francisco*, and *City of Angels*, among others. Baxter made her film debut in the movie *Stand Up and Be Counted*, which features a huge cast that included Jacqueline Bisset, Steve Lawrence, Gary Lockwood, Stella Stevens, Loretta Swit, and Hector Elizondo. Baxter landed additional film roles in movies such as *Ben* and *All the President's Men*. Based on her appearance in *All the President's Men*, she was named by *Screen World* as one of twelve promising new actors in 1976. Baxter made her transition from supporting roles to leading actress in *Bridget Loves Bernie* and then *Family*. She met her future husband, David Birney, as her co-star on *Bridget Loves Bernie* and changed her screen name to Meredith Baxter Birney. (The couple was divorced in 1989 after fifteen years of marriage, and she changed her screen name back to Meredith Baxter.)

Superstars in the making: Michael J. Fox and guest star Tom Hanks in a scene from *Family Ties*, 1984. Photo courtesy of Globe Photos, Inc.

The Keatons celebrate the 100th episode of *Family Ties*, 1986. (From left to right) Meredith Baxter (Elyse), Michael Gross (Steven), Brian Bonsall (Andy), Michael J. Fox (Alex), Tina Yothers (Jennifer), Justine Bateman (Mallory). Photo courtesy of Globe Photos, Inc.

Family Ties patriarch Michael Gross. Photo courtesy of Michael Gross.

To play Keaton patriarch Steven, the producers first looked to actor Ed O'Neill but decided instead on Michael Gross. Gross came to *Family Ties* via past appearances in dramatic television. Gross was born on June 21, 1947, in Chicago (on the same day as his *Family Ties* co-star Meredith Baxter). In high school, he was involved with a teenage gang before turning his life around and serving as the president of his senior class. Gross graduated with a Bachelor of Arts degree from the University of Illinois at Chicago, and then earned a Masters of Fine Arts from the School of Drama at Yale University. Continuing to appear in theater productions (he won an Obie in 1982 for his performance in the off-Broadway production of *No End of Blame*), Gross also landed roles in such television movies as *A Girl Named Sooner*, *F.D.R.: The Last Year*, *Dream House*, *The Neighborhood*, and the film *Just Tell Me What You Want*, with Ali MacGraw.

"My association with the show was a combination of both frustration and elation," remembers Michael Gross. "I came from repertory theater and, accustomed as I was to playing seven characters per year, playing one character for seven years took some getting used to. On the other hand, to have been a part of such a quality television show for any length of time is something for which I will always be grateful."

Gross would be thankful for landing the role but also for something additionally personal. "The most unique and life-changing experience for me was meeting and falling in love with Elza Bergeron, my wife of over twenty years," Gross says. "She was Paramount's Associate Director of Talent at the time and, in addition to casting one of the *Star Trek* films, she was responsible for overseeing Paramount's television shows, including *Family Ties*, *Cheers*, and others. She negotiated my contract on the studio's behalf. She was pretty tight-fisted, and had she known what she knows now, she would have done a lot better for me!"

Teenage actress Justine Bateman was cast in the role of Mallory Keaton. Bateman is the daughter of film producer, director, and writer Kent Bateman (*Headless Eyes* and *Land of No Return*, starring Mel Torme and William Shatner). Her mother, Victoria, was a flight attendant. The sister of actor Jason Bateman (*Valerie*, *Arrested Development*), Justine was born on February 19, 1966, in Rye, New York. The family moved to Boston when Bateman was three, then relocated to Salt Lake City. Bateman began her acting career when she was twelve, after her family moved to California, appearing in productions of *A Midsummer Night's Dream* and *Up the Down Staircase*. At the age of sixteen, Bateman landed a Wheaties commercial and shortly thereafter was cast in *Family Ties*.

Tina Yothers played the Keatons' youngest daughter, Jennifer. She may have been young—she was only nine when she was cast in the show—but Yothers didn't come without experience. She was born on May 5, 1973, in Whittier, California. Her three brothers, Jeff, Randy, and Bumper, had acted in commercials, and Tina appeared in commercials for Doritos, McDonald's, and Bell Telephone. Her television debut was in the movie *The Cherokee Trail* in 1981. Later that year Yothers landed the role of Molly Dunlap in the Alan Parker film *Shoot the Moon*, which starred Albert Finney and Diane Keaton. After an appearance in the television movie *Your Place . . . or Mine*, Yothers was cast in *Family Ties*. (During the first day of filming, Yothers was ill with the flu. She feared the producers would fire her for the necessary interruption to filming, but the producers understood and accommodated the talented young actress.)

Family Ties was cast and ready to go. The show would be shot live before a studio audience, as were the other Paramount Television comedies. *Family Ties* opened with the theme song "Without Us," written by Jeff Barry and Tom Scott, and sung in the first episode by Mindy Sterling and Dennis Tufano. The first episode aired on Wednesday, September 22, 1982, at 9:30 P.M.

The complexity of the show made it hard for the series to find a home with the viewing audience right out of the box. Viewers had to learn about the Keaton family and come to appreciate both their individual differences and the strong ties that bound them as a family. The show was moved to Monday nights in March 1983. (It wasn't until *Family Ties* was coupled with the ever-popular *Cosby Show* as a lead-in on Thursdays in September 1984 that the show would finally find its fan base and start to rank high in the ratings. By the 1985–1986 season *Family Ties* placed number 5 in the ratings. The show would rise to number 2 by the end of the following season, where it would remain through 1987.)

While the intricacies of the characters made the series a more difficult sell to the public, that same quality allowed the producers and writers to explore a number of complicated social issues. *Family Ties* was not adverse to controversy, nor were the producers afraid to approach issues that might make the audience slightly uncomfortable. Both ends of the political spectrum were represented, although conservative Alex was sometimes revealed to be well-read but naïve. At the same time, well-intentioned Steven and Elyse seemed to know that theirs was a world that was holding on by its fingertips in the power- and wealth-seeking America of the 1980s. Still, as they sought to both educate their children about their past social involvement and their hopes for the future, Steven and Elyse appreciated Alex's independence and desire to reach not the goals of his parents but those that he himself had set. While sometimes poles apart in their personal philosophies, the members of the Keaton family were loving toward and involved with each other. Gary David Goldberg demonstrated that a family divided by ideology and political differences could remain a caring, concerned entity. In an age of diversity, change, and strong opinion, the Keatons would love one another and endure as a family.

"The show premiered two years into the 'Reagan Revolution,' and I think the portrayal of a set of idealistic, liberal parents dealing with the new conservatism couldn't have been more timely," says Michael Gross. "The show tackled tough issues, with both liberals and conservatives coming in for their share of laughs. It gave the country a humorous perspective that is sadly lacking in today's overwrought, often bitter, political climate."

While the interactions between the Keaton kids and their parents could often be quite funny, the writers of *Family Ties* balanced the comedy with drama and the exploration of important issues. Season One episodes delved into teen pregnancy, gun control, dating older women, nuclear power, sex abuse, cheating, risky investments, and cultural differences. All that in just the first season. Yet the plotlines were carefully drawn and executed in such a manner that they didn't come off as preachy. If nothing else, the show was ambitious. The viewing audience eventually became aware of *Family Ties*, and by Season Two the show was a solid hit.

The show's stars got along exceedingly well. Michael J. Fox and Meredith Baxter Birney even car-pooled to the studio that first season. "The cast members were as kind as they were talented, making the creative process relatively easy," remembers Michael Gross. "Whatever 'chemistry' we shared as a cast was a product of both talent and a certain generosity of spirit. People were there to share what they did best, and egos seemed always to take a back seat to the overall success of the show. There are some people in the industry who seem to think that creativity works best in an atmosphere of paranoia and fear. I think we proved otherwise."

From August 1983 through December 1983 *Family Ties* aired on Wednesday nights at 9:30. The change in day and time didn't affect the show. By now it was solid. In January 1984 the show was switched to Thursday, where it would remain for the next three and a half years. In 1983 Tina Yothers was nominated for a Young Artist Award from the Young Artist Foundation. In 1984 *Family Ties* was nominated for an Emmy for Outstanding Comedy Series. Gary David Goldberg and Ruth

Bennett won the film and television industry's Humanitas Prize in the thirty-minute category. (The Humanitas Prize honors writing that affirms human dignity, explores the meaning of life, pays testament to human freedom, and enriches and unifies society.) Tina Yothers, Justine Bateman, and Marc Price were nominated for the Young Artist Award

The writing of the show continued to be outstanding, and the kudos awarded those behind the camera were certainly deserved. "It was producer Gary David Goldberg: his vision, his talent, his tenacity, which inspired *Family Ties* for [the long run of the series]," says Michael Gross. "That being said, he couldn't have done it alone, and so surrounded himself with a group of talented individuals who helped to implement that vision. Though the cast was the most visible part of the creative team, and while our opinions were valued, I always felt that it was Gary, along with his fellow producers, writers, and directors, who were the true heart and soul of the show."

The complex and serious issues would continue in the storylines of the second season, but there was also more humor. Even so, topics included child abduction, drug abuse, gambling, adoption, alcoholism, and violence. The talented writers were able to deliver dialogue that was both engaging and cause for contemplation, yet also laugh-producing when indicated.

A new character was introduced in teenage neighbor Skippy Handleman in Season One. By Season Three, Skippy was made a regular character, played by actor Marc Price, the son of stand-up comedian Al Bernie, who had made several appearances on *Toast of the Town* in the forties and fifties. Price had appeared on the BBC series *Juliet Bravo* and had also appeared on *One Day at a Time* and *Archie Bunker's Place*. Skippy's interchanges with Mallory, on whom he had a giant crush, and Alex, of whom he was in awe, brought lighter scenes to the show.

The show's cast members fit in perfectly with the camaraderie of the other actors and personnel on the Paramount lot. "We'd frequently cross paths with cast members coming and going on the lot," recalls Michael Gross. "*Happy Days* was still on the air. I had known Henry Winkler from our days together at Yale, and I saw him from time to time. I had worked with *Taxi* cast member Marilu Henner some years earlier, so would drop by her set. My friend Brian Dennehy was starring in a short-lived show titled *Star of the Family*, and another actor friend, Leonard Frey, worked on some bizarre little show titled *Mr. Smith* in which he starred with an orangutan!"

As with others who worked at Paramount Television in that magical decade, the history of the Paramount lot was very special to Michael

Gross. "Working there gave me the feeling that I was a part of Hollywood history," says Gross. "I'd roam the property past darkened sound stages or through the streets of the old back lot imagining 'The Marx Brothers worked here,' 'Bing Crosby may have stood on this spot,' or 'Mae West could have taken on the entire USC football team in this very dressing room!' When I arrived in 1982, the old water tank, which had once stood on the RKO property [adjacent to the Paramount lot and now a part of that lot], was still painted with the faded logo 'Desilu.' A great source of Paramount lore was 'Fritz', an ancient security guard who had worked on the lot for as long as anyone could remember. He was the unofficial Paramount historian, and his golf-cart tours of the property were legendary. He'd point to a spot and say, 'When Carole Lombard died in that plane crash, Clark Gable read the telegram, sat on that fire hydrant, and cried his eyes out.' How much of what Fritz said was true and how much fabricated, I've no idea; but like any great storyteller, he made you believe. The studio threw him a huge ninetieth birthday party the first year I worked there. Days later I stood near him one afternoon as the old back lot, and a great deal of his personal history, went up in flames. I think poor Fritz took it harder than anyone."

The third season of *Family Ties* began with the September 27, 1984, episode "Here We Go Again." In this episode Elyse learns she is pregnant with a fourth child. In real life, Meredith Baxter Birney was pregnant with twins, and the producers decided to write the pregnancy into the show. Alex by this time is in college at Leland University. The storylines were less obvious in the morals department but still very worthwhile. As would be expected, the parents and the children react in different ways to the addition to their family and the changes that they are experiencing in their individual lives. The themes of most of the shows of the third season somehow relate to growing up and addressing the experiences of life's evolution. Issues such as suicide, materialism, personal gain at the expense of public service, death, teen pregnancy, and jealousy are explored. The birth of baby Andrew is cause for both celebration and confusion in the Keaton household.

An interesting side note to the production of *Family Ties* is that during the third season Paramount Television guaranteed the companies involved with the syndication of their shows the commitment that they would be provided with a minimum of ninety-five episodes of the show. Only seventy *Family Ties* episodes had been completed at the time of the promise. The guarantee committed Paramount Television to produce the additional shows, whether or not NBC—or any other network—agreed to continue to air *Family Ties* as a first-run series. The series continued well past that mark, and everyone involved was a winner.

The show was again nominated for an Emmy, for Outstanding Comedy Series of 1985. Michael J. Fox was nominated for an Emmy for Outstanding Lead Actor in a Comedy Series. Justine Bateman and Tina Yothers both won Young Artist Awards. The hard work of the writers and actors was paying off.

Season Four of *Family Ties* began as a two-hour movie that aired on September 23, 1985. The Keaton family visits England, and all manner of minor adventures await them. An addition to the show is the character Nick Moore, who is first introduced during this season. Nick is Mallory Keaton's rough-and-tumble sculptor love interest. The young man is poignantly portrayed by actor Scott Valentine.

Scott Eugene Valentine came to *Family Ties* with an interesting and inspirational back story. He was born on June 3, 1958, in Saratoga Springs, New York. Valentine was interested in acting from the time he was a child. He appeared in a few plays in high school and pursued his interest at Adirondack Community College in Queensbury, New York. Valentine moved to New York City to attend the American Academy of Dramatic Arts. He landed a few off-Broadway roles and was delighted when he won a role in a daytime soap and a screen test for a role in the film *The Lords of Discipline*, based on a novel by Pat Conroy and starring David Keith. Tragedy struck when Valentine was hit by a truck in 1981. Over the course of three years, the young actor worked to rebuild his body and reclaim his life. Eventually he had recovered enough to move to Los Angeles and read for the role of Nick Moore.

Another new cast member arrived in the person of a love interest for Alex. Ever practical, Alex decided to methodically choose a college student from the freshman directory to be his girlfriend. He was instead attracted to Ellen Reed, the roommate of the girl he chose. The love-hate relationship that resulted was good fodder for the comedy. Tracy Pollan was cast in the role of Ellen and had terrific chemistry with Michael J. Fox.

Tracy Pollan was not new to acting. She was born Tracy Jo Pollan on Long Island, New York, on June 22, 1960, to Stephen M. Pollan and writer Corky Pollan. Tracy attended the Dalton School in New York City with actress Jennifer Grey. Her first acting appearance was in the after-school special *The Great Love Experiment*. Pollan was well-received as an actress and soon landed roles in the television movies *For Lovers Only*, *Sessions*, *Trackdown: Finding the Goodbar Killer*, and *The Little Sister*, in which she got second billing, after actor John Savage. Roles in other made for television movies led to Pollan being one of five actresses considered for the role of Ellen Reed. (At the time Tracy Pollan came to *Family Ties* to play Alex's girlfriend, she was dating actor Kevin Bacon, and Michael J. Fox was dating *Facts of Life* actress Nancy McKeon. Little did the two actors know that eventually they would fall in love, marry, and become parents to four children.) Pollan, unfortunately, wouldn't be on the show for very long. After her first successful season on *Family Ties*, Gary David Goldberg wanted to sign her for two more years. Pollan instead decided that she wanted to return to New York City.

Some of the themes the series delved into during the fourth season centered on peer pressure, martial jealousy, self-awareness, stress, shoplifting, plagiarism, and nationalism. The audience continued to support the show, and so did friends in high places. *Family Ties* finished the season again second in the ratings, behind *The Cosby Show*. The producers didn't know if it was a good or bad thing when Alex P. Keaton's hero President Ronald Reagan declared *Family Ties* his favorite television show.

Guest stars were often brought in to expand the cast and relate to the Keaton family members. Some of the actors who appeared on *Family Ties* over the years were *Bosom Buddies'* Tom Hanks, Wil Wheaton (*Stand by Me*), Maura Tierney (*ER*), *Mork & Mindy's* Jay Thomas and Jim Staahl, Dick Sergeant (*Bewitched*), David Paymer (*City Slickers*), Tracey Nelson (*Father Dowling Mysteries*), Judith Light (*Who's the Boss?*), Crispin Glover (*Back to the Future*), Jamie Gertz (*Sixteen Candles*), *The Bad News Bears'* Corey Feldman, Stephen Dorff (*Blade*), Tate Donavan (*The O.C.*), Geena Davis (*Thelma & Louise*), James Cromwell (*Babe*), Ronny Cox (*Total Recall*), Hank Azaria (*Huff*), and Christina Applegate (*Married . . . with Children*).

Season Five of *Family Ties* debuted in October 1986. To account for the departure of Tracy Pollan, Alex's girlfriend, Ellen, decides to leave Columbus to pursue her education in Paris. The stories this season continued to evolve around humorous incidents and moral dilemmas that included elopement, discrimination against senior citizens, office romance, ethics, hazing, and sexism. One episode in particular stood out. "A, My Name Is Alex," which aired in two parts on March 12 and 19, 1987, was a heartrending story that dealt with the death of Alex's best friend and the young man's quest for the meaning of life. It was basically a one-man show for actor Fox. The episode won an Emmy Award for Outstanding Writer in a Comedy Series for Gary David Goldberg and Alan Uger.

The series continued to fly high in the ratings. Awards also abounded in 1896 for *Family Ties*. Michael J. Fox won an Emmy for Outstanding

Actor in a Comedy Series, a Q Award for Best Supporting Actor in a Quality Comedy Series, and a Golden Globe nomination. The Television Academy also honored the show with Emmys for Outstanding Technical Direction for Parker Roe, Paul Basta, Richard Price, Eric Clay, Tom Dasback, and John Repczynski. Will MacKenzie was nominated for Outstanding Director in a Comedy, Gary Anderson and John Bellis were nominated for Outstanding Editing, and Justine Bateman was nominated in the Supporting Actress, Comedy category. The show itself was nominated as Outstanding Comedy Series. Marc Price won a Young Artist Award that year.

By Season Six the storylines may have been a bit harder to come by, but they were still quality. The show somehow found new issues to explore, such as Alzheimer's, mid-life crises, book banning, racism, obsessive love, family estrangement, and deafness. The producers and writers were able to continue to feature hot-button topics and maintain the integrity of the series.

Brian Bonsall was playing young Andy Keaton by this time. Brian Eric Bonsall was born on December 3, 1981, in Hawthorne, California. He began his career on *Family Ties*, which was his first real acting experience, and stayed with the show through 1989. Bonsall, who had appeared in commercials, was selected from more than 400 actors for the role of Andy.

Courteney Cox, who of course would rise to great fame as one of the stars of *Friends*, was brought in to play Alex's new girlfriend, Lauren Miller. (That episode would be the centerpiece of a 1989 ninety-minute PBS special, hosted by Henry Winkler, that provided a look behind the scenes of the popular series.) Cox clearly clicked acting with Fox and was given quite a bit of screen time.

Courteney Bass Cox was born to Richard and Courteney Cox of Mountain Brook, Alabama, on June 15, 1964, in Birmingham. She attended Mountain Brook High School, where she participated in tennis, swimming, and cheerleading. When she was a senior, Cox modeled for Parisians Department Store. She decided to study architecture and interior design at Mount Vernon College but soon realized that she had a greater interest in pursuing a modeling career. Moving to New York City, Cox landed a contract with the Ford modeling agency. She appeared as a book cover model and appeared in commercials for such products as Maybelline and Noxzema. Cox appeared on the television soap *As the World Turns* but was noticed more for her appearance in 1984 as Bruce Springsteen's dancing partner in his video for "Dancing in the Dark." She moved to Los Angeles the following year and made appearances on several television shows. Cox was cast as the fourth lead in a Dean Paul Martin vehicle, the short-lived television series *Misfits of Science*. After appearances in such movies as *Masters of the Universe* and *Down Twisted*, Cox auditioned for the role of Lauren Miller.

Even with the addition of new characters, *Family Ties* was starting to run out of steam. It slipped in the ratings and ended up in seventeenth position for the 1987–1988 season. The ratings didn't matter to the Television Academy, as Michael J. Fox would again win an Emmy for Outstanding Actor in a Comedy Series and the actor was also nominated for a Golden Globe. The show was nominated for a Golden Globe as Best Comedy Series. Additionally, Tom Scott and Jeff Barry won the BMI TV Music Award, as they had the previous year.

What would become the final year of *Family Ties* started off with a touching two-part episode revolving around Steven's heart attack and subsequent surgery. Steven—and his family—confronted the physical and psychological changes involved in his near-death and recovery, and those issues were examined over an arc of several episodes. Young Andy was old enough now (how children grow up so fast in televisionland is an interesting phenomena) to be a tiny version of his older brother, Alex. By this time Jennifer was old enough to date, so some of the earlier themes were revisited from a different, female perspective. In fact, many of the same themes were dealt with once again. The producers and writers were trying to maintain the distinctive mark of the show, but *Family Ties* had little left to explore.

In 1988 Michael J. Fox once again was awarded an Emmy as Outstanding Actor in a Comedy Series and a Golden Globe nomination for Best Performance by a Leading Actor in a Comedy Series. *Family Ties* was nominated for a Golden Globe for Best Comedy Series. Will MacKenzie, Tony Csiki, and Andrew McCullough were awarded a Directors Guild of America win for Outstanding Directorial Achievement in a Comedy Series. Brian Bonsall won the Young Artist Award. The fact that a series into its seventh season continued to receive acclamation was a testament to the creative talent involved.

When the producers of the show decided that the best verification of the show's worthiness would be to let it end on a high note, it became time for the folks at *Family Ties* to say good-bye. The last show focused on Alex leaving the family to take a job in New York City. In a poignant end to a series that succeeded in its goal to explore the inner workings of a complex but loving family, the cast took a final bow on May 14, 1989. The television industry honored the efforts of Gary David Goldberg and his writers, actors, and creative crew even for that last season. In 1989

Michael J. Fox was once again nominated for an Emmy. Rick Caswell, Paul Basta, Parker Roe, Hank Geving, Eric Clay, and Richard Price were nominated for Technical Direction, and Robert F. Liu was nominated for Lighting Direction. Michael J. Fox tied with *Dear John*'s Judd Hirsch and *Empty Nest*'s Richard Mulligan for a Golden Globe. Brian Bonsall once again took home the Young Artist Award.

The Keatons were a family that would not be forgotten by viewers. Steven Keaton ranked #12 in *TV Guide*'s list of Greatest TV Dads of All Time, published on June 20, 2004. Michael Gross says he believes that the effect the show had on his career began the moment the show was picked up. "In the spring of 1982, I was being considered for a role in an NBC mini-series, but the producers were hesitant to cast me because I was a 'nobody.' My fortunes changed the moment *Family Ties* received the order for its first thirteen shows, presumably because by the time the mini-series aired, Family Ties would have already been on for several months, making me a 'somebody.' I was the same actor, with the same abilities, but *Family Ties* provided visibility, and doors began to open. On the other side of that coin, a certain amount of type-casting was inevitable. Though I played 'edgier' roles in telefilms and some motion pictures, the character Steven Keaton had so saturated the airways that the very success of the show sometimes worked against me." Even so, Gross, like Fox and Baxter in particular, would continue productive careers beyond *Family Ties*.

Family Ties would long be remembered for its creative approach to the classic sitcom and its overall creativity and outstanding achievement. The issues that the series tackled were thought-provoking and complex, but all that the Keaton family was and had been through would remain in the hearts of viewers.

"I think I took the show for granted," muses Gross. "Before *Family Ties* I had worked steadily, lived comfortable, and had never been a 'starving artist.' I also watched little television in those days and so had no idea just how rare it was not only to land a hit series but to be a part of a show with such quality. I'd no idea that the level of our writing, the camaraderie of our cast, was often the exception and not the rule. It took me a while to realize just how blessed we were."

When it was all said and done, *Family Ties* was definitely a bright spot in television history.

Chapter 14

CHEERS TO YOU

E ven though they had realized success with *Family Ties* and a producer who had not been previously tried and tested at Paramount
Television, the studio had an abundance of creative talent already
working on the lot and didn't have to look beyond that realm to find stellar writing and production that they could back for another potential hit
series. One of the writers the Paramount executives looked to for new
product was Earl Pomerantz, who had begun his writing career with the
MTM shows and had also contributed to *Taxi* and *The Associates*.
Pomerantz's first outing as an executive producer was *Best of the West*, a
one-season Paramount Television–produced comedy series that debuted
in September 1981. Jim Burrows directed the first episode of the show,
which was the saga of Sam Best, a Civil War veteran who moves out west
with his wife and son and soon finds himself serving as marshal of
the town of Copper Creek. One of the key plotlines is that Best prefers
diplomacy to gunplay and has to deal with the shifty Parker Tillman, the
self-proclaimed town "boss."

 Best of the West starred Joel Higgins as Sam Best. Higgins had begun
his acting career in 1975 as Bruce Carson in the soap *Search for Tomorrow*,
and he co-starred with Andy Griffith in the television adventure series
Salvage 1. Joel Franklin Higgins was born on September 28, 1943, in

Bloomington, Illinois. After studying advertising in college and serving a stint in the Army, Higgins turned to public relations and commercial copywriting, creating jingles for such products as M&Ms and Kool-Aid. Higgins's first love was singing, and a change in career had him landing roles in the Broadway productions of *Oklahoma!* and *Shenandoah*, for which he won a Theater World Award.

Appearing as Sam Best's wife was actress Carlene Walters, who had appeared in such television series as *The Rockford Files*, *BJ and the Bear*, *Dukes of Hazzard*, and *The Bionic Woman*. Walters also came to the attention of the *Best of the West* producers through a guest appearance on *Taxi*. Born on June 4, 1952, in Hartford, Connecticut, Walters would later appear on *Dear John* with *Taxi*'s Judd Hirsch, Bob Newhart's 1992 series *Bob*, and the *Cheers* spin-off *The Tortellis*, starring Dan Hedaya. Rounding out the Best family was Meeno Peluce from *The Bad News Bears*; he starred as Best's son, Daniel.

Leonard Frey played Best's nemesis, Parker Tillman. Frey had previously appeared in such films as *Finnegan's Wake*, *The Boys in the Band*, and *Where the Buffalo Roam*, as well as on television. Frey was born on September 4, 1938, in Brooklyn and studied with Sanford Meisner at New York City's Neighborhood Playhouse. He played Mendel in the 1964 Broadway production of *Fiddler on the Roof* but was cast as Motel in the film version of the play. His performance landed him an Academy Award nomination for Best Supporting Actor. Frey was also nominated for a Tony Award in 1975 for his appearance in *The National Health*.

Tracey Walter, who had also appeared on *Taxi*, was cast as Tillman's henchman, Frog. Walter had appeared in numerous television shows, such as *Starsky & Hutch*, *Charlie's Angels*, and *WKRP in Cincinnati*, and in films, including *Annie Hall* and *Goin' South*. Born on November 25, 1942, in Jersey City, New Jersey, Walter would later become a popular character actor and appear in the films *The Two Jakes*, *Batman*, *Silence of the Lambs*, *City Slickers*, and *Philadelphia*.

Best of the West, a comedic approach to the genre of the television western, featured such guest stars as *Taxi*'s Christopher Lloyd as the Calico Kid, Slim Pickens, Richard Moll (*Night Court*), Andy Griffith, Chuck Connors (*The Rifleman*), Betty White (*Lou Grant*), Dixie Carter (*Designing Women*), and Al Lewis (*The Munsters*). The talent of the show was solid. Unfortunately, there didn't seem much to explore through the storylines, and the show went off the air in June 1982.

During the time the creative talent at Ubu Productions was getting *Family Ties* ready to roll, Paramount Television was making room for another production from the *Taxi* gang. *Taxi*'s director Jim Burrows and writers Glen and Les Charles were inspired by working on *Taxi* but felt the need to stretch their wings and head a series of their own. They formed Charles/Burrows/Charles Productions to pursue their own dreams. "We made a deal with Freddie Silverman at NBC, I think the second year of *Taxi*," Burrows recalls. "Glen and Les, ever since we worked together on *Phyllis*, we had wanted to do a show together. During *Taxi* we figured that was the time. So we got a two-for-one deal with NBC. We got to make two pilots, and they would have to put one on the air. When we were leaving *Taxi*, we started talking about what the show should be. We went through a number of permutations. We loved *Fawlty Towers*, and we thought about doing a show in a hotel. Then we thought about a show in a bar, then we thought about a bar in Barstow, then we thought about it maybe being a sports bar, then we had to get a great city. We thought about Philadelphia, but we liked Boston because there was an accent. Then we needed one more wrinkle, so we tried to do Tracy/Hepburn, 'Mr. Downtown,' 'Miss Uptown,' the pragmatist and the idealist. We combined those two, and it became a very successful show."

Grant Tinker, formerly associated with MTM and its subsequent hit productions, was now head of NBC. Tinker was eager to put his own brand on the network and bring in quality television of which he could be proud. Knowing that Burrows and the Charles brothers had a firm background in superior television, Tinker was happy to honor the deal Charles/Burrows/Charles had earlier struck with Silverman. No concept pitch or script was required. Tinker's confidence paid off more than even he could imagine. Debuting on September 30, 1982, at 9 P.M. on NBC, just one week after the first episode of *Family Ties*, was a little show they called *Cheers*.

The premise centered on the Boston sports bar of Sam "Mayday" Malone, a former Red Sox baseball player and ladies man. (The set was fashioned after a real Boston pub named the Bull & Finch that was located in Boston at $112^1/_2$ Beacon Street.) Burrows, Charles, and Charles enjoyed the BBC series *Fawlty Towers* and thought that a show set in an American hotel with guests passing through could also be quite funny. After they realized that most of the scenes they were writing for the NBC show took place in a bar, they reconsidered and changed the setting to a neighborhood tavern. The interactions between recovering alcoholic Sam and his employees and patrons would create a variety of individual and co-dependent storylines. *Cheers* would focus on clever dialogue and the intriguing stories of an oddball bunch of characters named Sam, Diane, Coach, Norm, Carla, and Cliff.

The first season was cast by Jeff Greenberg, Jim Burrows, and Les and Glen Charles. They decided to cast a strong lead and then go with actors who were fairly new to television in order to give the show a different, unique feel. For the swaggering, yet likable lead character Sam Malone, the producers looked to Ted Danson. Danson had appeared on *Taxi* early that year and had also auditioned for the series *Best of the West*.

Edward Bridge Danson II was born on December 29, 1947, in San Diego, California. His father, an archaeologist, relocated the family to Flagstaff, Arizona, the site of numerous American Indian ruins. In 1961 Danson attended the Kent School for Boys in Connecticut, where he became interested in the possibility of playing professional basketball. Danson changed his mind about his future after he began appearing in plays while attending Stanford University. He decided to transfer to Carnegie Mellon University in Pittsburgh to pursue acting. After graduation Danson was hired as an understudy in the off-Broadway production of *The Real Inspector Hound*. He was soon appearing in theater productions and TV commercials, and he landed a role in 1970 on the soap *Somerset*, portraying Tom Conway.

By 1978 Danson had relocated to Los Angeles and was studying at the Lee Strasberg Actors Institute. Danson began finding steady work appearing in television shows such as *BJ and the Bear* and *Mrs. Columbo*. He made his feature debut as Ian Campbell in the Joseph Wambaugh–written *The Onion Field*. Although his acting career was beginning to significantly develop, Danson devoted most of his time to his wife, Casey, who had suffered a stroke during the birth of their daughter Kate. As Casey recovered and he resumed his career, Danson appeared in the 1981 film *Body Heat*, with William Hurt and Kathleen Turner. Shortly after that appearance, he landed a role on *Laverne & Shirley* as Laverne's boyfriend Randy and in such other television series as *Benson*, *Magnum, P.I.*, and *Taxi*.

After the producers seriously considered casting actress Karen Valentine to play the role of Diane Chambers and ultimately decided against that actress, Shelley Long was cast to play the affected and opinionated waitress. Although she is an aspiring novelist, Diane takes the job at Cheers after being dumped by her fiancé. She wants Sam and the others at the bar to believe that she is employed at Cheers only temporarily as she waits for publishers to realize her astonishing talent. Perhaps in deference to the MTM pattern of a division between male bosses and female employees, Les and Glen Charles wrote an arc that would explore a love-hate relationship between owner/bartender Sam and his cocktail waitress, Diane.

Long came to *Cheers* via appearances on *Family*, *M*A*S*H*, and *Trapper John, M.D.*, and films such as *A Small Circle of Friends*, *Caveman*, and Ron Howard's *Night Shift*, which also starred Henry Winkler. Shelley Lee Long was born on August 23, 1949, the only child of teachers Leland and Evandine Long in Fort Wayne, Indiana. After graduating from South Side High School, she enrolled in Northwestern University as a drama major. Long supported herself during her college days working in the school's cafeteria. She decided to leave college to pursue a career as an actress and model. In Chicago by 1975, Long became a member of Second City and also wrote, produced, and co-hosted the television program *Sorting It Out*, a popular show that ran on the local NBC affiliate station and won three local Emmys for Best Entertainment Show.

Long pursued her acting career by relocating to Los Angeles. Her first nationwide appearance was on *The Love Boat* in 1978. Parts in television shows such as *The Dooley Brothers* and the made-for-television movies *The Promise of Love* and *The Princess and the Cabbie*, both starring Valerie Bertinelli, followed. Long was tapped to play the lead in a pilot Paramount Television was financing called *Ghost of a Chance*. The show was brought to Paramount by Irma and Austin Kalish, who had produced *Good Times*, *Carter Country*, and *The Facts of Life*. The Kalishes also brought with them years of sitcom experience, having been writers on *Gilligan's Island*, *My Favorite Martian*, *My Three Sons*, *F Troop*, *The Bob Newhart Show*, and many other shows. *Ghost of a Chance* featured Long as a newlywed haunted by the ghost of her dead first husband. The show also starred Barry Van Dyke (son of Dick Van Dyke), Steven Keats (*The Awakening Land*), and Gretchen Wilder (*Private Benjamin*). The projected series was not picked up by a network, and the actors were left looking for other projects.

Even though *Ghost of a Chance* failed to sell, it turned out to be a good year for Shelley Long. After a previous marriage that ended in divorce, Long married securities broker Bruce Tyson in October 1981. Professionally, Long was in for the break of a lifetime. Her appearance in Howard's *Night Shift* as a jovial hooker brought her to the attention of the producers of *Cheers*.

Charles/Burrows/Charles was out to achieve an attitude-driven presentation for their show, and the casting of each individual character was critical to achieve that goal. The actors selected to support Danson and Long were top-notch. One of the characters whose very presence epitomizes the Cheers patron is that of Norm Peterson, a CPA who makes the bar his home away from home. The viewing audience is never sure if Norm is a happy person, as he seems to rally as an individual only when

Where everybody knows your name: on the set of *Cheers*. Top (left to right): Woody Harrelson (Woody), Kelsey Grammer (Frasier), Rhea Perlman (Carla), George Wendt (Norm), John Ratzenberger (Cliff). Bottom (left to right): Ted Danson (Sam), Shelley Long (Diane). 1986. Photo courtesy of Globe Photos, Inc.

Ted Danson (Sam) and Shelley Long (Diane) welcome *Cheers* guest star Senator Gary Hart, 1986. Photo courtesy of Globe Photos, Inc.

Emmy Award–winning director James Burrows. Photo courtesy of NBC Universal Photo; photo by Chris Haston.

he has a beer in his hand and is away from his much-maligned wife, Vera. If anyone personifies the *Cheers* mind-set, it's Norm. Cast to play this pivotal role was George Wendt. Like Long, Wendt came to comedy television via Second City.

George Robert Wendt was born, one of six children, on October 17, 1948, in Chicago. His father, Tom Howard, was a noted Chicago *Tribune* photographer. (Howard's photo of murderer Ruth Snyder being electrocuted at Sing Sing was published worldwide in 1927.) Wendt attended a Jesuit prep school in Chicago and set his sights on a college education. After first attending Notre Dame University, Wendt decided to complete his higher education at Rockhurst College in Kansas City, Missouri. He graduated with a degree in economics and decided to take off two years to travel throughout Europe. In 1974 the adventurous young man returned to Chicago, where he took an improvisational acting class with Second City. He excelled as an actor and was asked to join Second City's troupe of comedians, with whom he toured for six years. (Wendt met his wife, actress Bernadette Birkett, during his involvement with Second City. Birkett would later be the voice of Norm's prickly wife, Vera.)

After moving to Los Angeles to pursue his desire to become a television producer, Wendt began to land small roles as an actor. He appeared in the Christopher Reeve–Jane Seymour movie *Somewhere in Time* and *My Bodyguard*, starring Matt Dillon and Adam Baldwin, and also in a film produced by Encyclopedia Britannica based on O. Henry's story *The Gift of the Magi* that was released in 1980. Wendt then secured roles on television in series such as *Hart to Hart*, *Soap*, *Alice*, and *Taxi*. Wendt caught Jim Burrows's eye when he appeared on *Taxi*, and Burrows was interested in the actor enough to offer him an audition for *Cheers*. Wendt impressed during the audition, and Burrows realized he was looking at two actors who might fill the role of Norm. While Wendt won the part of the beer-drinking cynic, the second actor would be asked to take the role of Norm's buddy, Cliff Clavin.

That second actor was John Ratzenberger. The producers liked Ratzenberger so much that they listened to his ideas for what would become the unique character Cliff Clavin. Cliff was initially perceived as a *Cheers* patron and buddy to Norm, but when Ratzenberger suggested another element to the character, Cliff grew into a more complicated personality. Cliff's the kind of person one might avoid socially, as his constant spouting of mundane trivia is enough to drive even the most patient of people up the wall. Yet this mailman who lives with his mother is one of the most loyal friends a person would want to have, and while it can sometimes be exasperating to be around Cliff, it's nearly impossible not to like him. It might have been a challenge for an actor to walk that thin line, but Burrows and the Charles brothers felt that John Ratzenberger could more than deliver.

Born in Bridgeport, Connecticut, on April 6, 1947, John Deszo Ratzenberger displayed his impressive sense of humor early in life entertaining his family and friends. Ratzenberger attended Catholic schools before earning a degree in English (would that come in handy!) at Sacred Heart University. During his college years Ratzenberger and a buddy started the improvisational group Sal's Meat Market. After graduation in 1971, Ratzenberger lived briefly in Boston, and then he and his friend took their act to England, where the Arts Council of Great Britain sponsored them for a European tour. During his decade-long stint in England, Ratzenberger decided to try his luck in films. His first role was in the Richard Lester movie *The Ritz*, starring Rita Moreno and Jack Weston. More British film appearances followed, in such films as Richard Attenborough's *A Bridge Too Far*, Ken Russell's *Valentino*, with Rudolph Nureyev and Leslie Caron, Richard Donner's *Superman*, with Christopher Reeve, Marlon Brando, and Gene Hackman, John Schlesinger's *Yanks*, starring Richard Gere, and George Lucas's *Star Wars: Episode V: The Empire Strikes Back*, as Major Bren Derlin. Ratzenberger's roles may not have been substantial, but the actor's affiliation with quality directors at such a pivotal point in his career was remarkable. While he was in England, Ratzenberger also co-wrote two BBC plays and was employed for a brief stint as an assistant to a tree surgeon. Back in the United States, Ratzenberger decided to audition for a role in *Cheers*, and the idiosyncratic Cliff Clavin was born.

Sam Malone could be such an irascible and shallow yet successful ladies man that the need for a character to serve as someone who might help Sam visit his more responsible and socially conscious obligations was evident. Sam's old buddy, former Red Sox coach Ernie "Coach" Pantusso, would fit that role. The slow-on-the-uptake, absent-minded, but lovable character was played by experienced actor-director Nicholas Colasanto. Colasanto was born on January 19, 1924, in Providence, Rhode Island. He entered the Navy during World War II, served in Europe and Africa, and became a decorated coxswain. After his discharge, Colasanto became an oil company accountant. While attending a stage performance by Henry Fonda in New York, Colasanto decided that he might like to become an actor. He moved to Phoenix, Arizona, where he was briefly involved with a theater company. Setting his sights on the big time, Colasanto relocated to New York, where he landed a few small roles in off-Broadway productions. He also appeared on such legendary television drama presentations as *Playhouse 90*, *Kraft Suspense Theater*, *The Alfred Hitchcock Hour*, and *Arrest and Trial*. In 1965 Colasanto tried his luck in Los Angeles. He must have done some amazing networking. Soon he was not only appearing in episodic television with roles on *I Spy*, *Run for Your Life*, *The Man from U.N.C.L.E.*, *The Fugitive*, *Mission Impossible*, *Ironside*, *Kojak*, *The Streets of San Francisco*, and *Lou Grant*, but he was also directing episodes of *Bonanza*, *Hawaii Five-O*, *McCloud*, *The Streets of San Francisco*, *Starsky & Hutch*, and *CHiPs*. Colasanto also landed roles in films such as Martin Scorsese's 1980 *Raging Bull*.

There is always at least one person in the workplace whom everybody has a problem with, and that person at Cheers was the sharp-tongued waitress Carla Tortelli, a single mother who works to support her many children. Jim Burrows knew just who he wanted for the role: Rhea Perlman. Switching from playing the sweet girlfriend of the disconcerting Louie De Palma to a character who is not only extremely bad-tempered but venomous was a challenge even for the talented Perlman. What was written on the page was only half of the ordeal in bringing Carla to life. Carla was, after all, someone who was intended to entertain viewers, so the character needed a vulnerability that would appeal. Burrows knew Perlman could pull it off, and that she did, in spades.

As had previously been the case with *Taxi*, the *Cheers* writers were exceptionally talented. Some of the most prolific writers over the run of the series were David Angell, Andrew Chulack, Douglas Hines, Dan O'Shannon, Tom Anderson, Dan Staley, Kathy Ann Stumpe, and Jim Burrows. (David Angell would die onboard one of the airplanes involved in the September 11, 2001, terrorist attack.) Over the course of the run of the show more than fifty writers contributed. *Cheers* focused on the lives and interactions of the people of the pub rather than on social issues. It was a formula that worked well with the viewing audience, and it was an exciting challenge for the writers.

The theme music for the show was written by Judy Hart-Angelo and Gary Portnoy, who also sang the ASCAP–winning song, "Where Everybody Knows Your Name." The catchy tune soon captured the public's attention. The song's slogan would enter into our national lexicon as viewers came to believe that Cheers represented a place we all might welcome as a retreat from our daily problems and concerns.

Paramount's Stage 25 was ready for action. Jim Burrows was embraced as the primary director of *Cheers*. His previous involvement with quality television comedy and his ability to work well with a variety of acting styles was appreciated by the cast. Ted Danson says that Burrows's knowledge of both sides of the equation—writers and actors—

enables him to get the best out of all concerned. Woody Harrelson, who would come on the show in the third season as bartender Woody Boyd, appreciates Burrows's humor, saying that if Burrows thinks something is funny it probably is, and if he doesn't find the humor it probably doesn't exist.

Burrows almost immediately felt *Cheers* would be a hit. The first exchange between the characters Norm and Coach drew exactly the kind of response that Burrows had intended. Norm responded to Coach's "Whatdaya know?" with "Not enough," and the audience roared. Burrows says that he knew then that rather than being joke-driven, *Cheers* would entertain viewers through the characters' dispositions and attitudes.

Television critics also knew right off the bat that the show was a keeper. Even back in the days when review copies didn't always precede a new show, the critics sensed that anything coming from Burrows and the Charles brothers had the potential to be special. Viewers were a different matter. To everyone's surprise, *Cheers* didn't immediately find its audience.

During that first year, the show hovered near the bottom of the ratings. NBC considered pulling the plug on the series, but Paramount Television executives believed that, given time, *Cheers* would find its audience and increase its ratings. The studio would be proved right. Viewers eventually were drawn to the show by the strong characters, and the series enjoyed a steady upward momentum.

"I had a great time," says Jim Burrows. "I loved doing *Taxi*, and I really loved doing *Cheers* because I was part of the creation of that show. At Paramount they were always very supportive. *Taxi* debuted, and it was a big show. It was a big number. *Cheers* debuted at a very low number, but [Gary] Nardino and his guys, John Pike and those guys, they loved the show. They fought for it, and I'm eternally grateful."

Industry acclaim for the first season of *Cheers* was phenomenal. Emmy wins and nominations were abundant in 1983. *Cheers* not only was acknowledged as Outstanding Comedy Series but also won Emmys in the categories of Directing (Jim Burrows), Lead Actress (Shelley Long), Writing (Glen Charles and Les Charles), and Graphic Design and Title Sequences (Bruce Bryant and James Castle). Emmy nominations for the show included in the Writing category, for the team of David Isaacs and Ken Levine, and also for David Lloyd. Ted Danson was nominated as Lead Actor, and other nominations included Supporting Actor for Nick Colasanto, Supporting Actress for Rhea Perlman, Film Editing for Andrew Chulack, Art Direction for George Gaines and Richard Sylbert, and Music and Lyrics for Judy Hart-Angelo and Gary Portnoy. The

Golden Globes ran on a different schedule, honoring the first season of the show in 1982 with a nomination for Best Comedy Series and a Golden Globe for Shelley Long as Best Supporting Actress in a Comedy. In 1983 both Long and Ted Danson were nominated for Globes, as was *Cheers* itself for Best Comedy Series. It was an excellent start for a new series, even if the ratings were low (in the seventies) that year.

NBC's Grant Tinker and his programming executive, Brandon Tartikoff, loved *Cheers*. They demonstrated their support by renewing the series for another season and allowing the show to gain momentum. The second season of *Cheers* began on September 29, 1983, with a different character each week proclaiming, "Cheers was filmed before a live studio audience." Paramount Television's tradition of live tapings for their comedies was now verbally acknowledged every week through the *Cheers* announcement.

Entertainment Weekly said that the second season of *Cheers* was a "template on how to build TV comedies to last." The producers struck gold with the continuing drama of Sam and Diane. Their involvement was the genesis of the "will-they-or-won't-they?" comedy arc for future sitcoms. "We premiered in 1982, and there were like three or four sitcoms on the air, and that was it," says Jim Brooks. "We were kind of the first new sitcom in this world that [was] basically dramatic shows. That was one thing [that was special about *Cheers*]. The other thing was the fact that we had done a romantic relationship at the head of a sitcom. That hadn't been done in a while or [maybe] ever. That was kind of the two imprints I think *Cheers* made."

By the end of the year, *Cheers*, along with *Family Ties*, *The Cosby Show*, *Night Court*, and *Hill Street Blues*, was firmly ensconced as part of the first "Must See TV" season for NBC. The network placed the show with *Family Ties* and *The Cosby Show* on Thursday nights. It was then the show began to hit its ratings stride, rising as high as number 13 that year.

Once again *Cheers* received a number of Emmy nominations by the end of the year. The show won in the categories Outstanding Comedy Series, Writing (David Angell), Supporting Actress (Rhea Perlman), and Film Editing (Andrew Chulack). Nominations included Jim Burrows for Directing, Glen and Les Charles for Writing, David Lloyd for Writing, Nick Colasanto and George Wendt for Supporting Actor, Shelley Long for Lead Actress, Ted Danson for Lead Actor, and Sam Black, Doug Gray, Tom Huth, and Gordon Kilmuck for Live and Tape Sound Mixing and Sound Effects. Shelley Long won another Golden Globe, this time for Lead Actress, and the show, Ted Danson, and Rhea Perlman were nominated.

Most of the cast remained the best of friends, although it was said that Shelley Long seemed to feel she never fit in with the others. The crew was dedicated and involved. "We shared a crew with *Taxi* the first year," remembers Jim Burrows. "Then the crew just evolved, because *Taxi* went off the air and it became my crew, and then it became [future hit series] *Frasier*'s crew. So most of those guys worked twenty years on the lot, but I would be insane not to try to take the crew I had on *Taxi* to *Cheers* because I had such a good working relationship with them."

Name guest stars were abundant over the years of the show. They ranged from political leaders and television icons to much-loved entertainment personalities. Speaker of the House Tip O'Neill, Johnny Carson, Dick Cavett, John Cleese, Alex Trebek (in a hilarious episode that featured Cliff appearing on *Jeopardy!*), and actor Gary Coleman all were guest stars.

The third season of *Cheers* brought some dramatic changes. The cast and producers were devastated when Nick Colasanto died on February 15, 1985, of heart failure. The actor had been in the hospital throughout most of the season, and during his illness Colasanto's voice was recorded to use on the show as if Coach was away from the bar for various personal reasons. After the beloved Colasanto passed away, it was decided to deal with his death on-screen. It was an emotional episode for all concerned.

Gone with the death of Coach was the antidote to the bar's fundamental cynicism. A gullible midwestern farm boy named Woody Boyd was brought in to fill the need for someone around the bar who would demonstrate a more positive approach to life. The actor who would play Woody was found in Woody Harrelson.

Woodrow Tracy Harrelson didn't really want to perform on television and initially focused his creative attention on theater. That said, after he was hired to join the cast of *Cheers* at $6,000 a week, Harrelson says his whole life changed, and he was thrilled to realize the power of comedy. The actor enjoyed the dialogue and making people laugh. "Man, it was heaven," he told *Entertainment Weekly*.

Harrelson was born in Midland, Texas, on July 23, 1961. His early years were complex and troubled. Harrelson's father, Charles Voyde Harrelson, deserted the family when Harrelson was just a boy. (Charles Harrelson is currently in prison for the 1979 murder of Judge John Wood. Wood was shot in the back as he was leaving his home to go to his chambers. The Judge's murder initiated an extensive FBI investigation that proved to be more costly than that of the assassination of President John F. Kennedy. The killing was said to have been contracted by a drug lord, who allegedly paid Harrelson $250,000.)

Woody moved with his mother to Lebanon, Ohio, where he started acting in high school after being "discovered" by fellow students who enjoyed his Elvis Presley imitations. Harrelson enrolled in Hanover College to study theology but soon discovered that he was meant more for the stage than the pulpit. He received a degree in theater arts and English in 1983 and relocated to New York City to see if he could launch a theater career. When Harrelson couldn't land a role after a year in New York, he bought a plane ticket, intending to return to Ohio. The day before he left, Harrelson landed a role in Neil Simon's production *Biloxi Blues*. He eventually married Simon's daughter Nancy. Moving to Los Angeles, Harrelson landed a job as an extra on the short-lived series *Harper Valley P.T.A.* and was soon asked to join the cast of *Cheers*.

As Woody was being introduced as Coach's bartending replacement, Diane broke up with Sam. Although her attraction to Sam would always simmer under the surface, Diane became involved with someone "more her style," psychiatrist Frasier Crane. Frasier was as self-important and snobbish as Diane, which allowed the audience to examine what might happen when someone is involved in a relationship with his or her mirror-image. Kelsey Grammer was chosen for the convoluted role of Dr. Crane.

Kelsey Grammer's early life was as complicated as his fictional counterpart's on-screen persona. Allen Kelsey Grammer was born on February 21, 1955, on St. Thomas, in the Virgin Islands. Grammer's father was murdered in the Virgin Islands, and Grammer was raised by his mother and grandfather Gordon, first in New Jersey and later in Florida. When Grammer was eleven, his grandfather died. Grammer's life continued to be plagued by tragedy. His sister Karen was later raped and murdered after leaving a Colorado Springs restaurant, and his brother was killed in a shark attack. Grammer attended Pine Crest School in Fort Lauderdale, no doubt being exposed to some of the self-important traits he would later attribute to Frasier Crane. He was accepted at Julliard, where he pursued an interest in Shakespeare. After two years at the school, Grammer performed in regional theater productions of *Othello* and *Macbeth*. He played Ross in a television production of *Macbeth* in 1981 and roles on *Kate & Allie* and the mini-series *George Washington* and *Kennedy* (as Stephen Smith) followed. Grammer had a distinctive talent that was recognized immediately by the producers and writers of *Cheers*. The producers were excited to watch him react in character to the lines delivered by their exceptional cast. Grammer had secured something unique in his limited contract to play Frasier Crane. The producers were obligated to let the actor know after his first episode whether or not he would be asked to join the cast on a more permanent basis. The answer was yes, and Grammer joined the cast. (As the writers got to know both the character and the actor, they would sometimes deliberately have the character Frasier Crane deliver corny lines because they knew that Grammer would make them special and funny.)

Shelley Long was not a great fan of Frasier Crane. Rather, she didn't want Frasier and her character, Diane, involved with one another. Long was very vocal about this, and her constant objections made those involved uncomfortable. During her acceptance of a Golden Globe for her performance in the role of Diane, Long declared that the year was difficult for her and that it broke her heart to go to work every day. Kelsey Grammer says that in her campaign against Frasier Crane, the actress consistently asked the writers to take out any jokes that Crane might try to deliver and that he couldn't help but take the assault personally. Grammer didn't dislike Long, realistically feeling that she was doing what she felt she had to do to for the sake of her character and her position on the show. The producers and writers liked Grammer, both as an actor and as a person, and despite Long's protestations; they decided to step up their writing for the Crane character.

Both Shelley Long and Rhea Perlman became pregnant during this season. While Perlman's pregnancy was written into the show, Long's was hidden through creative camera work. The show didn't miss a step. With ratings as high as the number 5 spot, *Cheers* continued to rack up awards. In 1985 an Emmy was awarded to Rhea Perlman for Supporting Actress, with nominations going to Peter Casey, David Lee, Glen Charles, Les Charles, and David Lloyd for Writing, Nick Colasanto, John Ratzenberger, and George Wendt for Supporting Actor, Michael Ballin, Sam Black, Doug Gray, and Tom Huth for Live and Tape Sound Mixing, Shelley Long for Outstanding Actress, Ted Danson for Outstanding Actor, and the show for Outstanding Comedy Series.

The prime-time drama arc of Diane and Sam still had appeal during the fourth season of *Cheers*. Frasier Crane returns to the bar to tell his sad story of Diane rejecting him at the altar in favor of traveling to Europe and "finding herself." Diane is soon back in Boston, though, asking for her old job. Although the season flirts with the possibility of a Sam and Diane romance, it isn't until the final episode that Sam calls someone on the telephone and asks that person to marry him. Is it Diane? (Several times throughout its run, the final episode of the season would result in a cliff-hanger ending, which during that time was unusual for sitcoms.)

The continuing interest and critical acclaim for *Cheers* was reflected in more Emmy nominations in 1986. Rhea Perlman once again won for

Supporting Actress, and Ted Danson, Shelley Long, Jim Burrows, Peter Casey, David Lee, Michael Ballin, Robert Douglas, Douglas Gray, Tom Huth, and the show itself received nominations. That year *Cheers* closed the season at number 3 in the ratings.

With the arrival of Season Five came the revelation that Sam had indeed asked Diane to marry him. Viewers were shocked when Diane turned him down. Evidently so was Diane, as she changes her mind, but by that time Sam isn't interested in having anything to do with her. As Diane pines for Sam, her old boyfriend, Frasier Crane, becomes more involved with the other patrons of the bar and is soon embroiled in an adventure of his own through his neurotically intellectual love interest, psychologist Dr. Lillith Sternin. Frasier and Lillith are quite a pair. The actors portraying the two characters could not have possessed more chemistry. Frasier and Lillith's war of words brought a completely new dynamic to the show. Whereas the regular characters often exchanged wisecracks and Carla was known for deep cynicism and the ability to deliver a well-placed barb, Frasier and Lillith brought new meaning to the term "effete snobbery." The viewing audience was allowed more than just a cursory look at the two eccentrics through hilarious sub-plots, and despite their superciliousness, the pair had great appeal. The *Cheers* writers allowed a closer look into the psyches of Frasier and Lillith, which permitted a glimpse not only of their inner angst but of their vulnerability. The characters were allowed to exhibit a certain poignancy, which was not easy for the writers and the actors to portray but which all concerned pulled off to entertaining bonanzas of comedy.

A strong actress was needed to perform the role of the convoluted Lillith Sternin. The producers found the perfect woman for the job in theater actress Bebe Neuwirth. Born in Newark on December 31, 1959, Beatrice Neuwirth grew up in Princeton, New Jersey, the daughter of a mathematician and an artist. Expressing an interest in dance at the age of five, Neuwirth was dancing with the Princeton Ballet Company by the time she was seven. After graduating from Princeton High School in 1976, she enrolled at Julliard to study modern dance. Neuwirth was cast in the Broadway production of *A Chorus Line* and began her professional acting career. She appeared in other Broadway musicals, including *West Side Story*, and won a Tony in 1986 for her performance in *Sweet Charity*. Neuwirth was then cast in the complicated role of Lillith on *Cheers*. She brought a confidence to the role that had been developed during her career on the stage. As an actress, Neuwirth said that she knew when she was bad, she knew when she was good, and she knew when she was everything in between.

Meanwhile, Sam again proposes to Diane. She once more turns him down, but finally the odd-ball couple decides to get married. The writers included a comical, yet moving, continuing storyline about the anticipated wedding. The season would close with the fate of the Diane-and-Sam romance once again up in the air. Although the show earned eight Emmy nominations, only John Cleese, as Guest Performer, and the sound mixers (Ballin, Douglas, Gray, and Huth) would win Emmys that year.

During this time, Kelsey Grammer was suffering a serious addiction to cocaine. It sometimes became a minor problem on the set, but the other actors stood by Grammer. Professing their love and regard for him, they joined together to suggest to Grammer that he get help for his problem. Grammer says their support saved his life. He was able to beat his addiction and return to being the professional actor he had once been.

The involvement of Sam and Diane seemed to be resolved with the departure of Shelley Long from the series before the debut of Season Five on September 25, 1986. Long's contract with the producers had ended, and she decided to seek work as a film actress. The show dealt with the absence of Diane by having the brokenhearted Sam selling Cheers to a corporation so that he can sail off into the sunset to reflect on his past and future. When his boat sinks, Sam takes it as a sign that he should return to Boston and to Cheers. He gets his job as bartender back but must now answer to a feisty manager named Rebecca Howe.

Jim Burrows had become interested in a young actress named Kirstie Alley when he saw her perform as Maggie in a production of *Cat on a Hot Tin Roof*. The brunette Alley, who was cast to play Rebecca, feared that the producers wouldn't recognize her comedy abilities and arrived at her audition dressed in a blonde wig as Shelley Long. Any doubts the producers may have had that Alley could do comedy were dispelled.

Kirstie Alley was born in Wichita, Kansas, on January 12, 1955. Upon graduation from high school, she attended first Kansas State University, then the University of Kansas. She pursued a career as an interior designer before moving to Los Angeles to work as an actor. Alley's first job on television was a 1979 appearance on the game show *Match Game P.M.*, followed by acting stints on *Masquerade* and in the television movies *Sins of the Past*, *A Bunny's Tail* (as Gloria Steinem), and *North and South*. Her first feature appearance was in 1982's *Star Trek: The Wrath of Khan*, followed by co-starring roles in *Blind Date*, with Timothy Bottoms, *Runaway*, with Tom Selleck, and Carl Reiner's *Summer School*, with Mark Harmon (husband of *Mork & Mindy*'s Pam Dawber.)

The network was concerned that viewers would have difficulty accepting a new central character in Rebecca Howe and that without the

Sam-and-Diane romance the show would suffer. NBC was relieved when Alley's characterization of the over-anxious Rebecca secured a spot in the hearts of *Cheers* fans and the show continued to thrive. Rebecca Howe was not initially drawn to Sam Malone, so the easing in of a new leading lady turned out to be fairly painless. (Rebecca would pursue a romance with the corporate boss, Robin Colcord, played by Roger Rees in subsequent seasons.) Even without the Sam-Diane dynamic, *Cheers* remained a hit. By the end of 1990–1991's Season Eight, the show would hit number 1 in the ratings.

Cheers continued throughout eleven seasons, from 1982 to 1993. All ten of the actors who appeared as regulars on the series received Emmy nominations for their portrayals over the course of that time: Ted Danson, Shelley Long, John Ratzenberger, George Wendt, Rhea Perlman, Nicholas Colasanto, Kirstie Alley, Kelsey Grammer, Woody Harrelson, and Bebe Neuwirth. By the time Paramount Television, the producers, and star Ted Danson decided that the show should exit the airwaves on a high note, *Cheers* had received a record 111 Emmy nominations and twenty-six Emmy wins. The ending of the long run of the show became inevitable when Danson decided that he wanted to pursue a career in films, and the producers decided that *Cheers* could not continue without Sam Malone. Additionally, because of the success of the show, the production costs were tremendous. Salaries alone were costing as much as $450,000 for one lead actor (Danson). *Cheers* had run its course, and although the viewers were attached to the patrons of that little Boston pub almost as though they were actually friends, everyone involved in the show wanted the end to come sweetly rather than, as for most series, with longevity that peaks, followed by a slow decline in the ratings.

Glen and Les Charles, who by this time had stepped back from their day-to-day involvement in the show, wrote the final episode of *Cheers*, which aired on May 20, 1993. The arc of the Sam-Diane love affair is fulfilled in the final episode, which has Diane winning an award for her writing and Sam calling to congratulate her. (Shelley Long returned to play Diane.) When Diane tells Sam she is married with children, he counters with the same. When it comes time for the two to meet each other's spouse, it's revealed that neither Sam nor Diane are married—and they still have feelings for one another. They decide to be together at last, but when their flight to California is delayed, they become involved in a heart-to-heart discussion and decide that their romance was not meant to be, after all. (An alternate ending was filmed in which Sam and Diane do get married. This was done to keep the audience—as well as industry insiders—in suspense as to whether or not the always-at-odds couple would get together or go their separate ways.)

Norm is the last person to depart the bar (leaving beer in his mug!) before Sam tells a would-be patron, "Sorry, we're closed," which would be the last words uttered on *Cheers*. The final show received the second-highest ratings of all time for an episodic program. Rhea Perlman was nominated for an Emmy in the Supporting Actress, Comedy category and Kirstie Alley as Outstanding Actress in a Comedy. Shelley Long was nominated as Outstanding Guest Actress, Comedy, and Tom Berenger as Outstanding Guest Actor, Comedy. James Burrows was nominated for directing and the show itself, once again, for Outstanding Comedy Series. Ted Danson would bring home the gold for Outstanding Actor in a Comedy Series, as would Robert Bramwell for Editing.

Thousands of fans gathered outside Boston's Bull & Finch Pub to celebrate the show. Kelsey Grammer remembers the night fondly. He also remembers the card that director Jim Burrows sent, with a line that summed up the experience of the creative forces of the show: Burrows wrote: "It was the best of times . . . it was the best of times." The set of *Cheers* was struck, and then transformed into the set of *Frasier*. And once again, Emmys abounded . . .

AFTERWORD

In 1983 producer Mel Harris told Garry Marshall that one of Marshall's shows was playing in syndication somewhere in the world every minute of every day. During the years 1974–1984 Paramount Television was the source of the most successful comedies on television. By the 1982–1983 season Paramount was producing eleven weekly prime-time shows. What was happening on the Paramount lot during that time was nothing short of pure magic. "The thing that was so interesting to me was that nobody realized it," says director Howard Storm. "You know, you were just doing your work. But when you look back at it, at one time Garry Marshall had five shows on the air at Paramount. That's phenomenal. Just major. It was *Laverne & Shirley*, *Mork & Mindy*, *Happy Days*, *Angie*, and *Bosom Buddies*. All were running at the same time. It was an amazing time."

What made that time so very special in the history of television continues to be a topic of interest even for the creative talents who experienced it. "I don't know if there is any constant," says director Jim Burrows. "I don't know how Garry Marshall came to the lot. He was already there when I was there. But Gary Nardino made a deal with the guys from Mary Tyler Moore, so he brought the right group in. And that spawned *Taxi*, and *Taxi* spawned *Cheers*, because I was the director of *Taxi*, Glen and Les were the producers of *Taxi*. Some of the creative personnel behind *Taxi* were at Paramount, so they made a deal with Paramount to do *Cheers*. Then *Cheers* spawned *Wings*, then the *Wings* guys went on to do *Frasier*. There were two power bases. The *Happy Days* power base and the *Taxi/Cheers* power base. Those two entities gave them a lot of shows. *Happy Days* spawned *Laverne & Shirley*, which spawned *Joanie Loves Chachi*, *Mork & Mindy*, *Angie*, *Blansky's Beauties*. All those shows are based on one show. It was just bringing the right people to the studio at the right time. A lot of it has to do with Gary Nardino, who made the deals with the creative people. I just think it was the sense of having the right creative people at the right studio at the right time. It was lightning in a bottle at that studio for that period of time."

The Marshall power base made all the right moves. "They were good shows, well written," says Storm. "The credit goes to Garry Marshall. He assigned shows to people he trusted. Garry knows how to run a show without tension."

Marshall's shows brought originality to Paramount Television that made those in charge sit up and notice. What a thrill to have such reliable hit-makers right there on the lot. One of the tenets of show business is that you're only as good as your last job. In a reversal of that mind-set,

Marshall and his team of creative talents could be counted on to deliver a new idea and a hit show time and time again. The same could be said of the John Charles Walters, Ubu, Miller-Milkis-Boyett, and Charles/Burrows/Charles production entities.

The talent discovered and nurtured by the Marshall and MTM-originated teams was enormous at that one place and time. That decade on "the lot" was magical, and even those who experienced the camaraderie and intense exchange of comedic ideas and tools remember the time as one of revelation and innovation. A great percentage of the actors, writers, directors, and producers who were involved in those years of unique and distinctive comedy at Paramount Television continued to awe and impress in their later careers. Many became superstar actors, while others excelled behind the camera in producing award-winning television and film. A handful even managed to do both. During that extraordinary decade at Paramount Television, Howard, Winkler, Marshall, Hanks, Williams, Fox, DeVito, et al. were just "kids" having fun and enjoying their first taste of success. Many of them remember that time as one of naïve newness and a dedicated brotherhood of novices. To their credit, most of the bonds formed in those early days of fame remained important professional friendships

The alpha and omega of Paramount Television's golden years, *Cheers*' Ted Danson and *Happy Days*' Henry Winkler pose at Paramount's 90th Anniversary party, 2002. Photo courtesy of Globe Photos, Inc.

that have continued to produce distinctive and substantial entertainment.

And it all began with *Happy Days*. Academy Award–winning director Ron Howard said that he learned comedy through *Happy Days*. Anson Williams, now also a director, said that Garry Marshall always encouraged his actors to wear as many hats as they could. Garry Marshall said that the cast of *Happy Days* had the immense popularity to turn guest-starring roles into spin-offs. No one involved with the show had a problem letting guest stars take center stage and display their talent, whereas on other shows, that might not have been the case. On *Happy Days*, *everybody* benefited.

On February 3, 2005, ABC aired *Happy Days: 30th Anniversary Reunion*, which reunited the cast with Garry Marshall. *People* magazine said that the get-together was a "pleasant diversion, thanks to the actors' camaraderie and the irreverence of series creator Garry Marshall." The reunion special was simply everything the original show had been.

As landmark television, *Happy Days* has been referenced in the television shows *The Fresh Prince of Bel Air*, *Friends*, *South Park*, *Saturday Night Live*, *3rd Rock from the Sun*, *Mad About You*, *Futurama*, *Boy Meets World*, *Family Guy*, *The Simpsons*, *Sesame Street*, *Step by Step*, *Dawson's Creek*, *The Nanny*, and *Seinfeld*. Homage has been paid to Fonzie with rock group Smashmouth's song "The Fonz," on a Will Smith rap song, and through a Weezer video for "Buddy Holly" that features footage from *Happy Days*. There are *Happy Days* references in the films *Pulp Fiction* (Samuel L. Jackson's character says, "We're all going to be like little Fonzies: cool"), *The Wedding Singer*, and *Austin Powers* (Mike Myers introduces himself as Richie Cunningham).

Happy Days has been syndicated in 126 countries, and Nick-at-Nite began its programming with the *Love, American Style* episode of *Happy Days*. *Entertainment Weekly* honored *Happy Days* by placing it at number 8 on their list of The Best Closers and Cliff-hangers of All Time for the final episode. American prisoner of war Terry Anderson told Henry Winkler that the American hostages watched reruns of *Happy Days* with their guards while they were being held captive. On a lighter note, when ABC aired the *Happy Days: 30th Anniversary Reunion*, Dalton Ross wrote in *Entertainment Weekly* that at last he had a reason to write the words Ralph Malph. Garry Marshall continues to work on mounting his stage show *Happy Days: The Musical*. A preview run featured New Kids on the Block's Joey McIntyre as Fonzie.

The other Paramount Television shows of the decade 1974–1984 continue to be immensely popular in syndication and through network specials. CBS aired a ninety-minute retrospective of *Taxi* on December

19, 1994. Even Penny Marshall and Cindy Williams—rather, Laverne and Shirley—reunited. There was *The Laverne & Shirley Reunion* in 1995 and *Entertainment Tonight Presents: Laverne & Shirley Together Again* in 2002. Tony Danza, Doris Roberts, Marilu Henner, Pam Dawber, Penny Marshall, Cindy Williams, Tom Hanks, Robin Williams, Andy Kaufman, Kelsey Grammer, Kirstie Alley, and other Paramount Television sitcom stars have been featured in television biographical documentaries. E! aired *Cheers: The True Hollywood Story* in 2000. In April 2005, NBC—*not* ABC, the network that aired the series—presented *Behind the Camera: The Unauthorized Story of Mork & Mindy*, featuring an amazing performance by Chris Diamantopoulos. (Robin Williams says he didn't watch it and further commented, "If they're going to make a bad movie about your life, you should wait for the Cartoon Network version.") The spin-offs from *Cheers* ranged from the less than enthusiastically received *The Tortellis* to *Frasier*, one of the most successful sitcoms of all time.

Today the Paramount Television shows of that magical decade are absent from first-run television but certainly are not forgotten by either viewers or the entertainment industry. The casts, producers, writers, and directors of those extraordinary and enduring sitcoms continue to play a very active role in entertainment. Emmys, Golden Globes, and Academy Awards attest to their unique and communal talents. While that enchanting time at Paramount from 1974 to 1984 was indeed lightning in a bottle, entertainment audiences worldwide will continue to enjoy the fruits of that bounty for years to come.

THE LEGACY

A shining example of the bonds that formed between writers, directors, producers, and actors who worked on the Paramount lot during the years 1974 through 1984 is what happened with *Bosom Buddies'* Tom Hanks and *Laverne & Shirley's* Penny Marshall. In 1988 Marshall directed Hanks, in *Big*, to his first Best Actor Academy Award nomination.

It is not uncommon for an actor on one of the Paramount Television sitcoms to show up in the casts of other Paramount actors, directors, and producers. Rather than partiality because the talent grew from the same roots, these creative individuals simply recognize genuine talent when they see it. Many of the leading actors in *Happy Days*, *Laverne & Shirley*, *Mork & Mindy*, *Taxi*, *Cheers*, and the other series featured in this book, such as Ron Howard, Tom Hanks, Robin Williams, Danny DeVito, and Michael J. Fox, have gone on to become mega-stars. Many of the others have become stellar, hardworking, popular, and award-winning entities in entertainment. The legacy of the Paramount Television comedy series from 1974 to 1984 is immense. The paths of the careers of the creative talent involved are an important manifestation of the diversity that abounds in Hollywood today.

HAPPY DAYS

Ron Howard (Richie Cunningham): Howard, who has said that if he hadn't been involved in entertainment he would have been a journalist, has created a tremendous career in the film industry. He formed Imagine Films Entertainment in 1986 with producer Brian Glazer, whom he met at Paramount Television. Howard has directed numerous films, many of which he also produced, including *Splash* and *Apollo 13* (both with *Bosom Buddies* star Tom Hanks), *Cocoon*, *Parenthood*, *Backdraft*, *Edtv*, *How the Grinch Stole Christmas*, *A Beautiful Mind*, *Cinderella Man*, and *The Da Vinci Code* (again with Hanks). Howard won an Academy Award in 2003 for directing *A Beautiful Mind*. He continued to be involved in television work through his association with *Arrested Development*, a critically acclaimed series he executive-produced and for which he provided the voice-over. The last episode of the show to air on Fox featured a statement of sorts on the unsupportive nature of television networks and the current trend of film-makers to turn to television for their "inspiration." Howard is seen in the last scene turning down a pitch for the show and says, "I just don't see it as a series. Maybe a movie?" Howard's next directing project is a remake of the film *East of Eden*.

Henry Winkler (Arthur "Fonzie" Fonzarelli): Continuing the friendship forged on *Happy Days*, Winkler appeared in Ron Howard's film *Night Shift*, and Winkler and his wife, Stacy, are godparents to Howard's children. Winkler told *Variety* that Howard was the best acting partner he ever had and that as a director Howard knows exactly what he wants and how to achieve it. Winkler starred in the television series *Monty* in 1994 and continues to make noteworthy appearances on such television series as *Arrested Development* and *Third Watch*. He produced the television game show *Hollywood Squares* and the television series *MacGyver* and appeared in the films *Little Nicky* and *The Waterboy*, with Adam Sandler. Winkler won an Emmy in 1977 as executive producer for the television movie *Who Are the DeBolts and Where Did*

They Get Nineteen Kids? and in 2000 was again nominated for an Emmy for his guest appearance on *The Practice*. He starred for nearly a year in the Broadway production of *The Dinner Party*. Winkler remains active as an executive producer (*Dallas Reunion: Return to Southfork*), as a guest voice on *King of the Hill*, and with appearances in such roles as the family lawyer in Ron Howard's *Arrested Development* and the voice of Dr. Maniac on the cartoon series *Duck Dodgers*. Winkler also is the author of the *Hank Zipzer* series of children's books. In 2005 Winkler received an Emmy for his voice work as Norville in PBS's *Clifford's Puppy Days*. He currently is seen in the hit sitcom *Out of Practice* and in the Adam Sandler movie *Click*.

Tom Bosley (Howard Cunningham): Bosley starred in the television series *Murder, She Wrote* from 1984 to 1988 and *Father Dowling Mysteries* from 1989 to 1991. He appeared as Bert in the soap *Port Charles* in 1999 and did the voice of Geppetto in the 2006 movie *Geppetto's Secret*, as well as that of Principal Warner for the series *Betsy's Kindergarten Adventures*.

Marion Ross (Marion Cunningham): Ross went on to star as Sophie in the series *Brooklyn Bridge*, for which she received two Lead Actress Emmy nominations (in 1992 and 1993). She was also nominated for an Emmy for her guest-starring role on *Touched by an Angel*. She appeared in Ron Howard's film *Skyward* and has been seen on television in such shows as *A Perfect Stranger*, *Postcards from Heaven*, and *The Gilmore Girls*. She was the voice of Marion Cunningham on the *Family Guy* episode "The Father, the Son and the Holy Fonz." In 2006 Ross appeared with Henry Winkler on the series *Out of Practice*. Winkler was delighted to have Ross on the show, telling *TV Guide* that she is "one of the great comedians ever."

Scott Baio (Chachi Arcola): Garry Marshall says Baio grew up to be a wonderful actor and a fine comedy director. Baio released two albums in the eighties: *Scott Baio* and *Boys Night Out*. In 1984 Baio starred in the series *Charles in Charge* and in 1993 played Dr. Jack Stewart in *Diagnosis Murder*. He made guest appearances in such shows as *The Nanny*, *Touched by an Angel*, and *Veronica's Closet*. He directed episodes of *The Jamie Foxx Show*, *Harry and the Hendersons*, *Unhappily Ever After*, *Nick Freno: Licensed Teacher*, and *The Parkers*. In 2004 Baio starred in the movie *SuperBabies: Baby Geniuses 2*, with Jon Voight. Baio was also seen on several episodes of *Arrested Development*, replacing co-star Henry Winkler as the family lawyer.

Al Molinaro (Big Al): Partnering with *Happy Days* co-star Anson Williams, Molinaro opened a chain of diners in the Midwest called Big Al's. He has appeared on such shows as *Family Man*, *Step by Step*, and *Punky Brewster*, and in more than forty-two commercials. Molinaro is currently writing his autobiography.

Erin Moran (Joanie Cunningham): Moran appeared over the years on the series *Hotel*, *The Love Boat*, *Murder, She Wrote*, and *Diagnosis Murder*, on game shows, and in Garry Marshall's 1996 film *Dear God*, which starred Greg Kinnear. She is involved with regional theater.

Pat Morita (Arnold): In 1987 Morita starred in *O'Hara*. He guest-starred on shows such as *Murder, She Wrote* and *Magnum P.I.*, co-starred with Ralph Macchio in the *Karate Kid* franchise, and appeared in movies, including *Honeymoon in Vegas*. Morita wrote the screenplay for the film *Captive Hearts* and voiced the Emperor of China in the movie *Mulan*. He owned a Japanese restaurant called Miyagi's on West Hollywood's Sunset Strip and toured nationally in 2003 with Sherman Hemsley in a production of *The Odd Couple*. Before his death of natural causes at age seventy-three on November 24, 2005, Morita was writing a book of autobiographical short stories. The actor appears in the films *Angst*, *Princess*, and *Coming Attractions*, all to be released after his death.

Donny Most (Ralph Malph): Most's *Happy Days*-era song "All Roads (Lead Back to You)" reached #97 on the *Billboard* chart. He appeared in the films *Teen Wolf*, *Edtv*, and *Planting Melvin*, and directed *The Last Best Sunday* and *Searching for Mickey Fish*.

Gavan O'Herlihy (Chuck Cunningham): O'Herlihy starred in the 1987 mini-series *A Killing on the Exchange* and in the films *Never Say Never Again* and *Superman III*. He also appeared in the Ron Howard–directed film *Willow*. O'Herlihy says that he has always liked Howard as Howard has a strong sense of values and priorities.

Linda Purl (Ashley): After *Happy Days*, Purl appeared in made-for-television movies such as *Secrets* and *Absolute Truth*. She also appeared in Jonathan Demme's *Crazy Mama* and Ron Howard's *Leo and Lorre*. A singer, Purl has her own cabaret act but returned to television in 2005 with roles in the series *Criminal Intent* and *Cold Case* and a starring role in the television movie *Maid of Honor*.

Misty Rowe (Wendy the Carhop): Rowe has returned to theater, where she has performed the part of Louise in the play *Always . . . Patsy Cline*. She also performs a comedy act, and has written and stars in a one-woman show called *A Misty Christmas . . . Finally, a Fruitcake You'll Like*.

Anson Williams (Potsie): William's song "Deeply" was #93 on the *Billboard* singles chart in 1977. Appearing only periodically on television as an actor, he is primarily a director and has been behind the camera on such series as *Beverly Hills 90210*, *The Pretender*, *L.A. Law*, *Melrose Place*, *Xena: Warrior Princess*, *7th Heaven*, *Sabrina, the Teenage Witch*, *Charmed*, and *Lizzie MaGuire*.

LAVERNE & SHIRLEY

Penny Marshall (Laverne DeFazio): In 1986 Marshall turned her career toward directing after being hired as a replacement director for the film *Jumpin' Jack Flash*. She served as director of the films *Big* (with Tom Hanks), *Awakenings* (with Robin Williams), *A League of Their Own* (again with Hanks), *The Preacher's Wife*, and *Riding in Cars with Boys*. She co-produced *Cinderella Man*, with Ron Howard and Brian Glazer, and was one of the producers of *Bewitched*, with Nicole Kidman and Will Ferrell. Marshall became the first woman to direct a film (*Big*) that grossed more than $100 million.

Cindy Williams (Shirley Feeney): Williams has played herself on many television programs and also appeared in the films *More American Graffiti* and *Rude*

Awakening. She starred in the television movies *Help Wanted: Kids*, *Save the Dog!*, *Tricks of the Trade*, *Big Man on Campus*, *Earth Angel*, and *The Stepford Husbands*, and in the series *Normal Life*, with *Barney Miller*'s Max Gail, *Getting By*, with *Bosom Buddies*' Telma Hopkins, and 1997's *Girls Across the Lake*. She appears with an all-star cast of comedians in *The Last Guy on Earth*, which stars Rob Schneider.

David L. Lander (Squiggy): Lander appeared in the film *Who Framed Roger Rabbit* and on such television series as *Twin Peaks*, *The Nanny*, *Highway to Heaven*, *Father Dowling Mysteries*, *Star Trek*, *Married . . . with Children*, *Mad About You*, and *Arli$$*, despite being diagnosed with multiple sclerosis. He also served as an associate scout for the Seattle Mariners baseball team and was once part owner of the Portland Beavers. In 2000 Lander was honored by the National Multiple Sclerosis Society as their Ambassador of the Year. In 2004 he appeared in *Christmas with the Kranks*, starring Tim Allen.

Michael McKean (Lenny): Next to his role as Lenny, McKean is perhaps best known as David St. Hubbins from the 1984 film *This Is Spinal Tap*. He also appeared in such films as *Coneheads*, *The Sunshine Boys*, *Best in Show*, *A Mighty Wind*, and *The Producers*, as well as on the television series *Grand*, *Sessions*, *Dream On*, and *Boston Legal*. McKean has directed for the series *Dream On*, *Tracey Takes On . . .*, and *Morton & Hayes*. In 2004 he replaced Harvey Fierstein in Broadway's *Hairspray*, and in 2005 he appeared in Woody Allen's play *A Second Hand Memory*. He is the only person to have been a musical guest, then a host, then a regular on *Saturday Night Live*, and he was nominated for an Academy Award in 2003 for the song "A Kiss at the End of the Rainbow" (from the film *A Mighty Wind*), co-written with his wife, actress Annette O'Toole.

Phil Foster (Frank DeFazio): Foster appeared in the Paramount Television/ABC dramatic pilot "Having Babies III," in the television movie *Gridlock*, and in the movie *The Happy Hooker*. His last film was 1986's *Sno-Line*, which starred Vince Edwards. Foster died on July 8, 1985, at the age of seventy-one.

Betty Garrett (Edna Babish): Garrett appeared in the television movies *All the Way Home*, with Sally Fields, and *The Long Way Home*, with Jack Lemmon. She has also appeared on such television series as *The Golden Girls*, *Union Square*, *Boston Public*, *Becker*, and *Grey's Anatomy*.

Eddie Mekka (Carmine "The Big Ragoo" Ragusa): Mekka has appeared on *Family Matters*, *The Jamie Foxx Show*, *Guiding Light*, and *24*, and has toured with productions of *The Goodbye Girl*, *Little Shop of Horrors*, and *They're Playing Our Song*. He also tours nationally with his Vegas-style cabaret show and appeared in the Las Vegas production of *Hairspray*.

TAXI

Jeff Conaway (Bobby Wheeler): Conaway starred in the television series *Wizards and Warriors* and in 1985's prime-time soap opera *Berrengers*. He played the role of Mick Savage in *The Bold and the Beautiful* and appeared as Zack Allen on

Babylon 5. In 2005 Conaway appeared in the film *Living the Dream*, with Sean Young, and starred in the film *Wrestling.* Conaway also had a memorable turn on *Celebrity Fit Club.*

Tony Danza (Tony Banta): After *Taxi,* Danza starred in *Who's the Boss?* (1984–1992), 1995's *Hudson Street*, and 1997's *The Tony Danza Show* (in all of which he once again played a character named Tony!). He produced such shows as *Hudson Street, George,* and *The Tony Danza Show.* Danza temporarily left television to appear in 1999's Broadway revival of *The Iceman Cometh*, with Kevin Spacey. In 1993 a skiing accident left him unable to walk. Danza spent a year and a half rehabilitating his body. After regaining the use of his legs, he decided he wanted to sing and dance professionally, and performed in a Las Vegas cabaret act. Danza appeared in the films *Cannonball Run II, Angels in the Outfield, The Whisper,* and *Crash.* He served as the host of daytime's *The Tony Danza Show* and contributed his voice to the animated comedy *Firedog.*

Danny DeVito (Louie De Palma): DeVito continued acting in films, including *Terms of Endearment, Romancing the Stone, Ruthless People, Tin Men, The War of the Roses, Batman Returns* (as The Penguin), *Hoffa, Get Shorty, L.A. Confidential, The Virgin Suicides, Death to Smoochy, Big Fish, Be Cool, Jack the Bear,* and *Jumpshot.* He made his feature directorial debut with 1987's *Throw Momma from the Train,* then directed *War of the Roses, Death to Smoochy, Hoffa, Duplex,* and *I Married a Witch.* He and his wife, Rhea Perlman, starred in the 1984 television movie *Ratings Game,* which he also directed. DeVito served as a producer on such films as *Hoffa, Pulp Fiction, Get Shorty,* the Best Picture Oscar–nominated *Erin Brockovich,* and *Along Came Polly,* and as executive producer on the television series *Mary, Kate Brasher, U.C. Undercover, American Embassy, Reno 911,* and *Karen Sisko.* In 2006 DeVito appeared as an actor in five films, including *Even Money* (with Kelsey Grammer), *The OH in Ohio,* and *Relative Strangers,* with (Michael McKean), and as a producer for six films.

Marilu Henner (Elaine Nardo): After *Taxi,* Henner appeared in the films *Hammett* with then-husband Frederic Forrest, *Johnny Dangerously,* with Michael Keaton, *Perfect,* with former boyfriend John Travolta, and *L.A. Story,* with Steve Martin. She has appeared on television in the movies *Mister Roberts, Fight for Justice: The Nancy Conn Story, Titanic* (as Molly Brown), and 2004's *Love Rules,* and in the pilot of Lisa Kudrow's television series *The Comeback.* Henner appeared in a guest-starring role on Tony Danza's *Who's the Boss?* and co-starred with Burt Reynolds in *Evening Shade.* Becoming proactive after both her parents died young of a degenerative disease, Henner studied nutrition and became a vegetarian and exercise spokeswoman. (During her time on *Taxi,* Henner was the first woman to use the Paramount gym.) She has published an autobiography titled *By All Means Keep Moving.*

Judd Hirsch (Alex Reiger): Hirsch won an Obie in 1979 for his off-Broadway appearance in *Talley's Folly* and won Tony Awards for his roles in *I'm Not Rappaport* and *Conversations with My Father.* Hirsch made his film debut in 1979's *King of the Gypsies* and was nominated for a Supporting Actor Academy Award for his role as the psychiatrist in 1980's *Ordinary People*. He appeared in the series *Detective in the House* and won a Golden Globe for *Dear John*, in which he played lead character John Lacey. In 1999 Hirsch starred in the Yasmina Reza play *Art* on Broadway with *Cheers*' George Wendt. He starred in the series *George & Leo* and is a co-star on *Numb3rs*. He has a son named Alex, which, of course, was also the name of his *Taxi* character.

Andy Kaufman (Latka Gravas): Kaufman continued to make comedy/performance art appearances and appeared on television in *The Rodney Dangerfield Special: I Can't Take It No More*. He was last seen on television in 1983 as Tony Clifton in *The Fantastic Miss Piggy Show*. Kaufman died of lung cancer on May 16, 1984, at the age of thirty-five. *Laverne & Shirley*'s David Lander remembers his doctor telling him about Kaufman's death while Lander was in the hospital with multiple sclerosis. Lander found Kaufman's passing hard to believe and told his doctor, "Andy was crazy, but you don't die of crazy." A year after the death of Kaufman, "Tony Clifton" (believed to be portrayed that night by Kaufman's friend Bob Zmuda) gave a performance at the Comedy Store. Many people expected Kaufman to show up at the event and declare his death a hoax. It wasn't a hoax. In 1999, Jim Carrey starred as Kaufman in *Man in the Moon*, a movie about Kaufman's life. All of his *Taxi* co-stars except Tony Danza appeared in the film as themselves.

Christopher Lloyd (Reverend Jim Ignatowski): After *Taxi*, Lloyd appeared in films such as *The Adventures of Buckaroo Banzai*, in which he played John Bigboote, and *Star Trek III: The Search for Spock*. He then co-starred as Doc Brown with *Family Ties*' Michael J. Fox in *Back to the Future* and its sequels. Lloyd appeared in a *Cheers* episode and in 1988 appeared in the films *Eight Men Out* and *Who Framed Roger Rabbit*, in which he was the evil Judge Doom. He played Uncle Fester in *The Addams Family* movie and won an Emmy for a guest appearance as a drama teacher/drifter on the series *Avonlea*. He appeared on the series *Stacked*, and voiced Mr. Sassafras in *Peter Cottontail: The Movie* and Mr. Clipboard in *Foodfight!* Lloyd has appeared in more than 200 plays.

Randall Carver (John Burns): In 1980 Carver co-starred in the Vietnam-based series *Six O'Clock Follies* as Lt. Vaughn Beuhler; the series, a black comedy about armed forces television, also starred Laurence Fishburne and Phil Hartman. During the show's debut episode, President Jimmy Carter pre-empted the show to announce the loss of eight soldiers during the attempt to rescue the hostages in Iran. The subsequent political climate caused the much-anticipated show to fade from the network's attention. Carver played a killer in the television movie *Detour to Terror*, which also starred O. J. Simpson. He has appeared on the series *The Norm Show* and *Malcolm in the Middle*.

Carol Kane (Simka Dahblitz-Gravas): Kane continues to appear in films, which have included *Jumpin' Jack Flash*, *The Princess Bride*, *Joe vs. the Volcano*, *Confessions of a Teenage Drama Queen*, and *Pacifier*. She has appeared on numerous television shows and starred in the 1990 series *American Dreamer*, 1991's *Brooklyn Bridge*, with *Happy Days*' Marion Ross, 1996's *Pearl*, with *Cheers*' Rhea Perlman, and 2002's *The Grubbs*. She continues to appear in films.

Pam Dawber (Mindy McConnell): Dawber appeared in the made-for-television movies *Remembrance of Love, Through Naked Eyes, Last of the Great Survivors, This Wife for Hire, Wild Horses,* and *American Geisha* before starring in the series *My Sister Sam.* She appeared in many other television movies and in the 1997 series *Life . . . and Stuff.* Dawber's last appearance was in the television movie *Don't Look Behind You,* co-starring with *Dallas'* Patrick Duffy. She is now retired and raising her children with actor Mark Harmon.

Robin Williams (Mork): Williams's second movie was *The World According to Garp,* and he went on to star in such films as *Moscow on the Hudson,* 1987's *Good Morning, Vietnam,* for which he was nominated for an Academy Award, *Dead Poets Society,* which resulted in a second Oscar nomination, and *The Fisher King,* for which he was again nominated for his performance, this time as a homeless medieval scholar. Williams also turned in memorable performances in the comedies *Mrs. Doubtfire* and *The Birdcage,* and received the Best Supporting Actor Academy Award for his role in *Good Will Hunting.* In 1997 he ranked #63 in *Empire* magazine's Top Movie Stars of All Time list and was voted Funniest Man Alive by *Entertainment Weekly,* which also chose him as one of its 25 Best Actors in 1998. Williams has won Emmys for his variety specials, and he co-hosted the *Comic Relief* shows that benefited the homeless. He served as director on *Comic Relief* and was a producer on *Mrs. Doubtfire* (with his wife, Marsha Garces Williams) and the film *Jakob the Liar.* Williams won Grammy Awards for his comedy albums, and he performed in *Robin Williams: Live on Broadway* in 2002. He has been dubbed the heir to Bob Hope for entertaining U.S. troops in Iraq.

Robert Donner (Exidor): Donner appeared in multiple episodes of the television series *Legend,* starring Richard Dean Anderson, and in such television movies as *With a Vengeance* and *Columbo: Undercover.* He last appeared in a 2000 episode of *Dharma & Greg.* Donner devotes himself to golf, performs stand-up comedy, and is a corporate speaker.

Gina Hecht (Jean DaVinci): Hecht appeared in films such as *Clockstoppers,* Ron Howard's *Edtv,* and *St. Elmo's Fire,* and co-starred on the television series *Everything's Relative* and *Heartbeat.* She has appeared on *The West Wing, JAG, Judging Amy, CSI, Will & Grace,* and *Everwood,* and produced the 2001 comedy movie *Odessa or Bust,* starring Red Buttons and Jason Alexander.

Conrad Janis (Fred McConnell): After *Mork & Mindy,* Janis appeared in such films as *Oh God! Book Two, Mr. Saturday Night,* and *The Cable Guy.* He had several guest-starring roles in *Frasier, Family Law, Murder, She Wrote,* and other series. He produced and directed the film *Bad Blood,* in which he starred with Piper Laurie. Janis plays jazz trombone in club appearances.

Elizabeth Kerr (Cora Hudson): Kerr appeared in the television movies *Something in Common,* starring Ellen Burstyn, and *Pleasures,* with Joanna Cassidy and *Happy Day's* Linda Purl. She had a cameo in Garry Marshall's film *Frankie and Johnny.* Ms.

Kerr died on January 13, 2000, at the age of eighty-eight.

Tom Poston (Franklin Bickley): Poston went on to co-star as George Utley in the series *Newhart*, in Howie Mandel's 1990 series *Good Grief*, in Newhart's 1992 series *Bob*, in *Grace Under Fire*, and in 2005's *Committed*. He also appeared in the films *The Princess Diaries 2* and *Christmas with the Kranks* and on such series as *ER, Becker, Will & Grace, That '70s Show*, and *8 Simple Rules . . . for Dating My Teenage Daughter*. In 2001, at the age of eighty, Poston married actress Suzanne Pleshette, who starred in the original *Bob Newhart Show*.

Jay Thomas (Remo DaVinci): Thomas won an Emmy for portraying Jerry Gold in the series *Murphy Brown*. He also starred in *Married People*, with Bess Armstrong, and *Love and War*, with Susan Dey and Annie Potts. He continued his acting career through guest appearances on *Ed, Law & Order: Special Victims Unit, Joan of Arcadia*, and multiple other series. Additionally, Thomas is a disc jockey in New York City. Traditionally, Thomas knocks the meatball off the Christmas tree during New Year's Eve on *The Late Show with David Letterman*.

Jonathan Winters (Mearth): Winters starred in *The Wonderful World of Jonathan Winters* in 1986 and appeared in the films *Moon Over Parador* and *The Flintstones*. He also appeared in the television series *The Completely Mental Misadventures of Ed Grimley*, which starred *The Associates*' Martin Short, *Davis Rules*, and *Fish Police*. Winters produced, wrote, and starred in *Spaced Out* for Showtime in 1992. He appeared in the film *Swing*, with Tom Skerritt and Jacqueline Bisset, and in the movie *National Lampoon's Cattle Call*.

ANGIE

Robert Hays (Brad Benson): Hays is perhaps best known for his performance as Ted Striker in the movies *Airplane* and *Airplane II*. He appeared in the films *Take This Job and Shove It, The Fall of the House of Usher*, and *Homeward Bound II*, and starred in the television series *Starman* in 1986, *FM* in 1989, and *Bette* in 2000. Hays starred in the television movie *Unabomber: The True Story*, as David Kaczynski, and appeared on such series as *Spin City* and *Robbery Homicide Division* and in the movie *Freezer Burn*. He served as a producer for 2006's *Nicky's Birthday Camera*.

Donna Pescow (Angie Falco Benson): Pescow appeared in the long-running comedy series *Out of This World*. She received three Emmy nominations for her role as Eileen Stevens in *Even Stevens*. She appeared in the film *Unsung Hero* and has directed episodes of *Even Stevens, Harry and the Hendersons*, and *That's So Raven*. She also directs theatrical productions.

Debralee Scott (Marie Falco): In 1999 Scott retired from acting to become an agent with Empowered Artists. She was engaged to a police officer with the New York Port Authority who was killed in the World Trade Center terrorist attack on September 11, 2001. Scott died suddenly on April 5, 2005, on Amelia Island, Florida, where she had moved to care for her sister, who was ill. Scott had been in a coma of unknown origin but awakened and returned home, only to quietly pass away during a nap several days later. The cause of her death is unknown.

John Randolph (Randall Benson): Randolph continued his career in television and film. He appeared in the films *Prizzi's Honor* and *You've Got Mail*, and played Roseanne's father in the sitcom *Roseanne*. Randolph won Tony and Drama Desk Awards in 1987 for playing the left-wing grandfather in Neil Simon's play *Broadway Bound*. He continued to be involved with politics and served as head of the Council of American-Soviet Friendship, a cultural exchange organization. He died at the age of eighty-eight on February 24, 2004.

Doris Roberts (Theresa Falco): After *Angie*, Roberts appeared regularly in the series *Maggie*, *Remington Steele*, and *The Boys*. She received Supporting Actress Emmy nominations for her roles on *St. Elsewhere* and *Remington Steele*, as well as for Guest Actress on *Perfect Strangers* and Supporting Actress in a Mini-series for PBS's *American Playhouse: The Sunset Gang*. Roberts was nominated five times for *Everybody Loves Raymond*, winning the award four times for her performance as Marie, a role for which she beat out 100 other actresses. She appears in the films *Grandma's Boy* and *Keeping Up with the Steins* (Garry Marshall also has a role), and starred in the television pilot "Our House."

THE BAD NEWS BEARS

Phillip R. Allen (Roy Turner): Allen appeared in the films *The Onion Field*, *Mommie Dearest*, and *Star Trek III: The Search for Spock*. He also appeared in the series *Alice* and *Center of the Universe* and in the television movies *A Very Brady Christmas* and *Marilyn & Bobby: Her Final Affair*.

Tricia Cast (Amanda Whirlitzer): Cast appeared as Christy Duvall on the soap opera *Santa Barbara* and, for fifteen years, as Nina Webster Chancellor on *The Young and the Restless*. She also has had roles on such series as *ER*, *L.A. Doctors*, and *Chicago Hope*.

Corey Feldman (Regi Tower): When he appeared in *Friday the 13th Part V: A New Beginning*, Feldman came to the attention of Steven Spielberg, who cast him in *The Goonies* as Clark "Mouth" Devereaux. He then appeared in Rob Reiner's film *Stand by Me* as Teddy Duchamp and in *The Lost Boys*, for which he won the 1987 Youth in Film award. Feldman overcame a drug addiction in 1991 and continues to appear in films. In 2005 he appeared in the stage production of *Fatal Attraction*. He also is a songwriter and recording artist.

Catherine Hicks (Dr. Emily Rappant): Hicks appeared in the television movies *Marilyn: The Untold Story* as Marilyn Monroe and *Jacqueline Susann's Valley of the Dolls* as Ann, and in the films *The Razor's Edge*, *Peggy Sue Got Married*, and *Eight Days a Week*, among others. Hicks co-starred in the 1982 television series *Tucker's Witch* and on the nighttime soap *Winnetka Road*. She played the role of matriarch Annie Camden for ten years on the hit series *7th Heaven*.

Meeno Peluce (Tanner Boyle): Peluce appeared in the television series *Voyagers*.

He attended the University of California at Santa Cruz to study American literature and taught history at Hollywood High School.

Kristoff St. John (Ahmad Abdul Rahim): St. John starred in the 1985 series *Charlie & Co.* and the soap *Generations*, and has appeared on *The Young and the Restless* as Neil Winters since 1991. He also appeared in the films *Carpool Guy* and *3 Day Test*.

Jack Warden (Morris Buttermaker): Warden continued his work in movies with such films as . . . *And Justice for All*, *Being There*, *The Verdict*, *The Three Kings*, *Problem Child*, *Toys*, *Bulworth*, and *The Replacements*. He starred in the series *Crazy Like a Fox* from 1984 to1986 and *Knight & Daye* in 1989. He appeared in the 2002 film *Abandon*, with Katie Holmes and Benjamin Bratt.

BOSOM BUDDIES

Tom Hanks (Kip "Buffy" Wilson): Hanks starred in Ron Howard's *Splash* in 1984 and was nominated for an Academy Award four years later for Penny Marshall's film *Big*. He appeared in numerous films, including *A League of Their Own* and *Sleepless in Seattle*, and then won consecutive Best Actor Oscars for *Philadelphia* (1993) and *Forrest Gump* (1994). He received two more Oscar nominations for *Saving Private Ryan* (1998) and *Cast Away* (2000). Although Hank's more substantial awards were for drama, comedian Chris Rock said in a 2005 *Entertainment Weekly* interview that Hanks was one of the funniest guys he's ever seen perform. Hanks starred in Ron Howard's film *Apollo 13*, wrote and directed *That Thing You Do* and segments of the mini-series *From the Earth to the Moon*, and co-produced the acclaimed film *My Big Fat Greek Wedding*. He stars in the Ron Howard–directed film *The Da Vinci Code* and co-stars with his son, Colin, in *The Great Buck Howard*. Hanks received the Distinguished Public Service Award in 1999 for his work in *Saving Private Ryan* and in 2002 was the youngest-ever recipient of the American Film Institute's Life Achievement Award. Hanks continues to rank high in *Premiere* magazine's Power 100 list and *Entertainment Weekly*'s Greatest Movie Stars of All Time list.

Peter Scolari (Henry "Hildegard" Desmond): In addition to appearances in *From the Earth to the Moon* and *That Thing You Do!*, Scolari continued his television career co-starring in the series *Baby Makes Five*, *Newhart*, *Family Album*, and *Dweebs*. He appeared in roles on the series *Listen Up* and the film *Mentor*.

Donna Dixon (Sonny Lumet): Dixon co-starred in the prime-time soap *Berrengers*, with *Taxi*'s Jeff Conaway, and in 1986's *Charmed Lives*, with Fran Drescher. She appeared in the films *Wayne's World*, *Exit to Eden*, and *Nixon*. She met husband Dan Ackroyd while appearing in his 1983 film *Doctor Detroit* (1983) and appeared on his series *Soul Man*. The couple has three daughters.

Telma Hopkins (Isabelle): Hopkins continues to be active mostly in television, co-starring in the series *Gimme a Break!* and appearing in sitcoms such as *Family Matters*, *Getting By*, *Half & Half*, and *The Hughleys*.

Wendie Jo Sperber (Amy Cassidy): Sperber co-starred on the series *Private Benjamin* and *Babes* and appeared in the movies *Back to the Future*, *Sorority Boys*, and

My Dinner with Jimi. She appeared several times on the series *8 Simple Rules . . . for Dating My Teenage Daughter,* and it was on that show that she would make her last appearance. After being diagnosed with breast cancer in 1998, Sperber headed the non-profit cancer support center organization weSpark, for which she organized celebrity golf tournaments and variety shows. She died of the disease on November 29, 2005. Tom Hanks said in *People* magazine that the memory of Wendie Jo Sperber "is that of a walking inspiration."

Holland Taylor (Ruth Dunbar): Taylor is a hardworking actress who has co-starred in the soap operas *All My Children* and *Ryan's Hope,* and in the series *Me & Mom, Harry, Going Places, The Powers That Be, Saved by the Bell: The College Years, The Naked Truth, Baby Bob,* and *Two and a Half Men,* among others. She has appeared in the movies *Romancing the Stone, The Jewel of the Nile, The Wedding Singer, The Truman Show, Legally Blonde,* and *The Wedding Date,* and has appeared regularly on the series *The L Word.*

FAMILY TIES

Michael J. Fox (Alex P. Keaton): After appearing in *Back to the Future* and its sequels, Fox starred in such movies as *Teen Wolf, Doc Hollywood,* and *Mars Attacks!* He married his *Family Ties* co-star Tracy Pollan; the couple has four children. Although diagnosed with Parkinson's disease in 1991, Fox starred in the television series *Spin City* from 1996 until 2000. He went public with his illness in 1998 and subsequently wrote his autobiography, *Lucky Man.* Fox voiced the starring animated character of all three *Stuart Little* films and made memorable appearances on the series *Scrubs* and *Boston Legal.* Fox has a theater named after him in his hometown, Burnaby, British Columbia, and in January 2005 came in at #23 on *TV Guide's* list of TV's 25 Greatest Teen Idols.

Justine Bateman (Mallory Keaton): After starring in the movie *Satisfaction,* Bateman appeared in several other films. She starred in the 1984 play *Journey to Day* with her brother, actor Jason Bateman; the play was directed by their father, Kent. Justine starred in the series *Men Behaving Badly* in 1996 and in 2004's *The Hollywood Mom's Mystery.* Bateman devotes most of her time to her design firm, which produces both a couture and a ready-to-wear line of women's clothing. She appeared in the series *Still Standing* and with her brother Jason on his series *Arrested Development.*

Meredith Baxter (Elyse Keaton): Baxter has appeared in more than thirty-five movies for television, including *Darkness Before Dawn, My Breast,* and *Winnie.* She executive-produced *The Faculty* for ABC. Baxter played former *Family Ties* co-star Michael J. Fox's mother in an episode of his series *Spin City.* She has a signature cosmetics line and is a social activist involved in women's rights, public awareness of breast cancer, and gun control. She continues to act, appearing in the films *Paradise, Texas,* and *The Mostly Unfabulous Social Life of Ethan Green,* and on the series *The Closer.*

Michael Gross (Steven Keaton): Gross appeared in several made-for-television movies, including *A Letter to Three Wives, A Connecticut Yankee in King Arthur's Court,* in which he starred as Arthur, and *The Making of a Hollywood Madam.* He won an Obie for his role in the stage production *No End of Blame*. Gross appeared in the popular movie *Tremors* and in the subsequent, short-lived 2003 series *Tremors*. He also became popular for his roles in the popular *In the Line of Duty* television movies and appeared in the television movie *Mrs. Harris* and on the series *The Drew Carey Show* and *CSI: New York*.

Tina Yothers (Jennifer Keaton): After appearing as skater Tonya Harding in the television movie *Spunk: The Tonya Harding Story* and 1995's *A Perry Mason Mystery: The Case of the Jealous Jokester*, Yothers semi-retired from acting to devote herself to music. She wrote the book *Being Your Best: Tina Yother's Guide for Girls* and appeared with her band Jaded. In 2004 Yothers played Linda Lovelace in the stage show *Lovelace: The Musical*.

CHEERS

Ted Danson (Sam Malone): Danson starred in the movies *Three Men and a Baby* and *Made in America*, and appeared in the film *Saving Private Ryan*. He won a Golden Globe for the television movie *Something About Amelia*, in which he played an incestuous father. Danson met his wife, Mary Steenburgen, on the 1994 film *Pontiac Moon*, and the two starred in the Danson-produced series *Ink*. He starred as Dr. John Becker on the sitcom *Becker* and has appeared in such films as *The Moguls* and the controversial television movie *Our Fathers*. Danson is active in environmental initiatives and is involved in a campaign to protect the oceans. In 2005, Danson starred in the series *Help Me Help You*.

Shelley Long (Diane Chambers): After appearing in movies such as *The Money Pit*, *Outrageous Fortune*, *Troop Beverly Hills*, and *Frozen Assets*, Long returned to television with the series *Good Advice*. She starred as Carol Brady in *The Brady Bunch Movie* and appeared on such series as *Joan of Arcadia*, *Boston Legal*, *Yes, Dear*, and *Complete Savages*, as well as in television movies. In 2006, Danson starred in the series *Help Me Help You*.

Kirstie Alley (Rebecca Howe): Alley returned to her film career with the *Look Who's Talking* franchise and in 1997 starred in the series *Veronica's Closet*, which ran for three years. She continues to star in made-for-television movies and created controversy with her television reality-drama *Fat Actress*, for which she also wrote and produced. Alley lost more than sixty pounds as spokeswoman for Jenny Craig.

Kelsey Grammer (Dr. Frasier Crane): Grammer not only starred in but directed several episodes of the *Cheers* spin-off *Frasier*, as well as becoming one of the show's executive producers. He was the first actor in television history to receive multiple Emmy nominations for appearing as the same character on three network series (as Dr. Frasier Crane on *Cheers*, *Wings*, and *Frasier*). Grammer also holds the record for the longest time an actor has played one role: twenty years. He received ten Emmy nominations as Frasier (and won four times), along with Golden Globes, People's Choice, and American Comedy Awards. Grammer did voice-overs in *Toy Story 2* and *Anastasia*, and is the voice of Krusty the Clown on *The Simpsons*. He created and produced *Kelsey Grammer Presents: The Sketch Show* in 2005, and appeared in the films *Even Money* (with Danny DeVito) and *X-Men:*

The Last Stand. In 2004 Grammer revisited Stage 25 on the Paramount lot, the old home of *Frasier* and *Cheers*, when he directed the pilot of *Out of Practice*, Henry Winkler's sitcom.

Woody Harrelson (Woody Boyd): A sought-after film actor, Harrelson starred in *White Men Can't Jump, Indecent Proposal, Natural Born Killers, The People vs. Larry Flynt, The Thin Red Line, North Country, A Prairie Home Companion*, and *A Scanner Darkly*. He continues to periodically appear on television and had a recurring role on *Will & Grace*. Harrelson writes, produces, and acts in theatrical productions. In 1990 he was chosen by *People* magazine as one of their 50 Most Beautiful People. Inspired by Ted Danson, Harrelson is involved with environmental issues, as well as efforts to legalize hemp.

Rhea Perlman (Carla Tortelli): Perlman appeared in the films *Sunset Park, Carpool*, and *Matilda*, and produced and starred in the series *Pearl* in 1996. She continues to appear on television and was seen in such shows as *Mad About You, Frasier*, and *Becker*, and in the television movie *Stroller Wars*.

Bebe Neuwirth (Dr. Lillith Sternin-Crane): Continuing her film career (while appearing on *Cheers*) with *Bugsy* and *Malice*, Neuwirth has since appeared in the films *Jumanji, Liberty Heights, How to Lose a Guy in Ten Days*, and *Game 6*. She reprised her role as Lillith with several appearances on *Frasier* and starred as ADA Tracey Kibre on the series *Law & Order: Trial by Jury*. Neuwirth continues to perform on Broadway and in 1996 won a Tony for her performance in *Chicago*.

John Ratzenberger (Cliff Clavin): Ratzenberger continues to act and has directed episodes of *Sister, Sister* and *Pearl*. He made guest appearances on the series *Murphy Brown, Caroline in the City, That '70s Show*, and *The Drew Carey Show*, and has done voice work in *Toy Story, Toy Story 2, A Bug's Life, Monsters, Inc., The Incredibles*, and *Cars*. Ratzenberger is active in the ecological movement.

George Wendt (Norm Peterson): After appearances in the films *Fletch* and *Man of the House*, among others, Wendt starred in the 1995 CBS series *The George Wendt Show* and later co-starred in *The Naked Truth*. Wendt and John Ratzenberger appeared as Norm Peterson and Cliff Clavin on six series: *Cheers, St. Elsewhere, The Tortellis, The Simpsons, Wings*, and *Frasier*. He sometimes appears in cameo parts on *Saturday Night Live* and appeared with Ted Danson on *Becker*. He and John Ratzenberger won a suit against Paramount Pictures in 2001 for illegal use of their likenesses in *Cheers*-themed airport bars.

BEHIND THE CAMERA

James L. Brooks: Brooks has had a very active and successful career in films. He wrote, produced, and directed *Terms of Endearment*, for which he won three Academy Awards, *Broadcast News*, for which he received two nominations, and *As Good as It Gets*, for which he received Oscar nominations for writing and producing. Brooks also received an Oscar nomination for producing *Jerry Maguire*. In 1984 Brooks founded Gracie Films and produced *The Tracey Ullman Show, The Critic*, and

The Simpsons, a legendary animated show that ironically pokes fun at domestic comedies on television. In 2004 Brooks wrote, directed, and produced the movie *Spanglish.*

James Burrows: Burrows is the most-nominated television director in the history of the Director's Guild, with twenty nominations. He is also the director with the best pilots-to-series record: Thirty-nine of the pilots he directed were picked up as series; in 1995 he directed six pilots, all of which went on to become series. Burrows is the winner of ten Emmys. He has directed *Night Court, Valerie, Dear John, Wings, Frasier, Friends, NewsRadio, Caroline in the City, Men Behaving Badly, 3rd Rock from the Sun, Dharma & Greg, Will & Grace, Veronica's Closet, Two and a Half Men,* and *Teachers.*

Michael Eisner: When Barry Diller hired Michael Eisner to join him at Paramount, the company was in sixth place in the film industry. Two years later, Paramount was the top studio and claimed half of the top box office films. After leaving Paramount in 1984, Eisner moved to Disney to become Chairman and CEO. He was at the helm when the Walt Disney Company bought ABC. He then controlled the company that had given him his start in television. Eisner left Disney in 2005. On October 7, 2005, he guest-hosted *The Charlie Rose Show*, where one of his guests was Barry Diller. He is currently involved with CNBC's *Conversations with Michael Eisner.*

Gary David Goldberg: Goldberg won critical acclaim for the television series *Brooklyn Bridge* and re-teamed with Michael J. Fox when Goldberg created and executive-produced *Spin City*. In 1998 Goldberg was awarded the Valentine Davies Award for Achievement by the Writers Guild. He established the Paramount Studio Child Care Center with Danny DeVito and Rhea Perlman in 1986; it was the first such facility on a studio lot. Goldberg wrote and produced the series *Battery Park*, and he wrote, produced, and directed the 2005 comedy film *Must Love Dogs*, starring Diane Lane and John Cusack.

Garry Marshall: Over the years, Marshall directed episodes of *Happy Days, Love, American Style, The Odd Couple,* and *Laverne & Shirley*, to name but a few television series. After writing, producing, and directing *Young Doctors in Love* in 1982, he decided that he wanted to devote his primary energy to film directing and subsequently directed *The Flamingo Kid, Beaches, Pretty Woman, Frankie and Johnny, Exit to Eden, Runaway Bride,* and *The Princess Diaries*. Marshall periodically appears in cameos in his films and had a role as Murphy Brown's boss, Stan. He voiced Bernie in *Father of the Pride* and Buck Cluck in the movie *Chicken Little*, and he appears in the film *Keeping Up with the Steins*, with Doris Roberts. In 2004 Marshall received the Golden Eddie Filmmaker of the Year Award from the American Cinema Editors, and he has received honors from the American Comedy Awards and the BAFTA Awards, a Lifetime Achievement Award from the Casting Society of America, a nomination for France's Cesar Award, nominations for four Emmy Awards, a Lifetime Achievement Award from the Producers Guild of America, a Lucy Award from Women in Film, a Valentine Davies Award from the Writers Guild of America, and a star on the Hollywood Walk of Fame.

Tony Marshall: Marshall had a cameo in Garry Marshall's 1986 film *Nothing in Common*. He died at the age of ninety-three on July 12, 1999, in Toluca Lake, California.

Jerry Paris: Paris directed the popular movies *Police Academy* and *Police Academy 2*. He died on March 31, 1986, in Los Angeles of a brain tumor.

Thomas L. Miller: Miller executive-produced and developed the series *Family Matters*, *Step by Step*, and *Going Places*, and executive-produced the series *Two of a Kind*, *Meego*, *The Hogan Family*, *Full House*, *Perfect Strangers*, and *Valerie*.

Gary Nardino: Heading Paramount Television for the mini-series *Shogun*, *Golda*, and *The Winds of War*, Nardino won Emmys for all three projects. He supervised the production of *Star Trek: The Wrath of Khan* for Paramount in 1982 and was executive producer for *Star Trek III: The Search for Spock*. Nardino left his position at Paramount Television in July 1983 to produce films and television programs of his own. He produced the series *Brothers* for Showtime and *Marblehead Manor* for NBC. Nardino was named Chairman and CEO of Orion Television Entertainment in 1988 and supervised the production of such shows as *Hearts Are Wild* and *American Detective*. In 1991 he moved to Lorimar to create television programming. While there he executive-produced *Time Trax*. Nardino died on January 22, 1998, from a stroke.

Howard Storm: Storm continued to direct television series, including *Mr. Belvedere*, *Perfect Strangers*, *Alf*, *Full House*, *Major Dad*, and *Everybody Loves Raymond*, and he also directed the film *Once Bitten*, which starred Jim Carrey. Storm has appeared as an actor in such films as *The Check Is in the Mail*, *American Hot Wax*, and *Take the Money and Run*. In 2004 he performed in a stage production with actor Pat Harrington called *Harrington and Storm: 2 Guys Doing a One-Man Show*, about growing up in New York City.

Ed. Weinberger: After the cancellation of *Taxi*, Weinberger co-produced *Mr. Smith*, a 1993 sitcom that featured a talking orangutan voiced by Weinberger. (The sigh in the John Charles Walters Company end logo is also his.) In 1984 Weinberger co-wrote the Emmy-winning pilot episode for *The Cosby Show*. He produced the series *Amen*, *Dear John*, *Baby Talk*, and *The Good News*, and co-wrote the 1984 Steve Martin film *The Lonely Guy*.

TIMELINE

Happy Days: January 15, 1974–May 8, 1984

Paper Moon: September 12, 1974–December 12, 1975

When Things Were Rotten: September 10, 1975–December 3, 1975

The Cop and the Kid: September 1975–January 1976

Laverne & Shirley: January 27, 1976–May 10, 1983

Blansky's Beauties: February 12, 1977–May 21, 1977

Busting Loose: January 1977–November 1977

Mulligan's Stew: October 25, 1977–December 13, 1977

Who's Watching the Kids: September 1978–December 1978

Taxi: September 12, 1978–June 15, 1983

Mork & Mindy: September 14, 1978–May 20, 1982

Brothers and Sisters: January 1979–April 1979

Struck by Lightning: September 1979–October 1979

Working Stiffs: September 1979–October 1979

Angie: February 8, 1979–October 2, 1980

The Bad News Bears: May 24, 1979–July 26, 1980

The Associates: September 23, 1979–May 17, 1980

Goodtime Girls: January 22, 1980–August 29, 1980

Here's Boomer: March 1980–August 1982

Fonz and the Happy Days Gang: November 1980–November 1981

Bosom Buddies: November 27, 1980–March 18, 1982

Laverne & Shirley in the Army: October 1981–January 1982

Joanie Loves Chachi: March 23, 1982–March 24, 1983

Family Ties: September 22, 1982–May 14, 1989

Cheers: September 30, 1982–May 20, 1993

SELECTED CREDITS

HAPPY DAYS

Cast
Ron Howard: Richie Cunningham
Henry Winkler: Arthur "Fonzie" Fonzarelli
Tom Bosley: Howard Cunningham
Marion Ross: Marion Cunningham
Erin Moran: Joanie Cunningham
Anson Williams: Potsie Weber
Donny Most: Ralph Malph
Pat Morita: Arnold Takahashi
Al Molinaro: Al Delvecchio
Scott Baio: Chachi Arcola
Lynda Goodfriend: Lori Beth Allen Cunningham
Cathy Silvers: Jenny Piccalo
Suzi Quatro: Leather Tuscadero
Ted McGinley: Roger Phillips
Crystal Bernard: K. C. Cunningham
Linda Purl: Ashley Pfister, Gloria
Heather O'Rourke: Heather Pfister
Billy Warlock: Flip Phillips
Misty Rowe: Wendy
Gavan O'Herlihy: Chuck Cunningham (1974)
Randolph Roberts: Chuck Cunningham (1974–1975)

Producers
Executive producers: Garry K. Marshall, Edward K. Milkis, Thomas L. Miller. Supervising producers: Lowell Ganz, Walter Kempley, Gary Menteer, Jerry Paris. Producers: Nick Abdo, Bob Brunner, Lowell Ganz, Mark Rothman. Co-producer: Ed Scharlach. Associate producers: William Bickley, Bob Birnbaum, Ronny Hallin, Michael Warren

Directors
Jerry Paris, Peter Baldwin, Frank Buxton, Mel Farber, Art Fisher, Jerry London, Garry Marshall, James Tayne, George Tyne, Herb Wallerstein, Don Weis, Joel Zwick

Writers
Al Aidekman, Sis Arthur, Art Baer, Cindy Begel, Dick Bensfield, Barbara Berkowitz, William Bickley, Beverly Bloomberg, Bobby Boswell, J. Elizabeth Bradley, Bob Brunner, Louise Bryant, Frank Buxton, Nancy Churnin, John B. Collins, Richard Correll, Anthony DiMarco, Charlotte M. Dobbs, David W. Duclon, Jim Dunne, Steven Dworman, Peggy Elliott, Judy Pidi Ervin, Ralph Farquhar, Marc Flanagan, Fred Fox Jr., Ron Friedman, Lowell Ganz, Stephanie Garman, Roger Garrett, Lloyd Garver, Joe Glauberg, Allen Goldstein, Perry Grant, Steve Grant, Sam Greenbaum,

Dixie Brown Grossman, Richard Gurman, Susanne Gayle Harris, Terry Hart, Ken Hecht, Craig Heller, Andrew M. Horowitz, Bob Howard, Bill Idelson, Bill James, Ben Joelson, Joel Kane, Robert Keats, April Kelly, Calvin Kelly, Walter Kempley, David Ketchum, Lesa Kite, Artie Laing, Ron Leavitt, Michael Leeson, Brian Levant, Michael Loman, Fred Maio, Alan Mandel, Babaloo Mandel, Garry Marshall, Bosco McGowan, Philip Mishkin, Samuro Mitsubi, Richard Morgan, Gary Murphy, Warren S, Murray, Marty Nadler, Ria Nepus, Barry O'Brien, Barbara Fredika O'Keefe, Michael O'Mahony, Robert Pekurny, Judy Pioli, Jerry Rannow, Rob Reiner, David Reo, James Ritz, Mickey Rose, Lorna Rosenberg, Richard Rosenstock, Mark Rothman, Paula A. Roth, Barry Rubinowitz, Pamela Ryan, Don Safran, Ed Scharlach, Patt Shea, Mary-David Sheiner, Bruce Shelly, Mel Sherer, Charles Shyer, Arthur Silver, George F. Slavin, Jeffrey Stamin, Nancy Steen, Greg Strangis, Larry Strawther, Neil Thompson, Michael Warren, Mike Weinberger, Yvette Weinberger, Shiela Judis Weisberg, Harriett Weiss, Holly White, Jack Winter, Tiffany York, Steve Zacharias

Theme song
Written by Jerry McClain and Truett Pratt

Casting
Bobby Hoffman

LAVERNE & SHIRLEY

Cast
Penny Marshall: Laverne DeFazio
Cindy Williams: Shirley Feeney
David L. Lander: Andrew "Squiggy" Squiggmann
Michael McKean: Leonard "Lenny" Kosnowski
Phil Foster: Frank DeFazio
Eddie Mekka: Carmine "The Big Ragoo" Ragusa
Betty Garrett: Edna Babish-DeFazio
Ed Marinaro: Sonny St. Jacques

Producers
Executive producers: Garry Marshall, Anthony Marshall, Edward K. Milkis, Thomas L. Miller. Producers: Nick Abdo, Robert L. Boyett, Ron Leavitt, Jeffrey Melman, Mark Rothman. Co-producer: Al Aidekman, Associate producers: Jeffrey Ganz, Tony Paris

Directors
Frank Alesia, James Burrows, Ray DeVally Jr., Michael Kidd, Dennis Klein, John Thomas Lenox, Garry Marshall, Penny Marshall, Michael McKean, Linda McMurray, Gary Menteer, Alan Myerson, Alan Rafkin, Jay Andrich, Gary Shimokawa, Howard Storm, John Tracy, Tom Trbovich, Cindy Williams, Joel Zwick

Writers

Al Aidekman, William Bickley, Eric Cohen, Wally Dalton, Nicholas DeMarco, Charlotte M. Dobbs, David W. Duclon, Phil Foster, Jeff Franklin, Lowell Ganz, Steve Granat, Buz Kohan, Barry Lange, Ron Leavitt, Deborah Leschin, Laura Levine, Jack Lukes, Babaloo Mandel, Emily Marshall, Garry Marshall, Holly Mascott, Monica Mcgowan Johnson, Dale McRaven, Gary H. Miller, Stephen Nathan, Judy Pioli, Paul B. Price, Richard Rosenstock, Marth Rothman, Paul A. Roth, Barry Rubinowitz, Ken Sagoes, Mel Sherer, Raymond Siller, Arthur Silver, Marc Sotkin, Greg Strangis, Chris Thompson, Michael Warren, Dan E. Weisburd, Jack Winter, Marion Zola

Theme song

Written by Charles Fox and Norman Gimbel, sung by Cyndi Greco

Casting

Ronny Hallin and Bobby Hoffman

TAXI

Cast

Judd Hirsch: Alex Reiger
Danny DeVito: Louie De Palma
Marilu Henner: Elaine Nardo
Tony Danza: Tony Banta
Andy Kaufman: Latka Gravas
Jeff Conaway: Bobby Wheeler
Christopher Lloyd: Reverend Jim Ignatowski
Carol Kane: Simka Dahblitz-Gravas
J. Alan Thomas: Jeff Bennett
Randall Carver: John Burns

Producers

Executive producers: James L. Brooks, Stan Daniels, David Davis, Ed. Weinberger. Supervising Producers: Glen Charles, Les Charles. Producers: Glen Charles, Les Charles, Ken Estin, Howard Gewirtz, Richard Sakai. Co-producer: Richard Sakai. Associate producer: Budd Cherry, Robin Green

Directors

James Burrows, Jeff Chambers, Stan Daniels, Joan Darling, Danny DeVito, Michael Lessac, Will Mackenzie, Harvey Miller, Noam Pitlik, Richard Sakai, Howard Storm, Michael Zinberg

Writers

Al Aidekman, Pat Allee, Larry Scott Anderson, Ruth Bennett, James L. Brooks, Glenn Gordon Caron, Glen Charles, Les Charles, Dari Daniels, Stan Daniels,

Dennis Danzinger, David Davis, Barton Dean, Barbara Duncan, Ken Estin, Howard Gerwitz, Katherine Green, Holly Holmberg Brooks, Mark Jacobson, Danny Kallis, Barry Kemp, Nancy Lane, Michael Leeson, Susan Jane Lindner, David Lloyd, Earl Pomerantz, Ian Praiser, Sy Rosen, Barry Rubinowitz, Sam Simon, Michael Tolkin, Ed. Weinberger

Music
Written by Bob James

Casting
Susan Arnold, Jennifer Jackson Part, Vicki Rosenberg, Joan Sittenfield, Joel Thurm, Rhonda Young

MORK & MINDY

Cast
Robin Williams: Mork
Pam Dawber: Mindy McConnell
Conrad Janis: Fred McConnell
Elizabeth Kerr: Cora Hudson
Robert Donner: Exidor
Ralph James: Orson
Tom Poston: Franklin Bickley
Jonathan Winters: Mearth
Jay Thomas: Remo DaVinci
Gina Hecht: Jean DaVinci
Jeffrey Jacquet: Eugene
Jim Staahl: Nelson Flavor

Producers
Executive Producers: Anthony Marshall, Garry Marshall, James O'Keefe. Producers: Dale McRaven, Bruce Johnson, Elizabeth Kerr Hudson, Crissy Wilzak Comstock

Directors
Howard Storm, Joel Zwick Don Barnhart, Frank Buxton, Jeff Chambers, Bob Claver, Garry Marshall, Harvey Medlinsky, Robin Williams

Writers
Cindy Begel, Gene Braunstein, John. B. Collins, Alan Eisenstock, Michael Endler, Stuart Gillard, Andy Guerdat, Richard Gurman, Winifred Hervey, Bruce Johnson, Bruce Kalish, April Kelly, Lesa Kite, Wendy Kout, Steve Kreinberg, Neil Lebowitz, Brian Levant, Dale McRaven, Larry Mintz, David Misch, Gordon Mitchell, Simon Muntner, David O'Malley, Ron Osborn, Bob Perlow, Deborah Raznick, Jeff Reno, Richard Rosenstock, Ed Scharlach, Ben Starr, Philip John Taylor, Roy Teicher, Tom Tenowich, Lloyd Turner, George Zateslo

Theme music
Written by Perry Botkin Jr.

Casting
Bobby Hoffman

ANGIE

Cast
Donna Pescow: Angie Falco Benson
Robert Hays: Brad Benson
Debralee Scott: Marie Falco
Doris Roberts: Theresa Falco
Emory Bass: Phipps
Valri Bromfield: Mary Mary
Susan Duvall: Mary Grace
Nancy Lane: Mary Katherine
Tammy Lauren: Hillary
John Randolph: Randall Benson
Diane Robin: Didi Malloy
Sharon Spelman: Joyce Benson
Tim Thomerson: Gianni

Producers
Executive producer: Leonora Thuna. Supervising producers: Robert L. Boyett, Edward K. Milkis, Thomas L. Miller

Director
Jeff Chambers

Writers
Ellen Guylas, Jeff Chambers, and others

Music
Written by Charles Fox, sung by Maureen McGovern

Casting
Joel Thurm

THE ASSOCIATES

Cast
Martin Short: Tucker Kerwin
Joe Regalbuto: Eliot Streeter
Alley Mills: Leslie Dunn
Shelley Smith: Sara James
Tim Thomerson: Johnny Danko
Wilfred Hyde-White: Emerson Marshall

Producers
Executive producers: James L. Brooks, Stan Daniels, Ed. Weinberger

Director
James Burrows

Writers
Stan Daniels, Charlie Hauck, Michael Leeson, John Steven Owen, Earl Pomerantz, Ed. Weinberger

Theme music
Written and performed by B.B. King

BOSOM BUDDIES

Cast
Peter Scolari: Henry "Hildegard" Desmond
Tom Hanks: Kip "Buffy" Wilson
Wendie Jo Sperber: Amy Cassidy
Donna Dixon: Sonny Lumet
Telma Hopkins: Isabelle
Lucille Benson: Lilly Sinclair
Holland Taylor: Ruth Dunbar

Producers
Executive producers: Robert L. Boyett, Edward K. Milkis, Thomas L. Miller, Chris Thompson

Directors
John Bowah, Herbert Kenwith, Will Mackenzie, Chris Thompson, John Tracy, Tom Trovich, Don Van Atta, Joel Zwick

Writers
Jack Carrerow, David Chambers, Bruce Ferber, Jeff Franklin, Roger Garrett, Howard Gewirtz, Terry Hart, David Lerner, Will Mackenzie, Gary H. Miller, Ian Praiser, Leonard Ripps, Stu Silver, Chris Thompson

Song
"My Life," written and sung by Billy Joel

FAMILY TIES

Cast
Meredith Baxter: Elyse Keaton
Michael Gross: Steven Keaton
Michael J. Fox: Alex P. Keaton
Justine Bateman: Mallory Keaton
Tina Yothers: Jennifer Keaton
Brian Bonsall: Andy Keaton
Tracy Pollan: Ellen Reed
Courteney Cox: Lauren Miller
Marc Price: Skippy Handleman
Scott Valentine: Nick Moore

Producers
Executive producer: Gary David Goldberg. Producers: Susan Borowitz, Lloyd Garver, Michael J. Weithorn. Associate producers: Dianne Edwards, June Galas. Line producer: Carol Sledz Himes

Directors
Debbie Allen, Peter Baldwin, Kent Bateman, Alan Bergmann, Matthew Diamond, Lynn Hamrick, Lynn Harrick, Asaad Kelada, Will Mackenzie, Dick Martin, Andrew McCullough, Tony Mordente, John Pasquin, Steven Robman, Rita Rogers, Barbara Schultz, Lee Shallat, Mark W. Travis, Sam Weisman, Michael Zinberg

Writers
Wendy Aaron, Lisa A. Bannick, Ruth Bennett, Susan Borowitz, Kate Boutilier, Jean Kraynak Brinck, Ben Cardinale, Stephen Curwick, Bruce David, Katie Ford, Shannon Gaghan, Lloyd Garver, Gary David Goldberg, Barbara Hall, Bruce Helford, Kimberly Hill, David Tyron King, Marc Lawrence, Lissa Levin, Lawrence H. Levy, Matthew Monaher, Joanne Pagliaro, Burt Prelutsky, Richard Raskind, Rich Reinhart, Jace Richdale, Michael Russnow, Peter Schneider, Bill Steinkellner, Alan Uger, Lawrence Uger, Alan Vejar, Trish Vrandenburg, Michael J. Weithorn, Jurgen M. Wolf, Paul Wolff, Douglas Wyman

Theme music
Written by Jeff Barry and Tom Scott, sung by Johnny Mathis and Deniece Williams

Casting
Allison Jones and Judith Weiner

CHEERS

Cast
Ted Danson: Sam Malone
Shelley Long: Diane Chambers
Kirstie Alley: Rebecca Howe
Nicholas Colasanto: Ernie "Coach" Pantusso
Rhea Perlman: Carla Tortelli
John Ratzenberger: Cliff Clavin
Woody Harrelson: Woody Boyd
Kelsey Grammer: Frasier Crane
Bebe Neuwirth: Lillith Sternin-Crane
George Wendt: Norm Peterson

Producers
Executive producers: James Burrows, Glen Charles, Les Charles, Rob Long, Bill Steinkellner, Cherie Steinkeller, Phoef Sutton. Co-executive producer: Dan Staley. Producers: David Angell, James Burrows, Peter Casey, Glen Charles, Les Charles, Ken Estin, David Lee, Rob Long, Heide Perlman, Sam Simon, Dan Staley. Co-producers: Tom Anderson, Larry Balmagia, Tim Berry, David Isaacs, Ken Levine, Dan O'Shannon, Brian Pollack, Mert Rich. Associate producers: Tim Berry, Mary Fukuto

Directors
Andy Ackerman, Rick Beren, Tim Berry, James Burrows, Thomas Lofaro, Tom Moore, John Ratzenberg, George Wendt, Michael Zinberg

Writers
Tom Anderson, David Angell, Nick Arnold, Larry Balmagia, James Burrows, Rod Burton, Peter Casey, Glen Charles, Les Charles, Chris Cluess, Andy Cowan, Jeffrey Duteil, Ken Estin, Fred Graver, Katherine Green, Norm Guzenhauser, Sue Herring, Kimberly Hill, David Isaacs, Stu Kreisman, Janet Leahy, David Lee, Tom Leopold, Ken Levine, Lissa Levin, David Lloyd, Rob Long, Tracy Newman, Dan O'Shannon, Joanne Pahliaro, Daniel Palladino, Jim Parker, Rebecca Parr Cioffi, Heidi Perlman, Brian Pollack, Earl Pomerantz, Tom Reeder, Mert Rich, Susan Seeger, Tom Seeley, Elliott Shoenman, Sam Simon, Dan Staley, Jonathan Stark, Bill Steinkellner, Cherie Steinkellner, Kathy Ann Stumpe, Phoef Sutton, Mark Tash, Miriam Trogdon, Michael J. Weithorn, David S. Williger

Music theme
Written by Judy Hart-Angelo and Gary Potnoy

SOURCES

Some of the information contained in *Happier Days: Paramount Television's Classic Sitcoms 1974–1984* is from the firsthand knowledge of the author, and some of the people who shared information remain anonymous.

BOOKS

Berman, Connie, *Penny Marshall & Cindy Williams*, New York: Grosset & Dunlap, 1977.

Crown, Lawrence, *Penny Marshall: An Unauthorized Biography of the Director and Comedienne*, Los Angeles: Renaissance Books, 1999.

David, Jay, *The Life and Humor of Robin Williams*, New York: Quill, 1999.

Grammer, Kelsey, *So Far*, New York: Signet Books, 1996.

Gray, Beverly, *Ron Howard: From Mayberry to the Moon—and Beyond*, Nashville, TN: Rutledge Hill Press, 2003.

Hill, Tom, *TV Land to Go: The Big Book of TV Lists, TV Lore, and TV Bests*, New York: Fireside, 2001.

Jacobs, Linda, *Henry Winkler: Born Actor*, St. Paul, MN: EMC Corp., 1978.

Lander, David L., with Lee Montgomery, *Fall Down Laughing: How Squiggy Caught Multiple Sclerosis and Didn't Tell Nobody*, New York: Tarcher/Putnam, 2000.

Lovece, Frank, with Jules Franco, *Taxi: The Official Fan's Guide—Taxi*, New York: Citadel Press, 1988.

Marshall, Garry, with Lori Marshall, *Wake Me When It's Funny: How to Break into Show Business and Stay There*, Holbrook, MA: Adams Publishing, 1995.

Masters, Kim, *Keys to the Kingdom: The Rise of Michael Eisner and the Fall of Everybody Else*, New York: HarperBusiness, 2001.

Sackett, Susan, *Prime-Time Hits: Television's Most Popular Network Programs, 1950 to the Present*, New York: Billboard Books, 1993.

Schneck, Paul D., *TV and Movie Tie-Ins: Mork & Mindy*, Mankato, MN: Creative Education, Inc., 1980.

INTERVIEWS

Jim Burrows, September 23, 2004; Randall Carver, November 18, 2004; Pam Dawber, September 22, 2004; Corey Feldman, March 17, 2005; Donna Frost, November 8, 2004; Michael Gross, March 21, 2005; Clint Howard, September 22, 2004; Donna Pescow, March 18, 2005; Misty Rowe, October 6, 2004; Rose Marie, January 31, 2005; Suzi Quatro, July 14, 2004; Howard Storm, November 15, 2004

INTERNET SITES

BBC, Cheers Central, Cinema, *Family Ties* On-line, *Happy Days* On-line, International Movie Database, Jim's Mario's Taxi, Jump the Shark, *Mork & Mindy* On-line, Sitcoms On-line, The Life and Times of Andy Kaufman, TVGuide, TVLand, TV Tome, davidlander.com, eddiemekka.com, lindapurl.net, meredithbaxter.org, tomposton.com

MAGAZINES

Biography: Summer 2004, "Tony Danza."

Entertainment Weekly: Oscar Guide, 2004, "Stupid Questions"; February 20, 2004; March 26, 2004, "The King of Comedy"; Fall TV Preview 2004, "Stupid Questions"; March 2004; September 24, 2004, "Hit List," "We're Dyin' for . . . Taxi"; November 5, 2004, "Pop Culture Quiz"; November 8, 2004, "Television"; November 12, 2004, "What, Him Worry?"; November 26, 2004, "TV on DVD"; December 3, 2005, "Something New from . . . Woody Allen; December 13, 2004; January 28, 2005, "Oscar 2005"; February 25, 2005, "Monster, Inc."; April 8, 2005.

Marietta [GA] Daily Journal: "The Fonz Is Having Fun with His Many Television Projects," by Dave Mason, February 2005.

People: January 9, 2004; January 19, 2004, "Chatter"; September 20, 2004, "Look Who's Talking"; September 24, 2004, "Look Who's Talking"; February 7, 2005, "*Happy Days* 30th Anniversary Special," "Disney War"; March 14, 2005, "Robin's Song"; December 12, 2005, "Pat Morita"; December 19, 2005, "Wendie Jo Sperber."

The Graphic, Pepperdine University (Malibu, CA): "*Happy Days* Films Reunion Special on Pep's Baseball Field," by Audrey Reed and Karen Sable, January 7, 2005.

TV Guide: April 29, 1976; , June 18, 1977, "Who Let Them In?" by Bill O'Hallaren; August 1982; June 20, 2004; April 18, 2005, "Robin Williams Reacts to NBC's Mork Movie"; February 13, 2006, "CBS Reunites *Happy Days* Duo," "Cheers & Jeers," "Kelsey Grammer Gets in Some Practice."

US: December 13, 2004, "Did Shelley Long Attempt Suicide?"; January 31, 2005, "Us Musts"; 2005, "MIA Men."

Variety: "Gary Nardino Dead at 62," by Nick Madigan, February 2, 1998.

ORGANIZATION ARCHIVES

Directors Guild of America, Hollywood Foreign Press, Museum of Broadcast Communications, National Academy of Television Arts & Sciences Screen Actors Guild, Writers Guild of America

TELEVISION

Happy Days: 30th Anniversary Reunion, February 3, 2005, ABC